Glencoe

INTERNATIONAL BUSINESS

COMMUNICATION

TRADE
GLOBAL ECONOMY

STANDARD &POOR'S

Glencoe:
Building the Future
of Business

In partnership with
BusinessWeek

Donald Baack, Ph.D.

McGraw Hill Glencoe

New York, New York   Columbus, Ohio   Chicago, Illinois   Woodland Hills, California

PHOTO CREDITS

Copyright © 2008 by The McGraw-Hill Companies. All rights reserved. Except as permitted under the United States Copyright Act, no part of this publication may be reproduced or distributed in any form or by any means, or stored in a database or retrieval system, without prior written permission of the publisher.

Printed in the United States of America.

Send all inquiries to:
Glencoe/McGraw-Hill
21600 Oxnard Street, Suite 500
Woodland Hills, California 91367-4906

ISBN: 978-0-07-868543-9 (Student Edition)
MHID: 0-07-868543-5 (Student Edition)

ISBN: 978-0-07-875704-4 (Teacher Annotated Edition)
MHID: 0-07-875704-5 (Teacher Annotated Edition)

2 3 4 5 6 7 8 9 079 12 11 10 09 08 07

About the Author

DONALD BAACK completed his Ph.D. degree in management at the University of Nebraska in 1987. Currently he holds the rank of University Professor at Pittsburg State University in Kansas, teaching management and marketing classes. He has authored and co-authored three college textbooks, four general audience books, and numerous academic papers.

Board of Reviewers

Glencoe/McGraw-Hill would like to acknowledge these individuals for their support and contributions during the development of *International Business*:

BLAKE BODENBURG
Anoka High School
St. Francis, Minnesota

LYNN A. HUGGINS
Institute for Global Commerce
and Government
Merrill F. West High School
Tracy, California

LISA R. MEYER
Williamsport High School
Williamsport, Pennsylvania

KIM POWELL
Fredonia High School
Fredonia, New York

SALLY ROTHENBERG
Roosevelt High School
Minneapolis, Minnesota

JENNIFER WEGNER
Mishicot High School
Mishicot, Wisconsin

Consulting Editor

LISA ERMETI HULL, B.S., M.B.A.
Zionsville Community High School
Zionsville, Indiana

Contributing Writer

JUDEE TIMM, Ph.D.
Monterey Peninsula College
Monterey, California

Business/Career Education Industry Advisory Board

PEGGY BRADFIELD
Vons, A Safeway Co.
Burbank, California

ANDY CHAVES
Marriott International Inc.
Washington, DC

MIKE DE FABIO
Otis Spunkmeyer
Torrance, California

BRIAN DUNN
JD Power & Associates
Westlake Village, California

DONNA FARRUGIA
CARRIE NEBENS
Robert Half International
Westlake Village, California

MARK HATCH
Ohio Association of Public School
Employees
Columbus, Ohio

MIKE KULIS
Sherwin Williams Co.
Cleveland, Ohio

DR. DAVID M. MITCHELL
Johnson & Wales University
Providence, Rhode Island

DEBBIE MORETON
JCPenney
Dallas, Texas

JOYCE WINTERTON
USA Today
McLean, Virginia

Table of Contents

Table of Contents

Table of Contents

Table of Contents

Exploring the World of
International Business

Welcome to the exciting world of international business. Get ready to learn about the expanding global economy. International business is a subject that you can relate to and make your own. After all, international business is everywhere, even in your hometown or city. You use products imported from countries around the world every day, and U.S. companies manufacture and send American products to other countries regularly. In addition, the Internet makes global e-commerce possible 24 hours a day, 7 days a week. You are part of the world of international business.

Organizing the Text

The units introduce you to the scope of international business. Each unit opens with a *BusinessWeek Global Business* feature and concludes with a unit-culminating thematic project, which is a business simulation. Each unit includes three to four chapters. The 16 chapters of *International Business* are divided into these five units:

UNIT 1 THE WORLD OF INTERNATIONAL BUSINESS

UNIT 2 THE INTERNATIONAL TRADE ENVIRONMENT

UNIT 3 INTERNATIONAL MANAGEMENT

UNIT 4 INTERNATIONAL MARKETING AND FINANCE

UNIT 5 YOUR FUTURE IN INTERNATIONAL BUSINESS

Understanding the Unit

Unit Opener Photo

The unit opener photo illustrates a unit concept. Ask yourself: "How does the photo preview the content of the unit?"

BusinessWeek | Global Business

Each unit opens with an excerpt from a real *BusinessWeek* article about an aspect of the unit material. To do the activity, go to the Online Learning Center through **glencoe.com**.

In This Unit

Titles of the unit chapters are listed on the lefthand side of the unit opener spread. Think about what you can learn in each chapter. A quotation helps you focus on what you will read.

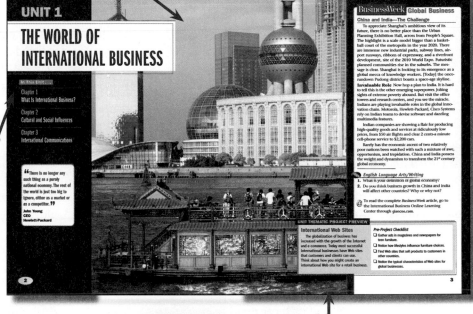

Unit Thematic Project Preview

This preview prepares you for the unit-closing thematic project, a real-world simulation and hands-on activity. A checklist helps you get a head start in doing the project.

Closing the Unit

Unit Thematic Project

At the end of each unit, this thematic project will take you on an exciting journey through the world of international business as you complete a real-world assignment.

Understanding the Chapter

Previewing the Chapter

The chapter opener resources introduce you to the chapter and can help set a purpose for your reading.

Chapter Opener Photo

The chapter opener photo focuses on the chapter topic and opening case study. Ask yourself: "How might the photo relate to the title and content of the chapter?"

Case Study

Standard & Poor's approved case studies provide learning opportunities about global companies listed on the Standard & Poor's indices. A critical-thinking question helps you to focus on chapter topics.

Chapter Objectives

The objectives help you identify exactly what you should know after studying the chapter.

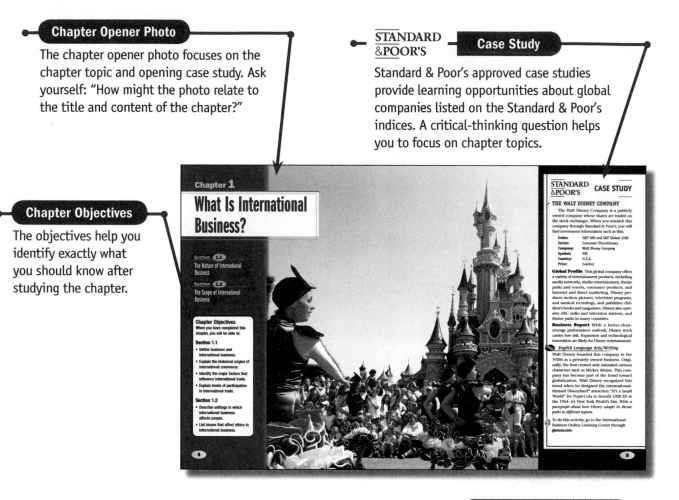

Using the Sections

What You'll Learn lists the objectives you will learn in the section.

Why It's Important explains how the chapter concepts relate to international business.

Key Terms list the major terms presented and highlighted in each section.

Academic Vocabulary highlights general terms you will see in most texts and on tests.

Reading Guide

Before You Read reading strategies provide questions to help you draw upon your previous knowledge to get ready for the section.

Main Idea states a main concept presented in the section.

Graphic Organizer provides a sample diagram you can draw and use to organize and understand each section's information.

Photographs and Figures

Throughout each section, relevant photographs and useful charts and graphs illustrate and reinforce the content. Captions with questions guide you.

Quick Check

The section-ending *Quick Check* assessments help you to respond, review, and apply what you have read.

Understanding the Features

Culture Corner

Spotlighting countries and their cultures, this feature includes a section with useful business etiquette tips. Critical-thinking questions before and after the feature text help you relate the information to the chapter topics.

Did You Know

Brief, memorable facts illustrate international business issues and trends.

International Business Careers

This feature provides insight and information about real careers. The "Career Data" section lists the needed education, skills, and outlook for each career. A chapter-related, critical-thinking question follows the feature. The Online Learning Center extends the material, providing career path information through **glencoe.com**

How Do You Say?

Typical phrases used in business, along with translations in 16 different languages are introduced.

World Market

You will learn about interesting businesses of all types and sizes around the world. This feature is illustrated with a real-world advertising image as well as a mini-map to help you find the featured business's location.

OUR MULTICULTURAL WORKPLACE

Globalization occurs around the world and at home. This feature focuses on diversity in the American workplace.

TECH Trends

Current and emerging applications of technology and the Internet used in international business are highlighted. An exercise directs you to the book's Online Learning Center through **glencoe.com**.

ETHICS & ISSUES

This feature links chapter content to current ethical issues in global business, influenced by cultural, legal, and ethical practices.

Understanding Assessments

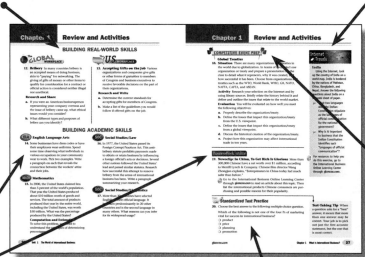

PORTFOLIO WORKSHEET Before each Review and Activities section, this write-on worksheet page provides review and skill-building activities related to chapter content. As you complete the worksheets, you build a portfolio. You can assess, reflect, and plan for your career as you complete activities that provide the foundation for a career plan portfolio.

KEY TERMS REVIEW Review the key terms you learn throughout the chapter by matching their definitions.

ACADEMIC VOCABULARY This writing activity helps you recall and apply the typical terms you will see in the chapter, in your other texts, and on tests.

CHAPTER SUMMARY This summary is a list of chapter highlights to help you review and recall topics. Each highlight relates to a chapter objective.

REVIEW ACTIVITIES *Critical Thinking*, *Discussion Starter*, and *Point of View* exercises help you apply chapter topics.

CONCEPTS REVIEW Concept Review questions correlated to the chapter objectives help you recall concepts and definitions.

BUILDING REAL-WORLD SKILLS Two activities ask you to use your critical-thinking, research, and writing skills. *The Global Workplace* focuses on career situations in other countries; *The U.S. Workplace* examines situations in the American workplace.

BUILDING ACADEMIC SKILLS Connect and apply academic subjects to international business.

INTERNET TRAVELS Find resources for each Web-based exercise through the Online Learning Center through **glencoe.com**.

COMPETITIVE EVENT PREP This activity allows you to research and role-play through real-world scenarios.

***BUSINESSWEEK* ONLINE** Go to the Student Center of the book's Online Learning Center through **glencoe.com** to read a complete chapter-related *BusinessWeek* article and do the activity.

STANDARDIZED TEST PRACTICE This exercise prepares you for standardized test-taking and provides proven tips to achieve the best results.

The International Business Online Learning Center

The Student Center at the Online Learning Center (OLC) gives you the tools and resources to open up the world of international business beyond your classroom. Use the materials on the OLC to help you do feature activities. Special Web links, practice tests, games, and eFlashcards will entertain you as you learn.

How to Get to the OLC

Step 1 Log on to **glencoe.com.** From the drop-down menu, CHOOSE your state. CLICK the "Student" radio button. CHOOSE the subject area "Business Administration." CLICK "Enter."

Step 2 You will enter the Business Administration site. CLICK "International Business."

Step 3 Welcome to the International Business Online Learning Center!

Focus on Reading

Reading Strategies

How can you get the most from your reading? Effective readers are active readers. Get involved with the text. Think of your textbook as a tool that helps you learn about the world around you. The material is a form of nonfiction writing—it describes real-life ideas, people, events, and places. Look for these reading strategies in the *Reading Guide*, in the margins, and in all of the section-ending *Quick Check* exercises.

Before You Read Make educated guesses about what the section is about by combining clues in the text with what you already know. Predicting helps you anticipate questions and stay alert to new information.

Ask yourself:

- What does the section heading mean?
- What is this section about?
- How does this section tie in with what I have read so far?
- Why is this information important in understanding the subject?

As You Read **Relate** Draw parallels between what you are reading and the events and circumstances in your own life.

Ask yourself:

- What do I know about the topic?
- How do my experiences compare to the information in the text?
- How could I apply this information in my own life?
- Why is this information important in understanding the subject?

As You Read **Question** Ask questions to help you clarify the reading as you go along.

Ask yourself:

- Do I understand what I have read so far?
- What is this section about?
- What does this mean?
- Why is this information important in understanding the subject?

After You Read **Respond** React to what you are reading. Form opinions and make judgments about the section while you are reading—not just after you have finished.

Ask yourself:

- Does this information make sense?
- What can I learn from this section?
- How can I use this information to start planning for my financial future?
- Why is this information important in understanding the subject?

More Reading Strategies

Use this quick-reference chart for reading strategies that will help you get the most from reading.

Before You Read

Set a purpose
- Why are you reading the textbook?
- How does the subject relate to your life?
- How might you be able to use what you learn in your own life?

Preview
- Read the chapter title to preview the topic.
- Read the subtitles to see what you will learn about the topic.
- Skim the photos, charts, graphs, or maps. How do they support the topic?
- Look for key terms that are boldfaced. How are they defined?

Draw from your background
- What have you read or heard concerning new information on the topic?
- How is the new information different from what you already know?
- How will the information that you already know help you understand the new information?

As You Read

Predict
- Predict events or outcomes by using clues and information that you already know.
- Change your predictions as you read and gather new information.

Connect
- Think about people, places, and events in your own life. Are there any similarities with those in your textbook?
- Can you relate the textbook information to other areas of your life?

Question
- What is the main idea?
- How do the photos, charts, graphs, and maps support the main idea?

Visualize
- Pay careful attention to details and descriptions.
- Create graphic organizers to show relationships that you find in the information.

Notice Comparison and Contrast Sentences
- Look for clue words and phrases that signal comparison, such as *similarly, just as, both, in common, also,* and *too.*
- Look for clue words and phrases that signal contrast, such as *on the other hand, in contrast to, however, different, instead of, rather than, but,* and *unlike.*

Notice Cause-and-Effect Sentences
- Look for clue words and phrases, such as *because, as a result, therefore, that is why, since, so, for this reason,* and *consequently.*

Notice Chronological Sentences
- Look for clue words and phrases, such as *after, before, first, next, last, during, finally, earlier, later, since,* and *then.*

After You Read

Summarize
- Describe the main idea and how the details support it.
- Use your own words to explain what you have read.

Assess
- What was the main idea?
- Did the text clearly support the main idea?
- Did you learn anything new from the material?
- Can you use this new information in other school subjects or at home?
- What other sources could you use to find more information about the topic?

UNIT 1

THE WORLD OF INTERNATIONAL BUSINESS

"There is no longer any such thing as a purely national economy. The rest of the world is just too big to ignore, either as a market or as a competitor."

John Young
CEO
Hewlett-Packard

2

China and India—The Challenge

To appreciate Shanghai's ambitious view of its future, there is no better place than the Urban Planning Exhibition Hall, across from People's Square. The highlight is a scale model bigger than a basketball court of the metropolis in the year 2020. There are immense new industrial parks, subway lines, airport runways, ribbons of expressway, and a riverfront development, site of the 2010 World Expo. Futuristic planned communities rise in the suburbs. The message is clear. Shanghai [pictured here] is looking to its emergence as a global mecca of knowledge workers. [Today] the once-rundown Pudong district boasts a space-age skyline.

Invaluable Role Now hop a plane to India. It is hard to tell this is the other emerging superpower. Jolting sights of extreme poverty abound. But visit the office towers and research centers, and you see the miracle. Indians are playing invaluable roles in the global innovation chain. Motorola, Hewlett-Packard, Cisco Systems rely on Indian teams to devise software and dazzling multimedia features.

Indian companies are showing a flair for producing high-quality goods and services at ridiculously low prices, from $50 air flights and clear 2 cents-a minute cell-phone service to $2,200 cars.

Rarely has the economic ascent of two relatively poor nations been watched with such a mixture of awe, opportunism, and trepidation. China and India possess the weight and dynamism to transform the 21st century global economy.

English Language Arts/Writing

1. What is your definition of the term *global economy*?
2. Do you think business growth in China and India will affect other countries? Why or why not?

To read the complete *BusinessWeek* article, go to the International Business Online Learning Center through **glencoe.com**.

UNIT THEMATIC PROJECT PREVIEW

International Web Sites

The globalization of business has increased with the growth of the Internet and e-commerce. Today most successful international businesses have Web sites that customers and clients can use. Think about how you might create an international Web site for a retail business.

Pre-Project Checklist

❑ Gather ads in magazines and newspapers for teen furniture.

❑ Notice how lifestyles influence furniture choices.

❑ Find Web sites that sell products to customers in other countries.

❑ Notice the typical characteristics of Web sites for global businesses.

Chapter 1

What Is International Business?

Chapter Objectives

When you have completed this chapter, you will be able to:

Section 1.1

- Define business and international business.
- Explain the historical origins of international commerce.
- Identify the major factors that influence international trade.
- Explain levels of participation in international trade.

Section 1.2

- Describe settings in which international business affects people.
- List issues that affect ethics in international business.

▶ THE WALT DISNEY COMPANY

The Walt Disney Company is a publicly owned company whose shares are traded on the stock exchanges. When you research this company through Standard & Poor's, you will find investment information such as this:

Index:	S&P 500 and S&P Global 1200
Sector:	Consumer Discretionary
Company:	Walt Disney Company
Symbol:	DIS
Country:	U.S.A.
Price:	(varies)

Global Profile This global company offers a variety of entertainment products, including media networks, studio entertainment, theme parks and resorts, consumer products, and Internet and direct marketing. Disney produces motion pictures, television programs, and musical recordings, and publishes children's books and magazines. Disney also operates ABC radio and television stations, and theme parks in many countries.

Business Report With a better-than-average performance outlook, Disney stock carries low risk. Expansion and technological innovation are likely for Disney entertainment.

✏ *English Language Arts/Writing*

Walt Disney founded this company in the 1920s as a privately owned business. Originally, the firm created only animated cartoon characters such as Mickey Mouse. This company has become part of the trend toward globalization. Walt Disney recognized this trend when he designed the Disneyland® attraction "It's a Small World" for Pepsi-Cola to benefit UNICEF at the 1964–65 New York World's Fair. *Write a paragraph about how Disney adapts its theme parks to different countries (such as France, pictured here).*

@ To do this activity, go to the International Business Online Learning Center through **glencoe.com**.

The Nature of International Business

WHAT YOU'LL LEARN

- To define business and international business
- To explain the historical origins of international commerce
- To identify the major factors that influence international trade
- To explain levels of participation in international trade

WHY IT'S IMPORTANT

International trade affects most companies and customers in the United States and around the world.

KEY TERMS

- business
- international business
- domestic company
- international company
- globalization
- global dependence

Academic Vocabulary

You will find these words in your reading and on your tests. Make sure you know their meanings. For defintions, go to the Glossary in the back of this book.

- establish
- factor
- individual

Reading Guide

Before You Read

What is your definition of international business?

MAIN IDEA

Though global trade has existed for centuries, today the business world is changing and becoming more international as a result of globalization.

GRAPHIC ORGANIZER

Draw this timeline diagram. As you read this section, write in major historical events in international commerce during the 1800s and 1900s.

U.S. Multinational Companies

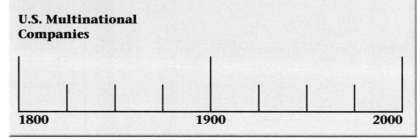

| 1800 | 1900 | 2000 |

Go to this book's Online Learning Center through **glencoe.com.** for a printable graphic organizer.

Understanding International Business

In the 21ˢᵗ century, people around the world are connected in many ways. Technology and new trading relationships between countries mean that everyone is affected by international business directly and indirectly every day. Your challenge as a global citizen is to find ways to live and work in the world's economy. Understanding international trade will help you work in business today.

Overview of International Business

In this text you will learn about the nature of international business. The first three chapters of this book discuss international trade and the international business environment. The later chapters examine management processes, marketing techniques, accounting and financial issues, and human resource management. You will also get a glimpse of the future of international business. After completing this course, you will better understand how companies and countries work together while competing with each other.

Business and International Business

Think about the basic term *business*. **Business** is any activity that seeks profit by providing goods or services to others. Doing business can be as simple as a boy or girl selling lemonade at a home-made stand or as complicated as a corporation expanding into new markets around the world.

International business is any activity involving business operations across national borders. The business activity can include a physical good, such as a tractor or T-shirt being sold in another country. Business activity can also involve offering a service, which is an intangible thing, such as telephone or Internet service. In addition, if someone in Canada logs on to an American Web site to read a *BusinessWeek* article online, that person is engaged in international business. Though the reader does not pay money to read the article, *BusinessWeek* earns money by charging fees to advertisers who place paid advertisements on its Web site. When more readers log on to the Web site, the magazine may charge higher fees to advertisers. Another term for international business is *global business*.

> **Reading Check** **Compare** What distinguishes international business from standard business?

Domestic and International Companies

Both domestic and international companies offer goods and services for sale. A **domestic company** is a company that conducts business in only one country, which is known as the *home country*. For example, if your favorite restaurant is a family-owned diner in your neighborhood, it would be considered a domestic company in a home country.

An **international company** is a company that conducts business across national borders. If you buy imported tea from China, the company that sold the tea is considered an international company. Importing or exporting a good or service is known as *international trade* or *foreign trade*. The number of international companies continues to grow. This growth contributes to the trend of **globalization**, which is the increasing integration of the world economy. Technologies such as the Internet, business software, PDAs, and cell phones make it possible for many companies to sell goods and services to customers in other nations.

Home and Host Countries

When a company sells products in another country, two terms apply. The first term is the *home country*, which is the country in which the selling firm is located. If an employee or representative travels to another country to market or sell goods or services, that country is known as the *host country*. For example, when a Japanese sales representative calls on a company in the United States, the home country is Japan and the host country is the United States.

How Do You Say?

Q: In Hindi, how do you say: "I am pleased to meet you"?

A: मुझे आपसे मिल कर खुशी हुई। (pronounced: Moo-jhā ăp-sā mĭl car coo-shē who-ē.)

To learn these words in other languages, go to the International Business Online Learning Center through **glencoe.com**.

As You Read

Relate Can you name a service that you or your family could use anywhere in the world?

The History of Global Business

You might be tempted to think that global trade is a recent development. It is not. Trade took place between China, India, and Japan as many as 15,000 years ago. There is evidence that Phoenician and Greek merchants traded with one another before the first century A.D. The expansion of the Roman Empire led to trade among many regions.

Since that time global trade has continued and grown steadily. During the 11th century, England, France, Spain, and Portugal all used ships to move products between countries. When Spain discovered North America in the late 15th century, explorers such as Columbus were searching for a better trade route between Spain and India.

The 1600s to 1800s

In 1599, the British East India Company was formed. That firm conducted trade through its branches in Asia. At about the same time, the Dutch East India Company was also operating in Asia, trading in products such as tea, spices, fabrics, and other sought-after goods.

Between 1600 and 1776, merchants in colonial America conducted trade and exported agricultural products and other goods to Britain and several European countries, despite British restrictions. After the Revolutionary War of 1776, British investors tried to **establish** companies in the newly independent United States.

By the 1800s, several multinational companies existed in the United States. In 1851, Samuel Colt opened a firearms plant in England and later in the United States. The Singer® sewing machine company became international by selling products in several countries. In 1855, Singer expanded to Paris, and in 1867, the company built a sewing machine factory in Scotland.

The 1900s to the Present

By 1920, more than 37 U.S. companies operated production facilities in two or more nations. Some of the companies included National Cash Register (NCR) and the Ford Motor Company. Soon after these companies became global, General Motors and Chrysler followed and became involved in international trade. During the 1920s, every car bought in Japan was made by a U.S. company.

As You Read

Question What were two multinational companies in the United States during the 1800s?

ANCIENT GLOBAL BUSINESS Global trade began as many as 15,000 years ago. *Why do countries trade goods and services with each other?*

Global Trendsetters in Switzerland

Think About It What factors affect business trends in the global business environment?

For a few days each year, the residents of an alpine village in Davos, Switzerland, host the world's policymakers for the World Economic Forum. Founded in 1971, the Forum is a powerful organization dedicated to improving the state of humanity. This "think tank" believes that a healthy world will produce a healthy economy. Leaders from business as well as the arts address issues that affect society. Forum members tackle such questions as climate change and disease, and mediate dialogue between groups with differing interests. The Forum also enlists Young Global Leaders. Each year more than 200 women and men under age 40, and from every region on Earth, participate in the 2020 Initiative to "remember the future."

Meeting and Greeting When doing business in Switzerland, shake hands firmly with people you meet, and again upon leaving. Use last names and titles unless invited to use first names.

Business Etiquette Give your business card to associates you meet, including the receptionist. Be punctual for meetings. Meetings are impersonal, quick, orderly, and well planned. Business luncheons are more common than business dinners.

Business Dress Wear neat and clean conservative attire. Men wear suits and ties, and women wear suits or dresses.

English Language Arts/Writing

Write a paragraph about a global issue that might affect the business environment by the year 2020, and include some strategies for addressing it.

Global Business Today Global business is everywhere in the 21st century. Many companies that began as domestic firms now sell products in the global marketplace. Everything from parts and supplies to finished goods and services moves from the United States to other countries. Large and small companies are able to reach customers in other nations.

The opposite is also true. American customers buy goods that are manufactured all over the world. Foods, drinks, clothing, and other products ship from various countries to the United States. This high level of global trade has raised the standard of living for some people around the world.

The Global Business Environment

Individual companies and countries are connected to each other in different ways through global business. **Factors** such as international events and business trends can influence these trading relationships. These factors fall into three categories:

- Cultural and social
- Political and legal
- Economic

International events or incidents can affect all three categories at the same time. Changes in technology and competition also influence the global business environment. (See **Figure 1.1** on page 10.)

Figure 1.1

The Global Business Environment

NOT JUST BUYING AND SELLING Many external factors and internal issues affect global business. *What is one example of one external and one internal factor?*

External Factors	Internal Issues
● Social and cultural factors	● Management and planning
● Political and legal factors	● Marketing
● Economic factors	● Human resource management
● Technology	● Competition
● Finance	● Accounting

Cultural and Social Factors

International business is influenced by many cultural and social trends. Changes in a country's education system or economic philosophy can have a big impact on international business. Some of the changes in the social environment result from religious influences. Some governments make decisions based on religion. Other governments may place less emphasis on religion when developing policies. Chapters 2 and 3 review many cultural and social factors that affect business, including ways that people communicate with one another.

Political and Legal Factors

On the international stage, political events can have powerful effects on business. Wars and international conflicts quickly alter political and business environments. Elections or revolts also affect the business climate. A new government might create new policies for doing business. Companies around the world must adjust to changing situations. You will learn more about governmental factors and their relationship to international business in Chapters 4 and 5.

Economic Factors

The economies of many countries around the world are connected in the business environment. A recession in Japan can affect business activities in many other nations. Inflation, economic growth or decline, investment levels, exchange rates for various currencies, and differences in interest rates all influence business relationships. Chapters 6 and 7 focus on these and other economic issues that may affect global business.

In addition, a natural disaster such as a major hurricane, flood, or earthquake can be a powerful force that may cause physical damage and hurt the local and international economies. In 2004, Florida was hit by four major hurricanes. In addition, the Tsunami disaster in Southeast Asia had an international impact. In 2005, Hurricanes Katrina and Rita, which hit the southern United States, were the most costly in U.S. history. They had a negative impact on many states' economies and business trade with many countries.

International Business Management

In the global business environment, businesses must adapt and adjust their management processes when they work in other parts of the world. Forms of business ownership and the legal requirements for operating businesses vary in different countries. In addition, the things that motivate employees vary around the world. Styles of business leadership also differ among nations. The ability to adjust to these aspects of a business culture is crucial for a manager who wants to be effective doing business globally. Chapters 8, 9, and 10 examine the key management issues and tools that help a company succeed in the international marketplace.

Marketing and International Trade

Another key activity in foreign trade is marketing. The four Ps of marketing (the marketing mix) are vital elements for successful marketing in international business:

1. Product
2. Price
3. Place
4. Promotion

Chapter 11 focuses on marketing and promotion in international business. Identifying different kinds of markets is crucial for the successful sale and distribution of products globally. The distribution of products and pricing methods are two elements of the marketing mix covered in Chapter 12.

Accounting and Finance

Effective businesspeople understand the importance of financial issues for international trade. Chapter 13 discusses currency exchange and the basics of accounting and finance. These are the major elements of money management in international trade.

Human Resource Management and Careers

The last three chapters of this book focus on the people side of doing international business. Chapter 14 examines human resource management. It explains how people are recruited, hired, and trained to succeed in both domestic and foreign companies. Chapter 15 focuses on you. It describes ways to build a successful career. To do well in international business, you will want to gain additional training and learn how to travel across international borders. To conclude, Chapter 16 discusses the use of new technologies.

It is fun and challenging to study international business and its many components. Understanding these components will help you to achieve success in the global marketplace.

TECH Trends

Translation Engines
Language barriers have always existed for businesses that span the globe, but the Internet has made them more obvious. Small companies on the Web need to make their information accessible to readers in other countries. Traditional professional translation can be expensive, but new technological tools may be chipping away at those costs by automating the process. Web sites such as freetranslation.com offer free "machine translations." However, a fee is charged for a more accurate translation by a person. Some search engines operate country-specific versions and free translation tools, so you can view any Web page in different languages. *Write a sentence you might use in conversation and translate it into Spanish through a translation Web site.*

@ For links to help you do this activity, go to the International Business Online Learning Center through **glencoe.com**.

Figure 1.2

The World of International Business

TRADING NEIGHBORS Trade relationships between nations exist around the globe. *Choose at least five countries that produce products that you use. Name the countries and products.*

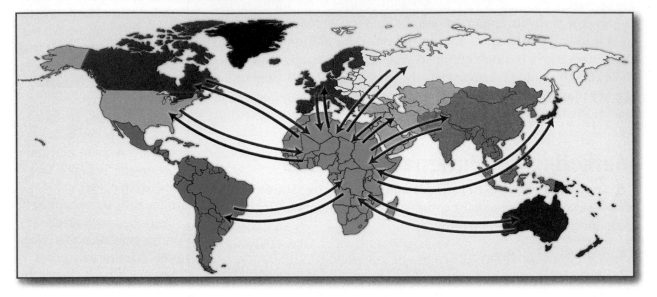

Trade Relationships

The United States is part of the global marketplace. International business affects most people who live in the United States. Many of the clothes people wear are imported from other countries. Shoes, socks, cars, radios, CD and DVD players, computers, and food can be imported goods. Services such as credit cards, banking, and investment and travel services are available to customers around the world.

Many well-known U.S. firms are global operations. American firms such as the Ford Motor Company, McDonald's, and Wal-Mart have international components. The relationships and ties between companies around the world have created **global dependence**, which is the concept that all countries depend on each other for trade. **Figure 1.2** illustrates trading regions around the world. International trade takes place between many participants:

- Individual consumers
- Companies
- States and provinces
- Countries

Individual Consumers

The first level of international trade occurs when one person buys a product that is from another country. The Internet and global shipping have dramatically increased the ability of **individual** consumers to participate in the global economy. In addition, people who travel to foreign countries buy many goods and services to use or to take home.

Companies

A great deal of international trade takes place between companies. Companies import and export goods every day. For example, a company such as IBM buys parts from other companies around the world to create its products. In turn, the companies buy IBM computers.

States and Provinces

Trading partners or relationships also develop between states and countries through regional connections. Many trading relationships exist between people in southern Texas or southern California and companies or customers in the country of Mexico.

Countries and Trade Relationships

Trade relationships evolve between various countries. Many of these relationships are based on geographic proximity—or how close one country is to another. Countries in North America, such as the United States, Canada, and Mexico, trade with each other. This international trade moves more freely than in the past due to the North American Free Trade Agreement (NAFTA), which took effect in 1994.

Other international trading regions include Latin America, South America, Asia, the Pacific Rim, the Middle East, the European Union region, Eastern Europe and the former USSR region, Australia and New Zealand, and Africa.

The Pacific Rim is made up of nations and states located along the coast of the Pacific Ocean. In the eastern hemisphere, it includes Japan, the Koreas, Indonesia, Singapore, Malaysia, Thailand, China, Taiwan, and Russia. Australia, New Zealand, and small island nations line its southern edge. In the western hemisphere, the Pacific Rim includes western provinces of Canada, western states of the United States and Mexico, and South American nations such as Colombia, Peru, and Chile. Many relationships between businesses cross the national borders of the region.

A Global Effect

International business and trade have long histories. Today the expansion of international trade affects the lives of most of the world's residents. The next section explains its impact in greater detail, as well as the challenges of ethics and social responsibility in business.

Did You Know ?

Volcanic Trade Region

The Pacific Rim is also called the "ring of fire." The name "ring of fire" is inspired by the many volcanoes located along the edge of the Pacific tectonic plate in the North Pacific Ocean.

Quick Check 1.1

After You Read Respond to what you have read by answering these questions.

1. What is international business? _____

_____

2. When did global trade first begin? _____

_____

3. What are three factors that influence trade relations? _____

_____

Academics / Social Studies/Geography

4. Explain the concept of geographic proximity and how it might affect trade in North America.

_____

_____

The Scope of International Business

WHAT YOU'LL LEARN

- To describe settings in which international business affects people
- To list issues that affect ethics in international business

WHY IT'S IMPORTANT

It is necessary to work in the global environment in an ethical and legal way in order to sustain effective global trade.

KEY TERMS

- ethics
- business ethics
- social responsibility
- code of ethics
- stakeholders

Academic Vocabulary

You will find these words in your reading and on your tests. Make sure you know their meanings.

- approach
- benefit
- create

Reading Guide

Before You Read

Are the concepts of global dependence and social responsibility compatible?

MAIN IDEA
International business impacts daily life around the world and also affects ethical decisions in business.

GRAPHIC ORGANIZER
Draw this diagram. As you read this section, use it to organize the factors that influence a nation's ethical decisions.

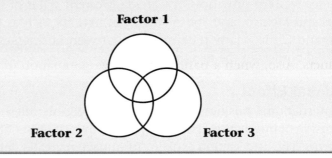

Factor 1

Factor 2   Factor 3

The Impact of International Business

International business has been a part of the history of many civilizations. In today's world, international trade affects most countries. It will continue to grow, affecting commerce and people in many settings:

- Local level
- State or provincial level
- National level
- International level

Local Level

At the local level, global business has changed the nature of shopping. Today people can buy products from firms around the world. Customers tend to expect local businesses to keep up with local trends in addition to national and international trends in goods and services. This means that local merchants must adapt to a rapidly changing world. The use of the Internet makes the world of international business move faster all the time.

State or Provincial Level

International business also affects commerce at the state or provincial level. Many state and provincial governments have commerce departments that actively seek ways to sell products made within their borders to countries around the world. In Wisconsin cheese producers export cheese to worldwide customers. In Nebraska companies sell beef products to many international customers. The state of Michigan is always looking to find ways to increase automobile trade in various countries. In addition, computer companies in California and Washington conduct a great deal of international trade with businesses along the Pacific Rim. Many businesses located in one state look to build relationships with international companies and national governments. You will learn more about these trade relations in Chapter 4.

National Level

At the national level, international trade has a major impact on the economy of an entire country. A country that imports more than it exports experiences economic difficulty because the balance of trade is unequal and unfavorable. Highly developed countries, such as the United States, need to keep a balance between exporting their products and importing products.

International trade also affects developing countries. Countries with few natural resources or goods to export have a difficult time building economic stability. They may need to rely more on imported products. Also, when a nation has a large population of untrained and under-educated people, economic conditions may not improve very quickly.

(A) **IMPORTS AND EXPORTS** **Importing and exporting affect your daily life. *Can you name a product that you ate today or that you are wearing right now that was imported?***

Coca-Cola® for the World

With 400 brands of beverages in over 200 countries, The Coca-Cola Company bottles and distributes one of the most recognized products in the world. How did a beverage with a secret formula created by a pharmacist in Atlanta, Georgia, become a global staple from Africa to Alaska? Dr. John Stith Pemberton concocted the syrup for Coke® in 1886 and sold it for five cents a glass mixed with carbonated water. The famous motto "Delicious and Refreshing" echoes today. He later sold the rights to the formula to Asa G. Candler, a savvy businessman. Since then, Coke has become one of the most widely recognized brand names around the world. Being aware of taste preferences and mindful of cultural differences, Coca-Cola has applied market research and adapted its advertising message to suit particular cultures. The first two countries outside the United States to bottle Coca-Cola were Cuba and Panama. It came to Asia after the turn of the 20th century, first in the Philippines. Besides being used as a thirst-quencher, it is served hot as a cold remedy in Hong Kong.

Wolfgang Kaehler/CORBIS

THINK GLOBALLY *Why might Coca-Cola have a different name in a different culture?*

@ To learn more about the country of origin for this business, go to the International Business Online Learning Center through **glencoe.com**.

International Level

Trade also affects the whole world on an international level. The term *trade war* applies to international business disputes. Governmental leaders try to make sure that international trade is fair. They impose taxes and tariffs if a country or company is gaining an unfair advantage by pricing products too low. Chapter 5 discusses the challenges of governmental relations and international trade.

Global trade affects individuals, families, social systems, economies, and even relationships between nations. A recession in one country or region, such as the Pacific Rim, can have a dramatic effect on economies in other countries near and far.

Ethics and Social Responsibility

The scope of international business encompasses additional challenges involving the issues of ethics and social responsibility. It is important to be open-minded about differences in culture. However, it is also important to avoid doing something that might be wrong or immoral in your culture as you conform to another culture. At times the balance may be difficult on a personal or professional level. Consequently, employees often look for a "compass," or guideline, to help direct their behavior and decision-making.

Ethics is a set of moral principles by which people conduct themselves personally, socially, or professionally. These principles do not provide an exact answer to every moral question. Instead, they serve as guidelines.

There are different ways to interpret an ethical principle or question. For example, should you never lie? Think about a situation in which someone is wearing clothing that is not appropriate or is unattractive. What if the person asks you, "How do I look?" What should you say? Resisting complete honesty may prevent hurt feelings.

Trying to do "the right thing" in the business world can be equally difficult. The best **approach** is to follow a set of ethical guidelines. **Business ethics** is a set of ideas about how a company should conduct business in relation to legal, social, and environmental issues. They include practicing business in a way that is legal, moral, and fair. **Figure 1.3** lists various ethical issues that challenge both domestic and international businesses today.

Social Responsibility

As members of society, employees of different companies need and want business organizations to benefit society. **Social responsibility** is the duty to do what is best for society. In the business world, companies can do two things to promote social responsibility:

1. Eliminate negative activities.

2. Perform positive activities.

Eliminating Negative Activities Negative activities include polluting or damaging the environment, practicing discrimination, breaking laws, and violating human rights. Unfortunately, problems such as unfair pay, dangerous working conditions, and the exploitation of young people occur around the world. Socially responsible companies condemn these practices and take ongoing action to eliminate them.

Figure 1.3

Ethical Issues Today

DOING THE RIGHT THING These are some of the typical ethical issues facing the business world today in many countries. *Which of these problems do you think is the most common or the most important for international businesses?*

Individual Level	Corporate Level
Theft	Discrimination
Lying and spreading rumors	Unfair pay
Accepting bribes	Sweatshop labor
Harassing others	Child labor
Stealing	Not paying taxes
Disobeying company rules	Pollution
	Selling defective products
	Unsafe work
	Paying bribes
	Misleading accounting statements

OUR MULTICULTURAL WORKPLACE

Appreciating Differences

Successful international businesses value and use workplace diversity. U.S. companies have an advantage because of the large number of immigrants who work in U.S. businesses. Projections for the 21st century show 70 percent of the people entering the U.S. workforce will come from cultures of other nations. As U.S. corporations become miniature global villages, they will employ more people from the countries where they conduct business. *How does diversity within a U.S. company give that company an advantage in the world marketplace?*

Performing Positive Activities Businesses can promote social responsibility by performing positive activities, such as creating programs that **benefit** people around the world. Sponsorship of charitable campaigns, training unemployed people for jobs, and allowing others to use company facilities for charitable events are a few examples of positive company activities.

A **code of ethics** is a statement that explains what a company or group believes is proper and improper conduct. This code applies to both individual employees and the whole company. Companies and business professionals can perform positive activities by following codes of ethics that help them stay on a socially responsible path.

Various professions **create** and sponsor codes of ethics. Accountants, business professors, physicians, literary agents, and many other professional groups strive to obey ethical codes. Along with codes of ethics, ethics counselors and ethics "hot lines" are available to employees around the world. These resources can help an individual identify and deal with ethical challenges.

Stakeholders

Ethical problems affect different people and groups in different ways. **Stakeholders** are the various individuals or groups of people who have a direct interest, involvement, or investment in something. Business organizations have many stakeholders. One set of stakeholders is made up of employees and the labor unions that represent them. Another set includes owners of businesses. Owners can be a family that owns a business or a set of stockholders. The government is another stakeholder group. Suppliers and customers are also stakeholders. In addition, the general public may have an interest in a company's activities and be considered stakeholders as well. A company with international operations has a larger set of stakeholders that includes more than one national government with additional sets of customers.

GLOBAL UNION POWER Labor unions are a key stakeholder group in many companies. *Are unions the same in the United States as they are in other countries?*

Ethical Issues and Stakeholders Ethical issues affect all of these stakeholder groups in different ways. For example, consider two basic issues: pollution and profits. Individual stakeholder groups will not respond to these two concerns in the same way. Owners or stockholders of a corporation may be more interested in profits and perhaps less concerned with pollution. Government regulators and the public are more likely to be worried about pollution and less concerned about a company's profits. Employees of the company may have another viewpoint altogether.

Every ethical issue, from unfair wages to tax evasion, has a specific impact on a stakeholder group. The different impacts result from the different interests of the group. As you think about ethical problems, examine each stakeholder's interest.

Factors Affecting Ethical Decisions

Ethical behavior is an issue in every country, because social rules and norms exist in every culture. At the same time, there may be stark differences in how ethical behavior is viewed by each culture.

Several factors affect ethical decisions in international markets. These factors include the culture and history of a country. International firms may also face pressure when dealing with union issues. In addition, the consequences of unethical business dealings depend on different governmental regulations. Thus, laws also influence businesspeople who must make ethical decisions.

✔ **Reading Check** **Recall** Name three factors that affect ethical decisions.

Culture and History National culture and history have dramatic effects on a nation's ethical climate. Culture is based on many things, including religion. For example, charging interest on a loan is unethical in Islamic cultures. Historical precedents, or past acceptance of certain actions, may also affect what is considered ethical or unethical.

Unions The presence of unions and the laws that regulate unions affect ethical decisions in many countries. For example, in some countries worker strikes are quite common. A strike may be an ethical expression of dissent that is legal. In other countries they are illegal and may be viewed as an expression of disloyalty and rebellion. Understanding ethics in a particular country requires examining the context in which that country operates.

Government Regulations National governments also view ethical issues in different ways. Child labor laws vary widely around the world. Paying a living wage, or enough money to live comfortably, is not required in every country. Some national leaders allow this, though people in the United States view it as unethical. Leaders may be trying to increase national exports, or are attempting to keep citizens employed. In a nation without a free enterprise system, there may be a strong emphasis on full employment rather than on allowing individual workers to accumulate wealth.

ETHICS & ISSUES

Eco-Entrepreneurship

Is it possible to make money and help the environment? Absolutely! Eco-conscious companies all around the globe practice eco-entrepreneurship—the concept that environmental protection and economic opportunity can go hand in hand. Many responsible companies limit hazardous emissions and protect water sources, but eco-entrepreneurs go one step further. Higher Grounds Trading Company in Leland, Michigan, is one example. To minimize its environmental impact, the company partners with small, farmer-owned, fair-trade coffee co-ops that produce shade-grown, organic beans. By protecting environmental resources, "green" businesses improve the world and turn a profit. *Why is it important for eco-entrepreneurs to prove that they can make money helping the environment?*

➤ **TRADE-OFFS** Health care has a price tag in most countries. In countries such as Denmark, workers' take-home pay is reduced in exchange for the assurance of universal health care. *Do you think it is ethical for a government to impose high taxes even if the proceeds go to helping people? Why or why not?*

Henrik Trygg/CORBIS

As You Read

Relate Do you think it is fair for one country to sell goods to buyers in other countries at much lower prices if companies in the seller's home country pay low wages to employees?

There may be other reasons for low wages. One major national debate concerns health care for every citizen. Most modern, industrialized nations offer health insurance to every citizen. Some national governments view full health coverage as an ethical issue. Workers in countries that provide universal health care generally earn less, but they do not have to pay for their medical care.

Consequences The consequences of "unethical" behavior vary widely. In some nations unethical practices are common. A government might ignore practices, such as allowing poor working conditions, or might even support them. Governments may be more interested in attracting business and making profits than in the rights of individual workers.

In other countries lawsuits and other forms of governmental intervention can combat activities that are deemed unethical. In the United States and other nations, it is possible to go to jail for doing unethical things. Everything from charging unfair prices to discrimination may have legal consequences. It is important to remember that what is ethical or unethical in one country or culture may not be the same in other countries. You need to understand how a culture views various acts if you work with or in a culture.

Also, there are different kinds of consequences that companies face when engaged in unethical or immoral business practices. Besides governmental action, individual consumers may stop doing business with a company or all businesses in an entire country. In addition, other partner companies may be less inclined to maintain relationships. Foreign governments may also take action if they believe a company is not doing things as it should.

International ✈ Business Careers

HOTEL MANAGER

Globalization is opening the doors to more international careers. Many of these jobs require travel, but some are home-based. Like all careers, these require education and certain skills. In addition to having world language skills, an individual must be able to adapt to different cultures.

Many of the same international careers can be found in a variety of countries. For example, careers in hospitality and tourism are global. A candidate who is willing to relocate has options in a variety of locales around the world. There is a wide range of lodging accommodations, from economy to luxury. With renewed business travel and domestic and world tourism, the field of hotel management needs competent, well-trained individuals.

Job Description

Hotel managers work directly with customers from many countries and oversee staff. A manager may work at night or during the day, supervising rooms, restaurants, entertainment, concierge services, finances, human resources, and bookings. Knowledge of the organizational structure of lodging facilities is necessary to coordinate all aspects of running a hotel, large or small.

Training

Managers can obtain training through in-house programs at hotels or through vocational schools specializing in hospitality. Some community colleges and four-year universities also offer in-depth training that can lead to certification as well as successful job placement.

📝 English Language Arts/Writing

What other careers in the tourism industry would you enjoy? What type of education might you need?

@ To learn more about hotel managers and their career paths, go to the International Business Online Learning Center through **glencoe.com**.

Career Data

Education: High school diploma, associate's degree, or bachelor's degree in lodging management

Skills: Computer, multi-tasking, diplomatic, and bilingual or multilingual skills

Outlook: Growth as fast as average in the next ten years

Local and Global Impacts

International business affects people at the local, regional, national, and global levels. Global business has expanded with the proliferation of the Internet, technology, and improved transportation. Customers can easily order and purchase products from around the world. States, provinces, and nations that once conducted business only within their countries' borders now seek trade and new opportunities with individuals, businesses, and governments in countries near and far. This growth of international business is part of an increasing globalization, which will continue to require responsible action by businesses around the world.

It is important to work within the ethical and legal limitations of each nation where business takes place. Codes of ethics can help individuals cope with ethical dilemmas. At the company-wide level, a business can maintain a socially responsible organization by eliminating negative activities and performing positive activities. Company leaders must balance the demands of many stakeholders as they try to build a successful and ethical business climate in the global business landscape.

Quick Check 1.2

After You Read Respond to what you have read by answering these questions.

1. How does international business affect ordinary people? _____

_____

_____

2. What are ethics and social responsibility? _____

_____

_____

3. What are stakeholders? _____

_____

_____

 **Academics**   *Science*

4. Use the Internet to identify the top three countries that produce emissions that pollute the air. Then research and list the effects of air pollution on the human body.

_____

_____

_____

_____

_____

Portfolio Worksheet

Career Preparation

Your dream is to work for an American company in the marketing department of its international division. Choose a country where you would like to work. Write a paragraph explaining how you would prepare yourself to live and work in that country. Use the Internet and library resources to research the language, culture, history, economics, and business environment of the country. Also research the various cities in the country and the cost of living and availability of housing there.

_____

_____

_____

_____

_____

_____

_____

_____

_____

_____

_____

_____

_____

_____

_____

_____

_____

_____

_____

ACADEMICS APPLIED Check off the academic knowledge you used to do this activity:

☐ English Language Arts ☐ Mathematics ☐ Social Studies ☐ Science

ACADEMIC AND CAREER PLAN Add this page to your Academic and Career Plan Portfolio.

CHAPTER SUMMARY

Section 1.1 **The Nature of International Business**

business (p. 7)

international business (p. 7)

domestic company (p. 7)

international company (p. 7)

globalization (p. 7)

global dependence (p. 12)

- Business is any activity that seeks profit by providing goods or services to others. International business is any activity involving business operations across national borders.

- The historical origins of international commerce are found throughout the world and in most of recorded history.

- The major factors that influence international trade include social, cultural, political, legal, and economic factors.

- The levels of participation in international trade are the involvement of individual consumers, companies, states or provinces, and countries.

Section 1.2 **The Scope of International Business**

ethics (p. 16)

business ethics (p. 17)

social responsibility (p. 17)

code of ethics (p. 18)

stakeholders (p. 18)

- Settings in which international business affects people include the local, state or provincial, national, and international.

- Culture, history, labor unions, and government regulations are all sources of issues that affect ethics in international business.

CONCEPTS REVIEW

1. **Define** the term *business*.

2. **Characterize** the growth in global trade from early civilization to modern times.

3. **Summarize** the political and legal factors that can influence international trade.

4. **Identify** the levels of participation in international trade.

5. **Describe** two settings in which international business affects people.

6. **List** the two things companies can do to promote social responsibility.

KEY TERMS REVIEW

7. Match each term to its definition.

_____ business

_____ international business

_____ domestic company

_____ international company

_____ globalization

_____ global dependence

_____ ethics

_____ business ethics

_____ social responsibility

_____ code of ethics

_____ stakeholders

a. a set of ideas about how a company should conduct business in relation to legal, social, and environmental issues

b. the duty to do what is best for society

c. a company that conducts business across national borders

d. individuals or groups of people who have a direct interest, involvement, or investment in something

e. any activity involving business operations across national borders

f. a statement that explains what a company or group believes is proper and improper conduct

g. the concept that all countries depend on each other for trade

h. a set of moral principles by which people conduct themselves, personally, socially, or professionally

i. a company that conducts business in only one country

j. the increasing integration of the world economy

k. any activity that seeks profit by providing goods or services to others

Academic Vocabulary

8. On a separate sheet of paper, write a sentence or two related to international business, using at least three of the academic terms you learned in the section openers:
- establish
- factor
- individual
- approach
- benefit
- create

Critical Thinking

9. A Japanese car manufacturer built a factory in the United States. It did so to reduce shipping and other costs. Make a list of who will benefit and who will not benefit from this factory.

Discussion Starter

10. Evaluate the quality and cost of products that are made overseas and sold in the United States. Give specific examples.

Point of View

11. Many American business leaders have supported the "outsourcing" of American manufacturing jobs to countries where the labor cost is much lower. They argue that this results in savings to consumers. Do you think American businesspeople will continue to "outsource"? Why or why not?

BUILDING REAL-WORLD SKILLS

12. Bribery In many countries bribery is an accepted means of doing business, akin to "paying" for networking. The giving of gifts of money or other items to qualify for consideration for a contract or official action is considered neither illegal nor unethical.

Research and Share

a. If you were an American businessperson representing your company overseas and the issue of bribery came up, what ethical issues would you consider?

b. What different types and purposes of bribes can you identify?

13. Accepting Gifts on the Job Various organizations and companies give gifts or other forms of gratuities to members of Congress and business executives to receive favorable decisions on the part of their organizations.

Research and Write

a. Determine the current standards for accepting gifts for members of Congress.

b. Make a list of the guidelines you would follow if offered gifts on the job.

BUILDING ACADEMIC SKILLS

ELA English Language Arts

14. Some businesses have dress codes or have their employees wear uniforms. Spend some time observing what individuals in various occupations in your community wear to work. Pick two examples. Write a paragraph on each that reveals the connection between the workers' attire and their jobs.

MATH Mathematics

15. In 2000, the United States claimed less than 5 percent of the world's population. That year the United States produced about $10 trillion worth of goods and services. The total amount of products produced that year by the entire world, including the United States, was worth $30 trillion. What was the percentage produced by the United States?

Computation and Estimation
To solve this problem, you need to understand the principles of determining percentages.

SOC Social Studies/Law

16. In 1977, the United States passed its Foreign Corrupt Practices Act. This anti-bribery statute prohibits payments made to obtain or retain business by influencing a foreign official's acts or decisions. Several other nations followed the United States' lead and passed similar statutes. Research how successful this attempt to remove bribery from the arena of international business has been. Write a paragraph summarizing your research.

SOC Social Studies/Linguistics

17. More than 30 countries have selected English as their official language. It is spoken predominantly in 20 other countries and is the second language in many others. What reasons can you infer for its widespread usage?

Global Treaties

18. Situation There are many organizations and treaties in the world due to globalization. In teams of two, select one organization or treaty and prepare a presentation for the class to detail what it represents, why it was created, and how successful it has been. Choose from organizations and treaties such as the WTO, World Bank, WHO, G8, NATO, NAFTA, CAFTA, and ASEAN.

Activity Research your selection on the Internet and by using library sources. Briefly relate the history behind it and define and outline the issues that relate to the world market.

Evaluation You will be evaluated on how well you meet the following objectives:

a. Properly describe the organization/treaty.

b. Define the issues that impact this organization/treaty from the U.S. viewpoint.

c. Define the issues that impact this organization/treaty from a global viewpoint.

d. Discuss the historical creation of the organization/treaty.

e. Project how this organization may affect international trade in ten years.

Internet Travels

India

Using the Internet, look up the country of India on a world map. India is bordered by the nations of Pakistan, China, Bangladesh, and Nepal. Answer the following questions about India on a separate sheet of paper.

➤ What two languages does the Indian Constitution stipulate as the languages of official communication for the national government?

➤ Why is it important to business that the Indian Constitution identifies such "languages of official communication"?

@ For resources to help you do this exercise, go to the International Business Online Learning Center through **glencoe.com**.

BusinessWeek online

19. Newsclip: In China, To Get Rich Is Glorious More than 300,000 Chinese have a net worth over $1 million, according to Merrill Lynch & Company. Chinese film director Wang Zhongjun explains, "Entrepreneurs in China today feel much safer than before."

@ Go to the International Business Online Learning Center through **glencoe.com** to read an article about this topic. Then list the international products Chinese consumers are purchasing and possible reasons for their popularity.

Standardized Test Practice

20. Choose the best answer to the following multiple-choice question.

Which of the following is not one of the four Ps of marketing vital for success in international business?
○ product
○ price
○ planning
○ promotion

Test-Taking Tip When a question asks for a "best" answer, it means that more than one answer may be correct. Your job is to pick not just the first accurate statement, but the one that is most correct.

Chapter 2

Cultural and Social Influences

Chapter Objectives

When you have completed this chapter, you will be able to:

Section 2.1

- Explain how culture affects international business.
- Describe the elements of cultures.
- Describe the elements of subcultures.

Section 2.2

- Explain how social institutions can help people adapt to a new culture.
- Identify ways to overcome stereotyping and cultural bias.
- Discuss how preparation and participation help improve cultural literacy.

▶ **EASTMAN KODAK®**

Eastman Kodak is a publicly owned company whose shares are traded on the stock exchanges. When you research this company through Standard & Poor's, you will find investment information such as this:

Index:	S&P 500 and S&P Global 1200
Sector:	Consumer Discretionary
Company:	Eastman Kodak
Symbol:	EK
Country:	U.S.A.
Price:	(varies)

Global Profile Eastman Kodak produces photography products and technology for images used in a variety of leisure, medical, business, entertainment, and scientific applications. Kodak provides goods and services to the photographic, graphic communications, and healthcare markets around the world.

Business Report With total sales of $14.3 billion in 2005, digital sales represented 54 percent of the total revenue. This was the first time in the company's history that digital revenue exceeded traditional revenue. Kodak's performance is due to strong demand for products from its consumer digital portfolio and its acquisition program to support its graphic communications business.

English Language Arts/Writing

With the slogan, "You press the button, we do the rest," George Eastman put the first simple camera on the market in 1888. Today wireless imaging is expanding our ability to capture and transmit images, such as this photo from Japan, and information, bringing people closer together. Kodak's focus on imaging science is converging with information technology to create "infoimaging." *How might this technology help people understand cultures and interact in business?*

@ To do this activity, go to the International Business Online Learning Center through **glencoe.com.**

Understanding Culture

WHAT YOU'LL LEARN

- To explain how culture affects international business
- To describe the elements of cultures
- To describe the elements of subcultures

WHY IT'S IMPORTANT

Understanding culture and its effect on international business provides a foundation for working in the global community.

KEY TERMS

- culture
- values
- norms
- folkways and mores
- role
- subculture

Academic Vocabulary

You will find these words in your reading and on your tests. Make sure you know their meanings.

- element
- respond
- similar

Reading Guide

Before You Read

What might be the difference between values and norms?

MAIN IDEA
Understanding cultural differences can help promote good global business.

GRAPHIC ORGANIZER
Draw this diagram. As you read this section, write in the elements and dimensions of culture.

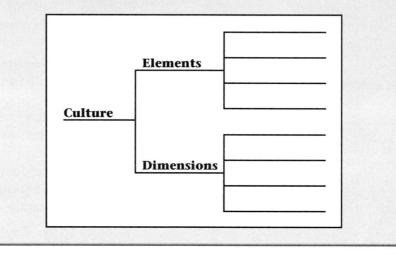

Culture in International Business

Imagine stepping off a plane in New Delhi, India. Would you know the history of that city and nation? Would you be aware of the influence of Great Britain? Would you know which religions are practiced in India? Who do people believe are their worst enemies or their best friends? Would you be able to avoid offending people? Would you feel comfortable in India? Whenever a firm does business with individuals or companies in other countries, its representatives must be aware of such cultural issues. This is because the cultures of both trading partners can affect every aspect of a business relationship.

This chapter presents and explains various aspects of culture. It also describes the concepts of subcultures within a culture and multicultural nations. Understanding culture is the foundation, or basis, of understanding every other aspect of conducting international business.

Understanding Culture

The term *culture* can apply to an entire country or part of a country, to a city, or even to a single business. **Culture** is the set of beliefs, customs, and attitudes of a distinct group of people. In addition, the shared values, beliefs, and goals in a company can also be a type of culture—a corporate culture.

Each level of culture—whether national, regional, or local—has an impact on the lives of people who live on that level. Culture also affects differences in how companies do business. Think about an activity that is as simple as eating a meal. If you go to a restaurant in Sitges, Spain, at 7:30 P.M. during the summer, there is a good chance that you might dine alone. In that culture, people fill the streets in the early evening. They walk, visit, or stop to get something to drink. A great deal of retail business takes place during the evening hours. People have dinner at 10 P.M. or later.

Figure 2.1 lists some of the most common characteristics of cultures. Study it carefully. Consider how each characteristic could have an impact on a business relationship. For example, in many countries the status of women in business is quite different than their status in the United States. In some cultures, women do not attend meetings. Succeeding in the world of international business requires:

1. Understanding culture
2. Preparing for and adjusting to culture
3. Participating in culture

Figure 2.1

Glossary of Cultural Components

CULTURAL INGREDIENTS Various characteristics make up a culture. *Have you been to a country where these characteristics were vastly different than in the United States? Share your observations with the class.*

1   aesthetics • social institutions

aesthetics what people in a culture consider to be beautiful

attitudes and beliefs commonly held views of persons, objects, and ideas

customs rituals performed in various settings, including celebrations of religious holidays, and political holidays

economic philosophy prevailing views of what an economy should be, whether it is free enterprise, socialism, or some other form

education approaches to teaching, including what is taught and how it is taught

language the native language(s) as well as dialects and slang

materialism views of what constitutes material wealth, and the importance of it

political philosophy the prevailing views regarding how people believe they should be governed

religion the most common faith or belief system in an area and people's tolerance of other religions

social institutions the official and unofficial practices of a country or region, including those that affect marriage, divorce, the status of women, and social standing

How Do You Say?

Q: In Italian, how do you say: "Hello, how are you?"

A: Salve, come sta? (pronounced: Sălvā, kōmā stă?)

@ To learn these words in other languages, go to the International Business Online Learning Center through **glencoe.com**.

Elements of Culture

To further understand culture, consider its basic **elements**: values, norms, folkways and mores, and roles. Culture is reflected in the values that people have. **Values** are strongly held concepts that are present in a culture. Values are connected to powerful emotions. For example, in the United States, many people value freedom. In other cultures loyalty may be the most important value. Freedom, democracy, justice, truth, social responsibility, love, marriage, and the roles of women and men in society are valued differently in various local, regional, and national cultures.

Norms may reflect values. **Norms** are social rules that affect behaviors and actions, and represent cultural values. In a culture where women are not considered equal to men, a married woman may follow the norm of walking a step or two behind her husband in public. The value is the society's concept about the role of women. The norm is the accepted behavior of walking behind, which represents the value.

Folkways and mores are cultural customs that dictate how people act socially. Some of these customs are relatively minor. Others have a major impact on people's daily lives. People in some cultures view time much differently than Americans view it. A simple invitation can reflect a folkway. In the United States, an invitation to a dinner scheduled for 7 P.M. asks a guest to arrive at 7 P.M., or a few minutes earlier. In Great Britain that same invitation is asking a guest to arrive between 7:30 and 8 P.M. In Argentina the host would expect the guest to be present after 8 P.M.

Mores are customs that reflect moral standards in a culture. They are strongly held by a group and include beliefs about forbidden acts, such as murder. Mores can influence controversial political topics.

> **DINNER TIME** Depending on the country, you need to know the appropriate time to arrive for dinner. *Give examples of typical dinner times in two countries.*

Figure 2.2

Factors that Create Roles

SHAPING YOUR ROLE Many elements help create the roles that people play in various countries. *What do you think are the main factors that influence the roles you play, as student, son or daughter, or friend in American culture?*

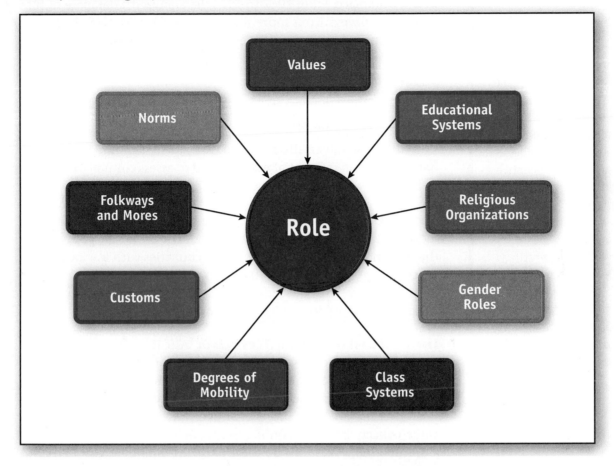

Roles A **role** is the part a person plays in a social situation. Values, norms, and folkways and mores all help shape the individual roles of people. The concept of a role is taken from the theater, where actors perform various parts. You play many roles each day. They might include son or daughter, friend, employee, or student in school.

Culture affects the types of roles in a community. A person's behavior might also depend on the nation in which the person lives and the customs or folkways associated with different events. For example, when a national anthem is played in most countries, many people play the role of "citizen" and **respond** by standing quietly or saluting a national flag. The role of "spectator" at sporting events, such as soccer games or tennis matches, may vary depending on the culture. The spectator's behavior might also depend on the nation in which the person lives and the customs or folkways associated with the event. In addition, the role of "police officer" may be very different in developing countries, compared to the role in most developed nations.

Understanding culture begins with recognizing the values, norms, and folkways and mores of a region. Then it is possible to examine the roles people play within a culture. **Figure 2.2** illustrates some factors that help shape the roles people play in their particular cultures.

As You Read

Relate In what ways might your personal values be influenced by living in an individualistic country such as the United States?

Value Dimensions of Culture

A management technique or philosophy that works in one culture may not be appropriate for another. To better understand cultural differences in the workplace, Dutch sociologist Geert Hofstede conducted a study to determine how national culture influences values in the workplace. From 1967 to 1973, he analyzed a database of IBM employee surveys from more than 70 countries. This study and its more recent follow-up studies describe differences based on five basic value dimensions:

- Power distance
- Individualism or collectivism
- Gender differentiation
- Uncertainty avoidance
- Short-term or long-term orientation

While not universally accepted, the Hofstede value dimensions have become an influential method used to assess cultural differences in businesses.

Power Distance In cultures with a large power distance among individuals, supervisors are "always right." The economic gap between the rich and poor may also be wide. In countries with low power distance, where people tend to have more rights, managers may have a collaborative style of leadership. They might view employees as "partners" and ask for advice from employees.

Individualism or Collectivism Another value dimension focuses on how people value the individual versus the group. In individualistic countries, such as the United States and Australia, people tend to take care of themselves and immediate families first. Organizations may rely on individual decision making. Cultures that value collectivism focus on being part of something larger, such as a family group, religion, political party, or employer company. An individual sees him- or herself as part of a collective of people and might sacrifice individual success to help the group or team. Many people in countries such as Japan, Colombia, and Venezuela value group acceptance.

Gender Differentiation Another value dimension reflects the extent to which a culture values assertiveness, acquisition of money and status, and achievement. In cultures with a high degree of gender differentiation, men tend to dominate society and power structures. The Hofstede system refers to this dimension as "Masculinity." Women usually do not enjoy equal status or rights in such cultures, such as those in the Middle East. In cultures with a lower degree of gender differentiation, such as those in the United States and the United Kingdom, there is less gender discrimination.

Uncertainty Avoidance In high risk-avoidance countries, such as Mexico, Portugal, and Japan, managers are less willing to take risks. This attitude may promote a stable environment, but it can sometimes prevent progress in businesses. Businesspeople in low risk-avoidance countries, such as the United States, Great Britain, and New Zealand, believe that taking risks can lead to success.

Short-Term or Long-Term Orientation This value dimension measures how businesspeople value short-term versus long-term results. In the United States, businesses tend to emphasize short-term results, such as high sales that provide immediate benefits. However, managers in many Asian nations believe that placing importance on short-term results causes a company to ignore long-term results. Managers focus on factors such as customer loyalty.

Understanding Subcultures

Not everyone in a country or nation behaves similarly or follows the same customs. People with varied behaviors within a culture make up a subculture. A **subculture** is a smaller group or subset within a larger culture. In the United States, one subculture might be a group of suburban men who enjoy football or golf. Subcultures can also form around music, religion, political affiliation, or other **similar** interests. In addition, age, race, or gender can differentiate subcultures. Regions and cities may also produce distinct subcultures. In France residents of Paris make up a subculture that is distinct from the subcultures existing in other towns and provinces of the country.

A key to working in international business is to be aware that people within the same nation and/or business organization may be quite different. Their diversity creates distinct subcultures.

✓ **Reading Check** **Recall** What are subcultures and why is recognizing them important?

World Market ITALY

The Vespa Culture

When Enrico Piaggio took over his father's transportation company in postwar Italy, he focused his attention on the mobility needs of the public. However, instead of making airplanes, trucks, or ships, he decided to create an elegant and comfortable two-wheeled vehicle. The product's shape, which was developed by aeronautical engineer Corradino D'Ascanio, prompted Piaggio to say, "It looks like a wasp!" *Vespa* is Italian for "wasp," so a brand name was born. By the end of the 1940s, production reached 35,000 units.

The decade of the 1950s saw a million Vespas buzzing around Europe and Asia. By the 1960s and 1970s, the scooters became a symbol of youth culture, appearing in movies such as *Roman Holiday*. Currently the company manufactures scooters, motorcycles, and mopeds in Italy, Spain, India, and China. Their vintage European styling and excellent gas mileage are fueling sales in the United States.

THINK GLOBALLY *How has the culture of Italy influenced Vespa products?*

@ To learn more about the country of origin for this global business, go to the International Business Online Learning Center through **glencoe.com**.

Promoting Pride of All Cultures

In the past immigrants often blended into American society and workplaces, forgetting their cultural heritage. Today's world is different. Many companies recognize that cultural differences can enhance an environment of creativity and innovation. Employees must think about business and developing strategies from a variety of perspectives. To create an environment that values and promotes pride and respect for differences, companies can display a variety of posters representing cultural celebrations. ***Think of three ways corporations can promote pride and respect for cultures. Why might these practices help companies be successful?***

Single Culture and Multicultural Countries

The concept of subculture is related to the ideas of homogeneity and heterogeneity in a country. These terms represent the level of diversity that is present in a country.

A *homogeneous* culture is one in which one group of people is dominant in the population. For example, this group of people may be one race or adhere to one particular religion. A homogeneous culture exists in a *single-culture* nation or region. For example, Mexico has a relatively homogeneous culture. The dominant religion is Catholicism, and the culture is relatively uniform. The culture of the United States is *heterogeneous* in a *multicultural* country, where there are many different groups of people.

The first step to working in a new country is to understand all of the elements of culture, both at the national level and the local level. However, even in a single-culture setting, such as Mexico, there are cultural differences in big cities as compared to outlying farming regions and small towns where subcultures exist.

Multinational Companies

The culture within a multinational company is not the same as the culture of a company operating in only one country. A single-country company's business decisions are more likely influenced by the culture of that country, including religious practices, traditions, customs, norms, and mores and folkways. In contrast, because a multinational company includes cultures from several nations, business decisions may be more inclusive and targeted to the variety of cultures. Employees may be more aware of cultural differences through doing business in an international community.

Quick Check 2.1

After You Read Respond to what you have read by answering these questions.

1. What cultural elements create individual roles in society? _____

_____

2. What are some examples of dimensions of cultures? _____

_____

3. What is the definition of the term *subculture*? _____

_____

 **Academics** / *Social Studies*

4. Explain how cultural issues may differ between multinational and single-country companies?

_____

_____

Participating in a Culture

Reading Guide

Before You Read

What is your definition of culture shock and how might it affect someone in a global business?

MAIN IDEA

By studying and preparing to adapt to a culture in another country, people can participate and benefit from doing business there.

GRAPHIC ORGANIZER

Draw this diagram. As you read this section, write in the three roadblocks to overcoming culture shock, providing an example of each, either from the text or from your own experience.

Roadblocks to Overcoming Culture Shock		
1._____	2._____	3._____

WHAT YOU'LL LEARN

- To explain how social institutions can help people adapt to a new culture
- To identify ways to overcome stereotyping and cultural bias
- To discuss how preparation and participation help improve cultural literacy

WHY IT'S IMPORTANT

The ability to adapt to cultural differences promotes personal and professional growth.

KEY TERMS

- social institutions
- culture shock
- cultural baggage
- cultural bias
- stereotyping
- ethnocentrism

Academic Vocabulary

You will find these words in your reading and on your tests. Make sure you know their meanings.

- region
- conduct
- tradition

Social Influences in Cultural Adjustment

How do you adjust to the culture of a new land so that you can fully participate socially and professionally? Identify the social institutions of the country and recognize how they operate. Learn how to overcome culture shock. Then prepare for, adjust to, and participate in the culture of a new country.

Social Institutions

The first step of adjusting to a culture is to identify the social institutions that are present in the country. **Social institutions** are the organizations that represent the patterns of activity that express the culture of a country. There are several basic social institutions:

- Educational systems
- Religious organizations
- Gender roles
- Class systems
- Degrees of mobility

Shehzad Noorani/Woodfin Camp/Independent Photography Network

Educational Systems

Educational systems as social institutions differ widely around the world. The main differences involve access to education and type of education. Some cultures favor males over females when offering educational opportunities. In other cultures only the more wealthy members of society have access to schools. In many parts of the world, formal academic education overlaps with religious teaching.

ACCESS TO EDUCATION In many countries, few students attend school beyond elementary or high school. *Do you think all people should have the "right" to go to college, regardless of wealth or social status? Why or why not?*

Both types of education are presented in the same school. In the United States and Great Britain, where separation of church and state is the law and a cultural value, public schools do not provide religious education.

In many countries only very successful students have access to education beyond elementary school. High school may be vocational with few academic courses available. In those countries, only the top students go to college. In the United States, most students, male and female, with a high school diploma are able to attend community colleges and some four-year colleges. These educational opportunities do not exist in many **regions** of the world.

Religious Organizations

Religious organizations are another key social institution of a culture. Because children may attend religious ceremonies when they are very young, religious influence can be long-lasting. Also, a country ruled by religious law has a legal system that differs from the legal system in a country that emphasizes the separation of church and state. Religious leaders are political forces in many countries today, even in those countries that foster a separation of church and state, or government.

Gender Roles

Gender roles are social institutions that affect many aspects of life, from family to work to government. These roles vary around the world. For example, in many African nations, women perform farm work. Farming was considered to be men's work in the United States for many years. Many cultures favor men over women in the workplace. This is still true even in some developed nations. Gender roles can also affect methods of parenting, housekeeping, and daily family activities, as well as how people **conduct** business.

Class Systems

Class systems and their related patterns of upward social and economic mobility are also key social institutions in a culture. In a nation where class differences are strong, people in the upper classes have better access to education, work opportunities, and the legal system. A person can belong to an upper class as a result of inheriting a family name (nobility) or family wealth. It is difficult for people in lower economic or social classes to move to a higher social status in such a culture. In cultures where the class system is weaker, such as in the United States and other countries, moving upward socially or economically is possible for more people.

Degrees of Mobility

The degrees of physical mobility within a country can also become a kind of social institution. Mobility relates to where people live and how easily they can move to live in different places. In a country with high mobility, people can relocate relatively easily and find a new home. In a region with low mobility, most people live and die close to where they were born, and do not often move to live in new places throughout their lifetimes. Understanding prevailing degrees of mobility can help you adjust to a new culture.

Overcoming Culture Shock

When you first encounter a new culture, you might experience what is called "culture shock." **Culture shock** is a reaction that newcomers to a culture may experience. Some reactions may include feeling uncomfortable, afraid, resentful, and/or intrigued. After being in the culture for a while, a newcomer begins to feel accustomed to the different environment and culture. At that point a newcomer may begin to enjoy the new culture.

To adjust to a new culture and overcome culture shock, newcomers must become very aware of their own mental and social reactions that can prevent successful adjustment. Three types of attitudes can become roadblocks to adjusting to a culture:

- Cultural baggage
- Cultural bias
- Stereotyping

By developing and using effective communication skills, most people can reduce and counteract negative attitudes and learn to adapt to a new culture.

✓ Reading Check **Recall** What reactions can be roadblocks to overcoming culture shock?

Cultural Baggage

Cultural baggage is a set of cultural attitudes that include the beliefs, values, and assumptions that people carry with them throughout life. These may include religious attitudes or dining habits.

Web logs, or "blogs," are Web sites that enable individuals to post their thoughts online in a sequential journal format. The blog has become a powerful tool for different uses. Some corporate executives create them to promote good public relations and to appear connected with customers. Corporate blogs show how the culture inside a company may differ from nation to nation. International businesses use blogs to gain insight into customer reaction in different countries. Regional blogs can provide information about which goods and services are most popular. *Find three different corporate blogs located in three different geographical regions. Write a one-page discussion about the differences and similarities between the three.*

@ For links to help you do this activity, go to the International Business Online Learning Center through **glencoe.com**.

For example, some people from the United States believe that "time is money." Consequently, they devote most of their time to business. When meeting people from certain cultures, some Americans become frustrated by their slower pace of doing business. In order to relate successfully, Americans may need to throw off their cultural baggage and adjust to the slower pace.

Cultural Bias

Cultural bias is a preconceived attitude of favoring or disliking a particular culture. For many years, a number of U.S. citizens had a negative cultural bias toward Japan and Germany after the countries opposed the United States during World War II. More recently some people developed cultural biases toward Islamic countries due to the events of September 11, 2001.

Stereotyping

Stereotyping is the practice of identifying a person or group by a single trait, or as a member of a certain group instead of as an individual. If you believe Brazilians are "hot blooded" or that Italians are "romantic," you are stereotyping. Each culture has tendencies that are rooted in its values, norms, and folkways. However, within a culture, there are many individuals who may not have those tendencies at all. For example, while people in Australia tend to be risk-takers, some Australians may avoid danger at all costs. It is never wise to assume that all people in any one group are the same.

When adjusting to a new culture, it is vital to prevent cultural baggage, cultural bias, or stereotyping from allowing you to cope with and appreciate a new country. It is worthwhile to make the effort to communicate with and understand people you meet in another culture or country.

ENJOYING A NEW CULTURE
Participating in a different culture can be exciting, fun, and educational. *Describe food that you have enjoyed from two countries. What countries?*

Culture Corner

Cultures Connect in Australia

Think About It Why should we respect cultural differences in the global business environment?

Australia is located in the Southern Hemisphere, where summer begins in December. In addition to distinctive animals and geographical features, Australia also boasts an ethnically diverse population. Australia's native people, the Aborigines, have their own unique culture. Also, the influence of British settlers remains strong. In addition, open immigration policies have transformed Australia into a multicultural nation. In fact, 43 percent of the population comes from more than 200 countries. The government's New Agenda for Multicultural Australia recognizes its diversity as "a source of economic benefit, cultural enrichment, and social stability." Companies such as IBM and Cisco Systems participate in this vision to cultivate good business through "community harmony."

Meeting and Greeting When doing business in Australia, shake hands at the beginning and end of a meeting. Address people by last names and titles until invited to use first names. Avoid using overused Australian terms, such as "G'day, mate."

Business Etiquette Present your business card when first introduced to people. Arrive on time for meetings. Do not emphasize your education or achievements. Be direct and good-humored in conversation.

Business Dress Wear conservative attire. Men wear ties and dark suits. Women wear dresses or skirt suits.

English Language Arts/Writing

Write a paragraph about ways in which businesses can use the skills of their diverse employees.

Communication Skills

Communication skills can counteract negative attitudes and broaden your perspective about different cultures. If you apply these skills in a new country, people may respond to you more favorably. There are a variety of languages used in various countries. A nation may have an official language, a common language, and a business language. By learning a few basic phrases as well as correct gestures and other forms of nonverbal communication, you show respect for another culture.

Nonverbal communication varies widely by culture. Gestures are different depending on the country. Body language also says different things. The concept of personal space varies. In the United States, people stand a certain distance apart. In some countries, not getting closer communicates distrust. Adjusting to a culture includes avoiding problems and taking advantage of opportunities.

Participating in Another Culture

Some people adapt to new situations easily while others may struggle. Still, anyone can improve his or her mental response to meeting different people. Before experiencing a culture that is new to you, consider a few cultural concepts that vary in different countries:

- Concepts of time
- Job prestige
- Directness in communication
- Change
- Achievement and work

Concepts of Time

To learn a culture's concept of time, become familiar with how people view punctuality and pace. Many cultures do not engage in multitasking to save time as people do in the United States. Also, moving too quickly can seem abrupt and rude in some countries.

In addition, some cultures value leisure time more than others do. Many people around the world work 40 hours per week, Monday through Friday. In countries with a strong emphasis on leisure, such as Germany and other European nations, spending time at work four days a week is common. Instead of 40 hours per week, workers are present for only 36 hours. Many employees in Germany work nine hours per day over four days per week. In contrast, Americans may work eight hours or more each day, five days per week.

Culture affects time at work in other ways. In Mexico and in countries of South America and Europe, the custom was to break from work after lunch for three hours during the warmest part of the afternoon. The break in Mexico is known as a *siesta*. This **tradition** is less common today. Still, some businesses continue the work schedule with the afternoon break.

Calendars and holidays vary by culture and the prevailing religion in the area. For example, only recently have people in Taiwan observed the New Year holiday on the same day as observed by western cultures. Traditionally, Taiwan follows the Chinese calendar, in which the New Year begins four to six weeks later.

To experience and participate in a new culture requires that you understand not only how people work but also at what times. Expect to adjust to different work times, work days, and work weeks.

Directness in Communication

Directness in communication is the tendency of people, especially in the United States, to "get right to the point." In some cultures, businesspeople engage in pleasant conversation over a drink or food before focusing on business matters. Forcing the point too directly is considered brash and rude. Learning to enjoy a slower pace in some cultures can be one step toward adapting to a culture.

Achievement and Work

Cultures value accomplishment and achievement in varying degrees. In Germany relationships and leisure time are valued. An impressive résumé is a major career asset in the United States.

Job Prestige

Manual labor may be disdained by people in some countries. Job prestige may come through working with one's mind, even when physical jobs, such as welding, may pay better wages. To understand a new culture involves being aware of these attitudes.

Change

Tradition is very important in many cultures. Change must be implemented slowly and carefully. To enjoy such cultures, recognize and appreciate their different traditions and customs.

International Business Careers

SALES REPRESENTATIVE

Sales representatives sell goods and services for manufacturers or wholesale distributors. Their job is to interest buyers and purchasing agents in their company's products. Sales representatives generate interest by making sales calls, giving presentations, demonstrating products, and entertaining possible customers and current clients. They represent everything from electronics to prescription drugs.

International sales representatives must understand different cultures in order to successfully pitch their products. For example, to be effective in Japan, a sales representative should know the proper greeting and what topics of conversation are appropriate for business dinners in that country. Because personal contact is extremely important in sales, extensive travel is required.

Skills and Training

Potential sales representatives should be able to work with people from different cultures. They must also be able to work independently. World language, communication, and negotiation skills are necessary for attracting clients and closing sales. They are responsible for analyzing sales statistics, preparing reports, and scheduling appointments. Successful sales representatives read trade magazines and attend trade shows to stay informed about trends and competition.

Sales representatives may enter the field with a high school diploma, but a college degree is becoming increasingly important. In addition to on-the-job training, sales representatives attend conferences, conventions, and seminars to improve their skills.

English Language Arts/Writing

Why is it important for international sales representatives to understand cultural and social influences?

@ To learn more about sales representatives and their career paths, go to the International Business Online Learning Center through **glencoe.com**.

Career Data

Education: High school diploma, associate's degree, or bachelor's degree

Skills: Computer, bilingual or multilingual, and communication skills

Outlook: Growth as fast as average in the next ten years

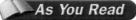

Question In what ways are ethnocentrism and cultural bias similar and different?

Cross-Cultural Literacy

If you can prepare yourself for these differences, you are beginning to develop a skill called cross-cultural literacy. This skill makes you a more valuable employee and may enhance your experience while living in another country. Most people begin to develop cross-cultural literacy by eliminating ethnocentrism from their thinking processes. **Ethnocentrism** is the belief that one's own culture is better than all other cultures. A culturally literate person replaces the idea that a culture is *better* with the idea that all cultures are *different*.

Exploring Cultures

To participate in another culture is to become involved in as many activities as possible. Enjoy the music, literature, art, architecture, foods, holidays, religious events, and patterns of living in the new country. There may be foods that you have never thought you would eat. Have you ever eaten a chocolate-covered ant or a grasshopper? You might enjoy trying a variety of fruits and vegetables not commonly served in the United States. Also, ask questions. Notice cultural differences without judging them. There may be some customs that are difficult to assimilate. Set aside those customs and participate in the activities that make the new culture rich.

 **Quick Check 2.2**

After You Read Respond to what you have read by answering these questions.

1. What are some social institutions present in a culture? _____
_____
_____

2. What attitudes can prevent overcoming culture shock? _____
_____
_____

3. What cultural concepts should you consider when adjusting to and participating in new cultures?
_____
_____

Academics *English Language Arts*

4. Define the term *cultural bias* in your own words and give an example of it from your personal experience or observation.
_____
_____
_____
_____

Culture Study

You have taken a management position in the United States with an international company whose country of origin is Malaysia. One of the senior company officials is arriving from the home office next week to inspect the company facilities. This will be the native Malaysian's first visit to the United States. Prepare a thorough briefing outline for the visitor on the culture of the United States. Use the questions in the first paragraph of the chapter to help you get started.

_____

_____

_____

_____

_____

_____

_____

_____

_____

_____

_____

_____

_____

_____

_____

_____

_____

_____

_____

ACADEMICS APPLIED Check off the academic knowledge you used to do this activity:

☐ English Language Arts   ☐ Mathematics   ☐ Social Studies   ☐ Science

ACADEMIC AND CAREER PLAN Add this page to your Academic and Career Plan Portfolio.

CHAPTER SUMMARY

Section 2.1 **Understanding Culture**

culture (p. 31)
values (p. 32)
norms (p. 32)
folkways and mores
    (p. 32)
role (p. 33)
subculture (p. 35)

- The cultures of both trading partners can affect every aspect of a business relationship.

- The basic elements of cultures are values, norms, folkways, mores, and roles.

- The subcultures of a country may be formed around geographical regions, political subdivisions, musical tastes, religious beliefs, and many other orientations.

Section 2.2 **Participating in a Culture**

social institutions
    (p. 37)
culture shock (p. 39)
cultural baggage (p. 39)
cultural bias (p. 40)
stereotyping (p. 40)
ethnocentrism (p. 44)

- The social institutions of a country are the organizations that represent and the patterns of activity that express the country's culture.

- The effects of stereotyping and cultural bias can be overcome by making efforts to communicate with and understand people from other cultures or countries.

- Cultural literacy can begin by eliminating ethnocentrism from an individual's thinking processes.

CONCEPTS REVIEW

1. **Explain** the term *culture*.

2. **Identify** the various elements of cultures.

3. **Provide** five examples of focal points around which subcultures may form.

4. **Give** three examples of social institutions that appear in most countries.

5. **Describe** how to overcome stereotyping and cultural bias.

6. **Summarize** how an individual would begin an attempt at creating a higher level of cultural literacy.

KEY TERMS REVIEW

7. Match each term to its definition.

_____ culture

_____ values

_____ norms

_____ folkways and mores

_____ role

_____ subculture

_____ social institutions

_____ culture shock

_____ cultural baggage

_____ cultural bias

_____ stereotyping

_____ ethnocentrism

a. a preconceived attitude of favoring or disliking a particular culture

b. strongly held concepts that are present in a culture

c. the part a person plays in a social situation

d. the practice of identifying a person or group by a single trait, or as a member of a certain group instead of as an individual

e. social rules that affect behaviors and actions, and represent cultural values

f. cultural customs that dictate how people act socially

g. a smaller group or subset within a larger culture

h. the organizations that represent the patterns of activity that express the culture of a country

i. the set of beliefs, customs, and attitudes of a distinct group of people

j. a reaction that newcomers to a culture may experience; reactions may include feeling uncomfortable, afraid, resentful, and/or intrigued

k. a set of cultural attitudes that include the beliefs, values, and assumptions that people carry with them throughout life

l. the belief that one's own culture is better than all other cultures

Academic Vocabulary

8. On a separate sheet of paper, write a sentence or two related to cultural and social influences, using at least three of the academic terms you learned in the section openers:

- element
- respond
- similar
- region
- conduct
- tradition

Critical Thinking

9. According to the International Labor Organization, 250 million children between the ages of 5 and 14 work in developing countries. Research child labor. Write a paragraph discussing the cultural reasons for this.

Discussion Starter

10. You are a citizen of a developing country that is experiencing a long drought. You want to emigrate to an industrialized country to find work. What factors would you consider in choosing a country?

Point of View

11. Ethnocentrism most often takes the form of one group imposing its cultural expectations on another. Give two examples of ethnocentrism drawn from your own observations.

BUILDING REAL-WORLD SKILLS

The GLOBAL WORKPLACE

12. Hospitality around the World
From the warmth of traditional Southern charm in the United States to the overwhelming attention paid to a guest, or *misafir,* in Turkish villages, hospitality takes many forms.

Research and Share

a. How guests are traditionally received in two countries other than the United States

b. How to properly thank your hosts upon receiving their outpourings of welcome in those countries

The U.S. WORKPLACE

13. Learning to Listen One of the greatest skills in the workplace is the ability to receive directions and carry them out. The most vital component in such a skill is the ability to listen. Without this ability, individuals may give their best effort to the wrong task.

Research and Write

a. Find examples of where mistaken commands have resulted in disaster.

b. Research and list tips that will improve a person's listening skills.

BUILDING ACADEMIC SKILLS

ELA **English Language Arts**

14. Identify a subculture in your school. Write two paragraphs describing the various identifying characteristics of this subculture. Read your description to the class and have them evaluate it for stereotyping.

MATH **Mathematics**

15. More than 7 million immigrants live in a country with open immigration. Of these, approximately 70 percent are from China. One province has almost one-third of the nation's immigrants. Approximately how many immigrants from countries other than China may be in that province?

Mathematical Reasoning and Operations To solve this problem, you need to understand the principles of determining and applying percentages.

SOC **Social Studies/Sociology**

16. One aspect of traditional culture in the modern state of India is the caste system. Research the background and current status of the caste system in India, and write a paragraph about it.

SOC **Social Studies/Archaeology**

17. Pompeii is one of the most informative archaeological sites ever discovered. This city on the Italian peninsula was entombed by an eruption of the nearby volcano, Mount Vesuvius. Pompeii's ruins reveal information about culture in the Roman Empire during 79 A.D. Research this topic and write a paragraph about how Roman culture in Pompeii was different from yet similar to current American culture.

COMPETITIVE EVENT PREP

Your Space or Mine?

18. Situation You are the head of the Human Resources Division of a multinational enterprise. It is your responsibility to prepare executives who must travel abroad to visit foreign subsidiaries. You have plants in six countries.

Activity Using a globe or world map, pick six countries in which you will build your foreign subsidiaries. Research and develop a grid to place in a protocol binder for your executives to reference. This grid should include the expectation in each country for eye contact, space maintained between businessmen carrying on a stand up meeting, voice intonation, practical advice for conversation starters, use of gifts, food and drink preferences, and other important cultural habits.

Evaluation You will be evaluated on how well you meet the following objectives.

a. Prepare a neat, clear, and well-organized presentation.

b. Provide sufficient quantity of informative facts and in-depth research.

c. Present your findings to the class.

Internet Travels

Italy

Using the Internet, find a map of Italy. Answer the following questions about this nation on a separate sheet of paper.

➤ What makes Italy's location ideal as a center for business and political power?

➤ What geographical factors would tend to isolate Italy's culture from those of the surrounding countries?

@ For resources to help you do this exercise, go to the International Business Online Learning Center through **glencoe.com**.

BusinessWeek online

19. Newsclip: Vive les Différences French business school HEC attracts MBA students from all around the globe. The multilingual and cosmopolitan student body allows for cultural exchange, while the small school's excellent reputation opens the door for opportunities in international business.

@ Go to the International Business Online Learning Center through **glencoe.com** to read an article about this topic. Then write a paragraph that cites some examples of cultural benefits gained from attending a school such as HEC.

Standardized Test Practice

20. Choose the best answer to the following multiple-choice question.

According to the chapter, which of the following is not a social institution?
- ○ An educational system
- ○ Gender roles
- ○ Class systems
- ○ All of the above are social institutions.

Test-Taking Tip When "all of the above" or "none of the above" appears as an answer to a multiple-choice question, it is likely not to be the correct choice. However, there are exceptions.

Chapter 3

International Communications

Chapter Objectives

When you have completed this chapter, you will be able to:

Section 3.1

- Explain the basic nature of communication.
- Identify the challenges of communicating in a world language.
- Describe verbal communication strategies.

Section 3.2

- Describe the forms of nonverbal communication.
- Discuss how culture affects nonverbal communication.
- Identify methods for overcoming communication problems and developing effective messages.

NESTLÉ

Nestlé is a publicly owned corporation whose shares are traded on the stock exchanges. When you research this company through Standard & Poor's, you will find investment information such as this:

Index:	S&P Europe 350
Sector:	Consumer Staples
Company:	Nestlé SA
Symbol:	NESN
Country:	Switzerland
Price:	(varies)

Global Profile Nestlé is one of the world's largest food companies. It produces beverages, milk, nutrition products, chocolate/confectionery, ice cream, prepared foods, and pet food. The Nestlé corporation has many brands, such as Nestlé, Nescafe, Nestea, Perrier, Maggi, Buitoni, and Purina.

Business Report Nestlé has been reshaping its products portfolio (a collection of brands and products) to expand its exposure to higher-growth products, such as water and pet care products. As a result, Nestlé has a strong and well-rounded portfolio. In addition, the company is actively cutting the costs of its business to increase profits steadily. Therefore, strong growth, profitability, and more cash flow are the attractions of Nestlé. The key risk of investing in Nestlé could be the possibility that sales and profits would not increase over the next few years.

English Language Arts/Writing

One of Nestlé's products is the French drinking water, Perrier. *Write a short paragraph about how and why Perrier's brand name might be communicated differently in various countries, such as England.*

To do this activity, go to the International Business Online Learning Center through **glencoe.com**.

Understanding Communication

WHAT YOU'LL LEARN

- To explain the basic nature of communication
- To identify the challenges of communicating in a world language
- To describe verbal communication strategies

WHY IT'S IMPORTANT

Communication skills are vital for people doing business globally.

KEY TERMS

- communication
- language
- verbal communication
- slang
- international trade documentation

Academic Vocabulary

You will find these words in your reading and on your tests. Make sure you know their meanings.

- process
- environment
- concept

Reading Guide

Before You Read

What is your definition of the word *language*?

MAIN IDEA
Effective communication creates bonds between people in all social settings, including the business world.

GRAPHIC ORGANIZER
Draw this diagram. As you read this section, write in the verbal communication strategies:

1. _____	2. _____
3. _____	4. _____

The Importance of Communication

How do you communicate each day? The answer is not as simple as it seems. You may think that you communicate only through the words that you speak and write, and through your gestures, facial expressions, and posture. But there are other methods as well. You also communicate through the clothes you wear, the way you style your hair, and in many other ways.

Effective communication holds things together—personal relationships, friends, organizations, and entire nations. People must be able to reach and understand each other to overcome differences, get along with one another, and accomplish goals.

Communicating Across Cultures

Understanding communication in a single culture is difficult. Trying to understand communication across cultures is a greater challenge. This chapter will describe the basic forms of verbal and non-verbal communication—and relate them to international business operations. Also, you will learn about the complications of communication between people who speak different languages. In business and in other international relations, the goal is effective communication when trying to send and receive messages across national borders and between different nationalities.

Verbal Communication

Verbal communication is one form of communication. **Communication** means transmitting, receiving, and processing information. When the **process** takes place between one person and another (or others), it is interpersonal communication. When it takes place in a company, it is organizational communication. **Language** is the medium of communication through words, symbols, numbers, characters, or nonverbal cues.

Figure 3.1 provides a model of individual communication. Note that the sender can pass along both verbal and nonverbal messages. At the same time, the receiver provides verbal and nonverbal forms of feedback. The receiver may be giving feedback by nodding in such a way that communicates, "I disagree," or the opposite, "I agree." The receiver may be giving feedback that says, "I am bored," or "You are making me uncomfortable." In any conversation between people, there is a constant back-and-forth transfer of information that is sent in both directions.

Verbal communication is sending messages by using words that are either spoken or written. This section examines different aspects of verbal communication used for international business:

- Language
- Challenges and complications
- Verbal communication strategies

Language and International Business

In international business, business people must first identify the language to use for communication. **Figure 3.2** on page 54 lists the most-used languages in the world.

There is a difference between the number of people who speak a language and the number of countries in which a language is spoken. For example, nearly a billion people speak the language Mandarin Chinese, but you will not hear it in many countries besides China. Fewer people speak Spanish and English, but they speak these languages in many more countries.

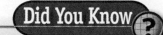

Did You Know?

Using the Right Language
Did you know that a single country may have several "languages"? They might include an "official" language that applies to government documents and laws, a "business" language for dealing with foreign companies, and a "common" language spoken by residents.

Figure 3.1

A Model of Communication

TWO-WAY MESSAGES Communication includes both verbal and nonverbal messages. *What nonverbal feedback do you give your teacher when he or she talks about international business?*

Figure 3.2

Major World Languages

MULTILINGUAL WORLD These languages are listed in approximate order of the total number of people who speak the language. *Which is the second most common language used in the world? The third?*

Language	Speakers	Where Spoken
Mandarin Chinese	1,052,000,000	China, Southeast Asia
English	508,000,000	United Kingdom, United States, Canada, Ireland, Australia, India, numerous European, African, and Asian countries (105 countries)
Hindi	487,000,000	India
Spanish	417,000,000	Spain, Mexico, most Central and South American countries, United States
Arabic	280,000,000	Saudi Arabia, Kuwait, Iraq, Syria, Jordan, Lebanon, Egypt
Russian	277,000,000	Russia, former republics of the Soviet Union
Bengali	211,000,000	India, Bangladesh
Portuguese	191,000,000	Portugal, Brazil, other South American countries
Malay-Indonesian	159,000,000	Malaysia, Indonesia
French	129,000,000	France, Belgium, Canada, various European and African countries
German	128,000,000	Germany, Austria, Switzerland, various European countries
Japanese	126,000,000	Japan

Source: Raymond G. Gordon, Jr. (ed.), 2005. *Ethnologue: Languages of the World*, 15th edition. Dallas, Texas: SIL International.

Language and Word Gender

Every language has unique features. For example, in most of the Romance languages, such as Spanish, French, and Italian, nouns are assigned a male or a female gender. For example, the noun for the word *cat* is masculine—*gato*. The preposition *the* also has different gender designations in Spanish, according to the noun it modifies. The masculine form is *el*, and the feminine form is *la*. So, the words *the cat* translate as *el gato* in Spanish.

Also, adjectives change to fit the gender of the noun. In French, the term for *the door* is feminine—*la porte*. The words *white door* are translated as *la porte blanche*. The masculine form of the adjective *white* is spelled *blanc*. The spelling and the pronunciation change with the gender.

In German, however, some nouns are male, some are female, and some are neutral. Such differences make learning a new language more difficult for English speakers. However, businesspeople can learn a few basic terms and phrases to promote courtesy and demonstrate interest.

Using Nouns and Verbs

Another complication in learning a language is the sequence, or order, of nouns and verbs. In English sentences the noun usually goes first, and the verb follows. In many other languages, the verb goes first, and the noun follows. In English, you would ask, "Do you like cake?" The same question in some other languages would translate literally as "Like, you, cake?"

Using Alphabets and Characters

Perhaps the biggest difference in many languages is their written forms. Certain languages have entirely different alphabets with different characters or letters. For example, **Figure 3.3** displays several alphabets for different languages.

Using English

Different languages make communication more difficult. However, many companies choose to use the English language when doing business, or they include text in English on their Web sites. English is becoming the most dominant language on the Internet.

Verbal Communication Challenges

There are several challenges that businesspeople must face when speaking various languages in other **environments**. They should consider various aspects of communicating in a world language:

- How people speak
- Technical terms
- Time for translations
- Social behavior

How People Speak

If you have learned a world language or have traveled, you know that people seem to speak very quickly in their native tongues. It may be difficult to understand them. One useful phrase to learn is: "Please speak more slowly." In Spanish, the phrase is: "*Hable por favor más lentamente*" (Ah-blay pour fah-vor maas len-ta-men-tay).

Another challenge when communicating in a world language is understanding **slang**, which is colloquial speech used on the street or in recreational situations. Even someone who has spent several years learning a world language can become frustrated by trying to understand everyday slang. Do you think that a visitor from Greece would understand an American term for extravagant jewelry, *bling*? An English speaker would experience the same type of confusion if he or she traveled to Greece and encountered Greek slang.

Technical Terms

Technical terms in world languages also vary. Everything is unique, from names for computer parts to math symbols and terms. It is important to learn these terms when communicating in another language.

How Do You Say?

Q: In Finnish how do you say: "How do you say ___?"

A: Kuinka sanotaan ___? (pronounced: Koo-ink-ă să-nō-tăăn _____?)

To learn these words in other languages, go to the International Business Online Learning Center through **glencoe.com**.

Figure 3.3

Diverse Alphabets

I am pleased to meet you.	English
我很高興見到你	Traditional Mandarin Chinese
أنا مسرور بلقائك	Arabic
Приятно познакомиться.	Russian

LANGUAGE IN WRITING These letters and characters do not look alike, but they say the same thing. *What other languages use alphabets that differ from the alphabet used for English?*

Culture Corner

Lingua Franca, Past and Present

Think About It What language do you think is the most used for business?

More than six hundred years ago, the "Franks" were the people of France and parts of Germany. They bought and sold goods, trading with people in the Mediterranean regions who spoke a variety of languages, including Italian, French, Spanish, Portuguese, Arabic, and Greek. To improve communication, the traders and sailors developed a "language" culled from all the languages they spoke. This language became known as *lingua franca,* a form of communication between peoples of different languages. It was shared by everyone who participated in commerce or diplomacy.

During the 20th century, English became the lingua franca for business. For example, when a Japanese company meets with an Italian company, they usually conduct transactions in English.

Though some cultures have resisted this trend, many businesspeople believe that knowing English is a strategic advantage.

Meeting and Greeting Today French is the official language in France, but many businesspeople speak English. However, the use of French is appreciated. When meeting people, shake hands with a quick, light grip. Use last names and titles unless invited to use first names. Address people as *Monsieur* or *Madame*.

Business Etiquette Give business cards to the receptionist and everyone you meet. Meetings follow an established format. Business entertainment takes place in restaurants.

Business Dress Wear conservative, stylish, and well-tailored clothing. French businessmen wear ties and suits in offices and restaurants. Women should avoid bright or gaudy colors.

English Language Arts/Writing

Why do you think the Franks' lingua franca was replaced?

As You Read

Relate Have you ever met someone who spoke only a different language than yours? If so, how did you communicate?

Time for Translation

A third challenge is the pace of a conversation. When someone speaks to you in a world language, and you wait for a translator to speak, there will be a pause. A few words in English may take several sentences to translate into another language. A short phrase may take a long time to interpret. Also, many people are not sure if they should look at the speaker or at the person who is providing the translation. Eye contact is a key element in communication. In this case, the listener should focus on the speaker, not the translator.

Social Behavior and Communication

Social behavior affects methods of communications around the world. For example, there are differences in behavior between high-context and low-context cultures. In a high-context culture, language is more figurative, or symbolic, than literal. The context of words is highly important. In a high-context culture, such as Japan, avoiding being embarrassed is a priority. One does not "bring dishonor" to oneself or one's household. Keeping a positive public image is crucial. A Japanese businessperson would never give a negative response in a direct manner. Businesspeople must allow people from this type of culture to maintain their sense of personal honor.

In low-context cultures, such as those in North America, words are taken more literally, and people are less concerned with personal embarrassment. Being self-effacing or telling jokes can be ways to create bonds with people from this type of culture.

Other Challenges

Complications can develop when you speak or interpret a language in a foreign country. These can lead to incorrect translations. It is important to pay attention to several language issues:

- Noun-verb agreement
- Singular-plural issues
- Imprecise translations

Noun-Verb Agreement One of the easiest mistakes to make in translating or speaking is in the area of noun-verb agreement. For example, It is not unusual for someone from another country to say, "I try hard," instead of "I am trying hard," or "I tried hard." People from the United States make similar mistakes matching the exact noun to the verb when speaking in languages other than English.

Singular-Plural Issues Sometimes, a person speaking a world language might not identify something as singular or plural. For example, a non-English speaker may be trying to say "my hair," referring to an entire head of hair. The translation, however, may cause the listener to think the speaker is talking about a single strand of hair. People who are learning to speak English as a second language may be unsure about adding an "s" to a word, since this practice varies in different languages. For example: "He bought three dozen rose" instead of "He bought three dozen roses." Likewise, English-speaking people may forget that the "s" at the end of plural nouns in many world languages is silent.

Imprecise Translations Business problems can occur when a phrase is translated imprecisely, or inaccurately. For example, in the 1980s, a popular ad for Pepsi in the United States advertised, "Come alive, with Pepsi." Due to imprecise translation, the German version read, "Come out of the grave, with Pepsi." Bank of America experienced a similar situation when the company posted an advertisement for an ATM, which was mistranslated into Chinese as "Great Wall of Money Bin."

English as a Second Language Remember to consider several aspects of communication when you talk to someone who speaks English as a second language:

- Pace
- Clarification
- Confirmation

Slow down your pace, or speed, when speaking. Give the other person time to process the words he or she hears that you are saying.

Then, look for clarification. If unsure, you should say, "I do not understand." Ask the person to rephrase. Many conflicts and problems result due to simply misunderstanding the intent or **concept** of a message. This is especially important if you believe the speaker may be using slang instead of more precise language.

OUR MULTICULTURAL WORKPLACE

The Languages of Business

The cultural diversity of the United States is increasing. By the year 2050, half the population will be of non-Anglo ancestry. This kind of globalization is also reflected in the U.S. workplace. Many businesses recognize the need to use the power of diversity as a source of new ideas and perspectives. However, challenges come with diversity. Organizations such as Massachusetts General Hospital have instituted foreign language training programs to help English-speaking employees better communicate with colleagues and clients who speak other languages. *How could employees benefit from better communicating with coworkers from cultures different than their own?*

Third, ask for confirmation. It is wise to ask courteously, "Do you understand?" You may wish to ask the other person to repeat or summarize what you said. Be sure the message received was the same one you meant to send. Be careful to avoid using slang.

Verbal Communication Strategies

It is clear that effective verbal communication skills are a vital part of working with companies in other countries. To succeed, it is helpful to apply several strategies:

- Learn key phrases.
- Use names, titles, and ranks appropriately.
- Use business cards appropriately.
- Consider other differences.

Learning Key Phrases

When preparing to do business with a company in another country, know what language is the most appropriate to use. Remember, a single country may have several languages. You will need to know which one best serves the business relationship. Then, when you know the most appropriate language, you should learn how to use key words and business phrases. These might include the phrases shown in **Figure 3.4**.

Using Names

Another communication issue is the use of names, titles, and ranks. In some countries it is extremely rude to call someone by his or her first name. You should use the more formal versions, such as "sir," "ma'am," "Mr. /Mrs." or even "Your Honor," "Mr./Mrs. President," or "Mr./Mrs. Secretary." Also, many cultures differentiate between a married woman (Mrs. or *Madame* in French) and a single adult woman (Ms. or *Mademoiselle* in French).

BUSINESS CARD ETIQUETTE Business cards are used differently around the world. *Are there times when handing someone a business card might be viewed as being rude? Explain your answer.*

Figure 3.4

Useful Terms and Phrases

IN ANY LANGUAGE These are some of the more common phrases used in international business. *Do you know how to say any of these words in a world language? What language?*

- Welcome
- Hello/Goodbye
- It is nice to meet you.
- Please/Thank you
- You're welcome.
- Yes/No (I agree/I disagree.)
- Do you understand?

- I don't understand.
- Friend
- I cannot answer your question now. Please be patient. (*or* Please wait.)
- Please speak more slowly.
- It is a pleasure doing business with you.
- What time should I arrive?

In some cultures workers from the rank and file, or lower-rank employees, in a company would not dare speak to a high-ranking person. In fact, it may be inappropriate to make eye contact. When greeting an executive from another business, you should know how to say "hello" and be aware of the type of relationship to expect—formal or informal.

Also, issues of courtesy vary in different cultures. For example, in the Japanese culture, a businessperson is not likely to directly say, "No." Instead, the individual may say, "I believe that would be very difficult." It would be rude to say anything more direct, even if the intent of the message is to say "no."

Using Business Cards

There are a variety of customs associated with the use of business cards. For example, in the United States, it is common practice to pass them around liberally. They are given out freely, even when a person does not ask for one. Giving out a card without being asked to do so may be inappropriate in some cultures. The culture may view such behavior as showing off.

In Korea and other Asian countries, governmental officials and high-ranking business leaders are very cautious about giving away business cards. They are wary of unscrupulous people who might take the card and use it to create the impression they know the cardholder very well, even if the person is a casual acquaintance.

In the United States, cards might be exchanged at the start of a meeting. In England cards are traded at the end of the meeting.

In some cultures businesspeople carry both "business" cards and "personal" cards. They give out a personal card whenever a relationship is not related to business. A personal card may be used for giving a phone number and address to a friend.

You should note that even something as seemingly minor as passing along a business card can have an impact on a business relationship. It is important to study the local culture before reaching for your card in a business situation.

Reading Check **Analyze** Why are high-ranking Asian businesspeople cautious about handing out business cards?

Other Differences to Consider

In addition to being aware of the appropriate use of key phrases, names and titles, and business cards, there are other differences to keep in mind. These differences relate to time zones, currency, the use of the variations in different measurement systems, such as the metric system, and trade document preparation.

Time-Zone Differences Consider time-zone differences. A person calling Spain from the United States should be aware that it is between six and nine hours later in Spain (depending on where the U.S. caller is located). A call placed at 6:00 P.M. in the U.S. arrives after midnight in Madrid.

TECH Trends

Cyberspace en Français

Should every Web site speak English? While the majority of Web sites now appear in English, the French government has spent considerable effort to stop the trend. The branch of government called the "Culture Ministry" has helped various groups file lawsuits to maintain the French language. One lawsuit was filed against a U.S. university for its "French" campus Web site prepared in English. The ministry also objects if products do not carry French labels. Another lawsuit noted that the instructions for products sold by an electronics chain appeared in only English. Countries want their native languages and cultures to remain alive and respected for their citizens. Mexico (for Spanish) and Canada (for French) have taken similar steps to maintain language integrity. *Find an article about this issue on the Internet. Write a one-page summary of it, including your opinion of the position.*

For links to help you do this activity, go to the International Business Online Learning Center through **glencoe.com**.

Currency Differences Monetary issues also affect communication. Negotiators must account for various currency rates when discussing finances. In England the currency used is the *pound*. However, in much of Europe, the standard currency is the *euro*. Each form of money can exchange with the U.S. dollar and other currencies—and the rates constantly change. For example, the exchange rate one day might be: US$100 = 80 euros. The exchange rate for another day might be the opposite. Trying to think in numbers, different currencies, and different exchange rates—and in a world language—is complex. It is wise to have someone with whom you can check your math.

The Metric System Remember that most of the world, except the United States, uses the metric system for measurement. For example, European countries use meters and kilometers; however, the United States uses feet and miles to measure distance. Therefore, it is a good idea to study and understand meters, liters, and the Celsius thermometer before starting any foreign journey.

Trade Documentation Finally, it is important to consider the legal side of business relationships. This includes **international trade documentation**, which is the papers and documents used to legally export or import goods. The papers must be prepared accurately. Fortunately, there are a variety of experts and software systems that can help a company meet the legal requirements of trade in clear and specific language for communicating globally.

Quick Check 3.1

After You Read Respond to what you have read by answering these questions:

1. What is the relationship between the sender and the receiver in the communication process?

_____

_____

2. What are at least three issues associated with verbal communication for international business?

_____

_____

3. What are some of the keys to effective verbal communication in international business? _____

_____

_____

Academics / Social Studies

4. Describe one American business practice that differs in Japan.

_____

_____

Nonverbal Communication

Reading Guide

Before You Read

How might a gift be a form of communication?

MAIN IDEA
When conducting international business, it is important to "build bridges."

GRAPHIC ORGANIZER
Draw this diagram. As you read this section, write in the nonverbal methods of communication:

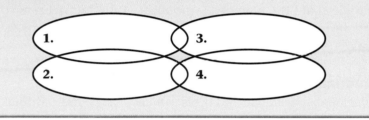

1.
2.
3.
4.

WHAT YOU'LL LEARN
- To describe the forms of nonverbal communication
- To discuss how culture affects nonverbal communication
- To identify methods for overcoming communication problems and developing effective messages

WHY IT'S IMPORTANT
Understanding the role of nonverbal communication contributes to building strong relationships.

KEY TERMS
- nonverbal communication
- gift
- bribe
- expatriate
- acculturation

Academic Vocabulary

You will find these words in your reading and on your tests. Make sure you know their meanings.
- impact
- analyze
- theory

Forms of Nonverbal Communication

Nonverbal communication can focus on facial expressions, gestures, and posture. **Nonverbal communication** is sending messages without the use of words. These expressions are major elements in nonverbal communication. However, beyond a smile, frown, blank stare, or good posture, a variety of other signals also send nonverbal messages. All of these signals are influenced by:

- Cultural factors
- Methods of communication
- Specific business activities

Cultural Factors and Nonverbal Communication

Many cultural factors affect communications in international business relationships. These nonverbal cultural factors can be extremely important:

- Numbers
- Emblems
- Personal appearance and dress
- Colors
- Smells
- Foods

Numbers

Certain numbers affect people of various cultures in different ways. In the American culture, the number 13 is considered unlucky. In fact, some office buildings or hotels do not have a 13th floor. The floor numbers skip from 12 to 14. The number 11 can have the same meaning in Asia.

In Europe the ground floor is not considered the first floor. The first floor is the floor immediately above the ground floor—or what would be the second floor in the United States. This applies to office buildings as well as to apartment dwellings. When traveling to another country, it is wise to research the significance of numbers.

Emblems

Emblems, or symbols, also **impact** business relations. The simple wearing of a cross as a piece of jewelry does not evoke much of a reaction in the United States. However, it might cause resentment in a country such as Saudi Arabia, where wearing non-Islamic religious symbols is illegal.

Consider emblems used in advertising. For example, one banking company decided to use a squirrel as its advertising symbol, when opening a branch in a South American country. The local people did not understand the intended symbolism of the squirrel as a "thrifty saver" because, in that country, squirrels are viewed as vermin, such as rats.

Personal Appearance and Dress

Personal appearance and dress can also affect international business. For example, there are different customs regarding shaving around the world. In some countries in Europe and other places, women do not shave their legs. In many parts of the world, religious customs dictate that men wear beards. Also, women in some cultures must keep their faces covered. The Jewish and Israeli tradition requires that a man covers his head, particularly during worship. In the United States, men might remove their hats while eating dinner or when entering an office or residence.

Colors

Colors also have different meanings, depending on the nation. In China and Taiwan, the color red indicates a celebration. In Italy the color purple indicates penance. The color white can symbolize death in some cultures (especially in Asia), whereas white may represent purity in other countries. A businessperson needs to be careful about choosing acceptable colors to wear.

CULTURAL SYMBOLS The color white is a symbol of different things in different cultures. *What might the color white symbolize in the United States?*

Royalty-free/Photodisc/Getty Images

Communicating with Nokia

Nokia is known for making cell phones with the latest designs and newest technologies, but surprisingly, the Scandinavian communications business began as a paper company in 1865. In fact, two other businesses contributed to Nokia's success—Finnish Rubber Works, founded in 1898 to facilitate the spread of electricity into homes, and Finnish Cable Works, founded in 1912 to support the telegraph and telephone industries. Decades later in 1967, the three businesses united as the Nokia Corporation. This collective company anticipated future technology, such as computer modems.

Predicting and adapting to new technology and market trends has proved to be Nokia's strength. When Scandinavia established the world's first international cellular phone network in 1981, Nokia created the first car phone. Then in 1987, the company introduced the world's first cell phone. Having dispensed with other business interests to focus on mobile phone production, Nokia has continued to lead the industry. The company creates not only small and efficient phones, but products that are also stylish and customizable by owners.

THINK GLOBALLY *How have Finland's technological contributions promoted global communication?*

@ To learn more about the country of origin for this global business, go to the International Business Online Learning Center through **glencoe.com**.

Smells

Business travelers should also be aware of different responses to smells, depending on the culture. A heavy dose of cologne might bother a businessperson in certain settings. In the United States, deodorants, perfume, and cologne are used to reduce or mask body odor. In many African and Middle Eastern countries, people do not mind the odor.

Foods

Food customs vary in different cultures. Some Taoists in Asia believe that onions and garlic are unhealthy and should not be eaten. In Islamic and other cultures, people do not eat pork or any of the by-products of pigs, such as lard. When traveling or dealing with international businesspeople, it is important to be aware of vegetarian cultures and those that prohibit specific foods or ingredients.

In addition, you should also know when you are being honored or flattered when served a delicacy. For example, in Russia high-quality caviar is reserved for important guests.

Each culture in the world has unique characteristics. Studying these elements can go a long way toward helping a company develop positive relationships with companies in other countries.

Nonverbal Methods of Communication

To develop successful international business relationships, be aware of the different methods of nonverbal communication. Nonverbal communication can take place in a particular culture through time, silence, space, and body and eye contact.

NONVERBAL COMMUNICATION This gesture could mean something different in another country. *Do you know how other people might interpret this gesture?*

As You Read

Relate What distance is too close for you when speaking to a new acquaintance?

Time

As noted in the previous chapter, there are many different views of time. These affect punctuality, or being on time and good or bad manners. Work days and work weeks have different times, depending on the country involved. Dining and resting also take place on different schedules in other parts of the world.

Silence

Silence can connote different meanings, depending on the nationality of the person who is communicating. In Taiwan a quiet room indicates lack of life, or liveliness. It is rude to sit quietly and not maintain an active conversation. The opposite is true in other cultures. Silence may indicate respect and attention.

Personal Space

Attitudes toward personal space are dramatically different in various cultures. In the United States, people stand fairly far apart when they speak. The distance is usually about the length of an arm. In Japan the distance is even greater. In Middle Eastern countries, such as Jordan and Syria, standing far away indicates distrust. When speaking to someone in that culture, a U.S. businessperson should not move away from the other person.

Body and Eye Contact

Body contact and touching may have profound effects on business relationships in different cultures. Would you feel comfortable doing business while holding hands with a colleague of the same gender? In many Arab countries, holding hands while working is commonplace. Touching and kissing customs also vary widely by nation. In the United States and some other Western cultures, inappropriate touching or kissing can be a form of sexual harassment.

Attitudes toward making eye contact also depend on the culture involved. In the United States, failing to make eye contact may be considered as rude or evasive. However, in many Asian countries, looking away while you speak is a sign of respect.

In summary, nonverbal methods of communication vary tremendously. Taking the time to learn and **analyze** which forms are appropriate will allow you to build bridges with individuals in other countries.

Business Behaviors in Other Countries

In the world of business, national and cultural factors play a major role in communication processes. Awareness of these factors is crucial to building long-term relationships with other businesses. However, building such relationships requires knowing about international behavior related to:

- Major holidays
- Giving and receiving gifts

Major Holidays

The United States has a tradition of holidays. Some are religious, while others are secular and established by the government. There are differences between holidays in the United States and other major holidays in other cultures. All business dealings are affected by the holidays in a particular country. The key thing to remember is that holidays involve more than just taking a day off from school or from work.

Religious Holidays For some religious holidays, fasting is a key element in observing the day. Many Catholics do not eat meat on Fridays during the season of Lent. Muslims fast during the entire month of Ramadan; this means no food, drink, or certain activities from the first light of dawn until after sunset for that month. The fasting process is less strict for those who are physically ill or traveling and for children.

In addition, some holidays require either giving or eating food. Buddhists bring gifts of food to a temple for worship and for special holidays, such as Buddha Day, which is celebrated on the night of the first full moon in May. Many religious holidays include feasts as part of their rituals. The religion of Judaism calls for celebrating the traditional feast of the Passover. Protestants and Catholics celebrate Easter and Christmas and usually include a festive dinner. Muslims note the end of the Ramadan holiday with the *Eid al-Fitr* feast, which includes giving food to the poor.

Secular Holidays Most nations have a national holiday similar to Independence Day, or the 4th of July, in the United States. Other national holidays depend on the history and culture of a country or region. For example, the Queen's birthday is a holiday in the Netherlands.

A businessperson visiting or living in a foreign land should be acquainted with the customs of holidays, from dining and appropriate dress to what gifts to give.

Giving and Receiving Gifts

Gift giving is an especially important aspect of conducting international business. Some common and acceptable gifts include flowers, small items such as pens or books, and chocolates. It is unwise to give flowers that are white or yellow, because in many cultures those colors are associated with death. Red roses are not an appropriate gift in Germany because they imply a strong romantic attachment. In some countries liquor is given as a gift; however, liquor is offensive to people in Islamic countries.

In Japan and Asia, good manners dictate bringing a gift when meeting a business partner. (Presenting gifts creates a sense of reciprocation in the person who receives the gift.) Remember, however, do not unwrap the gift in front of the person giving the gift. It is the gesture, not the value or content of the gift, that matters the most. The idea, or **theory**, is to never embarrass the person giving the gift, in case the receiver does not like the gift.

Grease Payments

The Foreign Corrupt Practices Act of 1977 (FCPA) makes it illegal for U.S. companies to bribe foreign officials in order to obtain or retain business. However, the FCPA draws a distinction between bribery and "grease payments." Grease payments are used to motivate officials to do a job they are already supposed to be doing. These payments keep products or services moving the way they would if the system worked as intended. U.S. law allows grease payments if they do not violate local laws. In addition, a company's legal department generally must approve such payments. *Are grease payments a form of bribery? Why or why not?*

Gifts or Bribes? There is a great difference between a gift and a bribe. A **gift** is an item given to convey good will. A **bribe** is an item or money offered to entice the receiver to do something illegal or unethical. For example, a bribe might be offered to get a buyer to purchase low-quality goods at an unfair price, when better, lower-priced goods are available.

The careful study of appropriate business behaviors is a major part of preparing to work in another country for an expatriate. An **expatriate** is a person who relocates in a foreign country to live and/or conduct business. This preparation is part of the process of acculturation. **Acculturation** is the process of understanding, adapting to, and operating in a foreign culture.

Business Behavior and Communication

Another aspect of acculturation includes understanding how to conduct business in other parts of the world. An expatriate manager or employee should understand two aspects of doing international business that relate to nonverbal communication:

1. Major business protocols and the proper steps for receiving business visitors
2. Business entertainment customs in various parts of the world

✔ **Reading Check** **Categorize** What aspects of international business function as nonverbal communication?

Business Protocol

There are several other business protocols that deserve attention. They include all of the items that are shown in **Figure 3.5**. The steps for receiving business visitors are a major part of correct business protocols. You can approach international business associates as visitors or as the hosts in their countries.

Figure 3.5

Business Protocols

GOOD BUSINESS MANNERS These are some typical aspects of business protocol around the world. *How would you conduct these activities in the American business culture?*

- Greetings and introductions
- Use of names and titles
- Business card etiquette
- Manners
- Type of dress
- Acceptable and proper gestures
- Gift giving
- Table manners
- Visiting the home of a business associate
- Conducting business meetings

GIFT GIVING Giving and receiving gifts is common practice in international business relationships. *Should the American businessperson receiving this gift open it right away? Why or why not?*

Before meeting, try to learn as much as you can about the businessperson and his or her culture to make the individual as comfortable as possible. Note that the visitor will probably try to follow your customs as well. Try to reach a middle ground by practicing the visitor's key customs while allowing that visitor to show you respect by acting out some of your country's customs. As a simple example, the two of you may first shake hands, and then bow.

When visiting another country, it is wise to be prepared. Remember that greetings vary from formal to informal. They can also take the form of a bow, curtsy, handshake, or salute. You will need to know how to be introduced. Find out if you should introduce yourself or if a third party should introduce you.

Knowing the proper forms of address and use of names and titles is vital for showing respect. The same is true for using proper manners and appropriate gestures. In addition, there are proper times and methods for visiting the home of a business associate.

Conducting a Meeting

When you begin doing business, follow the right steps for conducting a business meeting:

1. Set an appointment.
2. Arrive at the appropriate time.
3. Arrange the office and materials.
4. Make introductions.
5. Present gifts.
6. Greet (touching or not touching) your business associate.
7. Speak formally or informally.
8. Make eye contact or not.
9. Signal that you have reached or not reached an agreement.
10. Close the meeting and say "good-bye."

Many international businesspeople make checklists of these items and review protocols before ever making contact with the client.

Business Entertainment

Business entertainment is different around the world. However, the following procedures are fairly consistent.

Goals Successful business entertaining begins with setting goals for the event. When entertaining a client, decide if the goal is business, pleasure, or a combination of both. The person from the visiting company should feel comfortable and not feel pressured by any high-powered selling tactics.

Typically, a business entertainment event is carefully planned. The organizers create a budget and set the day and time of the event. They carefully communicate the information to the guest, accounting for differences in arrival times, depending on the culture involved.

Location Selection Smaller events are likely to be held in a restaurant, private venue, or an office. Large-scale entertainment programs may be held in a hotel, convention center, or under a tent. It is important to arrange transportation for your guest. The arrival of the visitor may be met with a celebration or a quiet reception. Remember to consider the culture of the guest when meeting and greeting that individual.

Menu items must be selected. Food may be anything from small snacks to an elaborate meal. Choose the best types of drinks to serve. Remember, in many cultures drinks are served at room temperature. The guest may or may not be used to very cold drinks, or drinks with ice.

Special Arrangements Business entertainment may also include special arrangements, such as music or other performances. The entertainment should be appropriate for the guests involved.

There may be other variations. For example, a round of golf, a tennis match, or luxury seats at a sports or entertainment event may be appropriate. The guest should have some interest in the activity.

Choosing the Gift Choose an arriving and/or departing gift that is appropriate for the occasion. Be sure not to "overdo" the gift or give something that would make the receiver uncomfortable in any way. Also, decide whether a photographer should be hired for the event.

Varieties of Business Entertainment

Companies in other countries also adapt their customs for foreign visitors. As a visitor, you may find yourself sitting on the floor rather than in a chair at a table. There may be elaborate toasting ceremonies. The foods may surprise you. It may be necessary to arrive with a gift and to know how to receive a gift gracefully.

You may also be entertained in ways you may not expect. In Spain bull fights are quite popular. Many Japanese people are fond of golf. In other parts of the world, horse racing or some other, more unusual sport might be popular.

INTERPRETER AND TRANSLATOR

Interpreters and translators play important roles in the world of international business as they translate one language into another language. Interpreters work with spoken language (and sometimes sign language) while translators work with the written word. Interpreters and translators work in the fields of business, government, education, social services, and entertainment.

Interpreters

Interpreters work as conference, guide or escort, judiciary, medical, or sign language interpreters. These positions require fluency in at least two languages, but interpreters do more than translate words. They must comprehend verbal as well as nonverbal expressions. Many of these positions also require the interpreter to understand complex subject matter such as medicine or law. Interpreters are required to travel.

Conference interpreters work in international business and government. Conference interpreters sit in sound-proof booths, listen to the speakers, and simultaneously speak in translation into a microphone. This requires a high level of concentration and a good memory.

Translators

Translators work as judiciary, literary, localization, and medical translators. They must know their subject matter. Translators are responsible for translating written words, meanings, concepts, and ideas.

Training

Prospective interpreters and translators should take English Language Arts, world languages, and computer courses. A bachelor's degree is usually required. Experience and proficiency are essential for success.

English Language Arts/Writing

For what purposes might multinational companies hire interpreters and translators?

@ To learn more about interpreters and their career paths, go to the International Business Online Learning Center through **glencoe.com**.

Career Data

Education: Bachelor's degree in world languages

Skills: Bilingual or multilingual, diplomatic, research, and analytical skills

Outlook: Growth faster than average in the next ten years

Methods of showing appreciation also vary by culture. Applause is not a universal phenomenon. There may be other customs to follow, including those for saying hello and good-bye. Make sure that you are aware of these customs before you arrive.

Successful Communication

Communication is a challenging aspect of doing international business. Successful businesspeople understand how to communicate in interpersonal settings and how to manage organizational communication. This includes overcoming the difficulties of speaking in a world language. It also means acting appropriately in business meetings and in other situations. Understanding the culture of a region can help with both verbal and nonverbal communication. Verbal communication is just one way to communicate. It involves sending messages by using words that are either spoken or written. By considering factors such as the languages, challenges, and strategies of verbal communication, you can achieve success in the international business community. Successful communication also depends on understanding nonverbal communication, which is sending messages without words through the connotations of time, silence, personal space, and body and eye contact. Following proper business protocols is crucial for conducting international business effectively.

Quick Check 3.2

After You Read Respond to what you have read by answering these questions.

1. What are the cultural factors that affect nonverbal communication? _____
_____
_____

2. What are the basic differences in nonverbal methods of communication across cultures? _____
_____
_____

3. How can an expatriate manager adapt to the business behaviors needed to succeed in an international relationship? _____
_____
_____

Academics *English Language Arts/Writing*

4. Define in your own words the term *nonverbal* and how it relates to international communication.
_____
_____
_____
_____

Portfolio Worksheet

Communication Issues

Choose one of these questions and write a one-page essay in response. Do research using the Internet and library for your essay and focus on the importance of the issue in global business.

1. If you are visiting with someone from a high-context culture, would joking be a good idea? Why or why not?

2. Someone from another country is talking to you. You feel like he is "crowding" you. Should you assume the person is being aggressive or angry? Why or why not?

3. How would you go about conducting a business meeting in Germany?

_____

_____

_____

_____

_____

_____

_____

_____

_____

_____

_____

_____

_____

_____

_____

_____

_____

_____

ACADEMICS APPLIED Check off the academic knowledge you used to do this activity:

☐ English Language Arts   ☐ Mathematics   ☐ Social Studies   ☐ Science

ACADEMIC AND CAREER PLAN Add this page to your Academic and Career Plan Portfolio.

(tl) Ulf Wallin/Getty Images; (tr) Royalty-free/David De Lossy/Getty Images; (b) Royalty-free/Getty Images

CHAPTER SUMMARY

Section 3.1 **Understanding Communication**

communication (p. 53)

language (p. 53)

verbal communication (p. 53)

slang (p. 55)

international trade documentation (p. 60)

- Verbal communication is sending messages by using words while observing the verbal feedback offered by the receiver.

- Verbal communication challenges include how quickly people speak as well as how much slang they use, differences in technical terms, waiting for translations, understanding how social behaviors affect communication, and other challenges such as noun-verb usage.

- Verbal communication strategies include effective use of key phrases, names, titles, ranks, and business cards; and consideration of differences in time zones and currencies.

Section 3.2 **Nonverbal Communication**

nonverbal communication (p. 61)

gift (p. 66)

bribe (p. 66)

expatriate (p. 66)

acculturation (p. 66)

- Nonverbal communication is sending messages without the use of words. There are many cultural differences that affect nonverbal communication, including interpretation of numbers, emblems, personal appearance, colors, smells, and foods.

- Nonverbal communication in a culture can take place through time, silence, space and personal space, and body and eye contact.

- Effective business behaviors include understanding major holidays that might affect doing business, the proper protocols for giving and receiving gifts, and the correct methods for conducting business meetings and business entertainment.

CONCEPTS REVIEW

1. **Describe** a model of individual verbal communication.

2. **Explain** differences in language, including gender, the order of nouns and verbs, and symbols and letters.

3. **Summarize** the ways to improve communication with someone who is speaking English as a second language.

4. **Identify** key words and phrases used in business relationships.

5. **List** at least three cultural factors that affect nonverbal communication.

6. **Identify** key differences in nonverbal communication around the world.

KEY TERMS REVIEW

7. Match each term to its definition.

_____ communication	**a.** the process of understanding, adapting to, and operating in a foreign culture
_____ language	**b.** the medium of communication through words, symbols, numbers, characters, or nonverbal cues
_____ verbal communication	
_____ slang	**c.** transmitting, receiving, and processing information
_____ international trade documentation	**d.** a person who relocates in a foreign country to live and/or conduct business
_____ nonverbal communication	**e.** sending messages by using words
	f. an item given to convey good will
_____ gift	**g.** an item or money offered to entice the receiver to do something illegal or unethical
_____ bribe	**h.** the papers and documents used to legally export or import goods
_____ expatriate	**i.** sending messages without the use of words
_____ acculturation	**j.** colloquial speech used on the street or in recreational situations

Academic Vocabulary

8. On a separate sheet of paper, write a sentence or two related to international communications, using at least three of these academic terms you learned in the section openers:

- process
- environment
- concept
- impact
- analyze
- theory

Critical Thinking

9. You are about to take an assignment working in the Sudan. Among the many aspects of this new job is the element of time. Describe how time differences could affect you as you travel.

Discussion Starter

10. Discuss how nonverbal gestures can communicate friendship, anger, or aggression in other countries.

Point of View

11. Some businesspeople in the United States are fond of using sports analogies when they conduct business. You may hear: "Take one for the team" or "This is our goal-line stand." Create a company policy addressing the use of these phrases, also explaining why using them might or might not be exclusionary to some female colleagues and to businesspeople visiting from other cultures.

BUILDING REAL-WORLD SKILLS

The GLOBAL WORKPLACE

12. Asian Tea In Taiwan and mainland China, an important ceremony is the sharing of tea. Tea has many health benefits. Brewing and drinking tea with others is a common social and business activity. Tea is brewed in a manner that is different from the way it is prepared in either the United States or England.

Research and Share

a. Explain how to brew tea in the Asian fashion.

b. Demonstrate how to cup your hand downward and tap your fingers on the table while being served tea, as a gesture to say "Thank you."

The U.S. WORKPLACE

13. The Corporate Culture A country's culture can be its history, dress, food, language, and art. However, culture can also exist in a smaller group, such as a company. Different companies have different corporate cultures, which include shared values, beliefs, codes of ethics, and goals. A formal culture may have many levels of management and a strict dress code. An informal culture may allow employees to make decisions on their own and dress casually.

Research and Write

a. Choose two companies, one small and one large. Find out if their cultures are formal or informal.

b. Find out if each company has a code of ethics and describe it.

BUILDING ACADEMIC SKILLS

ELA English Language Arts

14. Have you ever considered dance as a form of communication? In Hawaii, the hula is a native dance that tells a story through body movements and hand gestures. Dance as a form of storytelling is common around the world. Research two other dances in other cultures. Write two paragraphs about how they are the same and how they are different from a dance like the hula.

MATH Mathematics

15. Convert the following: 10 miles into kilometers and 100 yards into meters. If you are driving 80 kilometers-per-hour, how fast are you going in miles-per-hour?

Measurement To solve this problem, you need to understand units of measurement for different systems of measurements and apply math formulas.

SOC Social Studies/History

16. Research and trace the spread of the Spanish language from Spain to other places where it is the most common language. Create a timeline that also notes the path the language took. Make a list of different Spanish dialects in various parts of the world.

SOC Social Studies/Geography

17. Choose three major cities around the world where global business takes place—one in the northern hemisphere, one in the southern hemisphere, and one near the equator. Name your cities. Use the Internet or a book to find a map. Then locate them on the map. Also research and list each city's population as well as its type of national government and industry.

COMPETITIVE EVENT PREP

Meeting in Kazakhstan

18. Situation You are the head of the production department in your company, which makes athletic shoes. A meeting has been scheduled in which you and some colleagues will meet with people in Kazakhstan who will learn about your company's production techniques. They will be building a plant in Kazakhstan.

Activity To prepare for this meeting, research and create a checklist of business protocol information for your colleagues. The list should focus on (1) greetings, (2) introductions, (3) the use of names and titles, (4) manners, (5) appropriate attire, (6) acceptable and proper gestures, (7) table manners, and (8) how to conduct a business meeting.

Evaluation You will be evaluated on how well you meet the following objectives:

a. Identify the appropriate greeting (formal/informal) in the language of Kazakhstan.

b. Identify differences in manners or table manners.

c. Identify how men and women should dress.

d. Clearly specify the time of the meeting and if the visitors are expected to be on time.

e. Notify management if a translator will be needed.

Internet Travels

Switzerland

Using the Internet, look up the country Switzerland on a world map. Switzerland is located on the borders of France, Italy, Austria, and Germany. Research and answer the following questions about Switzerland on a separate sheet of paper.

➤ What are the four main languages spoken in Switzerland?

➤ Which language is most common in Swiss business transactions?

@ For resources to help you do this exercise, go to the International Business Online Learning Center through **glencoe.com**.

BusinessWeek online

19. Newsclip: Entering the Chinese Market Names are serious business in Chinese culture. There are important factors to consider when picking a suitable brand name for products. Businesses need to have knowledge of business, linguistic, market, and cultural needs.

@ Go to the International Business Online Learning Center through **glencoe.com** to read a *BusinessWeek* article about this topic. List some important factors for communicating the right name in Chinese.

Standardized Test Practice

20. Choose the best answer to the following multiple-choice question.

What is the process of understanding, adapting to, and operating in a foreign culture?
- ○ acculturation
- ○ global adaptation
- ○ evolution
- ○ nesting

Test-Taking Tip Always read the question and all of the answer choices carefully. Avoid answers that seem extreme.

International Web Sites

Success Model: IKEA
Country of Origin: SWEDEN
Business: HOME FURNISHINGS

The IKEA Concept began when Ingvar Kamprad, an entrepreneur from the Småland province in southern Sweden, had an innovative idea. In Småland the people have a reputation for working hard, living frugally, and making the most out of limited resources. Ingvar applied the lessons he learned in Småland to the home furnishings market. His innovative idea was to offer home-furnishing products of good function and design at prices much lower than competitors' prices by using simple cost-cutting solutions that did not affect the quality of products. He opened the first IKEA store in 1943.

Today a visit to the IKEA Web site illustrates why IKEA represents the leading home furnishings brand in the world with more than 200 stores in more than 30 countries. International customers can find store locations around the world and review an extensive catalog in numerous languages tailored to the global market.

● Situation

For the past two years, you have been working for a company that manufactures and sells stylish, mod furniture for teens and young adults. You have just been assigned the task of developing a Web site for your company. The Web site will facilitate trade between your company and retail customers in several foreign countries. To develop the first phase of the Web site, it is your responsibility to study the culture of another country so that you can effectively market the furniture through a well-designed, practical, and culturally appropriate Web site.

● Assignment

✓ Research information on cultural factors that will affect the design and implementation of an international retail Web site.

✓ Plan your Web site with one or two unique features to attract customers.

✓ Create a final report.

● Resources

SKILLS NEEDED

✓ *Academic Skills:* reading, writing, math, and social studies

✓ *Basic Skills:* speaking, listening, thinking, problem-solving, and interpersonal skills

✓ *Technology Skills:* word-processing, keyboarding, spreadsheet, presentation, telecommunications, and Internet skills

TOOLS NEEDED

✓ Newspapers and magazines, such as *BusinessWeek* and *U.S. News and World Report*

✓ The Internet and library

✓ Paper, pens, pencils, and markers

✓ Poster board

✓ Word-processing, spreadsheet, and presentation software

● Procedures

STEP 1 REAL-WORLD RESEARCH

Do cultural research on a country of your choice:

- Rooms for teens
- Primary language
- Main ethnicity and subgroups
- Major religion and holidays
- Hours of the typical work day and work week
- Where and how people shop for furniture

STEP 2 COMMUNITY RESEARCH

Visit two furniture stores in your community and ask the managers or owners what information and features they would provide on a Web site.

STEP 3 INTERNET RESEARCH

Find two similar retail Web sites for furniture.

- Find out the typical information provided on a furniture company's Web site.
- Find out the top ten languages used on an international company's Web site.

STEP 4 GRAPHIC ORGANIZER

On a separate sheet of paper, create a site map that outlines the features for your Web site.

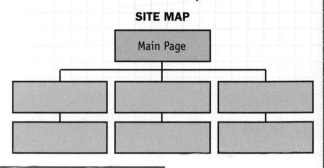

SITE MAP

● Report

Prepare a written report of your findings using the following tools, if available:

- *Word-processing program:* Prepare a 3-page written report about your cultural research. Include your Web-site plan with the site map outline and diagram, listing features, sections, and other elements.
- *Spreadsheet program:* Prepare a chart comparing other competitor Web sites with yours.
- *Presentation program:* Prepare a ten-slide visual presentation with key points, some visuals, and text.

● Evaluation

Present your report to the class and/or hand it in to your teacher. Use this chart to assess yourself before and after your presentation.

PRESENTATION SELF-CHECK RUBRIC	1 Needs Work	2 Average Quality	3 Good Quality	4 Excellent Quality	Totals
Knowledge of Web sites for foreign markets and their components					
Continuity of overall report					
Voice quality					
Eye contact with audience					
				TOTAL =	

0–6 Needs Work; **7–10** Average Quality; **11–14** Good Quality; **15–16** Excellent Quality

● Academic and Career Portfolio

Add this report to your Academic and Career Portfolio.

UNIT 2

THE INTERNATIONAL TRADE ENVIRONMENT

❝To succeed in business, to reach the top, an individual must know all that is possible to know about that business.❞

J. Paul Getty
Founder
Getty Oil Company

Piggybanks Full of Pesos

Lucia Jimenez and Benjamin Macias have been married for just a month, but they're already buying their first home: a newly built two-bedroom bungalow in an attractive subdivision a half-hour's drive from Mexico City. "Before, it was more difficult to buy your own home," says Lucia. "Things have gotten better."

American conceptions of Mexico usually focus on the country's poverty. But another Mexico is starting to emerge: a middle-class nation where millions have access to mortgages, solid jobs that provide security, and a class of strivers who save to put kids through college. The ranks of that middle class, or those making between $7,200 and $50,000 a year, have swelled to around 10 million families. For almost a decade, wages have been rising faster than inflation. Homeownership is the other key factor in Mexico's transformation, because it allows families to build equity, establish credit histories, and move up the economic ladder. Banks big and small are tripping over one another to offer mortgages.

Mexicans are buying more than homes. A record 1.13 million cars and small trucks were sold last year. "Sales of home appliances have tripled in the last ten years," notes Ernesto Cervera, director of a think tank. "Who's buying all those 37-inch TVs at Sam's Club? The middle class." There is more disposable income nowadays. Normal stuff north of the border, but a major change in a country that has endured so many crises.

English Language Arts/Writing

1. How might an improved economy in Mexico affect companies interested in exporting goods to Mexico?

2. How might it affect a U.S. company interested in importing goods from Mexico?

@ To read the complete *BusinessWeek* article, go to the International Business Online Learning Center through **glencoe.com**.

UNIT THEMATIC PROJECT PREVIEW

Export Expansion

As the world becomes "smaller" with globalization, international trade expands. Many businesses, large and small, go global and find new markets by exporting their products. Think about what information you would need to gather to help a company sell its food products in another country.

Pre-Project Checklist

❑ Research information about the type of food consumed in Brazil, Japan, and Morocco.

❑ Ask friends and family if they have traveled to these countries. If so, what foods did they notice or like?

❑ Find out if people in Brazil, Japan, and Morocco consume American food. What kind?

❑ Look at Web sites of U.S. food products that are sold globally.

Chapter 4

Importing, Exporting, and International Trade

Chapter Objectives
When you have completed this chapter, you will be able to:

Section 4.1
- Describe the processes of importing and exporting.
- Explain the differences between goods and services.
- Identify the steps of the importing and exporting processes.

Section 4.2
- Explain why companies and countries trade.
- Discuss the importance of having balance of trade for countries.
- Describe the roles played by international trade organizations.

SANRIO

Sanrio is a publicly owned corporation whose shares are traded on the stock exchanges. When you research this company through Standard & Poor's, you will find investment information such as this:

Index:	S&P Japan 500
Sector:	Consumer Discretionary
Company:	Sanrio Co. Ltd.
Symbol:	8136
Country:	Japan
Price:	(varies)

Global Profile Sanrio Company Limited manufactures, distributes, imports, and exports children's gifts, greeting cards, and stationery decorated with original characters such as Hello Kitty. Sanrio's Social Communication Gift division offers kitchen appliances, clothes, gift books, magazines, video software, and films. The Theme Parks division provides theme park services, including restaurants.

Business Report Sanrio employs over 1,400 people and has a presence in Asia, Europe, and North America. Sanrio's 2005 sales totaled 101.1 billion Japanese yen (about $859.8 million).

English Language Arts/Writing

In 1974, Sanrio introduced the first Hello Kitty design to Japan on a small vinyl purse. The mouthless mascot was an immediate hit. However, it took time for Europe and America to accept this character. Sanrio's export business improved with products tailored to cultural preferences. In the United States, Sanrio designs products matching characters with cultural images, such as DJs, leopard prints, and snowboarding. In Europe, Hello Kitty appears on commemorative Euro coins. *Name five countries that import Sanrio's products and describe them.*

@ To do this activity, go to the International Business Online Learning Center through **glencoe.com**.

The Nature of International Trade

WHAT YOU'LL LEARN

- To describe the processes of importing and exporting
- To explain the differences between goods and services
- To identify the steps of the importing and exporting processes

WHY IT'S IMPORTANT

International trade opens new markets for companies from many nations and provides access to products some people would otherwise never use.

KEY TERMS

- international trade
- imports
- exports
- good
- service
- FOB
- CIF
- C&F

Academic Vocabulary

You will find these words in your reading and on your tests. Make sure you know their meanings.

- purchase
- item
- require

Reading Guide

Before You Read

What is your definition of *exports*?

MAIN IDEA

Individuals, companies, and countries participate in international trade by importing and exporting goods and services.

GRAPHIC ORGANIZER

Draw this KWL chart. As you read this section, fill it in to track what you *know, would* like to know, and have *learned*:

K	W	L

What Is International Trade?

In your career, it is likely that you will do business with a company located in another country. At that moment, you will be participating in international trade. **International trade** consists of all business activities conducted between individuals, companies, and governments from different countries. Business activities include buying, selling, shipping, receiving, paperwork, granting credit, making payments, servicing products, and a wide variety of additional tasks.

International trade can occur between one nation and another nation. For example, when a company from Norway trades with a company from Yemen, both countries are conducting international trade.

International trade also takes place within groups or clusters of countries, such as member nations of the World Trade Organization, or WTO. Business is conducted both within the group and outside the group. Member countries of trade groups enjoy certain benefits. As discussed in this chapter, many countries in Europe are part of the European Union (EU). Within the EU member countries do not have to pay certain taxes on international trading. However, members also cannot trade some products, such as military arms, with certain countries.

Importing and Exporting

Most countries have abundant supplies, or surpluses, of some products and have shortages of others. Businesses export the extra products and supplies. Needs are met by importing. Much of international trade can be described by using two terms:

1. Imports
2. Exports

Imports

Imports are goods and services that people in one country buy from people in another country. This includes purchasing individual products, such as those you might buy through the Internet from a company in a foreign country. If you order an MP3 player directly from a Japanese company, you are importing that product. Importing also occurs when one company purchases from another company. General Motors buys many parts for its automobiles from other companies around the world. Governments also import goods and services from foreign governments and companies. Many governments **purchase** food from farms and food companies in the United States. The United States imports goods and services, such as crude oil and customer-relations call centers.

Exports

Exports are goods and services that people in one country sell to people in another country. The same pattern of buying and selling imports holds true for exports. Purchases can be made by individuals, companies, or governments. Notice that one country's exports are always another country's imports. The United States exports agricultural products, technology, and financial services, among other products to many countries.

Often the amounts of imports and exports are not equal. For example, the United States imports more fuel than it exports, and it exports far more food than it imports.

Goods and Services

International trade provides more than just physical goods. Services are also traded between countries. In fact, providing services across national boundaries is a rapidly growing part of the world's economy.

Goods

A **good** is a tangible **item** that is made, manufactured, or grown. When a good is imported or exported, a method of transportation must be chosen to move the item across national boundaries. Usually goods are inspected as they cross borders.

A company must pay shipping costs in order to transport goods. Because products can be lost or destroyed during shipping, the companies involved must agree how to insure or pay for damaged or missing goods. If the product is not exactly what the customer had in mind, there should be some kind of procedure for returning it.

Figure 4.1

Services Sold Internationally

SERVICES EXPORTED BY THE UNITED STATES These services are used by people around the world. *How many of these services have you or your friends used this month?*

Services Sold Internationally		
Banking and financial services	Hotel services	Repair and maintenance
Stock market services	Shipping services	Rental services
Credit	Accounting services	Real estate services
Insurance	Consulting	Legal services
Travel services	Healthcare	Education and training

Middlemen A physical good "changes hands" as it moves from one country to another. A middleman company, such as a distributor, wholesale outlet, or retailer, moves the product from the producer to the customer. This is part of the channel of distribution. If a company acting as the middleman buys the product and then resells it, that company is called a "merchant middleman." If the company just represents the product without owning it, the company is called an "agent middleman."

Services

A **service** is an intangible benefit or task provided by a business to its customers. A service is different from a physical good. Physical items may accompany a service, such as a contract, but the service is something you cannot touch. The benefit comes from the service being provided. **Figure 4.1** lists services that international customers receive. A service may not **require** a middleman.

Most services are marketed in somewhat different ways than goods. A customer can examine a physical good. Selling services usually involves convincing the customer of the benefits of the particular service. Also, the customer must believe that the service provider is a reliable source.

Individuals, companies, and governments purchase services. Certain services, such as hospitality and tourism services, might appeal more to individual consumers. Companies are likely to purchase services such as consulting, insurance programs, and banking and financial services. Individual governments might hire healthcare service providers or employ consultants to train employees for international assignments.

Goods with Services

Often a good is sold with a service. When you buy an extended warranty on an automobile, you purchase a good (the car) and a service (repair as needed). Services are also sold with other services, such as flight insurance with an airline ticket.

Importing Process

As companies and countries trade with each other, there are several key steps involved. The importing process consists of five steps:

1. Identify need.
2. Search for suppliers.
3. Create and finalize a purchase agreement.
4. Receive goods.
5. Confirm the purchase.

Individual companies work with governments from both countries to carry out the importing process.

Identify Need

An individual customer, a company, or a government can have a need. If you are opening a new Ethiopian restaurant, you might have a need to buy spices from Ethiopia. A need can be for a good or for a service.

Search for Suppliers

Looking for suppliers is both easier and more difficult in the 21st century. The Internet makes a search much easier, since there is ready access to numerous companies. It is also more difficult to decide which company is the best, since there are so many choices.

Create and Finalize Purchase Agreement

A purchase agreement is a contract between the buyer and the seller. The agreement spells out the items involved, the price, the exchange rate, who will pay for shipping, and the delivery method. The due date for payment is noted, as are provisions in case the goods are damaged or not acceptable.

International trade documentation refers to the papers and documents that companies must send to customers with their products to legally export or import goods. If the companies have different national languages, they must choose a common language for the contract.

TECH Trends

B2B Online Marketplaces

Business-to-business, or "B2B," marketplaces on the Internet are communities where companies can find goods and services to buy or sell. On some B2B sites, manufacturing is the primary focus. For example, many commercial products are made in Asian countries where labor is less expensive. As a result, factories in those countries may put assembly-line time up for auction on the Internet.

Products are also traded in huge volume on B2B sites. A manufacturer might have an extra truckload of computer parts. The maker will use a B2B site to find a company willing to buy the surplus. *Find three online B2B marketplace sites. Make a list of the products traded.*

@ For links to help you do this activity, go to the International Business Online Learning Center through **glencoe.com**.

◀ **TECHNOLOGY AND INTERNATIONAL SERVICES** New technologies have changed the ways many services are delivered. *Why might an X-ray be sent halfway around the world for someone to read?*

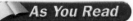

Relate What imported products do you buy and use? What countries export those products?

Receive Goods

When goods are shipped, they arrive at a specified place. This place can be a shipping dock or a company's front door. There, someone checks the order to make sure all items are included and are not damaged.

As goods pass across national borders, companies may owe a tax or duty. A customs agency working for the government of the receiving company collects duties. The agency also checks to make sure no illegal items are being shipped with the order.

Confirm the Purchase

Finally, the importing company confirms the purchase and makes payment when it agrees that the terms of the contract have been met. Most of the time, the company makes a courtesy call to accompany the payment. Its goal is to build good relations for the next purchase.

Exporting Process

While exporting processes share many common aspects with importing, there are some differences. The exporting process consists of five steps:

1. Assess demand.
2. Identify potential customers and make sales contacts.
3. Create and finalize a purchase agreement.
4. Deliver the goods or services.
5. Complete the transaction.

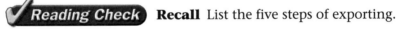 **Recall** List the five steps of exporting.

Assess Demand

The process of assessing demand for a product has two steps. The first is to effectively analyze the export potential for a good or service—whether people want to buy it. The second is to assess the company's ability to follow through and provide that good or service.

Assess Export Potential To assess a product's export potential, company leaders analyze the level of demand. There must be enough demand to support an international operation. Then they study the additional costs of meeting that demand, such as shipping costs, taxes or tariffs, and marketing and communications costs.

Assess Company Potential The selling company must be able to tailor a product to the country and customer who are importing it. For example, because most countries use the metric system, metric sizing for parts and equipment is critical. In addition, because types of electricity vary, a product may need to be adapted to operate on the electrical current of the destination country. Some countries use AC, or alternating current, while others use DC, or direct current.

The company must also have sufficient contacts to distribute the product as well as access to transportation to deliver the goods. The product must conform to national and local laws and customs.

Handcrafted in Armenia

> *Think About It* What one item representing the United States would you export? Why?

A hand-woven Armenian carpet is a work of art developed with the skills of an ancient people. More than a thousand years before 14th-century globe trekker Marco Polo proclaimed that Armenians "weave the choicest and most beautiful rugs in the world," travelers had noticed their beauty and brilliant colors. Rich blues, shades of yellow, vivid greens, and beige, brown, and black are processed from native plants, flowers, leaves, and grass. The spectacular color red, known as *kirmiz,* is extracted from a red worm found only in Armenia. The rich color palettes of Armenia's crafted rugs blended with a variety of patterns have led to global recognition. Today Armenian rugs have a permanent niche in the international market.

Meeting and Greeting When doing business in Armenia, men greet with a handshake and may embrace; women hug and kiss each other once on the left cheek. Maintain eye contact when conversing. There is no formal method of giving business cards.

Business Etiquette When arranging business, provide a letter of introduction. Expect delayed responses in communications. Because punctuality is not essential, arrive within 30 minutes of meeting time. Gift giving and business dining are typical. Table manners are formal.

Business Dress Wear casual but stylish attire. Never wear tight clothing.

English Language Arts/Writing

> Do you think a small country such as Armenia might have trade quotas? Why or why not?

Identify Customers and Make Contacts

The second crucial step of the exporting process is to identify potential customers and make sales contacts. Companies meet and get to know prospects through trade show exhibits (industry conventions), visits by salespeople, telephone calls, e-mails, teleconferences, and Internet solicitations. Once a company identifies potential customers, it must sell enough products to justify operating an international business.

Create and Finalize Purchase Agreement

The purchase agreement lists amounts, prices, exchange rates, methods of shipping, dates, and provisions for damaged or missing goods. The purchase agreement also specifies who pays for shipping.

Shipping Costs Different types of shipping terms give the seller and buyer different responsibilities. Most shipping terms are **FOB**, which means *free on board* or *freight on board,* and signifies that the ownership of merchandise in transit determines if freight charges are free. *FOB-loading dock* means the seller will pay all shipping until the goods reach the loading dock. Shipping charges can add to the price of the merchandise if the buyer has to pay shipping. If the seller pays shipping costs, the seller's profit will decrease.

CIF and C&F are other terms in a purchase agreement. **CIF** (cost, insurance, and freight) is the price quoted to the buyer, including cost, insurance, and freight. **C&F** (cost and freight) is the price quoted to the buyer, signifying the buyer pays separately for insurance.

Deliver Goods and Services

The seller must arrange to transport goods every step of the way to the buyer's location. The seller must also comply with legal and accounting requirements.

Many goods require a certificate of origin. It identifies the country in which a good was produced. This information allows customs agents to determine duties or import taxes, based on trade agreements between the nations of the buyer and the seller.

A bill of lading (BL) identifies exactly what is being shipped. Companies use this for accounting purposes. After inspecting the shipment, the buyer signs off on the bill of lading, signifying that all promised items have been delivered in good shape.

Complete the Transaction

The transaction is completed when the buyer and seller agree all terms are met and payment is made. To help facilitate payments, many countries rely on the International Monetary Fund (IMF), an institution whose goal is to maintain orderly exchange relationships. The IMF works on exchange rate problems.

The World Bank Group can lend money to support an international trade relationship. Part of the World Bank is the International Development Association (IDA). Its primary purpose is to help companies in less-developed nations. In some cases, the IDA uses other financial institutions, such as individual banks in neutral countries, especially Switzerland, to finalize payments.

To succeed in international business, company leaders must identify items to import and those to export. Many companies sell both goods and services. Often services are sold to support the goods. The steps of importing and exporting have several similar steps; the most noticeable is the crucial step of creating and finalizing a purchase agreement.

Quick Check 4.1

After You Read Respond to what you have read by answering these questions.

1. What is the difference between an import and an export? _____

_____

2. How is selling goods different from selling services in the international marketplace? _____

_____

3. What are the steps of importing? _____

_____

Academics / Mathematics

4. The purchase agreement lists the CIF as $74,000. If the cost of insurance is $23,500, how much is the C&F?

_____

_____

International Trade Relationships

Reading Guide

Before You Read

Can you predict what the term *isolationism* means?

MAIN IDEA
International trade organizations facilitate and regulate international trade.

GRAPHIC ORGANIZER
Draw this table. As you read this section, write in the benefits and risks of direct and indirect exporting:

	Direct	Indirect
Benefits		
Risks		

WHAT YOU'LL LEARN
- To explain why companies and countries trade
- To discuss the importance of having balance of trade for countries
- To describe the roles played by international trade organizations

WHY IT'S IMPORTANT
Success in international business depends on knowing the benefits and costs of importing and exporting. It also depends on help from various international groups and trade associations.

KEY TERMS
- dependency
- balance of trade
- trade barriers
- protectionism
- dumping

Academic Vocabulary

You will find these words in your reading and on your tests. Make sure you know their meanings.
- partner
- domestic
- focus

Understanding Trade Relationships

Companies and countries trade with each other for a variety of reasons. Trade relationships can be difficult and complex. Politics, economics, and social factors are all part of trading with another country. Still, most of the time, the benefits of trade outweigh the potential problems.

Why Companies Export

Exporting offers a variety of opportunities for individual companies that open new markets. Once a product has saturated, or flooded, one market, the only way to increase profits is to find new markets for the product. Many products can be adapted to foreign markets, which can become new sources of profits for the company.

Exporting also can "smooth out" sales. For example, the ideal selling seasons for lawn mowers are spring and summer. If a U.S. company also sells lawn mowers in Australia, where the seasons are reversed from the United States, it is possible to have strong sales all year. Winter coats, sports equipment, and other items can be sold year-round.

Some products tend to "grow old" and get replaced by other newer products. Companies frequently improve technologies in electronic products like computers, software, and sound equipment. A company may be able to sell the older version in a less demanding country.

Multinational Companies A company that exports has a different level of commitment to the international environment than does a company with global operations in several countries. An exporting company is more likely to maintain an allegiance to a single country. A business with operations in several countries focuses less on a home country and more on the company and all of the nations where it is located.

A single-country company is more likely to be influenced by the culture of that country, including views of religious practices, traditions, customs, norms, and mores and folkways. A multinational company will account for cultures across nations and its employees may be more attuned to cultural differences.

Why Companies Import

Companies import goods and services when the company has an unmet need or finds an opportunity in a product from another country. For example, a computer manufacturing company in Europe may need to import components, such as microprocessors, because it cannot produce its own components with equal quality.

Companies also import when an opportunity is present. If a Japanese company develops a new technology that can be sold in the United States, a U.S. company will quickly move to import it.

Why Countries Import

A country will import goods and services when there are unfulfilled needs. If the cheapest, best, or only way to meet those needs is to import an item, the country will choose that approach.

At the national level, importing also serves important purposes. For one, when a country does not have sufficient supplies of an item, importing is the only choice. American aluminum producers must import bauxite in order to make products, because there is no bauxite in the United States.

Imported goods meet people's desire for luxury goods or variety. For example, while people from all around the world do not need Swiss chocolates, they enjoy them. The same is true for a wide variety of products that can only be found in other places. Because companies have the ability to import items, products that would only be available for part of the year are available year-round. For example, oranges that farmers might harvest locally during one season of the year are available year-round from other countries with different climates or seasons. When two nations engage in trade, the standard of living in both nations can improve.

Why Countries Export

A country's leadership will encourage exporting for several reasons. First, additional sales spell economic growth. Economic growth often leads to job creation and a higher standard of living. Countries also engage in trade to form political and economic ties. When the United States exports wheat and farm products to nations in Africa, countries on both sides of the transaction benefit. The two nations may feel more strongly allied as a result of international trade.

Billabong Style

Surfboard shaper Gordon Merchant and his wife Rena started their clothing company Billabong in 1973 by cutting and sewing board shorts for surfers, and then selling them to local shops. Since then Billabong has become Australia's biggest surf-gear brand. Products include T-shirts, wetsuits, backpacks, wallets, jewelry, and other items, in addition to trunks for surfing.

Because surfers form a global community, the company also does business in Europe, Asia, Africa, and the Americas. A wave rider in Huntington Beach, California, knows about surf conditions from Malaysia to Costa Rica. Billabong promotes its products around the world through sponsoring world-class pro athletes, videos, global surf contests, and magazine advertisements.

Billabong also serves surfers of the Web. The company's Web site, which promotes Billabong's surfers, events, and global culture, has won awards from Microsoft and Macromedia. However, despite all the growth, the founders remain focused on what counts—they go surfing whenever possible.

THINK GLOBALLY *How has Billabong's type of products promoted international trade?*

@ To learn more about the country of origin for this global business, go to the International Business Online Learning Center through **glencoe.com**.

Direct Exporting

Companies can use two different methods to sell and distribute their goods and services: direct exporting and indirect exporting. A company that exports its own products uses direct exporting. Usually, a sales manager develops the export business. Employees handle the billing, credit, and shipping. In larger businesses, the company may establish an export department or a complete sales company. Smaller companies use freight forwarders.

As You Read

Question Why do nations export goods and services?

Benefits of Direct Exporting

A key benefit of direct exporting is control. A company has a great deal more control over negotiations, prices, distribution, and marketing programs with direct exporting. The seller is able to choose how and where products will be sold.

Costs of Direct Exporting

The primary cost or shared cost of direct exporting is shipping. Direct exporters must also keep inventory and payment records. They have to pay their sales force to keep the lines of communication open with companies in other countries. Direct exporting often raises a product's price. Each separate seller in the process, such as the distributor trading company, or retailer, adds a mark-up, or additional charge. Distributors, retailers, and trading companies all facilitate direct exporting.

Indirect Exporting

Indirect exporting often requires less work than direct exporting. A company hires another company located in the importing country, or the companies may have an agreement. To export goods through indirect exporting, a business must find and select one of four types of independent exporters to represent the goods and/or services:

1. **Manufacturer's Export Agents**—A manufacturer's export agent represents a company's goods without buying them. The company usually pays the agent a commission to sell its goods to firms in another country. A manufacturer's agent is an agent middleman.

2. **Export Commission Agents**—Independent exporters based in their own home country do the work of buying for their overseas customers.

3. **Export Merchants**—As indirect exporters, export merchants purchase and sell the company's products for their own profit.

4. **International Firms**—International firms can become independent exporters of goods they procure from other exporting companies in their home countries. Many mining, construction, and petroleum companies are examples of international firms that become exporters of other companies' products.

Benefits of Indirect Exporting

The primary benefits of indirect exporting are volume and simplicity. When an export management company or an international trading company buys and resells a product, it operates on a much larger scale than it would through direct exporting. Hiring an independent company to manage exporting operations is also simpler than setting up direct exporting operations within an established company. Commissions paid to export agents and export management companies are often lower than all of the costs associated with direct exporting. The lower costs result in a lower retail price for the consumer.

Disadvantages of Indirect Exporting

The major disadvantage of indirect exporting is that a company has less control over the export process. The various representative agencies may not find the best places to sell the product. They also carry competitors' products and may show a company's product alongside the competition's product.

Direct versus Indirect Exporting

Choosing the direct or indirect method of exporting is a key decision for managers. Businesses must carefully weigh the benefits and costs of each exporting option. It is not unusual for a company to start with indirect exporting, and then transition to direct exporting as sales increase.

Exporting and Risk

Whenever two nations trade, there are numerous risks that can affect profits and the success of a company. Four types of risk are associated with exporting:

- Time risk
- Economic risk
- Product risk
- Country risk

Time Risk

Time risk refers to how long it takes to "get your money back" on an investment. The longer it takes, the greater the risk. A company that builds a major plant in a foreign country that will take 30 years to pay off has a time risk to consider.

Economic Risk

Economic risk results from the possibility that downturns in economic conditions can affect business locally, nationally, or globally. The Asian economy suffered a major downturn in the 1990s and early 2000s. Many companies from other countries had lower profits as a result.

Product Risk

Product risk results from the fact that some products are more risky to sell than others. For example, there have been many failed attempts to sell electric cars over the years. Only recently have sales of hybrid automobiles (powered by electricity *and* gas) been profitable. Fashion and clothing are also items that carry product risk, because tastes and styles change often.

Country Risk

Country risk is the possibility that an investment will be lost due to political changes in a country. A new government may close or take over a plant. This practice is called "expropriation." In addition, a government may raise taxes on a company's products or services. Wars can also change business practices quickly.

▼ DIRECT OR INDIRECT
Managers must carefully choose between direct and indirect exporting. *What are the benefits of indirect exporting?*

How Do You Say?

Q: In Bahasa-Indonesian, how do you say: "Hello" and "Goodbye"?

A: Halo (pronounced: Hă-lōw) and Selamat tinggal (pronounced: Slă-măt tēng-gŭll)

@ To learn these words in other languages, go to the International Business Online Learning Center through **glencoe.com**.

Importing and Risk

The biggest risk in importing is dependency. **Dependency** is the practice of relying too much on one trading **partner**. Dependency can occur at the corporate or national level. When a country or company is dependent on one supplier, any price increase and supply reduction can cause major problems.

The Role of Trade Balances

The difference between how much a country imports and how much it exports is its **balance of trade**. A nation that exports more than it imports has a *trade surplus*. A nation that imports more than it exports has a *trade deficit*.

For many years the United States has experienced trade deficits, or an unfavorable balance of trade. Its trade deficits are caused by importing large quantities of oil and increased world competition in other products. Even though the United States has favorable trade balances and trade surpluses with many countries, its trade deficits with countries selling oil outweigh all those surpluses.

Most economists believe that a negative balance of trade, or a trade deficit, is bad for a nation's economy. The nation loses jobs, and its companies are less likely to succeed if international competition wins. Consequently, many national leaders will take steps to reduce or eliminate trade deficits. They may increase exports or decrease imports.

Reading Check **Analyze** Why is a trade deficit not beneficial for a nation's economy?

Increasing Exports

To increase exports, governments may become involved in subsidy programs or promotional programs for products or companies. Businesspeople who receive government subsidies may use them to start up companies. They may also reduce costs of established companies. The government can also give money in the form of a grant that does not have to be repaid. Sometimes the government offers low- or no-interest loans to businesses if a business has the potential to export products.

Promotional programs, sometimes called "trade junkets," occur when government officials visit other nations and companies to promote products. In the United States, the Commerce Department, led by the Secretary of Commerce, is the federal government's organization that is involved in promoting goods.

Decreasing Imports

To decrease the amount of imported goods, governments may take several steps. The most common method is to establish trade barriers. **Trade barriers** are restrictions that reduce free trade and limit competition from imported goods. Four types of trade barriers include:

- Tariffs
- Quotas
- Embargoes
- Boycotts

Tariffs A tariff is a tax on an imported good. The added tax raises the price of the good and gives local products a cost advantage.

Quotas A quota is a regulation that limits the number of items that can be sold in a country. Many farmers are protected by quotas limiting imports of various crops.

Embargoes An embargo is a complete ban on the import or export of products to a particular country. Embargoes are rare. Most of the time, governments use them for political or military reasons. For example, the United States government imposed partial and full embargoes on goods made in Iraq.

Boycotts A national government may also try to boycott goods from another country—they simply do not buy them. They can do this for trade reasons or for political reasons. During the apartheid rule of South Africa, many nations boycotted South African products.

Other Trade Barriers Trade barriers can be created in other ways. For example, a country may establish licensing requirements. It may set up licenses for radio and television stations in order to prevent foreign investors from buying media outlets.

Exchange rate controls are another form of trade barrier. A national government can require a certain rate of exchange for money. This prevents a company from taking advantage of a weak currency to make profits.

Protectionism

Trade barriers are part of a program called **protectionism**, which is a system of imposing extra costs on imports to protect the interests of local businesses. Governments and company leaders justify protectionism for many reasons. They argue that local workers lose jobs when too many imports come into a country.

Protectionism may also defend against unfair competition. Protectionism policies counteract certain advantages enjoyed by other countries. For example, some countries may have lower wages and labor costs or weaker environmental standards. Businesses in these countries pay less money to their workers and do not spend money to meet environmental standards. Because their expenses are lower, they can offer lower-priced products. Conversely, a non-polluting company that pays good wages to its workers might face a pricing disadvantage. Protectionism seeks to address this disadvantage.

TRADE BARRIERS Trade barriers protect domestic markets. *How might a tariff protect farmers?*

International Trade Agreements

Modern strategic trade alliances began to form following World War II in the late 1940s. Many national leaders recognized that protectionism and trade wars did not advance their countries' long-term interests. During this era international leaders began to use two terms:

1. Economic integration
2. Globalization

Economic Integration

Economic integration is the practice of removing trade barriers and establishing cooperation to connect businesses and businesspeople across national borders. Economies grow when there is interdependence, and the standard of living for the countries' citizens improves.

Globalization

With globalization, many companies today have operations in a variety of nations. When there is economic interdependence between nations and within multinational companies, several good things can happen. Investments are easier to make in new areas. More people can share technological innovations. Everyone has access to more and better goods and services.

Formation of Alliances

Major political alliances formed after World War II, combined with increasing economic integration and globalization, contributed to several strategic trade alliances. Peace-time negotiations made them possible.

Free trade has helped many nations form stronger political connections and enhanced economic opportunities for many people. Several international trade organizations help to implement them:

1. General Agreement on Tariffs and Trade (GATT)
2. World Trade Organization (WTO)
3. European Union (EU)
4. North American Free Trade Agreement (NAFTA)

General Agreement on Tariffs and Trade (GATT)

The General Agreement on Tariffs and Trade (GATT) was one of the first agreements reached between a group of mostly Western allies after World War II. Their goal was to reduce tariffs between member organizations. GATT was actually a series of negotiations called "rounds." In the first round in 1947, only 23 nations participated.

Almost 40 years later, one round that greatly increased the scope of GATT is called the "Uruguay Round." The organization had 114 member nations. In those sessions, which lasted from 1986 through 1994, many new products received tariff relief. Members established clear procedures for settling trade disputes. They also established protection for what is now known as *intellectual property,* which is anything that is a valuable idea. As a final outcome, members established a new organization—the World Trade Organization (WTO).

World Trade Organization (WTO)

Founded in 1995, the World Trade Organization grew from GATT members' goal to accomplish several lofty goals. They wanted to expand international trade, raise the standard of living around the world, fight discrimination, and make companies more transparent and predictable in international trade. By 2002, member nations in the WTO accounted for nearly 95 percent of world trade. The WTO addresses four key areas:

1. Most-favored-nation (MFN) treatment status
2. National treatment
3. Escape clauses
4. Dumping policies

Most-Favored-Nation Status Renamed *normal trade relations* (NTR) in the United States, most-favored-nation (MFN) status means that any favor or privilege granted to one member of the WTO must be given to all others holding that status. If Brazil reduces tariffs on imports of olive oil from Greece, tariffs on olive oil from anywhere else in the world must be reduced by the same amount.

National Treatment National treatment is the principle that once a product has cleared customs at a member nation's borders, the member nation will treat the product as a **domestic** good. The government may charge customs duties, but no additional charges will be added when a product enters the market. National treatment applies to goods, services, and intellectual property.

Escape Clauses Escape clauses or exceptions to these policies are given to developing countries. An escape clause provided by the WTO allows a developing country to charge higher tariffs to develop new and growing companies and industries in that country.

Dumping Policies The WTO also offers some protection against dumping practices. **Dumping** is the practice of selling goods in another country for less than the cost of manufacturing them, or for less than their market price. The WTO allows a country to impose import duties (fees) on products, such as cars, sold by countries that are dumping them.

Criticism of the WTO Some people object to the WTO, believing that it is beneficial only for richer, more developed nations. Protesters confront most WTO meetings with concerns about human rights violations, discrimination, environmental damage, and other problems. For example, in 1999, more than 40,000 anti-globalization advocates protested WTO meetings in Seattle, Washington.

European Union (EU)

Over the years, countries in various regions of the world have entered into treaties and arrangements to facilitate free trade and other forms of economic cooperation. These agreements supplement agreements between other international organizations.

ETHICS & ISSUES

Getting Dumped

Competitive pricing offers great advantages in the foreign marketplace, but sometimes those low prices are the result of questionable, even illegal, practices. Flooding the marketplace with products priced well below normal allows a company or government to undercut the competition and develop a strong market share. The company or government can then raise prices to normal levels. To curb this practice called "dumping," the EU fined China for dumping handbags on the European market. *Is it ethical to dump products on a foreign market? Why or why not?*

One of the most powerful of these groups is the European Union (EU). It has more than 25 member nations that are geographically close together. Many EU members share a common currency called the "euro." They also share more open trade with few tariffs or restrictions. See **Figure 4.2** for a list of member nations.

In matters of trade, the U.S. government negotiates with the EU as the representative of all EU member nations. Many individual businesses in the United States realize trade opportunities in the EU. The member nations of the EU represent major export markets for the United States. In addition, EU member nations also have major foreign investment in the United States.

The EU created two new sets of agreements, known as the *EC Free Trade Agreements* and the *EC Association Agreements*. "EC" stands for European Community. These two arrangements promote more open trade and investment with nearby nations outside the EU. As a result, the European Union is a powerful trading bloc, and member countries are allied with strong economic partners.

North American Free Trade Agreement (NAFTA)

The North American Free Trade Agreement (NAFTA) was the first free trade agreement that combined industrialized countries, the United States and Canada, with a developing nation, Mexico. It was signed in 1992 and implemented in 1994. NAFTA eliminates most trade barriers for industrial goods, services, investments, intellectual property, and agriculture. Separate arrangements cover wages, the environment, and import increases.

NAFTA creates a free trade district covering more than 360 million people. As a result, many companies have shifted their **focus** from just their home company to the entire North American region.

Figure 4.2

EU Member Countries

EUROPEAN UNION MEMBERS The EU is a powerful free trade alliance. *Why might a country wish to join the European Union?*

- Austria
- Belgium
- Cyprus
- Czech Republic
- Denmark
- Estonia
- Finland
- France
- Germany
- Greece
- Hungary
- Ireland
- Italy
- Latvia
- Lithuania
- Luxembourg
- Malta
- The Netherlands
- Poland
- Portugal
- Slovakia
- Slovenia
- Spain
- Sweden
- United Kingdom

WHOLESALE BUYER

Merchant wholesale companies import manufactured goods to businesses or governments. These companies employ wholesale buyers to purchase goods from manufacturers for resale. International travel is required. International wholesale buyers are responsible for importing goods and services from other countries.

Wholesale buyers must know their company's needs in order to decide what to buy. They must also understand their customers' needs to predict what products will sell. Purchasing professionals consider many factors when choosing manufacturers and goods, including price, quality, availability, reliability, and technical support. They negotiate for the best goods and services at the lowest possible price.

Skills and Training A candidate who has world language skills and the ability to work with people from different cultures will do well in the merchant wholesale field. Buyers need leadership and good decision-making skills because they often supervise assistant buyers. Good communication and negotiation skills are vital for dealing with manufacturer's representatives. To match products with customers, buyers must stay informed about other cultures and market trends.

Many wholesale buyers enter the merchant wholesale field with a high school diploma. Wholesale buyers may begin their careers as trainees, purchasing clerks, expediters, junior buyers, or assistant buyers. Training and experience are very important in this field. The field of wholesale trade offers good advancement opportunities.

English Language Arts/Writing

List the five steps of importing and describe the role wholesale buyers play in the importing process.

@ To learn more about wholesale buyers and their career paths, go to the International Business Online Learning Center through **glencoe.com**.

Career Data

Education: High school diploma, associate's degree, or bachelor's degree

Skills: Computer, negotiation, bilingual or multilingual, and mathematical skills

Outlook: Growth slower than average in the next ten years

Criticism of NAFTA Critics in various governments oppose NAFTA and the practice of free trade. Opponents argue in favor of protectionism because they believe that NAFTA gives an unfair advantage to countries that allow lower wages, ignore environmental protections, and flood the U.S. market with lower-priced goods. In addition, they believe this advantage causes the loss of jobs in America.

Other Trade Agreements

Several other trade alliances are in place. One agreement is between the Caribbean Community and the Common Market (CARICOM). Central America has a similar arrangement, the Central American Common Market (CACM). Other Latin American countries founded the Latin American Integration Society (LAIA in English; ALADI in Spanish). Countries in South America created the Southern Common Market (MERCOSUR in Spanish; MERCOSUL in Portuguese). In addition, countries throughout the Pacific Rim area formed the Asia Pacific Economic Cooperation (APEC) forum. In 2006, the Central America Free Trade Agreement (CAFTA) was approved by the U.S. Congress to promote trade between the United States and Costa Rica, El Salvador, Guatemala, Honduras, and Nicaragua.

The goals of a regional trade alliance are basically the same—to promote freer trade and investment across national borders.

The Future of International Trade Agreements

The future of trade, free trade agreements, and economic alliances is somewhat uncertain. Those who believe in protectionism work to create national laws and policies that reduce free trade. In the 2004 U.S. elections, several groups called for the United States to leave the WTO and NAFTA. These oppositions are likely to continue.

Quick Check 4.2

After You Read Respond to what you have read by answering these questions.

1. What are the main reasons that a company or a country would export goods? _____

_____

2. What are the main differences between direct and indirect exporting? _____

_____

3. What are four major trade agreements around the world? _____

_____

Academics / Social Studies/Geography

4. South America has a common market called "MERCOSUR." Name three countries in South America.

_____

_____

Import Business Research

After graduation you plan to go on a one-month tour of Europe. You have always been interested in importing. You decide to use the tour as a way of spotting products you might be able to import into the United States to sell. You must set up a trip journal to help organize your research while you are abroad.

Prepare a Chart In the space below or on a separate piece of paper, prepare a chart to use on each page of the journal. Include categories such as: product, description, price, customers, manufacturer and contact information, marketing ideas, and any other categories that might be helpful. Fill in one table with a hypothetical product.

Product	Description	Price	Customers	Manufacturer Contact	Marketing	Miscl.

ACADEMICS APPLIED Check off the academic knowledge you used to do this activity:

☐ English Language Arts   ☐ Mathematics   ☐ Social Studies   ☐ Science

ACADEMIC AND CAREER PLAN Add this page to your Academic and Career Plan Portfolio.

(tl) Ulf Wallin/Getty Images; (tr) Royalty-free/David De Lossy/Getty Images; (b) Royalty-free/Getty Images

CHAPTER SUMMARY

Section 4.1 **The Nature of International Business**

international trade
(p. 82)

imports (p. 83)

exports (p. 83)

good (p. 83)

service (p. 84)

FOB (p. 87)

CIF (p. 87)

C&F (p. 87)

- The processes of international trade include activities such as buying, selling, shipping, receiving, paperwork, granting credit, making payments, servicing products, and a wide variety of additional tasks.

- A good is a tangible item that is made, manufactured, or grown. A service is an intangible benefit provided by a company to individual customers, other companies, and governmental organizations.

- Importing involves identifying the need, searching for suppliers, creating and finalizing the purchase agreement, receiving the goods and confirming the purchase is complete. Exporting involves assessing the demand, identifying customers and making sales contacts, creating and finalizing a purchase agreement, delivering the goods and services, and completing the transaction.

Section 4.2 **International Trade Relationships**

dependency (p. 94)

balance of trade (p. 94)

trade barriers (p. 94)

protectionism (p. 95)

dumping (p. 97)

- Companies and countries trade with each other for a variety of reasons that include earning profits, adding unsaturated markets, and smoothing out seasonal sales.

- It is important for countries to maintain a positive balance of trade because most economists believe that a negative balance of trade, or a trade deficit, is bad for a nation's economy.

- International trade organizations play many roles such as helping to expand international trade and raise the standard of living in the participating countries.

CONCEPTS REVIEW

1. **List** five of the activities included in the process of conducting international trade.

2. **Explain** the difference between a good and a service.

3. **Contrast** the steps in importing with the steps in exporting.

4. **Identify** two reasons that countries and companies trade with each other.

5. **Explain** why a negative balance of trade is undesirable.

6. **Describe** two of the many roles played by international trade organizations.

KEY TERMS REVIEW

7. Match each term to its definition.

_____ international trade

_____ imports

_____ exports

_____ good

_____ service

_____ FOB

_____ CIF

_____ C&F

_____ dependency

_____ balance of trade

_____ trade barriers

_____ protectionism

_____ dumping

a. goods and services that people in one country buy from people in another country

b. free on board, or the ownership of merchandise in transit determines if freight charges are free

c. the practice of relying too much on one trading partner

d. restrictions that reduce free trade and limit competition from imported goods

e. a tangible item that is made, manufactured, or grown

f. all business activities conducted between individuals, companies, and governments from different countries

g. the price quoted to the buyer, including cost, insurance, and freight

h. the difference between how much a country imports and how much it exports

i. a system of imposing extra costs on imports to protect the interests of local businesses

j. the practice of selling goods in another country for less than the cost of manufacturing them, or for less than their market price

k. an intangible benefit or task provided by a business to its customers

l. goods and services that people in one country sell to people in another country

m. the price quoted to the buyer signifying the buyer pays separately for insurance

Academic Vocabulary

8. On a separate sheet of paper, write a sentence or two related to importing, exporting, and international trade using at least three of the academic terms you learned in the section openers:

- purchase
- item
- require
- partner
- domestic
- focus

Critical Thinking

9. Write a short paragraph identifying why it is difficult to prove that dumping has occurred and difficult to punish.

Discussion Starter

10. Do you think the United States will continue to have trade deficits as a result of its dependence on foreign oil? Explain.

Point of View

11. Research and evaluate the groups who are protesting the WTO.

BUILDING REAL-WORLD SKILLS

12. Working Conditions As the effects of NAFTA become more apparent, you can draw conclusions about the effectiveness of agreements between industrialized (the United States and Canada) and developing countries (Mexico).

Research and Share

a. How have wages and working conditions improved or become worse in Mexico since NAFTA was established?

b. How has the availability of inexpensive labor in Mexico affected the American and Canadian workforces?

13. Networking Communicating with and helping others of like interests is often the key to success in business. This can be accomplished through networking.

Research and Write

a. Research the benefits of networking.

b. Prepare a short report on how you would go about establishing and maintaining effective business contacts in a network.

BUILDING ACADEMIC SKILLS

 English Language Arts

14. Look up countries in the following organizations: CARICOM, CACM, LAIA, MERCOSUR, and APEC. Look up the countries in the EU. Prepare a report describing the most used language in each of these organizations. Do you think there is a relationship between language and free trade? Why or why not?

MATH Mathematics

15. For the year 2005, China reported an average monthly trade surplus of more than $8.5 billion. Approximately how much was China's trade surplus for the entire year of 2005?

Computation and Estimation To solve this problem, you need to understand the principles of multiplication.

SOC Social Studies/History

16. Since the late 1970s, China's economy has blossomed as a result of a major shift in economic philosophy. China moved from a centrally planned economy to a more decentralized one, with an emphasis on international trade. This move has paid off for the Chinese. Research and write a paragraph about how this situation occurred over the last 25 years.

SOC Social Studies/Geography

17. Research the trade balances that the United States has with ten other countries. Then make a photocopy of a political map of the world. On the map, mark in blue the countries with which the United States enjoys a positive trade balance. Indicate in red the countries with which the United States enjoys a negative trade balance. What conclusions can you draw from the results?

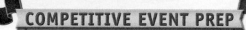

COMPETITIVE EVENT PREP

Exporting Products, Importing Profits

18. Situation Your state government has hired you to find a product that your state could export to increase its profits, market share, and employment statistics. This might include agricultural, manufactured, or technology products, or any service. Your job is to determine the product (good or service), identify the providers and their usage, and prepare an effective marketing campaign.

Activity Select and research an appropriate product by using your state government Web site, local resources, the Internet, and your school library. Develop a grid of other states and nations that will be your competition, and list the advantages and disadvantages they have compared to your state. How can your state market the product?

Evaluation You will be evaluated on how well you meet the following objectives:

a. Identify the good or service your state can export.

b. Evaluate different ways your product can be used.

c. Identify customers, domestic and international.

d. Identify the competition and its advantages and disadvantages.

e. Develop a market plan for the domestic market.

f. Develop a market plan for the international market.

Internet Travels

European Union
Using the Internet, answer the following questions about the EU bloc of nations on a separate sheet of paper.

➤ What are the member countries? (See Figure 4.2 on page 98.)

➤ What is the combined population and the combined gross domestic product of these countries?

@ For resources to help you do this exercise, go to the International Business Online Learning Center through **glencoe.com**.

BusinessWeek online

19. Newsclip: Europe's Utilities Stay Close to Home

The French government recently purchased a private French utility company over an Italian one. Does protectionism have a place in the European Union?

@ Go to the International Business Online Learning Center through **glencoe.com** to read an article about this topic. Then write a paragraph that discusses why EU regulators disapprove of "economic nationalism."

Standardized Test Practice

20. Choose the best answer to the following multiple-choice question.

Which of the following is NOT a trade barrier?
○ tariff
○ quota
○ currency
○ embargo

Test-Taking Tip Be sure to consider the appearance of a negative word such as NOT that reverses the meaning of the question.

Chapter 5

Governmental and Legal Influences

Chapter Objectives
When you have completed this chapter, you will be able to:

Section 5.1
- Identify different types of governments.
- Discuss the ways in which governments influence international trade.

Section 5.2
- Describe the different forms of legal systems.
- Identify the impact of laws and regulations on international business.
- Explain some ways to settle differences in international trade relationships.

ESPRIT

Esprit is a publicly owned corporation whose shares are traded on stock exchanges. When you research this company through Standard & Poor's, you will find investment information such as this:

Index:	S&P Global 1200
Sector:	Consumer Discretionary
Company:	Esprit Holdings Limited
Symbol:	330 (HK)
Country:	Hong Kong
Price:	(varies)

Global Profile Esprit Holdings Limited designs, licenses, sources, wholesales, and retails fashion clothing and ecology-based gear under the ESPRIT brand name. The company also sells Red Earth cosmetics, skin, and body care products. European stores are in many countries, such as Germany, Netherlands, Belgium, Switzerland, Austria, France, Great Britain, Denmark, and Luxembourg. Store locations in Asia include Hong Kong, Taiwan, Singapore, Malaysia, and China.

Business Report Susie and Doug Tompkins founded the Esprit brand as Esprit de Corp. Doug eventually sold his stake. Michael Ying founded Esprit Far East Group in 1971, which became the sourcing agent for the U.S. business. Though Asia suffered a SARS epidemic scare in 2003 and an economic slump, Esprit experienced strong sales in Europe. By 2005, sales totaled 20.6 billion Hong Kong dollars (or $2.7 billion). Esprit's success is helping to fuel investment in China.

English Language Arts/Writing

Having global appeal attracts counterfeiters who produce products to sell illegally. *Write a paragraph about three brand names, including Esprit, that imitators might use to sell phony products around the world.*

To do this activity, go to the International Business Online Learning Center through **glencoe.com.**

Governmental Influences on Trade

WHAT YOU'LL LEARN

- To identify different types of governments
- To discuss the ways in which governments influence international trade

WHY IT'S IMPORTANT

Understanding a country's form of government is an integral part of doing business globally.

KEY TERMS

- democracy
- totalitarianism
- theocracy
- free trade zone
- free trade agreement

📖 Academic Vocabulary

You will find these words in your reading and on your tests. Make sure you know their meanings.

- legal
- policy
- administration

Reading Guide

▶ Before You Read

What is your definition of the term *free trade*?

MAIN IDEA

Governmental policies and regulations affect trade.

GRAPHIC ORGANIZER

Draw this diagram. As you read this section, write in types of government.

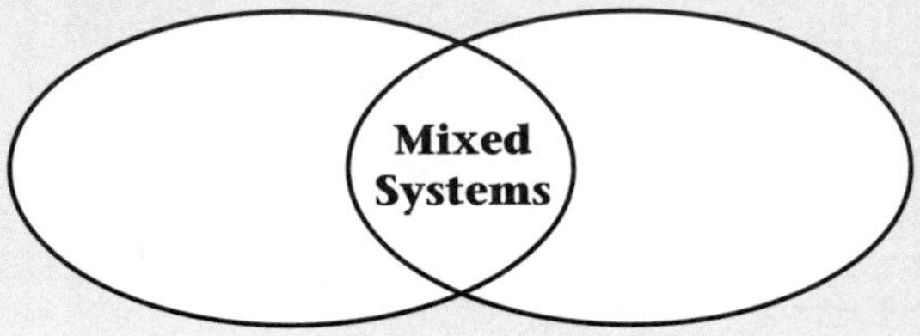

Mixed Systems

Government and International Business

Governmental policies and regulations play major roles in international trade. They affect all aspects of importing and exporting. **Legal** systems regulate trade. Every company must be able to work within various political and legal systems to be a competitive international player.

Of course, to work within foreign political and legal systems, you must understand the nature of different types of government. You need to be familiar with legal requirements unique to international trade. You must also be aware of the ways governments shape economic policies and practices that affect international commerce.

Types of Governments

A nation's form of government has a major impact on business. Political systems affect a government's economic policies and practices. While national governments are almost as unique as fingerprints, there are two basic types: democratic and totalitarian.

Most governments have characteristics that fall somewhere in between democracies and totalitarian governments. Such governments are mixed systems. **Figure 5.1** illustrates the political spectrum. Each government type has different political, social, legal, and economic environments.

Democratic Governments

A **democracy** is a government system in which the nation's citizens hold political power. It is a government by the people. Most democracies stress the rights, freedom, and responsibilities of the individual. A republic is a kind of democracy; its leaders are elected representatives. Democratic political systems share characteristics:

1. Freedom of opinion, expression, press, and freedom to organize
2. Elections in which voters choose officers of the government
3. Limited terms of elected officials
4. An independent and fair court system with respect of individual rights
5. A nonpolitical bureaucracy and defense infrastructure
6. Access to the decision-making process available to citizens

Elected leaders are accountable in key ways. Regarding business, elected officials are more likely to create policies and laws to help the country's economy. When they do not, their constituents, the voters who elected them, can vote them out of office.

Many democracies use an economic system based on supply and demand, which is a known as a *market economy*. It is common for a democracy to be linked to a free-enterprise economic system.

Totalitarian Governments

Totalitarianism is a type of government system in which citizens have no influence on the government's policies and laws. Such governments control all aspects of life, including attitudes, values, and beliefs. They deny religious freedom and other rights.

There are several types of totalitarian governments, including fascism, authoritarianism, and communism. Such governments can be theocratic or secular. In theocratic governments, religious leaders are the political leaders. A secular dictator can come from the military or rise through the country's single political party. Often the leader rules by force. A pure monarchy can be a kind of totalitarian state.

Figure 5.1

Types of World Governments

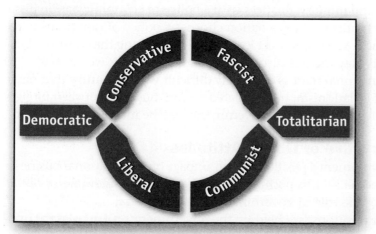

THE POLITICAL SPECTRUM Purely democratic and totalitarian governments are at opposite ends of the political spectrum. *Why are most governments considered mixed systems?*

A totalitarian state tightly controls the activities of its citizens by controlling most businesses and all trade. When a nation's government directs the economy, it is known as a *command economy.* Communist countries, such as Cuba, also have command economies.

Theocracy A **theocracy** is a type of totalitarian government whose leaders claim to be inspired by divine guidance. Such governments are not always totalitarian dictatorships and may include a mixture of elected officials and religious influences. The governments of Iran, Afghanistan, and the Vatican are examples of theocracies. Leaders rule according to the religious principles of the dominant faith. Members of other faiths may be excluded from the economic system or treated as second-class citizens. The policies of theocratic nations can affect international trade.

Mixed Systems

Few countries have purely democratic or purely totalitarian governments. Most countries are a combination and fall somewhere between democracies and totalitarian governments. For example, the government of the United Kingdom (U.K.) is democratic, but the Royal Family plays a role, even if that role is mostly ceremonial. The U.K. is a constitutional monarchy. Most countries have a mixed political system and a mixed economy. For many decades, China has been an example of a totalitarian state with a command economy. At the beginning of the 21st century, however, the government began encouraging some individual businesses. Citizens are freer to trade and create companies than in the past, though the government still directs the economy.

 **Reading Check** **Recall** What is a mixed system?

Political Environments

A nation's values, attitudes, and actions shape the nation's political environment. Two main factors guide governmental actions:

1. Isolationism
2. Conservative or liberal attitudes

Isolationism

Isolationism is a foreign **policy** that combines an avoidance of political and military alliances with a policy of economic nationalism or protectionism. When a nation chooses a policy of isolationism, its government seeks to protect its economy by closing the country's borders. This may include discouraging immigration as well as trade.

International trade is extremely difficult with a country that has a policy of isolationism. In an isolated nation, business between foreign companies and the home government may be marked by suspicion.

Conservative or Liberal Attitudes

A government's position has an impact on international business. In a broad sense, this position may be termed as *conservative* or *liberal* regarding the role of government in international trade. These attitudes, or positions, are held by the government's **administration**.

They can shape and guide a nation's trade policies. Though the terms are not global, it is important to understand their meanings because they are commonly used in the United States, especially when describing the spectrum of political parties.

Conservative Attitudes A conservative attitude favors limits on government activities and promotes private ownership and business domestically and internationally. Conservative leaders allow the marketplace to operate as freely as possible. They favor fewer government controls and regulations.

A nation that trades with a nation that has a conservative position deals with less "red tape," or government paperwork. However, product quality in conservative countries might not be well controlled. The government may be less concerned about product liability.

Liberal Attitudes A liberal position favors more government involvement in business. Liberal governments tend to impose stronger quality and safety regulations than do conservative governments. When doing business with a nation that takes a liberal position, it is important to know its laws and policies regarding liability. Consumer protections are likely to be strong.

▲ **FREEDOM OF THE PRESS** Isolationist countries often restrict access to information. *Why might an isolationist country have a state-run news organization?*

Economic Policies and Practices

J ust as a nation's system of government shapes its political environment, a nation's political environment shapes its economic policies and practices. The political environment of a country dramatically affects importing, exporting, and international trade through that nation's economic policies regarding international taxes, trade barriers, and free trade. Of course, a political environment can change.

International Taxes

Tax policies influence how people and businesses invest money. For example, some people who earn large incomes may prefer to live in Florida or Texas where there is no state income tax.

International businesses may operate in the same way. If a company's leaders can find places where business tax rates are lower, either in another country or in an "enterprise zone" in the United States, they tend to locate in those places. An enterprise zone is a geographical area in which local or state governments give businesses favorable tax credits, financing, or other incentives to encourage economic development. There are various types of international taxes:

- Income tax
- Payroll tax
- Sales tax
- Value-added tax
- Excise tax

Swiss + Watch = Swatch

Faced with stiff competition from Japanese manufacturers who had introduced new, cost-effective technology, Swiss watch companies ASUAG and SSIH were on the verge of dissolving in 1983. That is when engineer Nicolas G. Hayek completed a study of these watch manufacturers. He proposed a way for them to survive. Hayek implemented many changes that eventually revived and revolutionized the Swiss watch industry. One innovation was the introduction of the Swatch watch. The slim and affordable timepiece became a rage in the late 1980s and early 1990s, when fans would wear more than one together. Celebrity artists fueled the frenzy by approving watch designs that used their art work.

By 1993, the fad faded, and the company was once again struggling for survival. However, by the year 2000, the Swatch Group had regained its position. To maintain prominence, Swatch Group has diversified its business with 18 brands, which range from luxury items to private-label companies that manufacture watches to specifications.

THINK GLOBALLY *What type of taxes might be added to the cost of Swatch watches, and why?*

@ To learn more about the country of origin for this global business, go to the International Business Online Learning Center through **glencoe.com.**

As You Read

Relate Have you ever paid income tax? Why do some people pay a higher rate of income tax than others?

Income Tax An annual tax on an individual's or a corporation's net profit is an income tax. These taxes may be progressive, regressive, or flat. A progressive tax is one in which people with higher incomes pay larger percentages of their income. A regressive tax requires the rich to pay smaller percentages of income than paid by people with low income. A flat tax requires everyone to pay the same percentage of their income, regardless of the size of income. The income tax structures in the United States and in many European countries are designed to be progressive. As incomes rise, so do tax rates.

Sales Tax A sales tax is a tax on the sale of a product. Sales tax is flat because everyone pays the same rate, regardless of his or her income.

Excise Tax Excise tax is levied on specific goods and services. Telephone service, airline tickets, automobiles, and gasoline usually carry excise taxes. The tax is included in the price of the product. So-called "sin tax" added to the price of cigarettes and alcohol is excise tax.

Payroll Tax A payroll tax is a tax that employers are required to withhold from employees' paychecks. Payroll taxes are levied by the state or by the national government. Some types are taxes withheld for Social Security, Medicare, and unemployment insurance.

Value-Added Tax A value-added tax, or VAT, is a sales tax paid on the increased value of a good. When iron ore becomes finished sheet metal, it has more value. That increase in value is taxed.

Trade Barriers

National leaders create policies to discourage international trade for many reasons. Isolationist countries may establish trade barriers to prevent outside influences. Embargoes and boycotts can also be used for economic protection or to make political statements. For example, the United States protests the government of Cuba by imposing a trade embargo against that country.

Duties Taxes on goods that cross national boundaries are called "duties." A customs duty is a tax on an imported good or service. Customs duty taxes can also be used as a type of a trade barrier.

Other Trade Barriers Other trade barriers include tariffs (or an import tax), quotas, embargoes, licensing requirements, and exchange rate controls, discussed in the preceding chapter. These protectionist policies limit trade. Countries use these and other foreign market rules and practices to limit access to trading in that country.

Free Trade

Trade policies serve several purposes. One is to increase trade. An increase in trade benefits a country in several ways:

- Trade can improve the economic well-being of people in the country.

- Trade can bring in goods and services that otherwise would not be available.

- Trade can build political alliances.

Duty-free zones, free trade agreements, and other forms of tax reduction are designed to encourage trade.

Free Trade Zone To spur trade, many countries have free trade zones. A **free trade zone** is a place where people can buy goods from other countries without paying extra taxes. Free trade zones can be found in duty-free shops in airports and at some harbors where ships dock.

Free Trade Agreement A **free trade agreement** is a treaty between countries in which the countries agree to not charge taxes, duties, or tariffs on goods that they trade. Governments enter into free trade agreements to encourage international business. If Australia enters into a free trade agreement with Indonesia, businesses in the two countries are able to ship goods back and forth more economically. The agreement helps hold down prices in both countries and makes it possible for them to export and import more goods. NAFTA in North America is one example of a free trade agreement.

Double Taxation Relief Double taxation occurs when a multinational company incurs taxes in both the home and other country. A country may offer to reduce this tax burden for a company in exchange for gaining the benefit of economic growth that the company can provide.

OUR MULTICULTURAL WORKPLACE

Beyond the Law: Global Ethics

Global managers understand that a business practice may be legally correct, but could have adverse effects on employees, consumers, competitors, or the environment. Therefore, in addition to considering a country's laws, they must also consider professional standards and values, which may be stricter than the laws of the country. For example, the law may allow toxic waste to be dumped into a river, but ethical global managers would prohibit polluting the river. Businesses must be governed by a common set of ethical values that include truth, fairness, tolerance, responsibility, and respect for life. *Investigate a multinational corporation. Explain how its business actions have or have not reflected ethical behavior.*

How Do You Say?

Q: In Dutch, how do you say: "What time is it?"

A: Hoe laat is het? (pronounced: Who lăwt ĭss hĕt?)

@ To learn this phrase in other languages, go to the International Business Online Learning Center through **glencoe.com**.

Political Risk

All multinational companies face some degree of political risk. Changes in the political climate of a country can negatively impact international business. There are several forms of political risk:

- Trade sanctions
- Political turbulence
- Expropriation
- War
- Economic nationalism

Trade Sanctions A trade sanction is the use of a tariff, boycott, or embargo to make a political statement. The country that is harmed by a trade sanction may retaliate in like manner.

Expropriation Expropriation is the act of taking control and ownership of a foreign-owned company or operation. When a government expropriates a company that is based in another country, that foreign company does not receive compensation for the loss.

Economic Nationalism Economic nationalism is one facet of isolationism. It is the practice of discouraging the importing of goods in order to protect a domestic product. Economic nationalistic policies also discourage or prevent ownership of businesses by people in other countries.

Political Turbulence Political turbulence is the generic name for types of disruption such as protests, strikes, and other social disorder. Civil unrest hinders business activities like production and transportation.

War Both civil war and war with other countries can devastate an economy. Mass destruction and revolution negatively impact international business.

Quick Check 5.1

After You Read Respond to what you have read by answering these questions.

1. What are the three main types of governments? _____

_____

2. How do a nation's values, attitudes, and actions affect the political environment? _____

_____

3. Why would a national government set up trade barriers? _____

_____

Academics / English Language Arts

4. Explain the term *isolationism* in your own words.

_____

_____

Legal Influences on Trade

Reading Guide

Before You Read

Have you ever helped settle an argument? What happened?

MAIN IDEA

Laws and regulations offer certain guidelines and protections for companies engaged in international business.

GRAPHIC ORGANIZER

Draw this chart. As you read this section, write in three methods of solving legal disputes and one benefit of each.

1.	2.	3.

WHAT YOU'LL LEARN

- To describe the different forms of legal systems
- To identify the impact of laws and regulations on international business
- To explain some ways to settle differences in international trade relationships

WHY IT'S IMPORTANT

Understanding foreign law will allow you to conduct international business and protect your interests.

KEY TERMS

- common law
- civil law
- theocratic law
- liability
- intellectual property
- litigation
- mediation
- arbitration

Academic Vocabulary

You will find these words in your reading and on your tests. Make sure you know their meanings.

- principle
- civil code
- register

Legal Systems and International Business

There are two kinds of laws. The first kind tells you what to do. The second tells you what *not* to do. One law tells you to drive on the right hand side of the road (what to do). Another law says speeding is illegal (what not to do).

In international business, laws do the same things. Some tell you what to do—how to trade. Others tell you what not to do—illegal trade practices. This section looks at several types of legal systems that are present in different countries:

- Common law
- Civil law
- Theocratic law

Common Law

Common law is a set of laws based on local customs, traditions, and precedent. Common law is found in the United States, Great Britain, and in many of Great Britain's former colonies. Legal history, previous cases, and national customs serve as guides for systems that follow common law. Common law, or case law, gives a judge flexibility to reach a fair or just decision.

Precedent A precedent is something that precedes, or has come before. A judge who follows precedent looks at decisions made by other judges in the past when judging a current case. The judge follows precedents when deciding how much a fine should be, how much jail time should be imposed, and how high a payment should be made in a lawsuit. More lawsuits are filed in common law countries because judges in common law systems can be flexible.

Civil Law

Civil law is a set of codes based on broad legal **principles**. It is the basis of law in many countries, including Germany, France, Japan, and Russia. Decisions are based on the codes, which have been written over time. Judges in common law systems interpret laws, whereas, in civil systems they apply the **civil codes**. Judges in civil law countries have less flexibility. Consequently, a lawsuit can be settled by applying the code, instead of looking to precedent. Businesses operating in countries with civil law must understand the country's codes.

Reading Check **Compare** How does common law differ from civil law?

Theocratic Law

Theocratic law is a set of laws based on religious teachings. Theocratic law regulates moral behavior, and to a lesser extent, business. The most common form of theocratic law is found in Islamic Law, which is based on the *Koran,* Islam's holy book. Islamic Law is also built around the *Sunnah,* another holy doctrine.

For example, Islamic law bans paying or accepting interest on a debt. This prohibition can greatly affect a business relationship with a country, such as Saudi Arabia, that is guided by Islamic law. All transactions would be made in one-time payments, unless both sides agree a debt can be paid without interest. In terms of what *not* to do, Islamic law says, "Do not charge interest."

Laws and Regulations

There are major differences in the laws and regulations affecting business around the world. These include legal differences in areas such as product safety and consumer protection, labor laws, intellectual property laws, and licensing requirements.

Product Safety and Consumer Protection

Individual countries have widely differing laws about product safety, product liability, and consumer protection. These laws apply to those who manufacture goods and those who purchase goods. Companies that manufacture goods must consider the importance of making safe products. They might also encounter laws that demand safety. **Liability** is legal responsibility for the financial cost of another person's losses or injuries. Those injured from unsafe or poorly made goods can sue violators for damages. Businesses can even face trials for criminal negligence. At the extreme, a business may be forced to close its doors because it has harmed others.

Culture Corner

Law and Fashion in Old England

Think About It Why might a government restrict the sale of an imported product?

For centuries in the kingdom of Great Britain, the monarchy ruled absolutely over the countries of England, Scotland, Wales, and Northern Ireland. Kings and queens controlled the state and commanded the military. They also influenced the cultural climate of the realm. A favorable nod from Queen Elizabeth I could set the stage for musicians, artists, poets, and playwrights. The aristocracy would follow the fashion of royalty, from attitude to dress.

Sometimes, however, such trends were influenced by law. To keep British money in the country, the government enacted the 17th-century Navigation Acts. These laws prohibited importation of certain foreign goods, such as the popular "Painted Earthen Wares" of Italy and the Netherlands. Long after the Acts were repealed, the simple cream-colored dishes, "Queen's ware," which replaced the imported dishware, could be found in most English homes.

Meeting and Greeting When doing business in England, shake hands lightly with everyone at business or social meetings, and again upon leaving. Use last names and titles until you are invited to use first names.

Business Etiquette Be punctual for meetings. Meetings are congenial, but Brits attend to business after a few moments of polite conversation. Gifts are not exchanged in business settings. Most business entertaining occurs in restaurants or pubs over lunch.

Business Dress Men wear dark suits and ties. Women wear suits, dresses, or skirts and blouses. A blazer is considered country or weekend wear.

English Language Arts/Writing

Think of a popular product that is currently imported into the United States. Would that product's success be affected by trade laws or regulations? Which ones?

People and companies who purchase goods should be aware of whether consumer protection laws are enforced in the country where goods are produced. Many nations do not hold businesses accountable as much as the United States does. It is always wise to know if you are in a country with a "buyer beware" environment.

Extensive consumer protection and liability laws sometimes put U.S. businesses at a financial disadvantage in the global marketplace. U.S. businesses must pay for liability insurance and pay to settle lawsuits. The result is that U.S. goods may be safer but cost more.

It is a balancing act for a government to try to protect citizens without unfairly punishing businesses. Lawsuits are expensive, and some awards are excessive. However, lawsuits that are not frivolous must be allowed to proceed to protect individuals.

As You Read

Question How does consumer protection affect price?

Labor Laws

Labor laws may vary significantly from country to country. These laws regulate:

- Minimum wage rates
- Length of the work week and overtime
- Hiring, firing, and layoff policies
- The age at which a person can work
- The right to form a labor union
- The right to strike

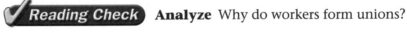
ANTI-PIRACY REGULATIONS Intellectual property laws protect artists against piracy. *Name three forms of intellectual property.*

Costs of Labor Laws Sometimes companies in the United States and other countries with strict labor laws face cost disadvantages. Some nations tolerate dangerous or unhealthy working conditions and very low wage rates. Child labor, sweatshops, and poor wages are common around the world.

Each government forms its position on labor laws. In countries with few or no protective labor laws, businesses may exploit workers. In contrast, companies operating in countries with strict labor laws may not be able to pay high wages. Governments may use trade agreements, embargoes, and other tactics to address these problems.

Reading Check **Analyze** Why do workers form unions?

Intellectual Property Laws

Intellectual property is an original work fixed in a tangible medium of expression that can be copyrighted, patented, or trademarked. *Piracy* is the illegal use of intellectual property such as illegal copying of films, books, articles, and music. Regulations to protect owners of intellectual property vary widely from country to country. Intellectual property protections include:

- Copyright
- Trademark
- Patent

Copyright A copyright is a legal protection of a creator's intellectual property or product. The creator might be an author, composer, playwright, artist, or publisher. A copyright gives the owner the right to publish and distribute the work in the way the owner thinks is best. The symbol © indicates that a work is copyright protected.

Trademark A trademark is a device that legally identifies ownership of a **registered** brand or trade name. It might be a design, name, or symbol registered by a merchant or manufacturer. The clothing brand Polo is a clothing trademark. McDonald's® arches are a trademarked design. The symbol ® indicates that a name or design is a registered trademark in the United States.

Patent A patent gives an inventor exclusive rights to manufacture, sell, or use an invention which can be a new physical product or something that improves an existing product. An invention can also be a process, such as a business process. Patents are granted for a limited time.

Rights Protection Many agreements exist to protect intellectual property, such as the Berne Convention for the Protection of Literary and Artistic Works, first signed in Paris, France, on September 9, 1886. Another major agreement is the Paris Convention for the Protection of Industrial Property, which was originally signed by 11 countries in 1883 and now has 169 member countries. In addition, the World Intellectual Property Organization (WIPO), an agency of the United Nations, administers these and 21 other international treaties. Also, a part of the General Agreement on Tariffs and Trade (GATT) accord is the Trade Related Aspects of Intellectual Property Rights (TRIPS) agreement.

The challenge of protection laws is enforcement. In fact, piracy and theft of intellectual property occurs globally. Many businesses demand that their governments impose sanctions on countries where intellectual property is stolen. Some governments cooperate more than others. It is important for business owners to know how much protection to expect.

Licensing Requirements

Multinational companies must comply with licensing requirements of other countries and international organizations when importing and exporting products. A business needs to obtain different types of licenses for different goods and services. These include licenses for physicians or dentists to provide medical services and driver's licenses to operate delivery vehicles. A business must also meet pollution specifications on company-owned automobiles. A license may be needed for specific business, such as a restaurant, radio station, or a retail store.

There are three licensing issues that businesses must address:

- Knowing the requirements

- Meeting the requirements in a cost-effective way

- Successfully completing the paperwork

Licensing Requirements as Trade Barriers In the United States, many furniture distributors have become concerned about the volume of furniture being imported from China. To slow this trend, the U.S. government imposed an import tariff and required China to have a special business license. Chinese officials complained that they were paying as much as $250,000 in legal fees to correctly file for the license, and also faced tariffs. China could retaliate by imposing fees and requiring licenses for goods that the United States might want to export to China. This situation illustrates how a licensing requirement can become a barrier to trade between two countries.

FOREIGN LICENSING REQUIREMENTS An international drivers license is an example of a foreign licensing requirement. *Why should multinational companies follow foreign licensing requirements?*

RESOLVING DIFFERENCES
There are other methods for resolving disputes, besides expensive litigation. *How can a company reduce the number of lawsuits and legal disputes it faces?*

Resolving Legal Disputes

As more and more companies do business across national borders, it is likely that the number of trade disputes will increase. There are three methods for resolving legal disputes:

- Litigation
- Mediation
- Arbitration

Litigation

Litigation is a legal process used to resolve a dispute through the court system. It is the process of bringing about a lawsuit or defending oneself from a lawsuit. Disputes can arise over the terms of a contract, whether goods meet specifications, payments, injuries from products, failure to properly service an item, and other matters.

A major issue in litigation is deciding which court system is the most appropriate. Should it be processed through the importer's court system or the exporter's system? In the United States, a case can also go to the state trial court, the district court, or to the federal court. Each has specific processes for working through cases as well as methods for appealing decisions. Most other countries have only one court system. Each country (and every state in the United States) has elaborate laws for determining which law should apply and where litigation should occur. The final decision on these matters rests with the court. Occasionally, courts in two countries will attempt to resolve the same dispute. Because these issues can be quite complicated, many businesses include specific clauses in contracts. A *choice-of-law* clause says which country's laws will apply to the suit. A *choice-of-forum* clause states the country in which the trial will take place. Both clauses are included in contracts between companies when they agree to trade with each other.

Litigation is slow, expensive, and complicated. Lawsuits are reserved for significant disputes and issues. Companies avoid litigation if possible.

Mediation

Mediation is a process of intervention between conflicting parties that promotes resolution of their conflict outside the court system. A mediator is a go-between who seeks ways to resolve trade disputes. The mediator is a negotiator and an advisor to the parties involved. For a successful resolution, both disputing parties must view the mediator as impartial.

U.S. FOREIGN SERVICE EMPLOYEE

The U.S. Department of State operates 265 offices throughout the world. Its purpose is to develop and implement U.S. foreign policy and to educate foreign cultures about the United States. The department offers four career categories: Foreign Service specialist, Foreign Service officer, civil services, and student programs.

Career Categories

Foreign Service officers live overseas and work with different cultures to promote U.S. foreign policy, protect American citizens, and help American businesses. They choose one of five career tracks: management affairs, consular affairs, economic affairs, political affairs, or public diplomacy.

Foreign Service specialists are experts in administration, construction engineering, information technology, international information and English language programs, medical and health, office management, and security. For example, a diplomatic security special agent protects the Secretary of State and other dignitaries.

Civil service employees work for the U.S. Department of State but live in the United States. They provide support to the department in jobs, ranging from passport and visa specialist to criminal investigator.

Student programs offer Foreign Service job experience in Washington, D.C., and at U.S. embassies and consulates around the world.

Skills and Training

These positions require the desire to learn about world cultures, adaptability, and world language skills. Foreign Service officers and specialists must be willing to live anywhere in the world and to change jobs every two to four years. The Department of State has a formal application process and provides training.

English Language Arts/Writing

How can Foreign Service officers help American businesses?

@ To learn more about Foreign Service employees and their career paths, go to the International Business Online Learning Center through **glencoe.com**.

Career Data

Education: High school diploma, associate's degree, or bachelor's degree

Skills: Bilingual or multilingual, diplomatic, research, and analytical skills

Outlook: Growth as fast as average in the next ten years

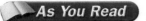
Arbitration

Arbitration is a process to resolve disputes in which each side presents its case to an independent individual, the arbitrator, who makes decisions that are binding. The arbitrator weighs the evidence, and then presents a resolution. All parties must abide by the arbitrator's decision.

Arbitration is less expensive, less complicated, and faster than a lawsuit. Many organizations now include arbitration clauses in business contracts. An organization known as the *International Court of Arbitration of the International Chamber of Commerce* in Paris oversees many hearings. When one side fails to comply with the arbitration award, a World Bank organization known as the *International Center for Settlement of Investment Disputes* may step in. The United Nations offers a similar service, sanctioned by the U.N. Convention on the Recognition and Enforcement of Foreign Arbitral Awards.

Contracts and Avoiding Disputes

Working within various legal systems is challenging. The best company policy is to be as cooperative as possible. Create quality goods and services that meet all legal requirements, and adhere to any intellectual property laws and licensing requirements. To avoid disputes, clearly discuss and write contracts and agreements, and then carefully follow the terms of those agreements. Forms of contracts may vary in different countries. In Japan, oral agreements are honored and considered binding. However, the Japanese have adopted the custom of writing contracts in doing international business. Avoiding litigation, mediation, and arbitration can promote good business relationships and future commercial endeavors.

Quick Check 5.2

After You Read Respond to what you have read by answering these questions.

1. What three types of legal systems are the most common? _____

_____

2. What are some examples of intellectual properties? _____

_____

3. What three methods are available to resolve legal disputes in international trade? _____

_____

Academics / Social Studies

4. Explain why the United States and the United Kingdom both use common law.

_____

_____

Location Study

You are a consultant on the placement of manufacturing plants. A large American company's newly created South American division wants to locate a factory on that continent. The company has hired you to advise it on locating the factory. The factory will produce a new type of hybrid automobile that uses electricity and hydrogen as fuels. The goal is to supply these vehicles to the South American continent for the next 20 years. Make a list of the governmental and legal factors that would affect such an effort. Then choose one South American country and research those factors in relation to that country. Write a short report on your findings.

_____

_____

_____

_____

_____

_____

_____

_____

_____

_____

_____

_____

_____

_____

_____

_____

_____

ACADEMICS APPLIED Check off the academic knowledge you used to do this activity:

☐ English Language Arts ☐ Mathematics ☐ Social Studies ☐ Science

ACADEMIC AND CAREER PLAN Add this page to your Academic and Career Plan Portfolio.

Chapter 6

Economic and Geographic Influences

Chapter Objectives

When you have completed this chapter, you will be able to:

Section 6.1

- Identify different types of economic systems.

- Explain how natural, human, and capital resources affect a nation's ability to trade.

- Explain the stages of economic development and their effects on trade.

- Differentiate between an absolute and a comparative advantage.

Section 6.2

- Identify geographic features and related advantages.

- Discuss the effects of location, time, and proximity.

▶ NIKE

Nike is a publicly owned corporation whose shares are traded on the stock exchanges. When you research this company through Standard & Poor's, you will find investment information such as this:

Index:	S&P Global 1200 or S&P 500
Sector:	Consumer Discretionary
Company:	Nike, Inc.
Symbol:	NKE
Country:	USA
Price:	(varies)

Global Profile Nike designs, produces, develops, and markets quality sports and fitness footwear, apparel, equipment, and accessory products. The Beaverton, Oregon-based corporation is known for its high-tech footwear, cutting-edge design, innovative marketing, and state-of-the-art Niketown and Nike Goddess boutiques. Nike distributes its products globally through 21 distribution centers in Europe, Asia, Australia, Latin America, Africa, and Canada. Customers include professional, collegiate, and recreational athletes around the world.

Business Report As the world's leading designer, marketer, and distributor of authentic athletic apparel and shoes, Nike employs more than 24,300 people. With $13.7 billion in annual revenue, analysts rate Nike as a good investment option.

✎ *English Language Arts/Writing*

Nike has outfitted star athletes and the World Cup soccer teams of Brazil, Australia, South Korea, the Netherlands, and Portugal. By sponsoring athletes from different countries, the company maintains interest among fans and customers in those regions. *Write about why sales of certain Nike products are influenced by the geographic area (such as India in this picture) where customers live.*

@ To do this activity, go to the International Business Online Learning Center through **glencoe.com**.

The Economy and International Trade

WHAT YOU'LL LEARN

- To identify different types of economic systems
- To explain how natural, human, and capital resources affect a nation's ability to trade
- To explain the stages of economic development and their effects on trade
- To differentiate between an absolute and a comparative advantage

WHY IT'S IMPORTANT

You must understand a nation's economic system in order to effectively conduct business there.

KEY TERMS

- economics
- market economy
- supply
- demand
- command economy
- mixed economy
- scarcity

Academic Vocabulary

You will find these words in your reading and on your tests. Make sure you know their meanings.

- resource
- trend
- demonstrate

Reading Guide

Before You Read

What is your definition of a marketplace?

MAIN IDEA
A nation's economic system greatly affects its trade relationships.

GRAPHIC ORGANIZER
Draw this diagram. As you read this section, write in the differences and similarities between the three major types of economic systems.

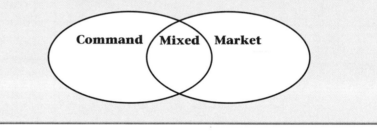

Economic Systems and International Trade

Every country has a political-economic system. There is a strong link between a country's form of government and its type of economic system. Chapter 5 examined political systems. This chapter looks at economic systems and the ways in which political systems influence them. **Economics** is the study of how a society chooses to use **resources** to produce and distribute goods and services for people's consumption. Economic systems influence the use of resources and have a major impact on a country's ability to compete in international trade.

Types of Economic Systems

Each nation has a unique economic system that dictates how goods and services will be produced and distributed. Many economies have common elements. There are three basic types of economic systems:

- Market economies
- Command economies
- Mixed economies

Market Economies

If you live in the United States, you are probably familiar with the idea of capitalism, or a free enterprise system. The more general term for this type of economy is *market economy*. A **market economy** is an economic system in which economic decisions are made in the marketplace. The marketplace is anywhere money changes hands. In a market economy, purchases are driven by two forces—supply and demand.

Supply One force that drives purchases by consumers and businesses is **supply**, which is the amount of goods and services that producers provide at various prices. Think of the differences between apples and oranges. Assuming the cost of growing apples and oranges is the same, if apples sell for 75 cents each, and oranges sell for 50 cents each, which fruit would you grow?

If the price of an orange rose to $1.00, it is likely that more people would plant orange trees, and eventually the supply of oranges would rise. The higher the price producers can charge, the higher the supply (see **Figure 6.1**).

Demand The other force that drives purchases is **demand**, which is the amount or quantity of goods and services that consumers are willing to buy at various prices. Assuming the price of apples dropped from 75 cents each down to 50 cents, people would probably buy and eat more apples. The lower the price that is charged, the more people will buy.

The market price is the meeting place between supply and demand. Sometimes the market price is also known as the *equilibrium price*. Figure 6.1 shows the intersection of the two forces.

Figure 6.1

Market Economy

SUPPLY + DEMAND = MARKET EQUILIBRIUM Supply and demand are tied to the prices people will pay to buy and sell goods. *If prices increased, would you be more willing to buy or sell products? Why or why not?*

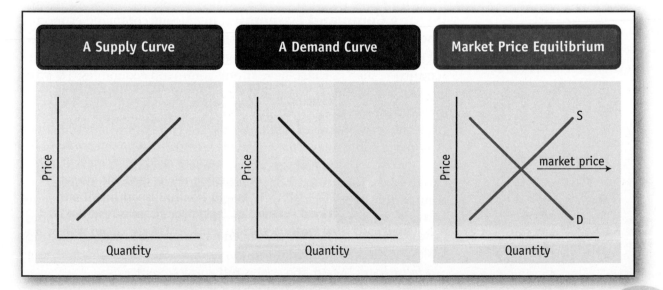

Profit The driving force of the market economy is profit. Profits take many forms, including personal, company, and governmental. As an individual consumer, you buy things because you believe the trade of your money for the item will make your life better. You profit from buying the item.

Companies make profits when the prices that they charge are greater than their costs. An orange grower makes a profit when the total amount of money received for an orange harvest is higher than the costs of purchasing land, planting the trees, watering and feeding the trees, and harvesting and shipping the fruit.

Other Forces In addition to profit, two other forces drive market economies:

1. Private property rights
2. Relatively free and competitive marketplaces

Private property rights allow individuals to buy land, machinery, and other goods. Some of these goods are for personal use, such as houses, while others can be used to start businesses.

In a free and competitive marketplace, nothing interferes with prices or sales activities. Government laws do not restrict a free and competitive marketplace. Large businesses and groups cannot use unfair advantages to increase prices. However, there are no pure market economies.

In any market, there are some goods that require governmental regulation, such as dangerous chemicals. Still, in most market economies, the government tries to play as small a role as possible while promoting fair business practices.

Command Economies

A **command economy**, or planned economy, is an economic system in which a central authority makes all key economic decisions. The government, or a national leader, decides what will be produced, how, and for whom. There are two forms of command economies—strong and moderate.

Strong Command Economies In a strong command economy, there is heavy governmental control. The government owns much of the land, and private property rights are limited. Many communist countries, such as Cuba, have strong command economies. They try to reach a goal of full employment, so that every citizen who can work has a job. Countries that transition from a command economy to a market economy may sell various government-owned companies to private companies. This process is *privatization*.

Moderate Command Economies In moderate command economies, the state owns all of the major resources, but there is some private enterprise. The state may control minerals and ores, airlines, and other assets. France and Sweden have moderate command economies. Moderate command economies are sometimes referred to as *socialist* states. Again, the goal is full employment.

Mixed Economies

A **mixed economy** is an economic system in which the marketplace determines some economic decisions, and the government makes some decisions. The government oversees defense, education, building and repairing roads, fire protection, and other general services. Everything else is bought and sold in the marketplace. Shirts, shoes, coats, most foods, televisions, radios, cars, and other consumer goods are subject to market forces. Some argue that socialism is also a type of mixed economy with similar characteristics.

Most countries have mixed economies. One force, either the marketplace or the government, tends to dominate. If you do business in another country, you need to know which force drives the marketplace.

Economic Resources

The study of economic systems is essential because these systems dictate how a country controls and distributes its economic resources. Economic growth depends on having natural, human, and capital resources available.

Natural Resources

Natural resources are raw materials found in nature. Each country has a unique number of these resources. They are located in two key places, on the ground and in the water (such as a river, lake, sea, or ocean).

Natural resources play a major role in a country's ability to trade internationally. Those nations with rich resources, such as the United States, are able to export raw materials and manufactured goods made from those materials. Oil is a very valuable resource. Oil-rich countries, such as Saudi Arabia or Venezuela, usually have major trade surpluses due to oil exports.

Countries with few natural resources have a disadvantage. They must import key resources from overseas, which makes everyday goods made from them more expensive. Leaders in regions where foods are imported must find ways to export something to achieve an acceptable balance of trade. Only then can a country hope to raise the standard of living for its citizens.

There are two kinds of natural resources:

1. Renewable
2. Nonrenewable

Renewable Resources Renewable resources are raw materials that can be replaced. Agricultural products come from the ground and can be renewed. For example, trees can be cut from a forest and new ones can be planted. Other renewable resources come from rivers, lakes, oceans, and seas. These include fish, seaweed, and, in some cases, water.

Nonrenewable Resources Nonrenewable resources are those that will not grow back. They consist mostly of items taken from the ground. These resources include iron ore, coal, oil, diamonds, gold, and other minerals. Once they have been mined, the resources are gone for eons.

Human Resources

In business, human resources are workers, managers, contractors, and other employees. The term *human resources* is distinct from the term *population*. A population is the number of people in a given region, such as city, state, or country. If a population is too high, it can become a disadvantage. Overpopulated areas can experience shortages of food, high unemployment, and many other problems associated with poverty.

The level of knowledge, ability, and skill that is present in a population has an effect on the available human resources. Employee labor can be:

- Skilled
- Unskilled
- Physical
- Mental

Skilled Labor Skilled labor is a key resource for a country. Regions that are rich in natural resources may not have enough educated people who are trained to take advantage of those resources. Governments that offer good educational opportunities seek to increase the number of skilled workers in their countries. There is a strong connection between a country's literacy level (ability to read and write) and the number of skilled workers in a population.

SKILLED LABOR Plumbers and electricians used to be considered unskilled laborers, but it takes significant technical education and experience to do these jobs. *Why does a country need skilled physical laborers?*

Unskilled Labor Unskilled labor refers to laborers and workers who have less education and fewer skills that require training. Businesses can utilize unskilled laborers. They might be employed at menial jobs and in physically difficult work situations.

Physical Labor Jobs that require physical labor often require unskilled and semi-skilled workers to perform tasks. Workers who perform unskilled labor jobs are paid very little. They may live in poverty in certain countries. Semi-skilled and skilled workers doing physical jobs tend to have better incomes. They may work as truck drivers, production plant employees (semi-skilled), and electricians or plumbers (skilled).

Mental Labor Jobs that require special knowledge, negotiation skills, and creativity utilize mental labor. Mental labor is often also skilled labor, since training and education are needed to do skilled jobs. Workers in these jobs tend to receive higher wages.

Most jobs require both physical and mental abilities. Even a surgeon needs physical stamina to stand by an operating table for long periods of time. In general, a country's economic well-being depends on having workers who are able to perform physical and mental tasks.

Coffee from Fertile Grounds

Batian Peak is a farmer-owned company that markets fine and exotic coffee, tea, and gift baskets. Batian Peak was founded by Peter Kagunye, son of a Kenyan coffee farmer. After relocating to Massachusetts from Kenya, Africa, Peter decided to use his connections with the coffee farms of his homeland to start this business.

One of Batian Peak's signature products is Batian Farms Kenya coffee. This coffee is grown in the rich volcanic soil of the Batian Farms in Kenya. Batian Peak also processes and sells gourmet coffees and teas from around the world. The company has such confidence in its products that it sends free samples to customers, who have responded with approval. In addition to coffee and tea, Batian Peak also sells gift baskets filled with exotic and unique African crafts, and tea and coffee accessories.

Peter is passionate about making a difference in his homeland. He is one of the founders of SAFI, a Kenya-based AIDS and youth leadership grassroots organization. Batian Peak also donates 10 percent of its after-tax profits to support SAFI.

THINK GLOBALLY *How has the geography of Kenya affected the Batian Peak Coffee Company's business?*

To learn more about the country of origin for this global business, go to the International Business Online Learning Center through **glencoe.com**.

Capital Resources

Companies use capital resources to produce goods and services. These resources include buildings, factories, materials, money, vehicles, and equipment.

Capital is the term for the money, or funding, that helps a company buy the items needed to start up and maintain a business. Capital comes from people who invest their money in a company. Businesses also raise capital by selling stock to outside investors and by getting loans from banks, organizations, and governments.

When a country has a high level of national debt and a large trade deficit, it is more difficult to obtain capital. Lack of capital can restrict the development of new businesses and economic growth.

Entrepreneurial Resources A crucial source of capital is entrepreneurial resources, or funds that help start new companies. The United States government runs the Small Business Administration (SBA), which helps new companies get started. The SBA also provides low-cost loans to worthy applicants. A country without entrepreneurial resources is at a disadvantage.

Infrastructure One component of a country's capital resources is its infrastructure. The term *infrastructure* refers to all the large-scale public systems and services necessary for economic activity. With an adequate infrastructure, a nation has access to shipping ports, rail systems, airports and airlines, and other ways of moving goods. It includes a solid transportation system with good roads. Good infrastructure provides for communication, electricity, and other services.

> **As You Read**
>
> **Question** How does capital affect economic progress?

Economic Decisions

Economic systems are affected by the decision-making skills of those in charge, but two factors never change. Every business and economic decision is affected by scarcity and opportunity costs.

> **Reading Check** **Recall** What two factors affect economic decisions made by businesses?

Scarcity

Scarcity is a term used to describe a situation in which there is a limited amount of a commodity. For example, on a spacecraft there is only so much air. Air is the scarce commodity. Scarcity can refer to time, money, natural resources, human resources, capital resources, and anything else you might need that is in short supply. For example, the United States is facing a shortage of nurses. Scarcity drives **trends** in decision making. It is vitally important to make the best use of scarce resources, such as capital.

Opportunity Costs

Opportunity cost is another factor that affects decision making. Opportunity cost is the cost associated with taking one course of action instead of another. For example, a government can invest money in a road system or in building new colleges. The opportunity cost of building roads is: money not spent on education.

Most managers and government officials use a method called "cost-benefit analysis" to determine whether the benefits are higher than the costs.

Economic Conditions

How can a leader **demonstrate** that he or she is making sound economic decisions? Economists and other experts look at several factors to describe the economic well-being of a country:

- Gross domestic product
- Cost of living
- Inflation rate
- Interest rate levels
- Levels of unemployment
- Purchasing power parity
- Balance of trade
- Level of foreign debt

Gross Domestic Product

The total value of goods and services produced in a country each year is known as the country's *gross domestic product (GDP)*. The rate of growth of the GDP is one measure of economic success. Productivity, which is output-per-worker, causes the GDP amount to increase more quickly. In other words, if each worker produces more goods and services in the same amount of time, the GDP will rise. To calculate the GDP, economists add the total value of goods and services sold:

- To consumers
- By businesses
- From the government
- To other countries

Cost of Living

The cost-of-living index is a measure of how much a typical family must spend to live. It includes housing, food, and other essentials. A rise in the cost of living means it costs more to live.

Inflation

Inflation is the increase in currency relative to the availability of goods and services. Inflation causes an increase in the average prices of goods and services. When inflation rises, so does the cost of living, since the same amount of money buys you less than it did before.

The standard of living is closely related to the cost-of-living index. If your standard of living improves, you can afford to buy more and better things. If your standard of living declines, due to inflation, you will have to spend even more money to buy the same things. Also, you might stop buying some products. The Consumer Price Index (CPI) measures a country's inflation rate.

Interest Rates

Another measure of economic well-being is interest rates. An interest rate is the cost of borrowing money, expressed as an annual percentage. Interest rates affect people in different ways. Those borrowing money have a harder time when interest rates rise. If you are going to buy a car or house, and the interest rate rises from 7 percent to 10 percent, then you will pay more in interest charges. Institutions or people who lend money and people who have savings accounts benefit when interest rates go up. Most economists believe that lower rates are better for the majority of people.

Unemployment Levels

The unemployment rate is a measure of the number of people who are looking for jobs but are unable to find them. The key factor in determining the unemployment rate is the difference between the current rate compared to the normal, or baseline rate. When too many citizens are unemployed, the economy is not doing well.

Purchasing Power Parity

Purchasing power parity (PPP) is an estimate of the exchange rate needed to equalize the purchasing power of currencies from different countries. When a dollar is traded for a *peso* or *euro*, how much does it buy? If parity, or equality, exists, then a U.S. dollar's worth of euros buys the same amount of goods in Europe as a dollar buys in the United States. If it is not equal, a dollar's worth of euros buys either less than or more than a dollar's worth of goods. Economic stability exists when PPP is stable and changes very little over time.

Balance of Trade

A balance of trade is based on the number of imports as compared to the number of exports in a country. If a country imports more than it exports, it has a trade deficit. If a country exports more than it imports, it has a trade surplus. A country is better off when the balance of trade is near zero, which means balanced.

How Do You Say?

Q: In Swahili (or Kiswahili), how do you say: "Where are you from?" and "I come from _____."

A: Unatoka wapi? (pronounced: Ŭnătōkă wăpēē)
Mimi ninatoka _____. (pronounced: Mēmē nĭnătōkă)

@ To learn this phrase in other languages, go to the International Business Online Learning Center through **glencoe.com**.

Developing Nations

The World Bank provides approximately $20 billion each year for international development. It uses the resources and knowledge of more developed countries to help less developed ones improve. The United States is the largest contributor to the World Bank, providing money for debt relief, loans, poverty and hunger relief, health and social services, technical assistance, environmental protection, and education. U.S. foreign aid comes from corporate and individual taxpayers, meaning U.S. workers indirectly contribute to international development. This aid can transform a country from underdeveloped to industrialized. In recent years, South Korea, Thailand, Morocco, and the Czech Republic have all graduated from borrower to donor of the World Bank. *Why do you think the United States gives money to developing nations?*

Level of Foreign Debt

When a national government owes money to foreign banks, individuals in other countries, and other national governments, it has foreign debt, or external debt. Countries with continuing trade deficits have high levels of foreign debt.

Economic Cycles

As you study the factors that measure the economic well-being of a country, be aware that these factors are subject to cycles. An economic cycle consists of four parts:

1. Recession/Depression
2. Rising
3. Peak
4. Decline

A recession occurs when the unemployment rate is very high; depression occurs at the most extreme level. Eventually, the economy begins to improve, companies begin hiring again, and economic activity increases. A peak economy means high employment, strong growth in the GDP, and a positive consumer environment. However, this phase eventually ends, and the economy declines, moving into another recession. A typical cycle takes four to seven years to run its full course.

Stages of Economic Development

Because various nations are in different stages of economic development, you cannot weigh economic factors equally for all countries. You must take into consideration a country's stage of economic development. There are four stages of economic development:

- Underdeveloped
- Developing
- Industrialized
- Post-industrial

Underdeveloped Economies

An underdeveloped economy has high levels of unemployment. A nation with an underdeveloped economy has very few natural and human resources, or it has not developed them due to a lack of capital. The poverty level is high. An underdeveloped country depends on other nations to help take care of its citizens. International trade is nearly impossible in an underdeveloped country. The country usually does not have anything to sell and export.

Developing Economies

Characteristics unique to developing economies include a disproportionately small middle class, technological dualism (some people use primitive technologies and others use current technology), regional dualism (some regions have strong economies and others do not), low savings rates, and poor banking facilities. Nations with developing economies require assistance to move forward economically. It is in the world's best interests to help these nations become more self-sufficient. This makes them better trading partners in the future.

Industrialized Economies

Nations with industrialized economies have an industrial base that enables them to establish trade relationships with foreign companies and governments. Physical goods are the most common products of an industrialized nation. These nations have manageable unemployment levels, and they are more self-sufficient than developing nations.

Post-Industrial Economies

In a nation with a post-industrial economy, the value of total sales of services is greater than the value of the physical goods that the nation produces. The United States is a post-industrial nation. However, there are not many other post-industrial economies. When seeking international trade partners, company leaders should examine a country's stage of development and its economic well being.

Absolute or Comparative Advantage

A country has an *absolute advantage* when it can produce a good or a service more efficiently than any other country in the world. Canada has an absolute advantage regarding wood, forest products, and paper pulp. An absolute advantage is a key trading resource for a nation and its leaders.

A country that does not have an absolute advantage should look for *comparative advantage,* which is an advantage gained by a product it makes most efficiently on a personal best level. Doing so will make the best use of the country's resources, even though the country has no absolute advantage. For example, South Korea may not have an absolute advantage in building cars, but South Korean companies may have a comparative advantage in producing these items.

When trading with companies in another country, it is important to know if they have an absolute or comparative advantage in a particular industry to make decisions about importing goods and services.

Quick Check 6.1

After You Read Respond to what you have read by answering these questions.

1. What are the three kinds of economic systems found in various countries? _____

_____

2. What are the three economic resources present in a country? _____

_____

3. What statistics are used to analyze the economic conditions present in a country? _____

_____

Academics / Mathematics

4. Calculate the percentage increase if the interest rate rises from 5 percent to 9 percent.

_____

_____

Geography and International Trade

WHAT YOU'LL LEARN

- To identify geographic features and related advantages
- To discuss the effects of location, time, and proximity

WHY IT'S IMPORTANT

A country's geographic layout determines how well its companies are able to trade. Success in international business means taking advantage of positive geographic features.

KEY TERMS

- topography
- cartography
- population density
- proximity

Academic Vocabulary

You will find these words in your reading and on your tests. Make sure you know their meanings.

- area
- overseas
- parameter

Reading Guide

Before You Read

What are some of the major geographical features of your state?

MAIN IDEA

Geographical features can be an advantage or a disadvantage in international trade.

GRAPHIC ORGANIZER

Draw this diagram. As you read this section, write in the possible benefits of these geographical features for a country.

Plains	Population Density	Bodies of Water	Mild Climate

Geographic Influences on International Trade

Doing business internationally requires an understanding of "the lay of the land," or the geography of an **area**. There are three aspects to study when considering how geography of a country plays a role in international trade:

1. Geographic features
2. Geographic advantages
3. Geography and trade alliances between countries

Geographic Features

Since every country is unique, it is helpful to look at common geographic features that might influence the ability of a country to engage in international trade. There are four basic geographical features:

1. Topography
2. Deserts and tropical forests
3. Bodies of water
4. Climate

Topography

Topography refers to the physical surface features of a geographic area. Topographic features include: mountains, plains, and the region's relationship to sea level. Mountains and mountain ranges can make trade more difficult. Roads are harder to build over mountains. Mountain ranges separate people. This leads to differences in language dialects, governments, and other areas, even in the same country.

Plains tend to be closer to sea level. As the land elevation rises, machines may operate differently due to altitude differences. It takes more horsepower to drive a truck at higher elevations. Many plains areas support agriculture, which helps a nation feed itself. Topography greatly influences a country's ability to be self-sufficient and its overall economic well-being.

Cartography is the science or art of mapmaking. Cartographers can use map-making software to produce topographical maps which use contour lines to show elevation. Maps are good resources for information about a country's topography.

Deserts and Tropical Forests

Higher transportation costs exist in deserts and tropical forests. Fewer people live in these areas as well. It is difficult to live in deserts and tropical forests, which means that people are likely to move to other, more hospitable areas. Large portions of Brazil are covered with tropical forests where the population is small due to thick vegetation and a hot, humid climate. The Sahara Desert in Africa also has a harsh climate. Two million people live in the Sahara, but most of them are located in oases where crops are grown with irrigation.

Population density is a measurement of the number of people living in a geographic area. Low population density, often found in deserts and tropical forests, means few people live in the area. High population density, found in cities and other places, means a large number of people live in the area. High population density creates opportunities for economic activities, including businesses such as restaurants and stores. Areas of high population density also can be susceptible to problems, such as poor sanitary conditions, crime, and other situations associated with overcrowding.

TOPOGRAPHICAL DISADVANTAGE Mountain ranges separate people and make trade difficult. *Would this body of water be more valuable if it were next to a plain instead of a mountain range? Why or why not?*

Culture Corner

The Extreme Geography of Tanzania

Think About It What are some kinds of geographic areas that have commercial value? Explain your answer.

Located on the east coast of Africa, the United Republic of Tanzania is a country of geographic extremes. It includes the highest peak, Mount Kilimanjaro, as well as the lowest point on the continent of Africa. Tanzania also has some of the most unspoiled beaches in the world. Its largest city and seaport is Dar es Salaam, located on the coast of the Indian Ocean. Most workers are employed in agriculture.

Tanzania's wildlife and natural beauty are a magnet to visitors worldwide. Year-round ecotourism offers a wide range of discovery trips. Ecotourism is an industry promoting travel that aims to preserve the natural world and sustain the human cultures that inhabit it.

One of the country's most captivating destinations is northern Tanzania's Serengeti, a vast region of grasslands and woodlands. The Serengeti is famous for the annual wildlife migration, protected by the Serengeti National Park. Seasonally, more than a million wildebeests and zebras crisscross the rolling plains to search for food and water. It "takes my breath away," says one onlooker.

Meeting and Greeting Swahili is the primary language; English is the language of commerce. When meeting, Tanzanians shake hands.

Business Etiquette Meetings may start a half an hour late. Begin conversations with small talk when socializing before doing business.

Business Dress Men and women wear modest or conservative attire. Men wear suits for formal business meetings. Lightweight clothing is the norm.

English Language Arts/Writing

Why might preserving the world's natural areas help promote international business?

As You Read

Question How does a country's access to water affect its economy?

Bodies of Water

There are many types of bodies of water, including rivers, lakes, oceans, peninsulas, harbors, and inner-coastal waterways. Bodies of water are a crucial resource for a country's economic standing. Rivers and lakes provide water for irrigation and support the movement of goods through the interior of a country. Shipping supports a wide number of industries and products. Without access to ports and sea routes, businesses must find other, more expensive ways to move products.

Climate

Climate is an area's prevailing set of weather conditions, such as temperature and humidity. A mild climate can promote industries, such as travel and tourism, which are major sources of revenue for a number of countries and regions.

Agricultural industries tend to do well in moderate temperatures. Extreme heat and cold may limit a nation's ability to trade by inhibiting crop growth and activities such as transportation.

Geographic Advantages and Factors

Geography affects one key factor in business—location. For example, a small business is best located on a busy street corner with easy access. Some cities or countries have a natural geographic advantage simply because they are in the right place. Geographic features affect both economic development and international trade.

Location and Trade Routes

Being located near bodies of water is one of the most important geographic advantages for international trade. The country of Panama is located between the Gulf of Mexico and the Pacific Ocean. The Panama Canal, opened in 1914, facilitates trade for the United States and other countries that previously had to ship goods around the southern tip of South America.

Many major cities around the world are built in places with natural geographic advantages. All across the United States, major cities developed near harbors and seaports. In cities such as New York, Boston, Miami, Charleston, New Orleans, and San Diego, seaports offer easier access for loading and unloading shipments.

This same pattern holds true worldwide. Montreal, Canada, is positioned along the St. Lawrence River, which is a pathway to the Atlantic Ocean. **Figure 6.2** lists some major cities in the world and the nearby bodies of water that facilitate commerce in their regions.

Other large cities are located along major trade routes, via water or land. St. Louis, Missouri, is located on the Mississippi River. Denver, Colorado, is located in the foothills of the Rocky Mountains along a key trade route over land.

These major cities are also important transportation centers. Airports, rail stations, highways, and shipping docks transform cities into international marketplaces. Good transportation systems make it easier to import and export goods **overseas**.

Reading Check **Analyze** Why do major cities need good transportation systems?

Figure 6.2

Bodies of Water

SELECTED MAJOR CITIES Many major cities have bodies of water nearby. *What is the advantage to having a lake or a river near a city?*

City and Country	Body of Water
Santo Domingo, Dominican Republic	Caribbean Sea
San Francisco, United States	Pacific Ocean/San Francisco Bay
Rio de Janeiro, Brazil	Atlantic Ocean
Buenos Aires, Argentina	Rio de la Plata (river)
London, England	River Thames
Paris, France	Seine River
Amsterdam, Netherlands	Waddenzee (bay)
Tokyo, Japan	Gulf of Tokyo

Time Zones

Location is a geographic factor that determines time zones, which affect international business. Have you ever noticed the complications created by time zones, just in the United States? Think about placing a telephone call at 10:00 A.M. in New York City. If you are trying to reach someone in Los Angeles, the phone is ringing at 7:00 A.M. in California. In addition, if you place the call to Honolulu, it would be 5:00 A.M. there.

The major television and news networks all must adjust to time zone differences. "Prime time" on the East Coast of the United States is 8:00 P.M. until 11:00 P.M., but it runs from 7:00 P.M. to 10:00 P.M. in the Midwest. News cycles all depend on airtimes of 5:30 (or 6:30) P.M. and 10:00 (or 11:00) P.M.

In the world of business, many companies begin operations at either 8:00 A.M. or 9:00 A.M. They stop at either 5:00 P.M. or 6:00 P.M. When time zones come into play, these times all require adjustments and calculations.

The farther away from a country you are, the greater the time zone disparity. Halfway around the world, it is daytime when it is night in the United States. Also, the actual date changes when you cross the International Date Line. This can lead to a confusing situation, such as departing on a flight from Taipei, Taiwan, at 11:00 P.M., flying for many hours to San Francisco, and arriving at midnight on the same day! When conducting international business, you should be aware of the time zones involved.

Scheduling In addition to considering the time zones involved, you should conduct business within the **parameters** of normal business hours. You do not want to call a foreign company in the middle of the night when it is closed, or at other inconvenient times. It is essential to account for time differences when scheduling conference calls and meetings.

Seasons around the World

Daylight is affected by a country's north/south location, that is, how close the country is to the North or South Pole versus the equator. In northern Finland during the summertime, there is sunlight for as many as 23 hours per day. In the winter it stays dark there for most of the day. The farther you are from the equator, the greater the difference will be in daily sunlight or darkness during certain seasons. If you are closer to the equator, the hours of daylight will be more equal to the hours of the night.

Seasons The seasons in the Southern Hemisphere are reversed from those of the Northern Hemisphere. For example, if you are planning a business trip to southern Australia in January, leaving from Minneapolis, you will need to take along completely different clothing for the visit. It will be the coldest time of winter in Minneapolis, Minnesota, but it will be summertime in Brisbane, Australia.

Ⓥ TIME AND TRADE Time difference can complicate domestic and international trade. *If it is 5 P.M. Pacific Standard Time, should you place a sales call from Portland, Oregon, to a customer in London, England? Why or why not?*

NEW YORK
LONDON
PARIS

ECONOMIST

Economists study how society chooses to use resources to produce and distribute goods and services. They conduct research and collect and analyze data in order to predict economic trends. Many economists specialize in a specific area of economics. For example, international economists study international financial markets, exchange rates, and the effect of trade policies.

Multinational corporations employ economists who study consumer demand and competition. They also monitor economic situations and analyze risk in the countries where their corporations operate. Economists employed by the U.S. Federal Government analyze economic conditions overseas and predict how changes in U.S. foreign policy might affect other countries. International organizations such as the World Bank, International Monetary Fund, and United Nations all employ economists. International travel is often required.

Economists also work in economic consulting or research firms. In addition, colleges and universities employ economics professors and instructors. The demand for high school economics teachers is expected to grow.

Skills and Training

All economists should have excellent mathematical, research, and analytical skills. Communication skills are important for writing reports and orally presenting research results. Success in the field of economics requires attention to detail, precision, patience, persistence, and the ability to work independently. Candidates should have a bachelor's degree, although those with a master's or Ph.D. in economics will have more opportunities.

English Language Arts/Writing

List the economic factors economists study in order to determine the economic well-being of a country.

@ To learn more about economists and their career paths, go to the International Business Online Learning Center through **glencoe.com.**

Career Data

Education: Bachelor's degree, master's degree, or Ph.D.

Skills: Mathematical, research, analytical, quantitative, and communication skills

Outlook: Growth slower than average in the next ten years

Geography and Trade Alliances

Chapter 4 explained several free trade agreements. Many of these agreements are based on geographic location. For example, NAFTA applies to countries in North America. The EU is a collection of closely-located countries in Europe. In addition, ASEAN is an association of ten allied member countries located in Southeast Asia.

Proximity is the physical nearness of one thing to another. In the world of business, proximity often leads to closer trade relationships and trading partners. Some of the more common trade regions in the world are: North America; Latin America; South America; the Pacific Rim; the Middle East; the European Union region; Eastern Europe and countries from the former U.S.S.R.; Africa; Australia; and New Zealand.

It makes sense for a country to trade with partners that are located near its borders. Sometimes partners also share a language. Thus, shipping expenses are lower, and communication is easier. Several of these economic alliances have counterparts in military partnerships, such as the alliance between NATO and the EU.

Economic and Geographic Influences

As you study international business, consider both economic circumstances and geographic characteristics. A nation's economic status largely determines its ability to trade. Geographic features also play a part in creating economic advantages and disadvantages for various countries. Geography also affects trade through location, time zones, and proximity. Close trading partners are often physically close together on a world map.

Quick Check 6.2

After You Read Respond to what you have read by answering these questions.

1. What four major geographic features have an impact on international trade? _____

_____

2. How does geographic location affect international trade? _____

_____

3. How does time affect doing business with companies in other countries? _____

_____

Academics / Social Studies

4. List six types of bodies of water and give an example of each one.

_____

_____

Portfolio Worksheet

Personal Evaluation

Choose any type of career you would like. Then imagine you are updating your résumé in order to seek a better, higher-paying position in that field. To help you find a job, you contact an employment agency. The agency asks you to prepare a list of your comparative and absolute advantages over other competitors for the type of position you are seeking. Create your list, applying the definitions of comparative advantage and absolute advantage you learned in this chapter.

_____

_____

_____

_____

_____

_____

_____

_____

_____

_____

_____

_____

_____

_____

_____

_____

_____

_____

_____

ACADEMICS APPLIED Check off the academic knowledge you used to do this activity:

☐ English Language Arts ☐ Mathematics ☐ Social Studies ☐ Science

ACADEMIC AND CAREER PLAN Add this page to your Academic and Career Plan Portfolio.

CHAPTER SUMMARY

Section 6.1 **The Economy and International Trade**

economics (p. 130)

market economy
(p. 131)

supply (p. 131)

demand (p. 131)

command economy
(p. 132)

mixed economy
(p. 133)

scarcity (p. 136)

- The most common types of economic systems are market economies, command economies, and mixed economies.

- The degree of development of the natural, human, and capital resources of a country determine its ability to trade.

- Four stages that define the level of economic development are underdeveloped, developing, industrialized, and post-industrial. Countries in the latter two stages of economic development are capable of doing the most international trading.

- An absolute advantage for a country means that it produces a good or a service more efficiently than any other country in the world. A comparative advantage for a country means that it specializes in producing goods and services that it can create most efficiently.

Section 6.2 **Geography and International Trade**

topography (p. 141)

cartography (p. 141)

population density
(p. 141)

proximity (p. 146)

- Four basic geographic features are topography, deserts and rain forests, bodies of water, and climate. Success in international business involves taking advantage of positive geographic features, such as having a trade center near a body of water and a flat plain.

- Geography affects trade through location, time zones, and proximity. Close trading partners often are physically close together on a world map.

CONCEPTS REVIEW

1. **List** the most common types of economic systems.

2. **Identify** the most important resources for a country to develop for trade.

3. **Explain** each of the four commonly used categories of economic development.

4. **Distinguish** between absolute advantage and comparative advantage.

5. **Describe** the various geographic features that are advantageous for a country.

6. **Discuss** how proximity affects trade.

KEY TERMS REVIEW

7. Match each term to its definition.

_____ economics

_____ market economy

_____ supply

_____ demand

_____ command economy

_____ mixed economy

_____ scarcity

_____ topography

_____ cartography

_____ population density

_____ proximity

a. an economic system in which economic decisions are made in the marketplace

b. or planned economy, an economic system in which a central authority makes all key economic decisions

c. the amount or quantity of goods and services that consumers are willing to buy at various prices

d. the physical surface features of a geographic area

e. a measurement of the number of people living in a geographic area

f. the study of how a society chooses to use resources to produce and distribute goods and services for people's consumption

g. a situation in which there is a limited amount of a commodity

h. the science or art of mapmaking

i. the physical nearness of one thing to another

j. the amount of goods and services that producers provide at various prices

k. an economic system in which the marketplace determines some economic decisions, and the government makes some decisions

Academic Vocabulary

8. On a separate sheet of paper, write a sentence or two related to economic and geographic influences using at least three of the academic terms you learned in the section openers:

- resource
- trend
- demonstrate
- area
- overseas
- parameter

Critical Thinking

9. Research examples of communism. List the pros and cons of a communist command economy. Would you prefer this economy?

Discussion Starter

10. The U.S. budget deficit is covered mostly by the government borrowing money from investors in its bonds and other securities. Is this method of funding a government advisable? Explain your answer in a class discussion.

Point of View

11. You live in a developing country with large reserves of natural resources. How might you view an elite class that takes bribes from foreign companies that use up these resources?

BUILDING REAL-WORLD SKILLS

12. Seasonal Adjustments When dealing in the global marketplace, a business must plan to supply goods for various seasons at the same time. When it is summer in the northern hemisphere, it is winter in the southern hemisphere. This places demands on planning and production cycles.

Research and Share

a. Pick an industry and research how businesses in the industry cope with such seasonal requirements.

b. Prepare a short report on what you have learned and read it to the class.

13. Regional Diversity Different regions of the United States feature different keystone industries. From the heavy industrial base of the Northeast to the farms of the Midwest, the United States' economy rests on many different and diverse regional business concentrations.

Research and Write

a. Research the various economic regions of the United States.

b. Prepare a short report on one of these regions emphasizing the dominant business types in it.

BUILDING ACADEMIC SKILLS

 English Language Arts

14. The topography of many countries contains some unique features. Choose a country from a continent other than North America and research its topography. Write a short paragraph describing one of that country's outstanding topographical features.

MATH Mathematics

15. In 2002, the United States imposed tariffs on imported goods from the Ukraine. The United States believed the Ukraine failed to comply with the international treaty protecting copyrighted materials. Because of this tariff, the cost to the American consumer for a pair of shoes from the Ukraine went from y to $2y$. What percentage of the original cost (y) was imposed as a tariff?

Algebraic Expressions To solve this problem, you need to use symbolic algebra to represent and explain mathematical relationships.

 Social Studies/Law

16. U.S. laws prohibit monopolies. The laws are called "antitrust laws." For example, if a business controls more than 90 percent of a type of commerce, the government can break up the company. Do you think such laws are typical of a market economy or of a command economy? Explain your answer.

SCI Science/Chemistry

17. Water is vital to international trade. Water also covers 70 percent of Earth's surface. The chemical symbol for water is H_2O, representing the compound of hydrogen and oxygen. Water is one of three compounds that occur in solid, liquid, and gaseous forms in Earth's environment. Water is ice in solid form, and actually floats on liquid water. This is due to its molecular structure. Do you think the molecular structure of ice is more or less dense than liquid water? Why?

COMPETITIVE EVENT PREP

Competition or Demolition?

18. Situation Walmart wants to open a new store on your Main Street. There is considerable controversy from the small merchants who fear they may be run out of business, as well as from citizens who worry about the traffic and aesthetic concerns. Research and identify the historical evolution of this mass merchandiser.

Activity Research the current statistics on Walmart including the implications of their global presence. Identify and outline the pros and cons of locating a Walmart in your town. Consider how many new jobs will be created and the impact and quality of the jobs. Also discuss the disadvantages of the new store.

Evaluation You will be evaluated on how well your report meets the following objectives:

a. Detail the relevant statistics.

b. Report on the issues that pertain to your town.

c. Define which issues will most impact the situation and why.

d. Develop a plan that you can present to all the stakeholders as an acceptable compromise.

Internet Travels

Australia

Using the Internet, look up the continent of Australia on a world map. Study the types of geographic features mentioned in the text. Then answer the following questions about Australia on a separate sheet of paper.

➤ Where are the main cities located?

➤ What geographic feature dictates the location of these cities? Why?

@ For resources to help you do this exercise, go to the International Business Online Learning Center through **glencoe.com**.

BusinessWeek online

19. Newsclip: Rise of a Powerhouse The countries of Central Europe have shrugged off communism and transitioned from command to market economies. The region is attracting foreign investors and driving an economic boom.

@ Go to the International Business Online Learning Center through **glencoe.com** to read an article about this topic. Then write a paragraph that identifies why Western companies are investing in Central European companies.

Standardized Test Practice

20. Choose the best answer to the following multiple-choice question.

If the gross domestic product in trillions of dollars was 12.5 for Asia, 2.1 for Africa, 17.0 for North America, and 0.7 for Australia/Oceania, what was the GDP of Australia/Oceania?

○ $17,000,000,000,000

○ $700,000,000,000

○ $17,000,000,000

○ $700,000,000

Test-Taking Tip Notice that these statistics represent trillions of dollars. Therefore, you must multiply these numbers by one trillion dollars ($1,000,000,000,000) to get the final answer.

Chapter 7

Currency and Risk Management

Chapter Objectives

When you have completed this chapter, you will be able to:

Section 7.1

- Identify the uses of money, currencies, and currency exchange rates.
- Explain how a fluctuating currency exchange rate affects international trade.
- Describe methods that nations use to manage currency exchange issues.

Section 7.2

- Identify the types of commercial risk in international trade.
- Identify the types of payment programs used when trading across international borders.
- Discuss ways to reduce risk when building international business relationships.

▶ **LLOYD'S OF LONDON**

Lloyds TSB Group, or Lloyd's of London, is a publicly owned corporation whose shares are traded on the stock exchanges. When you research this company through Standard & Poor's, you will find information such as this:

Index:	S&P Global 1200 and S&P 500
Sector:	Financials
Company:	Lloyds TSB Group
Symbol:	LLOY and LYG (NYSE)
Country:	Great Britain
Price:	(varies)

Global Profile Lloyds provides banking and financial services internationally. It operates three segments: U.K. Retail Banking and Mortgages, Wholesale and International Banking, and Insurance and Investments. Its insurance division specializes in 62 risks, including marine, aviation, catastrophe, and motor. Offices are located in more than 25 countries, including Argentina, Australia, Hong Kong, the United States, and South Africa.

Business Report Lloyds generates an annual revenue of about 15.7 billion pounds sterling ($27.5 billion), employing 82,953 people. Lloyds cut costs, eliminating 2,700 jobs to save $480 million a year. Analysts generally rate Lloyds as a strong investment option.

English Language Arts/Writing

The company formed in 1688 outside Edward Lloyd's London coffeehouse. Merchants, traders, and ship owners gathered there to buy insurance. Today Lloyds is the world's leader in specialist insurance. When the World Cup of soccer takes place, Lloyd's of London insures broadcasters against cancellation. Lloyds also focuses on less-established sports, such as downhill mountain biking, with insurance called "SportsGuard." *Write about an emerging sport and a new insurance to cover it.*

To do this activity, go to the International Business Online Learning Center through **glencoe.com**.

Currency and Currency Exchange

WHAT YOU'LL LEARN

- To identify the uses of money, currencies, and currency exchange rates
- To explain how a fluctuating currency exchange rate affects international trade
- To describe methods that nations use to manage currency exchange issues

WHY IT'S IMPORTANT

Buying from and selling to international partners requires knowing how to manage money. This includes understanding the impact of exchange rates on trading relationships.

KEY TERMS

- money
- currency
- currency exchange rate
- hard currency
- soft currency
- currency value fluctuation
- capital

Academic Vocabulary

You will find these words in your reading and on your tests. Make sure you know their meanings.

- ratio
- compensate
- technology

Reading Guide

Before You Read

What might happen to the value of the dollar if the value of the *euro* drops?

MAIN IDEA

Businesses that sell products to businesses in other countries must consider the value of money in other countries.

GRAPHIC ORGANIZER

Draw this chart. As you read, write in the four types of statistics that reflect economic conditions and include a brief description of each one.

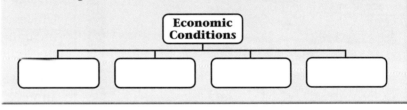

Currency Management

This chapter examines two related topics—money and risk. Investors know that greater risk is associated with greater return. If you take greater financial risks, you might earn more money. The down side is that greater risk increases the chance you will lose money. The first section of this chapter examines how money and the currency exchange system affect international transactions.

Money and Currencies

A market is any place where money is exchanged for things of value. Markets can be as uncomplicated as a farmer's fruit-and-vegetable stand or as complex as an international financial institution. To understand the roles of money and currency in international business, it is important to know what the two terms mean.

Money is anything that people accept as a form of payment. Money has taken many forms, including salt, stones, seashells, and beads. To be money, an item must have five characteristics: acceptability, scarcity, durability, divisibility, and portability.

Acceptability

To be used as money, an item must be accepted as such by a group of people. In our culture, a merchant will accept a paper five-dollar bill in exchange for a can of soda, and give you some money back as change. That same merchant would not accept a piece of plain paper with your signature on it.

Scarcity

Scarcity means there is a short supply of a product, causing the product to become more valuable. In the early years of the United States, coffee and tea were so scarce that they could be measured and used as a form of currency to make exchanges.

Durability

Durability means an item will not easily spoil or become damaged. It is not surprising that most money today is made out of strong paper or metal. These materials are durable.

Divisibility

Divisibility means that you can divide something into smaller units. A diamond or a stone would not be a suitable form of currency because it cannot be divided to make change.

Portability

Portability is a characteristic of being small enough that people can carry the item around easily. Euro bills easily fit into a pocket or wallet, as do various kinds of coins.

Uses of Money

Money serves three main purposes in the world of business. It can be 1) a measure of value, 2) a medium of exchange, and 3) a savings mechanism.

Measure of Value

As a measure of value, money tells you what something is worth. Would you pay $10 for a 2-liter bottle of Pepsi? Probably not. But if you were dying of dehydration in the desert, would you pay $10 for a 16-ounce bottle of water? Everyone assigns a relative value to goods and services.

Medium of Exchange

As a medium of exchange, money works only if people are willing to trade goods or services for it. Euro and *yen* currencies are not acceptable forms of exchange in the United States.

Savings Mechanism

A crucial use of money is storing it as savings. Some people save gold, because they believe it will hold value in the future. Confidence in a form of money is an important part of financial stability.

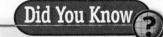

Did You Know ?

> **Selling for Seashells**
>
> In Asia and Africa, cowrie shells were used as money for centuries. These tiny seashells from the Indian Ocean became symbols of currency, even appearing as pictographs in Chinese script. Today the currency of Ghana in Africa is called *"cedi,"* a form of the Ghanaian word meaning "cowrie shell." As late as the 1990s, cowrie shells appeared as currency in remote parts Africa.

Barter

Barter is an exchange of goods or services without the use of money. A trade of a haircut for a baseball cap is barter. While barter expresses value and is a medium of exchange, it is difficult to save for the future. So barter has some characteristics of money, but not all of them. Barter can frustrate governments because it is difficult to tax, even though it may be a common form of economic activity. Most bartering takes place within a country rather than between countries.

Currency

The form of money used by a specific country or region is called **currency**. **Figure 7.1** lists some of the world's major currencies. Currencies can change and evolve over time. When East and West Germany reunited as one nation in 1990, the *Deutsche mark* took the place of the former East German currency. Currently, Germany uses the euro. In the past, the U.S. government introduced a one-dollar coin and a two-dollar bill, but they were discontinued. Today the symbol "$" represents the U.S. dollar, but it is also the symbol for the Mexican *peso*. In addition, it is the symbol used for currency in Canada, Hong Kong, Australia, and New Zealand. When conducting international business, do not assume that the symbol "$" means only the U.S. dollar. It is important to know the currency used in the country where you intend to trade.

 **Reading Check** **Recall** What is currency?

Currency Exchange

The **currency exchange rate** is the rate at which one country's currency can be traded for another country's currency. If the exchange rate is US$1.00 to € .82, then it takes one U.S. dollar to buy .82 euro. (€ is the symbol for the euro.) The **ratio** is 1 to .82.

➤ **A FAIR TRADE** Money serves as a medium of exchange. *What are other functions of money?*

Figure 7.1

Major World Currencies

THE LANGUAGE OF MONEY These are the names of currencies used in other countries. *Find a currency conversion Web site on the Internet. Choose one of these currencies and find out what it is worth in U.S. dollars.*

Brazil *real*	**Great Britain** *pound*	**China** *yuan*	**European Union** *euro*	**India** *rupee*
Israel *new Israeli shekel*	**Japan** *yen*	**Saudi Arabia** *riyal*	**South Africa** *rand*	**United States** *U.S. dollar*

Hard Currency

Currency rates fluctuate based on a number of factors described later in this section. An international businessperson most often uses hard currencies in business transactions. A **hard currency** is a currency that can be exchanged for other currencies at uniform rates in financial centers around the world. Both the U.S. dollar and the euro are hard currencies. Dollars can be traded at uniform rates for euros, *riyals, yen,* and other foreign hard currencies, whether the trade is made in New York, Paris, London, or Tokyo. Another name for a hard currency is *convertible currency*.

Soft Currency

What is a soft, or nonconvertible currency? A **soft currency** is an unstable currency that is not exchanged at major financial centers. A soft currency may be used to buy and sell goods within a country, but it has limited or no use in other countries. Soft currencies are found in underdeveloped and developing nations.

Exchange Rates and International Business

Why are currency exchange rates such a vital issue for international businesspeople? To answer this question, think about the uses of money. Money establishes the relative value of goods and services. When the value of one currency changes, its price in international markets fluctuates.

SUNNY EXCHANGE Prices may change when international currencies fluctuate. If these sunglasses were made in Mexico, what would happen to their price if the value of the peso rose in relation to the dollar?

Royalty-free/CORBIS

When Currency Changes Value

Consider, for example, a U.S.-based company that makes and sells sandals. A retail company in Spain sells the sandals for nine euros (€9), which is roughly equivalent to ten U.S. dollars ($10). If the exchange rate suddenly changes, with the euro losing value compared to the U.S. dollar, then those nine euros may suddenly be worth only nine dollars. The new price means the retailer loses one dollar per pair of sandals. As a result, the Spanish company can do one of two things. It can raise the price of sandals to **compensate** for the loss, which means fewer people are likely to buy them. Or the company can keep the retail price the same but make less profit, or possibly lose money, on each sale.

Imagine the U.S. company's situation: It has a contract stating the wholesale price of the sandals is six euros each. So the Spanish retailer has the opportunity to mark up the price by three euros, to the nine-euro retail price. When the U.S. company receives Spain's payment, those six euros, instead of being worth about seven U.S. dollars, will be worth only about six dollars. When the value of the euro dropped, it meant someone could lose profits, either the vendor from the United States or the retailer in Spain. This illustrates how exchange rates have a significant impact on international trade.

Factors Affecting Exchange Rates

Currencies and their exchange rates play a key role in international business. **Currency value fluctuation** is the change in value of one country's currency when it is traded for another country's currency. When currency values fluctuate, the value of one currency, such as the British *pound,* changes when it is traded for another currency, such as the Mexican peso. Several factors affect exchange rates and cause currency fluctuations:

- Balance of payments
- Economic conditions
- Political conditions

Balance of Payments

A country's balance of payments is the difference between the amount of money the government pays to other countries and the amount it receives from them. If the amount of money coming in is greater, the country has a favorable balance of payments. If the amount of money going out is greater, the country has an unfavorable balance of payments.

What does "unfavorable" mean? The country with an unfavorable balance of payments is importing more products than it is exporting. In other words, it is buying more than it is selling. This has a negative impact on the country's employment, interest rates, and other key economic conditions. Also, the country's money develops a lower value because it has moved into another country as payment for imports. Less currency is available in the home country to pay for goods and services to local merchants.

An unfavorable balance of payments can also occur when residents leave the country with money and spend it in other countries. When the U.S. dollar is strong, it can "buy" more of a foreign currency. U.S. citizens may feel encouraged to travel to other countries and purchase items in other countries. This can potentially drain the United States of money. Some nations restrict the amount of money that people and businesses can spend when traveling in other countries.

Culture Corner

Luxembourg's Central Role

Think About It What is the advantage of sharing the same currency with other countries?

What if all of Europe shared a common currency? Luxembourg was one of the original six founding members of the European Union. Its prime minister originally introduced this idea in the late 1960s. At that time, a common currency was an improbable dream. However, New Year's Day 2002 saw the dream realized. In the world's largest monetary exchange ever, billions in *euros* were circulated throughout the continent, replacing the currency of individual countries. All but the United Kingdom, Sweden, and Denmark have traded in their own money for colorful paper money—one color for each value—and shiny metal coins.

The euro's design reflects Europe's unity. Windows symbolize openness and cooperation, 12 stars represent energy and harmony, and bridges stand for communication. Unlike the paper money, one side of each coin displays different national symbols for each member country. Coins representing Luxembourg depict its head of state, Grand Duke Henri of Luxembourg.

Meeting and Greeting Shake hands with everyone present and again when you leave. Luxembourgers are friendly but reserved.

Business Etiquette Meetings start on time; call with an explanation if you will arrive late. Meetings are usually brief. People begin doing business immediately.

Business Dress Men wear suits and ties, or a sports coat and dress pants. Women wear dresses or suits.

English Language Arts/Writing

If you were designing a new currency for the United States or another country, what symbols reflecting national pride would you include and why?

Economic Conditions

Economic conditions can have an impact on what people trade and how much they are willing to pay. Economic conditions are reflected in four statistics:

- Interest rates
- Inflation rates
- Economic growth and decline (GDP levels)
- Unemployment rates

Relate Do you and your friends lend to and borrow from each other? Do you charge interest for borrowing?

Interest Rates In general, higher interest rates slow down purchases and investments. This is because people who borrow money to buy items pay more money as interest when interest rates are high. As a result, they cannot afford to spend as much on the items. Higher interest rates make it harder for individuals to buy cars or houses, which are usually paid by installments. The higher interest payments also make it more difficult for an expanding business to buy new machinery or office equipment.

Inflation Rates Inflation is a rise in price of goods and services. It directly affects the value of a currency. If the annual inflation rate in a country is 5 percent, then one dollar today will be worth ninety-five cents next year. Because of inflation, you must pay more money to buy the same amount of goods or services than you bought in the past. For example, if the annual inflation rate is 10 percent, the price of a ten-dollar T-shirt will be $11 next year ($10 × 10% or .10 = $1; $10 + $1 = $11).

Economic Growth and Decline Economists measure growth and decline by rising or falling Gross Domestic Product (GDP) levels. GDP is the total value of all goods and services sold in a country during a year. When the GDP rises, a country's economy is strong. When the GDP is flat or drops, the economy is weak. A weak economy affects imports, prices, and other things that influence the value of a country's currency. Underdeveloped and developing countries with weak economies suffer from having currencies that cannot hold their values.

GNP vs. GDP To assess economic conditions, many economists watch both the GDP and the GNP (Gross National Product) levels of a country. How are the terms different? The GDP is the total value of all goods and services sold in a country, but the GNP level is more specific and is based on the value of the GDP. To calculate GDP, add the value of goods and services generated by the country's businesses in other countries. Then subtract the amount that foreign businesses generated in the home country. To calculate the GNP of the United States, add its GDP to the value of everything made and sold by the United States in other countries (including movies, cars, and clothes). Then subtract the value of goods and services that other countries made in the United States. For example, subtract profits earned by Honda in U.S. plants, if those profits are returned to Japan.

Unemployment Rates Unemployment is another measure of economic well-being. In the United States, the unemployment rate measures the percentage of workers currently looking for a job. A high unemployment rate is one sign that a nation's economy is weak. Usually, unemployment has a negative impact on the value of a nation's currency.

Political Conditions

Political conditions in a country can affect a business in many ways. The possibility of war or the overthrow of a government will cause a country's currency to lose value. Expropriation occurs when a government takes over a foreign business. Concern about possible expropriation means there is a major political risk involved in doing business in that country.

Exchange Rate Problems

Currency value fluctuations are one problem associated with dealing in foreign currencies. Other problems, mentioned previously, include rising levels of inflation, rising interest rates, and other economic changes in a country.

Exchange rate problems can lower profits. They can make it more difficult to sell items, since prices will change. Fluctuating values may discourage trade. Companies seeking to trade with other countries are affected by exchange rates and currency values.

Consequently, in the world of international business, a key issue for businesses to consider is the potential for problems associated with a given country's currency. A company can take steps to manage the risks involved and to make trading easier.

Managing Exchange Rates

National governments take two approaches to making sure exchange rates are at least a neutral factor in business transactions. The approaches involve:

1. Market measures
2. Nonmarket measures

These measures are designed to maintain a "level playing field" when it comes to currency exchange.

Market Measures

A government can use certain market measures, or strategies, to manage exchange rates, including devaluing its currency or intervening in its economy.

When currency is devalued, it takes more of another currency to make an exchange for the local currency. Devaluation helps local vendors protect sales and profits.

A government can also use devaluation to change the money system so dramatically that its economy experiences deflation instead of inflation. With deflation, goods and services cost less because the government lowers the value of its money. This may result in reduced importation of goods and other national currencies.

TECH Trends

Changing Money

Using a "one-world currency" may be as impossible to put into practice as establishing a single world language. Regional areas have cultural and geographic differences as well as distinct ways of doing business and conducting commerce. As a result, differences in types of currency require people to convert one unit of money to another in order to operate in another country.

Technology provides many resources to accomplish currency conversion, including calculators and software programs. However, values of currency change daily; Web sites can provide the most current quotes with numerous online tools to convert one country's money to another. In addition, most banks offer online calculators for major currencies. Several Web sites provide holistic calculators that can convert any type of money. *Locate a Web site that allows conversion from any common form of money into another.*

@ For links to help you do this activity, go to the International Business Online Learning Center through **glencoe.com**.

Competitive Devaluation

Devaluation is the reduction in value of a currency relative to other currencies. A country's central bank sometimes reduces the value of its currency to become more competitive. Devaluation reduces the cost of exports to foreign buyers and increases the cost of imports for domestic buyers.

However, devaluation often leads to competitive devaluation. When one country sees that another country has devalued its currency and become more competitive, it must also devalue its currency or risk losing business. This can create international financial chaos. The International Monetary Fund (IMF) discourages competitive devaluation. *Should the IMF be able to control the way a country's central bank values its currency? Why or why not?*

Nonmarket Measures

Nonmarket measures include tariffs and quotas, discussed in Chapters 4 and 5, as well as exchange controls. Exchange controls can limit the amount of money or currency that can be taken out of a country. Governments can place these limits on individual travelers as well as entire companies. Exchange controls can also set the exchange rates of currencies when individuals and companies trade for other currencies. These limits affect tourists, who must exchange the country's currency for foreign currencies at a set rate. Governments use exchange controls instead of freely operating foreign exchange markets. Foreign exchange markets are networks of banks and financial institutions that buy and sell currencies at floating market rates.

International Financial Organizations

The international monetary system is a network of international organizations that try to help individual countries create and participate in trade. The system includes various organizations:

- International Monetary Fund
- World Bank
- European Economic and Monetary Union
- Other exchange organizations

International Monetary Fund

The International Monetary Fund (IMF), created in 1946, is actually an organization with over 180 member countries. The IMF serves as a deposit bank. It allows member countries to facilitate trade at established exchange rates.

Some member nations experience trade deficits each year. This leads to greater debt based on an unfavorable balance of trade. The IMF tries to help these countries by doing three things:

1. Monitors purchases and sales of goods to observe the balance of trade
2. Suggests economic policies that might help improve trade
3. Makes loans

The third area is vital. The IMF offers low-interest loans to help protect countries from becoming overburdened by debt and interest.

World Bank

The World Bank was formed in 1944 at about the same time as the IMF. The official name of the World Bank is the "International Bank for Reconstruction and Development." Its activities include providing loans and helping to build and improve communication and transportation systems and energy plants in disadvantaged countries.

A goal of the World Bank is to help various countries develop international trade through its organization, the International Development Association (IDA).

Soft Loans The IDA provides money to promising new businesses through "soft loans." These loans have long grace periods, which extend the due dates for payments. The total repayment periods are very long—up to 40 years. Having a long repayment period can reduce the amount of each payment, or loan installment, making the loan manageable for the borrower.

Hard Loans The other major goal of the World Bank is to provide low-interest loans to finance new businesses in developing countries. A segment of the World Bank, called the International Finance Corporation (IFC), offers "hard loans." A hard loan must be paid back on a regular schedule without any grace period before payments must begin. A hard loan has a shorter time period for repayment.

The IFC looks for joint ventures. A joint venture is an agreement between two or more parties to start a business and share in its profits and losses. In a joint venture with the IFC, a company or government puts up some of the money to start a business, while the IFC provides the rest. The IFC also provides technical assistance by showing a business owner different management methods and ways to achieve success.

European Economic and Monetary Union

The European Economic and Monetary Union (EMU) is the financial agreement that guides the economies of the European Union (EU). The European Central Bank provides most of the financial support for the EU's member nations. Three of the EU's members, England, Denmark, and Sweden, do not use the euro. Leaders in these countries do not believe it is in their nations' best interests to convert to the currency.

Other Exchange Organizations

There are other organizations that help with international trade activities. They include the Asian Development Bank (AsDB), the European Bank for Reconstruction and Development (EBRD), and the Inter-American Development Bank (IDB). The AsDB helps develop trade between Asian and other countries, especially the United States, Japan, and countries in Europe. The EBRD promotes economic investment in the former Soviet Union and Eastern European allies. The IDB finances projects in Latin America.

Financing an International Business

When a company starts, the original funds are **capital**, or money needed to establish a business and operate it for the first few months, or to expand an existing business. Many financial institutions, especially the World Bank, help businesses in underdeveloped and developing countries obtain start-up capital. Capital is used to buy a building or plant, equipment and office supplies, and other items to get started. A business might also buy inventory and advertise the opening of the business with capital.

OUR MULTICULTURAL WORKPLACE

Culture and Currency

A country's national currency is rooted in culture and history. Great men and women, national treasures, and cultural beliefs all can be found on a culture's currency. In Roman times, the generals minted coins with their likeness on one side and a legend about them on the other side. Currency is a source of cultural pride and identity. When the European Union transitioned to a common currency—the euro—it took years of negotiations, because European countries feared losing their national identity. *Explore how the euro—the common currency of the European Union—has preserved the cultural identity of the participating countries.*

In the world of international business, it is important to know how to raise capital, no matter where your company is located. There are several ways to obtain these funds:

- Intercompany financing
- Equity financing
- Debt financing
- Local currency financing

Intercompany Financing

There are two ways to obtain capital by using intercompany financing. The first is to borrow or receive it from an existing parent company. For instance, if Procter and Gamble's management team decided to manufacture and sell furniture polish in Angola, the parent company would provide all of the necessary resources to get started. A large number of spin-off companies got their start using intercompany financing from a parent organization.

The second way to obtain capital through intercompany financing is through loans from other corporations. The interest on these loans is a legitimate business expense for the new company. That means that the interest is tax-deductible for the company. Often a company will obtain short-term financing from other companies in the early days of operating a business.

Equity Financing

Equity financing is the method a company uses to raise capital by selling shares of stock. A share of stock is a unit of ownership in a company. If a company sells one million shares of stock, and you own one of those shares, you own one millionth of the company.

Owning Stock Owning one share of stock gives you one vote to elect the company's board of directors, which is the group that decides a company's direction. If the company makes a profit, you are entitled to your portion of the profits. The company can either pay you the profit as a monetary dividend or as stock. It may also reinvest your profits in the company, thus making the company more valuable. Over time, the reinvestment of profits may make the share you own worth more money.

Selling Stock When a company expands into international trade, the management team can issue new shares of stock. The company can sell these new shares in the company in the home country, in the new country where the business will expand, or in both places. People and businesses can sell shares of stock in the United States through the New York Stock Exchange or through NASDAQ, in Japan through the Tokyo Stock Exchange, or in the European Union through Euronext. **Technology** such as the Internet enables the buying and selling of stock worldwide. There are also smaller outlets for new stock sales besides these major national and international stock exchanges.

Debt Financing

Debt financing occurs when a company takes out long-term loans to obtain capital. There are three sources of debt financing for international operations:

1. International bank loans
2. Euronote markets
3. International bond markets

International bank loans can take the form of Eurocredits. Some companies obtain loans from other countries. U.S. bonds are also called "Yankee bonds." Japanese bonds issued by the Japanese domestic market by a non-Japanese company are sometimes called "Samurai bonds." Bonds sold in England are also called "bulldogs."

Local Currency Financing

Sometimes the best place to look for capital is at local banks. Banks may provide loans to new businesses as a way to develop local commerce. In many countries a bank will allow a new business to write a check, or overdraft, even when the business does not have money in the bank to pay the check. By covering the check, the bank is giving that company a "loan" until the company can deposit money to fund the check. In the United States, this practice is known as *kiting*, which is illegal.

Non-bank loans come from private local companies. Companies can offer short-term credit to help a new business get started. When a company offers credit to another company, it may be in the form of commercial paper—a short-term loan for less than nine months.

All aspects of the international monetary system and the various organizations that provide capital to companies play a role in international trade. Careful management of capital and investment money is key to a successful international business operation.

Quick Check 7.1

After You Read Respond to what you have read by answering these questions.

1. List five characteristics associated with money. _____

_____

2. Identify the factors that affect exchange rates. _____

_____

3. Name the sources of capital a new company can use. _____

_____

Academics / English Language Arts

4. What is the role of the International Monetary Fund?

_____

_____

Risk Management

YOU WILL LEARN

- To identify the types of commercial risk in international trade
- To identify the types of payment programs used when trading across international borders
- To discuss ways to reduce risk when building international business relationships

WHY IT'S IMPORTANT

Understanding risk and how to reduce it can promote successful international business.

KEY TERMS

- risk
- commercial risk
- exchange rate risk
- transaction risk
- insurable risk

Academic Vocabulary

You will find these words in your reading and on your tests. Make sure you know their meanings.

- invest
- economy
- formula

Reading Guide

Before You Read

What is the biggest financial risk you have ever taken?

MAIN IDEA
If a business does not receive payment for any reason, it risks losing money.

GRAPHIC ORGANIZER
Draw this chart. As you read, write in the ways to reduce transaction risk.

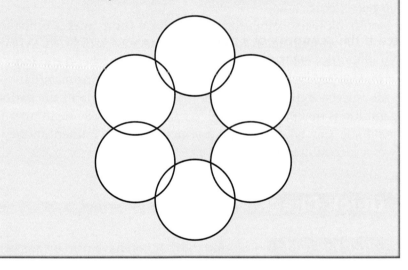

Ways to Reduce Transaction Risk

Risk vs. Return

Risks can be high or low. For example, an individual might place $100 in a money-market savings account that pays interest tied to the prime rate. That is a low-risk investment. Another person might **invest** $10,000 by buying stock in a company that is making a new invention that might or might not be successful. That is a high-risk investment.

So, what is a risk? A **risk** is the possibility of loss when there is uncertainty associated with the outcome of an event. International business includes five basic forms of risk—time, economic, product, country/political, and dependency (see **Figure 7.2**). In addition, there are several other types of risk in international trade, which involve commercial risk.

Commercial Risk

On the company-to-company level, a **commercial risk**, or trade risk, is a risk present in day-to-day buying and selling processes between companies. Businesses can use different methods to reduce or manage risk. There are three types of commercial risks:

- Exchange rate risk
- Transaction risk
- Insurable risk

As You Read

Question Do investors expect more or less interest when lending money to a high-risk company?

Exchange Rate Risk

Whenever a company makes a sale to a business in another country, there is risk. The **exchange rate risk** is a risk that occurs when the currency exchange rate fluctuates as a transaction takes place. As a result, one trading partner or the other will lose money because of changes in currency values, rather than business activity. This is the exchange rate risk. Exchange rates can be affected by political turbulence, economic events, and the passage of time.

Political risk, or country risk, can have a strong impact on exchange rates. A war, the overthrow of a government, or even the results of an election can change a country's degree of stability. The currencies of unstable countries often lose value.

An economic event, such as a recession, can also change exchange rates. If the **economy** of a trading partner experiences rising inflation, unemployment, or some other negative economic trend, the odds are that the country's currency will lose value.

As time passes, risk rises. Long-term contracts with a company from another country can be affected by both time risk and exchange rate risk.

Figure 7.2

Forms of Risk

CONSIDER THE POSSIBILITIES Doing international business involves many types of risk. Which of these risks is most difficult to manage?

Time Risk	The longer it takes to "get your money back" on an investment, the greater the risk.
Economic Risk	Downturns in economic conditions can affect business locally, nationally, or globally.
Product Risk	Some products are more risky to sell than others.
Country Risk/Political Risk	There is a possibility that an investment will be lost due to political changes in a country.
Dependency Risk	Relying too much on a single trading partner is a risk on the importing side of international business.

Reducing Exchange Rate Risk

To manage exchange rate risk, the manager must understand different types of currency exchange rates, such as a "spot rate" and a "forward rate." A spot rate is the rate between two currencies for an immediate trade. A forward rate is the rate that is agreed upon in advance for a future transaction. Forward rates are usually fixed for only 30, 60, 90, or 180 days. To manage a forward rate, a manager can use a currency future, which is a contract to buy a currency at some point in time in the future at today's exchange rate.

Transaction Risk

A **transaction risk** is a risk associated with a buyer making installment payments on a purchase. If the buyer receives the merchandise and fails to pay for it, the seller experiences a loss. Transaction risks are a good example of the how uncertainty affects risk. If you sell something to a well-known company with a solid financial and ethical history, the risk is low. When you sell to a company that has a poor history of repayment, the transaction risk increases.

Reducing Transaction Risk

Individual companies use various methods to reduce transaction risk by setting up different types of payment programs for goods and services. Some methods include:

- Cash in advance (CIA)
- Letter of credit (LC)
- Bill of exchange
- Sale on account
- Promissory note
- Electronic Funds Transfer (EFT)

Cash in Advance (CIA) Cash in advance is a simple way to complete a sale. The buyer pays for the goods before they are shipped. This provides the greatest level of risk protection to the seller, who may be worried that the buyer will have problems paying for the goods. Cash in advance is also a good choice when the buyer's country has political or economic instability.

Letter of Credit (LC) A letter of credit is a legal document that a bank sends to the seller guaranteeing the seller will receive payment. It is written and signed by a bank that represents the buyer. The bank usually protects its interests by making the buyer deposit the money for the payment before it writes the letter of credit.

Bill of Exchange A bill of exchange is similar to a letter of credit. The bill states when and where the buyer should make the payment. Usually "when" is within 90 days. "Where" is a bank or some other financial institution. The buyer deposits the money into the seller's account at the bank or financial institution.

Sale on Account A sale on account is a form of short-term credit. The buyer has an account with the seller. The buyer is able to "charge" merchandise but must pay the bill within 90 days or less. A sale on account is risky, since the seller is granting credit.

Promissory Note A promissory note is a type of contract used to finance a large sale. If you have ever bought a car on credit, you have signed a promissory note. You (and probably your parents) signed a contract stating that you would pay a set amount on a month-by-month basis until the bill is completely paid. Another term for the payments is *installments*.

A promissory note works the same way in international business. The seller prepares a promissory note when the buyer is going to make a series of payments, either monthly or each year for several years, for a major purchase. The buyer makes payments instead of a one-time payment for the entire item. It is normal for the seller to charge interest on this type of loan. A promissory note includes time risk: The longer the time granted in the repayment contract, the greater the risk.

Electronic Funds Transfer Many buyers pay bills by using the Electronic Funds Transfer (EFT) method, or a "wire." Using a bank or financial institution, the buyer orders the money to be sent electronically to the seller after the buyer receives the goods. EFT is simple, secure, and quick, often moving funds within hours. When the buyer and seller trust each other, it is a good way to finish a sale. EFT transactions are growing in popularity for individual buyers and for companies that are trading partners. Many large multinational companies, such as General Motors, do business using only "electronic paper," or EFTs.

✓ **Reading Check** **Analyze** Explain the advantages of EFTs.

World Market SINGAPORE

Singapore Air Flying High

In 1947, the governments of Singapore and Malaysia started Malayan Airlines as a joint venture to serve Southeast Asia. When the two countries separated in 1965, it was agreed that each would handle its own airline— Singapore Airlines was launched in 1972. As a small city/country, Singapore the country was faced with doing international business and having international competition. So, Singapore Airlines assembled one of the newest and best fleets in the industry. It was among the first to have Boeing 747s and Boeing 777s custom-made into 747 Megatops and 777 Jubilees. The airline also strived to provide the best service, offering hot meals, beverages, and video on-demand. Its stewards and stewardesses originally wore Sarong-inspired uniforms by Paris designer Pierre Balmain. By offering top technology and service, Singapore Airlines has managed to cruise through the ups and downs of the travel industry.

THINK GLOBALLY *What are some risks a company such as an airline may encounter as a result of depending on international business?*

@ To learn more about the country of origin for this global business, go to the International Business Online Learning Center through **glencoe.com**.

Commercial Invoice

Most payment methods require a commercial invoice. The invoice is a written statement of what was sold, the terms of the sale, and other details. The invoice includes the quantity of goods, the price, how the merchandise should be shipped, dates for the sale and shipment to take place, the form of payment, and the terms of payment, including any discounts given or interest charged.

A commercial invoice might include an early payment discount, which is recorded on the invoice as 2/20 net 90. This means that the discount is 2 percent if the bill is paid in 20 days or less. (The **formula** example would be $420 \times .02 = \$8.40$; $420 - \$8.40 = \$411.60$ due.) If the buyer does not take advantage of this discount, the full amount is due in 90 days. A 3/10 net 60 discount allows a 3 percent discount if the bill is paid in 10 days; otherwise the full amount is due in 60 days.

Each method of financing implies different levels of trust and different kinds of involvement between the buyer and the seller. Each method also has a different level of risk. Cash in advance is, essentially, the least trusting type of financial relationship. When the buyer and seller have worked together over time and have developed trust, they may use other payment options.

Insurable Risk

Businesses purchase insurance to be protected against a few specific types of risk. An **insurable risk** is a risk that insurance companies will cover, including an "act of God" and other less-random events. They cannot be predicted. They cause damage to goods being shipped or stored in a warehouse, dock, or harbor. There are several types of insurable events that are completely random:

- Fires
- Weather or storms
- Earthquakes
- Natural catastrophes

Less-random events include theft and damage due to negligence. A boat that runs ashore and damages its cargo due to the negligence of the captain is a more preventable risk. A ship that sinks during a hurricane is less preventable. Theft is more preventable through the use of security measures. The newest type of insurable risk is loss due to terrorism. A company may pay a premium (fee) to insure goods against being lost, damaged, or stolen during a terrorist attack.

Insurable business risks hinge on one key question: Who owned the property when the loss occurred? Did the merchandise still belong to the seller, or had it changed hands to the buyer? If an agent middleman is involved, representing goods without ever holding the title, the issue of ownership is even more clouded. These concerns are typically resolved by insuring the items from the beginning to the end of the sale and shipment period.

FINANCIAL ANALYST

Financial analysts are professionals with strong backgrounds in accounting and finance and a firm grasp of global business operations. Analysts help banks, insurance companies, mutual or pension funds, securities firms, and other businesses make investment choices. To do so, they consider all available information about a company or government to advise companies about the potential failure or success of a business deal. They assess risk. This requires gathering and analyzing information, preparing spreadsheets, and writing reports.

Advising an international firm involves understanding where the company is invested worldwide, and the different cultures and currencies involved. Analysts also consider how a company's plans for future growth might be affected by changes in foreign markets. This often requires international travel and "face time" with clients.

Skills and Training

Successful financial analysts must be detail-oriented and possess self-confidence, good interpersonal skills, and the ability to work both independently and in a team. Strong communication skills are necessary for working with clients, preparing reports, and giving presentations.

Interested candidates should take mathematics and economics courses in high school and obtain a bachelor's degree in business administration, accounting, statistics, or finance. Companies provide training to new analysts. A financial analyst can advance by gaining experience, becoming certified as a Chartered Financial Analyst (CFA), and earning an MBA degree.

English Language Arts/Writing

Describe how financial analysts help multinational companies manage risk.

@ To learn more about financial analysts and their career paths, go to the International Business Online Learning Center through **glencoe.com.**

Career Data

Education: Bachelor's degree or master's degree in business, finance, statistics, or accounting

Skills: Mathematical, computer, analytical, and communication skills

Outlook: Growth faster than average in the next ten years

Reducing Insurable Risk

The two major forms of risk that are insured in international trade are loss and liability.

Losses occur when merchandise is broken, stolen, lost, or damaged. The seller usually prepares an insurance certificate for goods that are about to be shipped. An insurance certificate states the amount of coverage (in dollars or some other currency) for losses due to fire, theft, water, or damage during shipment. The certificate also names the insurance company providing the coverage.

Liability is present when a good or service injures someone or another company. For example, if a company ships microwave ovens overseas, and those ovens have electrical shorts that can cause fires, the manufacturing company has a liability risk. That type of liability is based on a defective product. Most companies take out insurance policies which pay for liability losses for both defective products and actions by employees. Those actions can be the result of negligence. If a UPS driver crashes a truck into a building or injures someone, UPS will most likely have a liability policy covering the company for injuries and property damage caused by the driver. Some countries take a hard stance when it comes to liability issues; others are more lax.

Insurance is the ultimate form of risk management. When insurance is combined with company practices that handle transaction risks and exchange rate risks, a business is in the best position to withstand all forms of commercial risk.

Managing Money and Risk

Money management and risk management have something in common: Both have manageable and unmanageable elements. Success in international business means carefully managing every aspect of currency exchange. It also requires managers to assess risks in transactions and to take steps to reduce those risks.

Quick Check 7.2

After You Read Respond to what you have read by answering these questions.

1. What are the three main elements of commercial risk? _____

_____

2. What methods can be used to make payment? _____

_____

3. What are the two main types of problems covered by insurance? _____

_____

Academics / Social Studies

4. Why might companies use EFTs?

_____

_____

Financial Planning

In two months your company plans to transfer you to a division in a developing country. You will be there for a year. There is considerable political unrest in the country. The currency fluctuates widely in value. Thieves steal money and valuables, and kidnappings occur frequently. Your pay will be doubled during the assignment. In addition, most of your living expenses will be covered by the company. To reduce risk, plan how, where, and in what form you will keep your own money while you are on this assignment.

_____

_____

_____

_____

_____

_____

_____

_____

_____

_____

_____

_____

_____

_____

_____

_____

_____

_____

_____

_____

ACADEMICS APPLIED Check off the academic knowledge you used to do this activity:

☐ English Language Arts ☐ Mathematics ☐ Social Studies ☐ Science

ACADEMIC AND CAREER PLAN Add this page to your Academic and Career Plan Portfolio.

(tl) Ulf Wallin/Getty Images; (tr) Royalty-free/David De Lossy/Getty Images; (b) Royalty-free/Getty Images

Chapter 7   Review and Activities

CHAPTER SUMMARY

Section 7.1   **Currency and Currency Exchange**

money (p. 154)
currency (p. 156)
currency exchange rate
    (p. 156)
hard currency (p. 157)
soft currency (p. 157)
currency value
    fluctuation (p. 158)
capital (p. 163)

- Money and the currency exchange system allow companies to conduct international business.

- When currency values fluctuate, the value of one currency changes when it is traded for another.

- National leaders use both market and nonmarket methods to make sure exchange rates are at least a neutral factor in business transactions.

Section 7.2   **Risk Management**

risk (p. 166)
commercial risk (p. 167)
exchange rate risk
    (p. 167)
transaction risk (p. 168)
insurable risk (p. 170)

- The types of commercial risks in international business include exchange rate risks, transaction risks, and insurable risks.

- Individual companies use various methods to reduce transaction risks. This is partially done by setting up different types of payment programs for goods and services.

- Insurance is used to cover a few specific types of risk such as damage from fires, weather or storms, earthquakes, and natural catastrophes.

CONCEPTS REVIEW

1. **Define** the term *money*.

2. **Identify** the factors that cause currency exchange rates to fluctuate.

3. **List** three nonmarket control measures used to neutralize exchange rates.

4. **Distinguish** between insurable risks and other types of commercial risks in international business.

5. **Describe** how transaction risks are reduced.

6. **Explain** the key question in insurable risk cases.

KEY TERMS REVIEW

7. Match each term to its definition.

_____ money

_____ currency

_____ currency exchange rate

_____ hard currency

_____ soft currency

_____ currency value fluctuation

_____ capital

_____ risk

_____ commercial risk

_____ exchange rate risk

_____ transaction risk

_____ insurable risk

a. the rate at which one country's currency can be traded for another country's currency

b. an unstable currency that is not exchanged at major financial centers

c. a currency that can be exchanged for other currencies at uniform rates in financial centers around the world

d. the change in value of one country's currency when it is traded for another country's currency

e. the possibility of loss when there is uncertainty associated with the outcome of an event

f. a risk that occurs when the currency exchange rate fluctuates as a transaction takes place

g. the form of money used by a specific country or region

h. a risk present in the day-to-day buying and selling processes that take place between companies

i. a risk that insurance companies will cover, including an "act of God" and other less-random events

j. the risk associated with a buyer making installment payments on a purchase

k. anything that people accept as a form of payment

l. money needed to establish a business and operate it for the first few months, or to expand an existing business

Academic Vocabulary

8. On a separate sheet of paper, write a sentence or two related to currency and risk management using at least three of the academic terms you learned in the section openers:

- ratio
- compensate
- technology
- invest
- economy
- formula

Critical Thinking

9. Assume the United Nations voted to create a world currency, the "uno." Unos will be exchanged for all major currencies. What might occur as a result?

Discussion Starter

10. In 1971, U.S. President Nixon imposed a wage and price freeze to combat inflation. Is a freeze a good idea in a market economy?

Point of View

11. Four out of five new businesses fail. Would the risk of starting a new business stop you from trying? Why or why not?

BUILDING REAL-WORLD SKILLS

12. The Japanese Bow Uncomfortable with physical contact when meeting someone, the Japanese substitute the polite bow. Such a bow can accompany statements such as "Thank you," "Hello," "Good-bye," "Congratulations," "Good night," "Good morning," "Sorry, " "Excuse me," and more. If the person to whom you are bowing is older and/or more important, your bow should be lower and held longer.

Research and Share

a. What traditions for polite greetings exist in other nations?

b. Would you shake hands or bow if you had a Japanese guest here in the United States? Explain your answer.

13. Risk Management A growing risk to employees is theft of their financial resources by electronic means. This danger becomes especially significant when one realizes that more than half of all U.S. employers deposit their employees' paychecks electronically every month.

Research and Write

a. What are the pros and cons of the electronic fund transfer system?

b. Make a list of useful tips that would help to maintain the integrity of electronic transfers and accounts.

BUILDING ACADEMIC SKILLS

 English Language Arts

14. Write a short essay on how you would determine how much money a person's life is worth for insurance purposes.

MATH Mathematics

15. When you barter you exchange goods or services without exchanging money. Say you do yard work for a dentist in exchange for dental services. According to the U.S. Internal Revenue Service, the fair market value of goods and services exchanged must be included in the income of both parties. The value of the yard work was $1,100, and the value of the dental services was $5,000. You are being taxed at a 10 percent rate on additional income, and the dentist is being taxed at a 30 percent rate. Who pays more in additional taxes?

Computation and Estimation To solve this problem, you need to understand the principles of taxation and incremental income.

SOC Social Studies/Sociology

16. The Yappese in Micronesia used stone money discs of great size and weight. Beaded shells called "wampum" were made legal tender in the Massachusetts Bay Colony in 1637. Today many cultures have transitioned from check writing to electronic transferring. What does the use of these forms of currency say about the cultures that accept them?

SOC Social Studies/Economics

17. Today almost two-thirds of the United States' basic money supply—in physical dollars of all denominations—is held overseas. What do people use for money here? Electronic fund transfers. List as many activities as you can for which you absolutely need cash.

COMPETITIVE EVENT PREP

Money Matters

18. Situation Countries often must design or redesign their currency to protect it from being counterfeited as well as to update it to fit the current economic situation. As a member of the Treasury Department of Estonia, you will study the current currency, and then issue a redesigned version that will be safer and present a fresh new look.

Activity Research the current currency's design. Discover how long this particular breakdown of coins and currency has been in use, and what and why particular designs are in use. Use the embassy Web site and research images of the currency. Study precautions in place in the country and in the United States to see if they can be updated. Consider the implications of adopting the euro and list the pros and cons.

Evaluation You will be evaluated on how well you meet the following objectives.

a. Describe the currency, its history, and its distribution.

b. Define the issues one might have with Estonian currency and develop a grid of the pros and cons of changing to either a new design or adopting the euro.

c. Present a design to the class. Detail the choices you made as well as why you made them.

d. Compare and contrast the security measures used in the new currency as opposed to the current currency.

Israel

Using the Internet, look up the nation of Israel on a world map. Study the topographical features. Answer the following questions about Israel on a separate sheet of paper.

➤ What physical resources does the nation have?

➤ How did the nation's history affect the naming and design of the current Israeli currency?

@ For resources to help you do this exercise, go to the International Business Online Learning Center through **glencoe.com**.

BusinessWeek online

19. Newsclip: Will India Free the Rupee? India may relax controls over its currency to allow full convertibility. This would make it easier for money to flow in and out of the country and encourage international business.

@ Go to the International Business Online Learning Center through **glencoe.com** to read an article about this topic. Write a paragraph about how convertibility will help India compete.

Standardized Test Practice

20. Find a world map on the Internet and choose the best answer to the following multiple-choice question.

Which stock exchange is located in South America?
- ○ Rio de Janeiro Stock Exchange
- ○ Australian Stock Exchange
- ○ London Stock Exchange
- ○ Tokyo Stock Exchange

Test-Taking Tip When the question includes a map, carefully read the question and the map itself. After selecting an answer, reread the question to ensure the accuracy of the answer.

Export Expansion

Success Model: CAFÉ MADRID
Country of Origin: COLOMBIA
Business: COFFEE

For more than 85 years, a small coffee plantation, owned by Don Abel Londoño, cultivated and roasted fine coffee known as *Café Madrid*. Nestled in the fertile hills of Colombia in South America, this farm supplied locals with fresh-roasted coffee beans wrapped in parchment paper and delivered via bicycle. As time passed, Café Madrid developed a reputation for high quality and state-of-the art production.

An original member of the National Federation of Coffee Growers (FNC) of Colombia, this small company supported the federation's efforts as its membership grew to 500,000 coffee farmers (*cafeteroes*). Today the FNC has over 800 agricultural advisors who help ensure consistent, high-quality coffee exported from Colombia. While helping to improve Colombia's local economy and biodiversity, the FNC provides an assurance of quality, represented by the "Juan Valdez" logo.

In the early 2000s, Café Madrid made the move to expand operations to export its products, providing all aspects of production and delivery of bulk coffee to top restaurants and hotels around the world.

● Situation

You have been promoted to the sales and marketing department of a mid-size wholesale food supplier, Sunny Daze. Your company sells granola and granola bars, whole-grain pancake mix, specialty cookies, and popcorn, and has decided to explore the international market. Your assignment for the next four months will be in Brazil, Japan, and Morocco. You will be conducting research so that Sunny Daze management can make a decision regarding exporting their products into these markets.

● Assignment

✓ Research the governments, economies, and geographies of Brazil, Japan, and Morocco.
✓ Determine what other types of products are currently exported to Brazil, Japan, and Morocco from the United States.
✓ Research the steps that a U.S. company must take to export products.
✓ Create a presentation of your findings.

● Resources

SKILLS NEEDED

✓ *Academic Skills:* reading, writing, and social studies
✓ *Basic Skills:* speaking, listening, thinking, problem-solving, and interpersonal skills
✓ *Technology Skills:* word-processing, keyboarding, spreadsheet, presentation, telecommunications, and Internet skills

TOOLS NEEDED

✓ Newspapers and magazines, such as *BusinessWeek* and *U.S. News and World Report*
✓ Access to the Internet and library
✓ Word-processing, spreadsheet, and presentation software

● Procedures

STEP 1 | REAL-WORLD RESEARCH

Using the library, the Internet, newspapers, and/or magazines, research facts about Brazil, Japan, and Morocco:

- Government
- Economy
- Geography
- Products imported into the country
- Products exported out of the country

STEP 2 | COMMUNITY RESEARCH

Locate a business in your community that exports any product. Interview the owner or manager to find out this information:

- The difference between doing business in the United States and with another country
- Export laws and regulations
- Future trends and global opportunities

STEP 3 | INTERNET RESEARCH

Access the U.S. Department of Commerce and U.S. Chamber of Commerce Web sites.

- Find out what information is available to businesses that wish to export products.
- Find out what tariffs and taxes have to be paid on products that are exported.
- Create a list of resources available to companies interested in exporting products.

STEP 4 | GRAPHIC ORGANIZER

On a sheet of paper, create a chart of the steps Sunny Daze should take as it considers exporting.

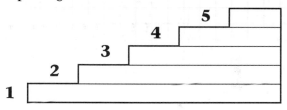

● Report

Prepare a report of your findings using the following tools, if available:

- *Word-processing program:* Prepare a 3-page written report about your research and include the step-by-step approach for exporting products. Offer your reasons that Sunny Daze should or should not export to each country.
- *Spreadsheet program:* Prepare a chart comparing the government, economy, geography, and exports of the three countries.
- *Presentation program:* Prepare a ten-slide presentation for your boss with key points, some visuals, and text.

● Evaluation

Present your report to the class and/or hand it in to your teacher. Use this chart to assess yourself before and after your presentation:

PRESENTATION SELF-CHECK RUBRIC	1 Needs Work	2 Average Quality	3 Good Quality	4 Excellent Quality	Totals
Knowledge of the three countries					
Recommendations to Sunny Daze					
Voice					
Eye contact with audience					
				TOTAL =	

0–6 Needs Work; **7–10** Average Quality; **11–14** Good Quality; **15–16** Excellent Quality

---

● Academic and Career Portfolio

Add this report to your Academic and Career Portfolio.

UNIT 3

INTERNATIONAL MANAGEMENT

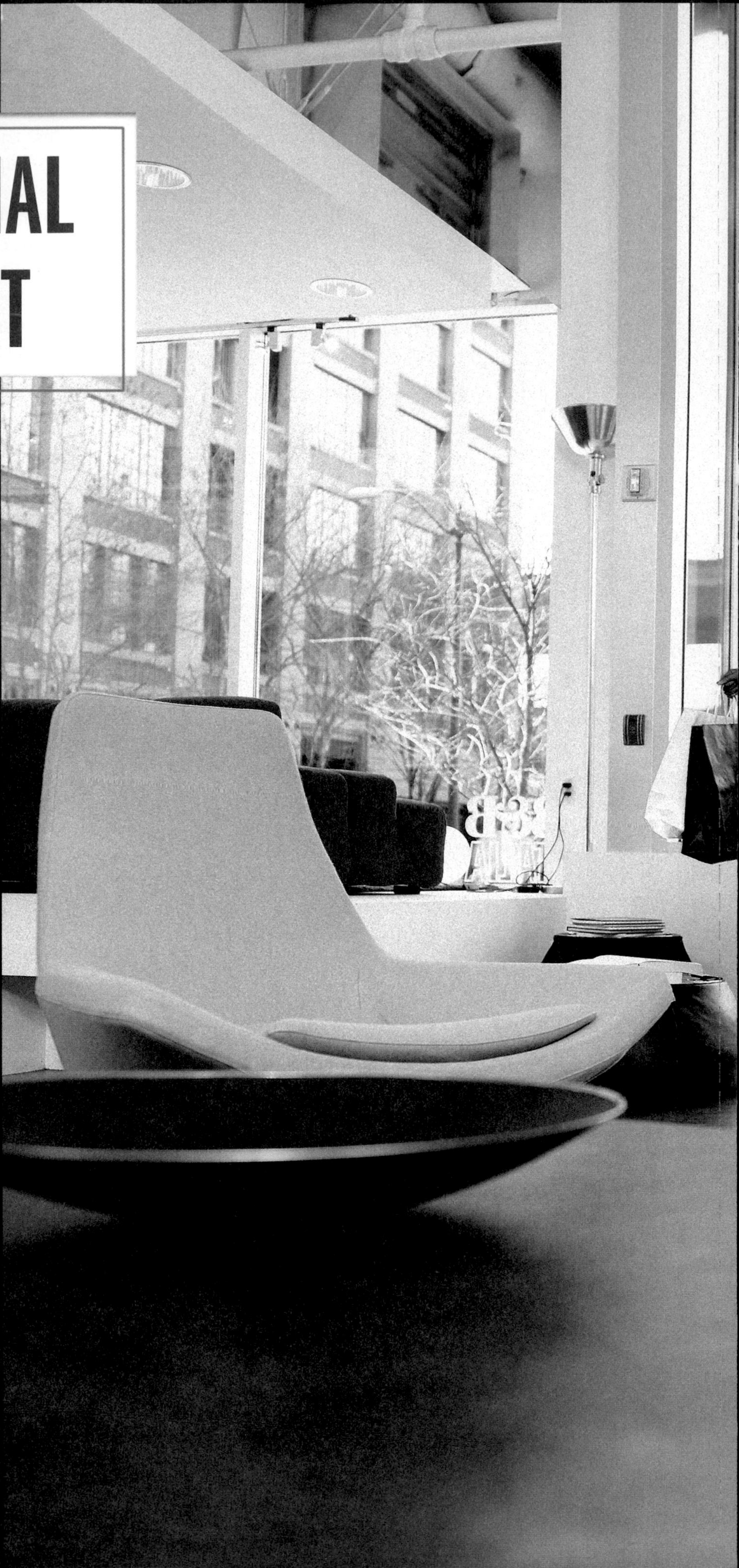

In This Unit . . .

Chapter 8
Business Ownership and Entrepreneurship

Chapter 9
Organizational Management and Strategy

Chapter 10
Production and Quality Control

> **"Nobody talks of entrepreneurship as survival, but that's exactly what it is and what nurtures creative thinking."**
>
> **Jeff Bezos**
> **Founder and CEO of Amazon.com**

"Made in Italy" Keeps Its Cachet

Italian specialty furniture companies are finding ways to survive in the face of cheaper wares from China. Ben Wals, a Dutch furniture retailer, has been coming to the Milan furniture fair for 30 years. He's admiring brightly colored metal chairs called "Mr. Bugatti." "Customers love Cappellini design," he says.

In 2004, a group of investors led by Luca Cordero di Montezemolo paid for a controlling stake in the furniture maker. Montezemolo's private-equity outfit, Charme, has spent three years assembling a portfolio of high-end Italian furniture brands that [also] includes Poltrona Frau, Cassina, Alias, Gebrueder Thonet Vienna, Nemo, and Gufram. Now these companies form Poltrona Frau Group. Montezemolo and his crew are betting the whole can amount to more than the sum of its parts: "We invested in an industry with incredible brands."

Companies like Poltrona Frau, a 94-year-old outfit famous for luxury leather sofas, find themselves threatened with extinction in the face of competition from lower-cost rivals, notably the Chinese. The business model promoted by Charme offers some hope for survival. The group functions like a loose federation. Each company offer[s] its own unique line of products, designers, production, distribution, and marketing.

Demand for high-quality work has not evaporated. Says Yosuke Watanabe, general manager of a Tokyo-based furniture retailer, "Poltrona Frau makes classic, modern furniture with a natural quality." Fine craftsmanship, apparently, is not lost in translation.

English Language Arts/Writing

1. Why did Montezemolo form Poltrona Group?
2. What is the Poltrona Frau business model?

@ To read the complete *BusinessWeek* article, go to the International Business Online Learning Center through **glencoe.com**.

UNIT THEMATIC PROJECT PREVIEW

Global Social Entrepreneurship

Businesses of all types are finding ways to benefit society and the environment—and make a profit. Known as social entrepreneurs and eco-entrepreneurs, these businessowners may start small and later go global. Think about a business you might start to benefit the world.

Pre-Project Checklist

❑ Using the Internet and publications, find three businesses that benefit society or the environment.

❑ Identify each business as owned by one person, a partnership, or a corporation.

❑ Find businesses in your community that help people or the environment and talk to their owners.

❑ Find a business plan format online.

Chapter 8

Business Ownership and Entrepreneurship

Chapter Objectives

When you have completed this chapter, you will be able to:

Section 8.1

- Identify three main types of business ownership.

- Describe the situations in which each type of business ownership is most effective.

- Differentiate between a company from a single country and a multinational corporation.

- Describe the modes of entry for selling goods and services in other countries.

Section 8.2

- Explain the nature of entrepreneurship.

- Discuss how to implement an entrepreneurial operation in another country.

CADBURY SCHWEPPES

Cadbury Schweppes is a publicly owned corporation whose shares are traded on the stock exchanges. When you research this company through Standard & Poor's, you will find investment information such as this:

Index:	S&P Global 1200 and S&P 500
Sector:	Consumer Staples
Company:	Cadbury Schweppes
Symbol:	CBRY or CSG (NYSE)
Country:	Great Britain
Price:	(varies)

Global Profile Cadbury Schweppes owns several long-established brands, such as Cadbury confections and Schweppes beverages, Dr. Pepper soft drink, Halls cough drops, and Dentyne gum, as well as other brands, including Trident, Bubbaloo, 7UP, Hawaiian Punch, Sunkist, A&W, Mott's, and Orangina. The business is organized by four regions: America's Beverages; America's Confectionery; Europe, Middle East, and Africa; and Asia Pacific.

Business Report Cadbury Schweppes has generated strong earnings for shareholders of its stock. Its revenue growth and annual earnings of 765 million British pounds ($1.33 billion) are due in part to its confectionary and beverage brands gaining market share.

English Language Arts/Writing

In the late 1700s, Jean Jacob Schweppe of Geneva, Switzerland, created the first carbonated water. He founded his business in 1783 and moved to England. In 1824, John Cadbury opened his chocolate shop. Decades later in 1969, Cadbury and Schweppes merged to become a global corporation. Today it maintains an ethics policy through efforts to reduce emissions, fight child labor, and create sustainable tree crops. *Write about differences between a corporation and a business owned by one person (such as this shop in Belgium).*

To do this activity, go to the International Business Online Learning Center through **glencoe.com.**

Types of Ownership

WHAT YOU'LL LEARN

- To identify three main types of business ownership
- To describe the situations in which each type of business ownership is most effective
- To differentiate between a company from a single country and a multinational corporation
- To describe the modes of entry for selling goods and services in other countries

WHY IT'S IMPORTANT

Certain types of business ownership are more effective for marketing certain products in different countries.

KEY TERMS

- sole proprietorship
- partnership
- corporation
- Subchapter S corporation
- limited liability company (LLC)
- multinational corporation (MNC)
- mode of entry

Academic Vocabulary

You will find these words in your reading and on your tests. Make sure you know their meanings.

- consist
- structure
- role

Reading Guide

Before You Read

What might be the definitions of the terms *direct exporting* and *franchising*?

MAIN IDEA

There are several types of business ownership, each with advantages and disadvantages.

GRAPHIC ORGANIZER

Draw this chart. As you read this section, write in the three types of business ownership and list one advantage and one disadvantage of each type.

Type of Ownership	Advantage	Disadvantage

Business Ownership

Have you ever thought about starting or owning your own business? Would you know how to comply with the legal requirements? Could your company market products to international customers?

New or existing businesses can take different forms of ownership. Sometimes, a single person or family owns a business. For other businesses, stockholders are the owners, who may be located across the country and even around the world. This section examines several types of business ownership:

- Sole proprietorships
- Partnerships
- Corporations
- Subchapter S corporations
- Limited liability companies (LLC)
- Multinational corporations

The section also discusses modes of entry, which are the ways in which all companies enter international markets. Section 8.2 examines entrepreneurship as a process of starting a business in both local and global markets.

Sole Proprietorships

A **sole proprietorship** is a type of business ownership in which one person owns the business. Most small businesses are sole proprietorships. These ventures may be small shops, restaurants, and dry cleaning stores, as well as farms and home-based businesses. Many families own and operate sole proprietorships. In the United States, almost 80 percent of all businesses **consist** of sole proprietorships.

Advantages of Sole Proprietorships

In the United States, there are several advantages to forming sole proprietorships. One is that you can be your own boss. Many Americans and people around the world love the idea of working for themselves. It means they can work the hours they wish and take vacations when they choose. Starting a sole proprietorship is relatively easy. There is limited paperwork in establishing this type of business and fewer regulations. All of the profits made by a sole proprietorship go to the owner.

Disadvantages of Sole Proprietorships

The biggest disadvantage of a sole-proprietor form of business is unlimited liability. With unlimited liability, the business owner is fully responsible for all company debts or negligence. The owner might have to use his or her personal savings to pay overdue bills. Also, a sole proprietorship requires capital to start operations. Many businesses fail because they do not have enough money to keep the company running in the beginning years when sales and profits are lower. The financial risks of starting a business are high.

Small businesses operate around the world. The business environment in various countries may or may not be the same as that in the United States. In many countries, taxes vary on small businesses. Government regulations may be more or less strict than in the United States. In some countries starting your own business is as simple as putting up a sign. In other countries, government officials may expect to receive bribes. Some governments may require numerous forms, applications, and certificates.

Selling products and services internationally by a sole proprietor company is challenging. There is a great deal of global competition. Using the Internet for communications, wholesaling, and retailing is one way to keep costs lower.

Partnerships

A **partnership** is a type of business ownership in which two or more people own the business. Partners share the risks of this type of business. They also share the rewards and profits. When a partnership business is started, the owners decide how much each will invest in the new company. The simplest arrangement is a 50/50 division, which means each of the two partners invests half of the start-up capital. Thus, each owns half of the company, sharing profits, responsibility, and risk.

OUR MULTICULTURAL WORKPLACE

All Business Is Global

A successful 21st century entrepreneur recognizes that today's business world is global. With increased access, via telecommunications and the Internet, global markets and global competitors are a click away. Many organizations, schools, and governments support global entrepreneurs with programs to help them grow in the international marketplace. The International Council for Small Business (ICSB) is one organization that provides worldwide research and support for entrepreneurs. *What strategies can small business owners use to successfully compete in a global environment?*

A DELL COMPUTERS Dell Computers began as a sole proprietorship, owned by Michael Dell, and grew into a major corporation. *Why might a sole proprietorship convert to a corporation?*

Advantages of Partnerships

There are several advantages to forming the partnership type of business. One is that each partner can bring different skills to the company. For example, a talented artist may start a souvenir T-shirt business. Her partners could include one person who is skilled at marketing and sales, and another who has accounting expertise. The three-person company will have a better chance of success than a sole proprietorship in which the artist is responsible for doing all of the jobs.

Partnership companies often try to sell products to international customers. They may have partners who are skilled at conducting international business. Also, having more partners can mean having more capital to expand a business to the global marketplace.

The partnership is a common type of business ownership for law firms, medical offices, and other small businesses. Ideally, the partners work well together.

Disadvantages of Partnerships

One disadvantage of a partnership is that breaking up partnerships is difficult. In the event of a personal conflict, the business could be destroyed. In addition, the death of a partner dissolves a partnership, requiring the survivor to reestablish the business as another entity. Another disadvantage is that each partner is liable for debts and injuries caused by the business to employees and customers. Each partner is fully liable if the business loses money. Like sole proprietorships, partnerships assume unlimited liability.

Partnerships across international boundaries are difficult to form and maintain. The biggest complication involves complying with the laws of different countries, depending on the partners' nationalities. It is also more difficult and complex to arrange financing for international partnerships.

Corporations

A **corporation** is a type of business ownership in which many people, whom the law treats as one person, own the business. A corporation can own property and enter into contracts, and must pay taxes on income or profit. There are different types of corporations. A *closely held* corporation is a private corporation whose shares are owned by a small group. A *publicly held* corporation is an organization that sells its shares openly in stock markets. The federal government must recognize a corporate **structure** to validate corporate status.

Characteristics of Corporations

Different types of corporations have several characteristics in common. For example, each type of corporation must have a set of officers, or board of directors, who meet at least once a year.

All corporations offer shares of stock, which are small pieces of ownership. If a corporation issues 1,000 shares of stock, then each share is worth one-thousandth of the ownership. One person may own every share of stock in a corporation, or many owners can invest in owning many shares. Each stockholder's percentage of shares is his or her percentage of ownership. For example, if one owner holds 400 of the total 1,000 shares, that owner has a 40 percent ownership of the corporation. Stockholders have a key responsibility. They elect a board of directors each year.

Stockholders earn profits from investing in corporations in two ways. The first way is that shareholders can receive dividends, which are a percentage of the corporation's profits. Another way is through an increase in stock value. A company can keep profits and reinvest them in the business. Thus, the value of the company increases, and each share of stock may be worth more money.

Advantages of Corporations

Corporations have several advantages. Most importantly, the owners, or shareholders, have limited liability. If the corporation loses money, stockholders lose only what they have invested. This is true even if the company goes bankrupt and does not pay its debts. Another advantage of the corporate type of ownership is that the business continues to exist no matter who owns shares of stock. Stockholders can sell shares, and they can also buy more shares. If a corporation needs to expand, it can collect new capital by selling additional shares of stock.

Disadvantages of Corporations

Corporations also have disadvantages. They are costly to start up and require a lot of paperwork. In addition, an individual or another company can take over a corporation by buying a majority of the shares of stock. The founder of a company can lose control through such a takeover. Another disadvantage involves taxes. Many corporations make profits that are double taxed. The corporation pays tax on its profits for the year. The remainder of the profits may be distributed to stockholders who must pay taxes on those dividends.

Subchapter S Corporation

The **Subchapter S corporation** is a corporation that is taxed like a partnership. It is not a taxpaying entity; the business owners pay taxes from personal earnings. Small cash businesses, such as restaurants, are usually Subchapter S corporations.

Limited Liability Company

This type of company is similar to a corporation and a limited partnership. A **limited liability company (LLC)** is a company whose owners and managers enjoy limited liability and some tax benefits.

ETHICS & ISSUES

Social Entrepreneurship

Social entrepreneurship combines traditional entrepreneurship with the values and goals of charitable groups. But this is not charity. Social entrepreneurs want to solve economic and social problems and believe they can do so and turn a profit—but they are not afraid to take risks. For example, Centro Ginecologico Integral (CEGIN SRL) is a private limited company in Jujuy, Argentina, that offers low-priced health services, focusing on women, children, and preventative health. CEGIN uses its profits to offer medical services to poor and geographically isolated communities. By applying sound business principles as well as innovative ideas and solutions to the world's problems, social entrepreneurs can address problems with education, health, human rights, and workers' rights, and provide economic opportunities for people in need. *Why might an entrepreneur choose this type of business?*

A MULTINATIONAL Toyota operates in countries besides its home country. *Where did this company originally start?*

Multinational Corporations

A large percentage of U.S. companies involved in international trade are corporations. Corporations exist in various forms around the world. They make it possible to sell products in international markets by managing the risks involved. They can also develop partner relationships with corporations based in other countries. This helps to increase international trade. A **multinational corporation (MNC)** is an organization that operates in more than one country. MNCs may also be called "global," "transnational," or "worldwide" companies or corporations.

Home and Host Countries

Many MNCs started by doing business in one country, or their home country. If a corporation becomes very successful, it may expand into other nations, or host countries. Some examples of corporations that developed into MNCs include Royal Dutch/Shell, Nestlé, Exxon, Ford Motor Company, IBM, Honda, Hyundai, and Toyota.

When a corporation evolves into a multinational corporation from a simple exporting company, the firm is no longer tied exclusively to a home country. Instead, the MNC leaders have a worldwide view of the organization and its **role**.

Characteristics of Multinational Corporations

When multinational corporations are effectively managed, they focus on creating products that are universally accepted or standardized. Their human resource (HR) policies are designed to include workers from each nation in which the company operates. Well-run MNCs try to be good guests in every country in which they do business. This type of corporation often has great economic and political power.

Modes of Entry

For all forms of business ownership, whether sole proprietorships, partnerships, or corporations, the decision to "go global" must consider a mode of entry. A **mode of entry** is the method a company uses to sell products in another country. The typical modes of entry include:

- Indirect exporting
- Direct exporting
- Turnkey projects
- Licensing
- Franchising

- Joint ventures
- Strategic alliances
- Wholly owned subsidiaries
- Foreign direct investments

Indirect Exporting

As discussed in Chapter 4, indirect exporting is managed by independent companies that handle exported goods for other companies. If a business chooses indirect exporting as a mode of entry, it must find an independent company in the destination country.

Direct Exporting

Direct exporting occurs when a company exports its own goods and services. The company may have its own department or a subsidiary company set up to handle all aspects of its direct exporting operations. Direct exporting is more expensive than indirect exporting. However, a business can have more control over its products and its message because it is overseeing the entire exporting process. If the business makes more sales this way, it may profit.

Turnkey Projects

A turnkey project is a special type of mode of entry. A company designs, builds, and starts up a business in another country. When the plant is up and running, the exporting company (that built and owns the new operation) sells the plant to a local client company. In return, the new owner does business with the export company.

Turnkey projects are found in many developing countries. For example, a non-prescription medicine company from the United States, such as Johnson & Johnson, might set up a facility in Zambia, Africa. The new plant would be designed to make medicines such as cough and cold remedies as well as pain medicines such as aspirin. Johnson & Johnson would eventually turn over the facility to a local Zambian medical supply company. In exchange, that company would buy most of its raw medical materials from Johnson & Johnson. The Zambian company would also pay a percentage of its profits to Johnson & Johnson for a specific time period. A turnkey operation allows a company to get its money back in the form of profits.

Licensing

Another way to export goods and services is to use a licensing agreement. Licensing means a company transfers the rights and grants permission to produce and sell its products overseas to a foreign firm. As payment, the licensing company receives a fee or royalty from the foreign firm. In addition, the licensing company provides any patent, trademark, formula, or design for the foreign company.

Licensing has been a successful and lucrative mode of entry for decades. During the 1950s, AT&T licensed its transistor technology to several international firms, which in turn created numerous products. Another example of licensing was RCA's agreement with Matsushita and Sony. RCA originally licensed its color-television technology to those Japanese companies, which used the technology to develop products. In the 1970s, the Xerox Corporation of the United States set up a licensing arrangement with the Fuji Photo Film Company of Japan. In exchange for allowing Fuji to use Xerox's photocopying technology, Xerox received 5 percent of Fuji's net revenues resulting from the arrangement.

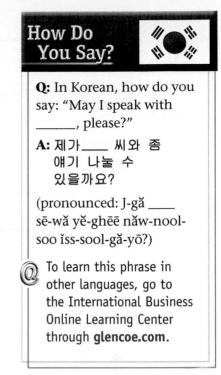

How Do You Say?

Q: In Korean, how do you say: "May I speak with _____, please?"

A: 제가___ 씨와 좀 얘기 나눌 수 있을까요?

(pronounced: J-gǎ ____ sē-wǎ yě-ghēē nǎw-nool-soo ĭss-sool-gǎ-yō?)

@ To learn this phrase in other languages, go to the International Business Online Learning Center through **glencoe.com**.

As You Read

Question How might a turnkey operation become a problem for the original owner?

Figure 8.1

Global Franchises

Businesses by Industry	Franchise Fee
Food Service:	
Baskin-Robbins	$30,000 – $60,000
Dunkin' Donuts	$12,500
KFC (Kentucky Fried Chicken)	$25,000
Retail:	
7-Eleven, Inc.	$10,000 – $194,800
The Athlete's Foot	$35,000
GNC (General Nutrition Centers)	$20,000 – $40,000
Service:	
Century 21 (real estate)	$25,000
Intercontinental Hotel Group	$40,000 minimum
The UPS Store	$14,950 – $29,950

Source: www.worldfranchising.com, Bond's Top 100 Franchises

Franchising

As a mode of entry, franchising is similar to licensing. The difference is that a license usually applies to a single good or service, such as Fuji using Xerox's photocopying. A franchise applies to the operation of an entire company or business. When a company (franchisor) sells a franchise, the purchaser (franchisee) agrees to use the brand name and to follow the standards and rules set up by the parent company. Any franchisee that does not keep the agreement may be forced to close. Fast-food restaurants and retail stores are two of the most common types of franchise operations. **Figure 8.1** lists some successful franchises operating globally.

One of the most well-known examples of the franchise is McDonald's®. This fast-food corporation sells franchises to individual owners and to groups of investors. In addition, McDonald's operates "company stores." The franchisee agrees to use the menu, cooking methods, ingredients, and physical appearance of the franchisor's restaurant. McDonald's allows some variations in menus, especially for international McDonald's units.

Reading Check **Analyze** Why might fast-food businesses be the most common form of international franchise business?

Joint Ventures

A joint venture is an agreement between two or more companies to work on a business project. The companies agree to share costs, risks, and profits. When two or more companies believe they can gain an advantage by relying on each other's strengths, a joint venture is an effective option as a mode of entry.

Culture Corner

Two Wheels to Four in China

Think About It Look around your classroom and select one object you think best represents the entrepreneurial spirit.

Photos of China often depict the country's wide boulevards filled with streams of bicyclists jockeying for position. Although bicycles are still a mainstay of everyday life, increased wealth and a growing respect for the concept of speed have encouraged many Chinese to take to the road in cars. The world's fastest-growing major market for automobiles, China has begun to export its own. One Chinese company, Geely Automotive, was the first Chinese automaker to appear at the world-famous Detroit Auto Show.

"Geely" (pronounced "JEE-lee") originates from a Chinese phrase meaning "I am lucky." It takes more than luck, however, to attract American buyers. By 2006, Geely faced major problems in its goal to export and sell low-cost cars to the United States:

Its automobiles failed a crash test and did not meet U.S. pollution standards. One consultant noted, "It took the Japanese 20 years to understand this market and build appropriate cars."

Meeting and Greeting Shake hands upon meeting. Chinese may nod or bow. If a group of Chinese greets you with applause when you are introduced, applaud back.

Business Etiquette Meetings begin on time. Use an interpreter. Exchange business cards upon introduction. Be prepared to exchange a modest gift at the first meeting.

Business Dress Simple, modest clothing is worn in China. Men wear sport coats and ties. Women wear dresses or pantsuits and avoid heavy makeup.

English Language Arts/Writing

Should Americans buy only products made in the United States? Write an editorial explaining why or why not.

American and Japanese automobile companies have participated in joint ventures for many years. This was especially true in the 1980s. U.S. manufacturers such as GM and Ford entered joint ventures with Japanese companies, such as Toyota and Subaru that were skilled at producing smaller, more economical cars. By combining efforts, the joint venture cars utilized Japanese technologies and American marketing and distribution systems. The joint ventures provided a mode of entry into foreign markets for U.S. and Japanese companies.

Large construction projects are also candidates for joint ventures. Construction companies from several countries may combine their skills and workers to complete a large building project. Joint ventures are also successful for oil-drilling operations.

Strategic Alliances

Closely related to joint ventures are strategic alliances. International strategic alliances are cooperative agreements between competitors or potential competitors from different countries. The companies agree to set up either a formal joint venture or a less formal collaboration on a project. This mode of entry benefits both competitors.

An example of a strategic alliance is General Electric's collaboration with the French aviation company Snecma Moteurs. The two firms developed a low-thrust commercial aircraft engine in 1974. Canon and Hewlett Packard are direct competitors producing many similar products. However, they also have a strategic alliance through which they share laser-print technology.

Wholly Owned Subsidiary

When a multinational corporation fully owns a company in another country, the company in the host country is called a "wholly owned subsidiary." Many MNCs own entire companies in countries around the world. The company in the host country runs as a local operation, usually hiring local employees, even though it is also part of a global corporation.

Foreign Direct Investment

Foreign direct investments (FDIs) are closely related to wholly owned subsidiaries. When a company from one country buys land or other physical property in another country, the purchasing company has made a foreign direct investment. This is another mode of entry into a country. Examples of FDIs include British, Japanese, or German ownership of hotels, shopping malls, and office complexes around the world.

Exporting Decisions

Around the world, companies use all of these modes of entry into new global markets, whether indirect exporting, direct exporting, turnkey projects, licensing, franchising, joint ventures, strategic alliances, wholly owned subsidiaries, or foreign direct investments.

Each type of business, whether a sole proprietorship, partnership, or corporation, analyzes and chooses the method of exporting that provides the most effective and efficient means for selling its goods and services in other countries.

Quick Check 8.1

After You Read Respond to what you have read by answering these questions.

1. What are the three main types of business ownership? _____

_____

2. What is the difference between a home country and a host country? _____

_____

3. What are the modes of entry for an export operation? _____

_____

 **Academics** / *Mathematics*

4. A privately owned natural pet food company recently incorporated its business and is offering 5,000 shares of stock for sale to the public. If the original owner retains 3,500 shares, what is her ownership percentage?

_____

_____

Entrepreneurship

Reading Guide

Before You Read

Do you think it is easy or difficult to start a business? Why?

MAIN IDEA
Entrepreneurial small businesses are the mainstay of economies around the world.

GRAPHIC ORGANIZER
Draw this diagram. As you read this section, write in the similarities and differences between the two types of entrepreneurial businesses.

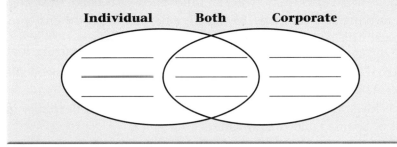

Individual   Both   Corporate

WHAT YOU'LL LEARN
- To explain the nature of entrepreneurship
- To discuss how to implement an entrepreneurial operation in another country

WHY IT'S IMPORTANT
Entrepreneurial companies are domestic and global, as are their potential benefits and problems.

KEY TERMS
- entrepreneurship
- entrepreneur
- intrapreneurship
- global entrepreneurship

Academic Vocabulary

You will find these words in your reading and on your tests. Make sure you know their meanings.
- seek
- corporate
- goal

What Is Entrepreneurship?

Starting a new business is a dream for many people. Though the process requires long hours of hard work and is risky, each year entrepreneurs start up companies around the world.

Entrepreneurship is the process of starting up a new company or business. Many new companies are started by individuals, or sole proprietors. However, new companies may also be created by companies that already exist. This section discusses entrepreneurial companies from two perspectives: 1) a company created by one person or a small group, and 2) a company that is "spun off" from an existing business.

Individual Entrepreneurs

An **entrepreneur** is a person who starts a new business. When a business begins, one of four results occurs:

1. The company survives but stays small.
2. The company grows and becomes a major corporation.
3. The company is purchased and merges with another company.
4. The company fails, which is the most common result.

Advantages of Entrepreneurship

Innovation and frustration motivate individuals to start new businesses. An innovation is a new product or a new and improved way of doing something. Perhaps someone has invented a product that fills a need or has discovered a way to improve an existing product. Many entrepreneurs start businesses because they **seek** to make new and innovative products.

The other motive is frustration. Many people form new companies because they became dissatisfied with former employers or workplace situations. Frequent layoffs, lack of opportunities to advance, and pay cuts can inspire an employee to form a business.

Many people believe that an entrepreneur is a risk taker, but he or she may actually be a *risk manager,* someone who is willing to take calculated or planned-for risks. This person is willing to take those risks to receive the benefits of entrepreneurship. Entrepreneurship has three advantages for individuals:

- Self-direction and self-reliance
- Flexibility
- Potential profits

Self-Direction and Self-Reliance An individual who has special skills or expertise may create an innovation or become frustrated with working for a company. By starting a new business, the entrepreneur leads the company and oversees all operations.

Flexibility A new business can operate during hours set by the owner. The entrepreneur can choose vacation days and holidays, as well as his or her work schedule. There is a great deal of flexibility in terms of opening and closing times.

Many entrepreneurs may begin their businesses at home and later move to a commercial office or building. Businesses such as delivery services, repair shops, and others may not require an office location. A professional writer, personal trainer, or consultant might set up a business in a garage, basement, or guest house.

Potential Profits The greatest incentive for starting a new company is that a sole proprietor keeps all the profits. Many small businesses generate substantial profits for their owners. Some owners pass on their businesses to their children. Others develop businesses that become so lucrative, they can sell the company to a new owner.

Advantages for Others

Small businesses owned by entrepreneurs are common worldwide. In the United States, small businesses and entrepreneurial operations provided nearly 75 percent of all new jobs during the 1990s. That trend is expected to continue domestically and internationally.

Most new products and services reach the market through entrepreneurships. Small business ownership is an alternative to **corporate** America. Entrepreneurs from diverse cultural backgrounds own small businesses. These enterprises have provided a source of goods, services, and income for people throughout the nation.

◄ OPPORTUNITY KNOCKS
With planning and effort, the door to the world of small business ownership is open to everyone. *Besides business opportunities, what other advantages do entrepreneurs have?*

Disadvantages of Entrepreneurship

Not all businesspeople want to start their own companies. Why? There are disadvantages to entrepreneurship. Starting and owning a business requires long hours, complete responsibility for the business, and financial risk.

Entrepreneurs say that when you own a small business, you are either there working or at home worrying about it. Because most entrepreneurs are sole proprietors who do most business tasks by themselves, they may work very long hours.

The level of responsibility is also very high. From the potential for a liability lawsuit to interpersonal problems with employees, a new business owner is responsible for every aspect of the business.

Personal funds are often the source of start-up funds for a small business. The owner can lose this investment because sole proprietors (and partners) have unlimited liability for debts. A major reason that most new companies fail is lack of capital.

✔ **Reading Check** **Recall** What are three disadvantages of entrepreneurial businesses?

Intrapreneurship

The process of starting a new business that is spun off from an existing business is **intrapreneurship**. Sometimes a company creates only a new good or adds a new service to current lines. General Electric, which owns the National Broadcasting Company (NBC), acted as an intrapreneur by creating new spin-off networks under the names MSNBC and CNBC.

A company might develop an entirely new division of its company. For example, General Motors created the Saturn automobile company. Intrapreneurship can mean a separate company is formed.

The primary advantages of intrapreneurship involve financing and expertise. A corporation has access to both internal and external capital as well as skilled and knowledgeable employees.

Political Risk Political risk includes the possibility that a foreign government could take over the company in the event of political upheaval. In addition, the government may change laws affecting business. Those in power who were favorable toward the company may also change positions, which can cause a negative impact on the company.

Economic Risk A company may be affected by a downturn in economic conditions. This economic risk could manifest as higher interests rates, rising unemployment, or other economic factors that could cause a global venture to fail.

Time Risk There is a greater risk of losing money when recovering an investment, or getting the money back, takes a long time. Building a large, expensive plant that will be paid off over many years increases the time risk.

Product Risk Product risk is linked to the product itself. Some products are risky, because they may or may not be accepted. Others are risky because the competition is strong and could dominate the market. Opening a pastry shop in Paris, France, or a computer software company in the United States involves product risk.

Financial Risk Financial risk involves the possibility of losing the money used for all of the costs associated with a global venture. In most cases, recovering an investment in a new business and making a profit can take several years. The global entrepreneur must arrange for distribution, buyers, and a new location in another country. Because the owner must pay for these things up front, there is financial risk associated with the new venture.

Support Systems

A chieving success in global entrepreneurship is more likely when there is support available. This support can come from both international sources and local sources. There is also a wide variety of entrepreneurial organizations that help new businesses, which are listed in **Figure 8.2**.

Figure 8.2

Entrepreneurial Support Organizations

BUSINESS AID These organizations are dedicated to helping entrepreneurs.
Which group might help global entrepreneurs?

- Entrepreneur America
- The Entrepreneur Network
- The Indus Entrepreneurs
- International Council for Small Business
- National Foundation for Teaching Entrepreneurship

- Service Corps of Retired Executives (SCORE)
- Springboard Enterprises
- United States Association for Small Business and Entrepreneurship
- Women Entrepreneurs in Science & Technology
- Young Entrepreneurs Organization

SMALL BUSINESS OWNER

Small business owners are not limited by the physical locations of their flower nurseries, warehouses, or boutiques. E-commerce can help small business owners reach international markets. Thanks to the Internet, small business owners may break into the international market without incurring the expense of opening overseas locations. They can construct cyber-locations in several countries, translate their Web sites into the appropriate languages, and use software technologies to process complex multicurrency sales transactions in seconds. Going global still requires planning, research, and money, but the Internet has made it feasible.

Small business owners hoping to attract international customers online must consider the culture, language, and currency of their target audiences. Products, Web-site design, and the site's communication system must all be tailored to the global marketplace. This requires research that may involve international travel. In addition, small business owners are responsible for knowing national and regional regulations and import and export restrictions.

Skills and Training

Small business owners must be creative, goal-oriented, persistent, independent, self-motivated, self-confident, and enthusiastic. The ability to create long-range plans and to manage risk is essential. Strong communication skills are necessary for working with clients and employees.

Prospective small business owners should take mathematics, accounting, computer technology, and other business courses in high school. They should also gain experience conducting research and developing business plans.

English Language Arts/Writing

How do small business owners benefit from participating in the global marketplace?

@ To learn more about small business owners and their career paths, go to the International Business Online Learning Center through **glencoe.com.**

Career Data

Education: High school diploma, associate's degree, or bachelor's degree

Skills: Mathematical, computer, problem-solving, and communication skills

Outlook: Growth as fast as average in the next ten years

International Support

The international monetary system is a set of international organizations that help individual countries create and participate in trade. There are two segments of the system that help global entrepreneurs: The World Bank and international exchange organizations.

The World Bank The World Bank helps countries develop and participate in international trade. This organization provides money to promising new businesses through loans. The World Bank also seeks out joint ventures: A company or government puts up a portion of the capital, and the World Bank provides the rest.

International Exchange Organizations Other support organizations include the Asian Development Bank (AsDB), the European Bank for Reconstruction and Development (EBRD), and the Inter-American Development Bank (IDB).

Local Support

Many cities in the United States have organizations that support global entrepreneurship. A local chamber of commerce can provide access to other governments and information. States also promote international business. National sources include the U.S. Department of Commerce and the Small Business Administration.

Growing Global Enterprises

Global entrepreneurship will continue to grow everywhere. Today small- to medium-sized businesses are able to compete internationally through means such as the Internet, unimagined 30 years ago. Through careful planning and assessment of all of the factors related to competition, costs, benefits, and risks, an entrepreneur can reach the **goal** of building a new global enterprise.

Quick Check 8.2

After You Read Respond to what you have read by answering these questions.

1. What are the advantages and disadvantages of entrepreneurship? _____

_____

2. On what four levels should a company consider its ability to compete? _____

_____

3. What kinds of support systems are available for global entrepreneurs? _____

_____

Academics / *English Language Arts*

4. Write a paragraph describing your dream global business and its product.

_____

_____

Evaluating a Global Expansion

Research and choose a large company that has not yet expanded into the global marketplace. Write a one-page paper for the president of that company. List the advantages and disadvantages of a global expansion. Also select two potential countries and recommend a mode of entry for each country.

_____

_____

_____

_____

_____

_____

_____

_____

_____

_____

_____

_____

_____

_____

_____

_____

_____

_____

_____

_____

ACADEMICS APPLIED Check off the academic knowledge you used to do this activity:

☐ English Language Arts   ☐ Mathematics   ☐ Social Studies   ☐ Science

ACADEMIC AND CAREER PLAN Add this page to your Academic and Career Plan Portfolio.

CHAPTER SUMMARY

Section 8.1 Types of Ownership

sole proprietorship (p. 185)

partnership (p. 185)

corporation (p. 186)

Subchapter S corporation (p. 187)

limited liability company (LLC) (p. 187)

multinational corporation (MNC) (p. 188)

mode of entry (p. 188)

- Three main types of business ownership are the sole proprietorship, the partnership, and the corporation.

- Most small businesses are sole proprietorships, owned by individual owners. Partnerships allow each partner to bring different skills to the business. Corporations have many owners and can attract large amounts of capital.

- A multinational corporation (MNC) is an organization that operates in more than one country.

- The selection of a particular mode of entry determines the approach a company will use to sell goods and services in another country. Modes of entry include indirect exporting, direct exporting, turnkey projects, licensing, franchising, joint ventures, strategic alliances, wholly owned subsidiaries, and foreign direct investments.

Section 8.2 Entrepreneurship

entrepreneurship (p. 193)

entrepreneur (p. 193)

intrapreneurship (p. 195)

global entrepreneurship (p. 196)

- Entrepreneurship is the process of starting up a new company or business.

- Global entrepreneurship is the process of selling new products, starting a new operating division, or starting up a new company in another country.

CONCEPTS REVIEW

1. **List** the three main types of business ownership.

2. **Describe** the situations in which each of the three main types of business ownership is most effective.

3. **Differentiate** between a solely domestic company and a multinational corporation.

4. **Explain** the term *mode of entry*.

5. **Discuss** the difference between entrepreneurship and intrapreneurship.

6. **Identify** the factors a company should consider regarding its ability to compete when expanding to another country.

KEY TERMS REVIEW

7. Match each term to its definition.

_____ sole proprietorship

_____ partnership

_____ corporation

_____ Subchapter S corporation

_____ limited liability company (LLC)

_____ multinational corporation (MNC)

_____ mode of entry

_____ entrepreneurship

_____ entrepreneur

_____ intrapreneurship

_____ global entrepreneurship

a. a type of business ownership in which two or more people own the business

b. an organization that operates in more than one country

c. a person who starts a new business

d. a type of business ownership in which one person owns the business

e. a corporation that is taxed like a partnership

f. the process of selling new products, starting a new operating division, or starting up a new company in another country

g. the process of starting a new business that is spun off from an existing business

h. the process of starting up a new company or business

i. a company whose owners and managers enjoy limited liability and some tax benefits

j. a type of business ownership in which many people, whom the law treats as one person, own the business

k. the method a company uses to sell products in another country

Academic Vocabulary

8. On a separate sheet of paper, write a sentence or two related to international business using at least three of the academic terms you learned in the section openers:

- consist
- structure
- role
- seek
- corporate
- goal

Critical Thinking

9. Research the history of the Chrysler Corporation under Lee Iacocca's leadership and the General Electric Corporation under Jack Welch. Report about how they resembled sole proprietors.

Discussion Starter

10. Using the Internet and print sources, do research on franchises available for less than $30,000. Report to the class on a franchise in which you would invest and explain why.

Point of View

11. Research the problems associated with the partnership type of business and sole proprietorships. Prepare a short report explaining why you would choose either form of ownership.

BUILDING REAL-WORLD SKILLS

 The GLOBAL WORKPLACE

12. Multinational Networking Some of the same principles of personal networking apply to establishing beneficial relationships between multinational corporations. For example, strategic alliances between General Electric and Snecma, Canon and Hewlett Packard, and Mitsubishi and Caterpillar have been successful.

Research and Share

a. Describe to the class an example of successful multinational corporate networking.

b. Discuss what draws the participants together in such relationships.

 **The U.S. WORKPLACE**

13. Prioritizing Tasks Prioritizing is a vital aspect of an efficient workplace. A good system helps a worker identify the relative importance of her or his tasks. The priorities then become the basis for scheduling and completion of the tasks. The best prioritization systems are those created by the user. However, using an existing system is a good place to start.

Research and Write

a. Research prioritization systems in use in the United States.

b. Create your own system with explanations of each level. Present it to the class.

BUILDING ACADEMIC SKILLS

ELA English Language Arts

14. Starting a small business may allow women who face the "glass ceiling" to avoid discrimination. Research and write a short essay on the origins of the term *glass ceiling* and how it applies to today's workplace.

MATH Mathematics

15. You need to order 1,500 cardboard boxes to ship tulip bulbs from your nursery to destinations around the globe. You would like to order 9" × 12" boxes, but the company from which you plan to buy the boxes is in Winnipeg, Canada, and uses the metric system. Calculate the size of each box in centimeters.

Measurement To solve this problem, you need to understand units of measurement for different systems of measurements and apply math formulas.

SOC Social Studies/Political Science

16. Political risk is a big concern for entrepreneurs expanding businesses to other countries. The potential loss of an entire investment due to change in government policies can deter plans. Research what happened to Cuba's business community, both domestic and foreign, after Fidel Castro took over leadership of that country. Write a two-page report on your findings for the class.

SOC Social Studies/History

17. One of the longest-running and most profitable entrepreneurial ventures in the history of international trade began in the early 1600s. The British East India Company grew from a small trading company chartered by the British Crown. It achieved the position of pseudo-ruler over India and other British colonies. Research and write a one-page report on the history of this company.

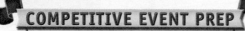

COMPETITIVE EVENT PREP

Choosing a Business Organization

18. Situation As the chief financial officer (CEO) for a small sporting goods company in your state, you see an opportunity to expand your business in South America. You want to raise capital to fund a new production facility in Chile, but you must examine how secure your company's investment would be. Your company is a Subchapter S corporation. Three members of a local family own the stock. One member holds a majority share of 54 percent, and the other two hold 26 percent and 20 percent.

Activity Research the financial situation in Chile. Research rules associated with Subchapter S corporations. Research other types of companies: partnerships, corporations, LLPs, and LLCs. Look at other funding methods.

Evaluation You will be evaluated on how well you meet the following objectives:

a. Discuss investing in Chile from a historical perspective.

b. Explain the pros and cons of each type of business.

c. Make a recommendation to the company.

Goa, India

Using the Internet, find the location of Goa. Notice its advantageous location for trade. Answer the following questions about Goa on a separate sheet of paper.

➤ Research Goa's unique role in international trade, past and present.

➤ Explain the advantages of entering the Indian market, utilizing Goa as a main port for trade.

@ For resources to help you do this exercise, go to the International Business Online Learning Center through **glencoe.com**.

BusinessWeek online

19. Newsclip: A Pocket-Size Famine Fighter Entrepreneur Fatchima Cissé has teamed up with the French company that invented vitamin-packed Plumpy'nut to help feed Niger's malnourished children.

@ Go to the International Business Online Learning Center through **glencoe.com** to read an article about this topic. Write a paragraph about what motivates social entrepreneurs.

Standardized Test Practice

20. Read the paragraph and choose the best answer to the following multiple-choice question.

When an entrepreneur starts a new business, typically, one of four results occurs: The company survives but stays small; the company grows and becomes a major corporation; the company is purchased and merges with another company; or the company fails.

What is the main idea of the paragraph?

❍ Starting a company can result in different outcomes.
❍ An entrepreneur is someone who starts a new business.
❍ New companies are started daily.
❍ Many companies merge with others.

Test-Taking Tip The main idea of a paragraph is usually a general statement. To identify the best answer to this question, note that most of the potential choices provide specific details, not a general idea.

Organizational Management and Strategy

Chapter Objectives

When you have completed this chapter, you will be able to:

Section 9.1

- Describe the job of manager at each level in a company.
- Explain the planning process.
- Explain the strategic management process.
- Represent the structure of a company in an organizational chart.

Section 9.2

- Explain how the processes of leadership and influence affect business organizations.
- Describe how control procedures benefit a company.

STANDARD &POOR'S — CASE STUDY

► AMAZON.COM

Amazon.com is a publicly owned corporation whose shares are traded on the stock exchanges. When you research this company through Standard & Poor's, you will find investment information such as this:

Index:	S&P Global 1200 and S&P 500
Sector:	Consumer Discretionary
Company:	Amazon Corporation
Symbol:	AMZN
Country:	USA
Price:	(varies)

Global Profile In Amazon's first month of operation during 1995, founder Jeff Bezos the e-tail pioneer received book orders from all 50 states and 45 countries. Since then Amazon.com has become the Web's premiere retail site, selling books, CDs, DVDs, video games, cell phones, electronic goods, toys, housewares, and sporting goods. Amazon.com operates Web sites in the United Kingdom, Germany, Japan, France, Canada, and China.

Business Report Employing more than 9,000 people globally, Amazon operates each Web site using a similar platform and strategy in every country: Sell a vast selection of items for a low cost with an emphasis on convenience. This strategy and the growth of the Internet have contributed to the increase in Amazon's stock value for investors in the corporation with annual sales of $8.5 billion.

English Language Arts/Writing

Amazon.com pioneered strategies for suggesting other items that a person is likely to buy while making an online purchase. When a customer selects an item, other items also appear which were ordered by customers with similar tastes. Returning customers see a selection of items that may fit their tastes. *Write a paragraph about strategies that you notice on other e-tail sites and why they are or are not effective.*

To do this activity, go to the International Business Online Learning Center through **glencoe.com**.

Planning and Organizing Processes

WHAT YOU'LL LEARN

- To describe the job of manager at each level in a company
- To explain the planning process
- To explain the strategic management process
- To represent the structure of a company in an organizational chart

WHY IT'S IMPORTANT

Understanding the role and processes of management will help you succeed in international business.

KEY TERMS

- management
- planning
- strategic plan
- differentiation
- organizing
- authority
- decentralization

Academic Vocabulary

You will find these words in your reading and on your tests. Make sure you know their meanings.

- perceive
- regulate
- feature

Reading Guide

Before You Read

What is the difference between doing and managing?

MAIN IDEA

Effective management and planning move a company toward its goals.

GRAPHIC ORGANIZER

Draw this chart. As you read this section, write in the three levels of management and a brief description of each.

Levels of Management	
1.	
2.	
3.	

Management Processes

In business, there is a huge difference between doing and managing. **Management** is the process of getting things done through other people. One of the most common mistakes made by new managers is not delegating tasks. Instead of showing others how to work effectively, many new managers try to do it all themselves. Successful managers help others perform quality work instead of doing it all themselves.

Usually, a manager gets promoted to that position because he or she is highly skilled and effective at some activity. A successful salesperson may become a sales manager; a gifted computer expert may become the manager of the company's information systems department; or a top-flight accountant might become the manager of the accounting department.

This chapter examines several key concepts from the world of management:

- The job of manager
- Management functions
- Strategic management
- Organizing processes

To succeed in international business, you need to clearly **perceive** the principles of management. Then you can apply those principles to the international environment.

The Job of Manager

A common analogy compares a manager to the captain of a ship. Managers are found at practically every level of a company. The highest-ranking manager is the president, CEO (chief executive officer), or executive director. This person is most like the captain of the ship. Managers on other levels, however, fill in the ranks. **Figure 9.1** illustrates three levels of management:

1. Top-level management
2. Middle management
3. First-line supervision

Top-Level Managers

Top-level managers are responsible for setting goals and planning for the future. The president, CEO, and key vice presidents make up what is called the "top-level management team" in large organizations and corporations. They provide the overall direction for a company.

Middle Managers

Middle managers carry out decisions and plans made by top management. They are normally involved with the different tasks that a company performs, such as production, human resources, accounting, or sales. A middle manager can be head of a region.

First-Line Supervisors

First-line supervisors, or operational managers, **regulate** the daily operations of the business. They hold titles such as office manager, crew chief, head server, nursing supervisor, shift manager, foreperson, and others. These managers directly supervise individual workers.

Figure 9.1

Levels of Management

MOVING UP The job of manager varies on different levels. *On what level does a manager do the most delegating?*

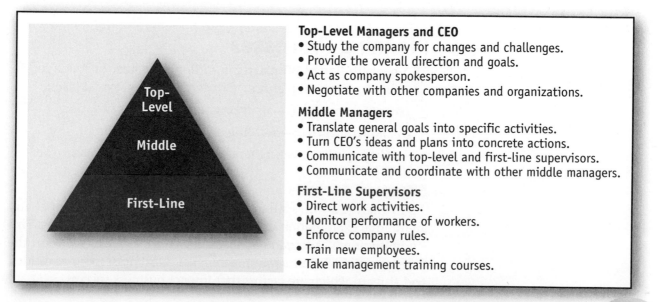

Top-Level Managers and CEO
- Study the company for changes and challenges.
- Provide the overall direction and goals.
- Act as company spokesperson.
- Negotiate with other companies and organizations.

Middle Managers
- Translate general goals into specific activities.
- Turn CEO's ideas and plans into concrete actions.
- Communicate with top-level and first-line supervisors.
- Communicate and coordinate with other middle managers.

First-Line Supervisors
- Direct work activities.
- Monitor performance of workers.
- Enforce company rules.
- Train new employees.
- Take management training courses.

Management Skills

Each level of management requires three skills: conceptual skills, human relations skills, and technical skills.

Conceptual Skills Top-level managers utilize conceptual skills. They should know how their part of the operation fits into the overall direction of the company and how all operations work together: Production has to mesh with quality control, sales, marketing, accounting, finance, and every other activity. Top-level managers anticipate financial needs for new plants and equipment. They are also skilled at working with others (human relations) and retain technical skills.

Human Relations Skills Managers use human-relations skills to manage workers. They must possess some technical skills so they can "speak the language" of first-line supervisors and workers. The human-relations skills required for middle managers are somewhat different from those needed by other managers. They must know how to manage and lead others—to be the boss. At the same time, they must also know how to carry out the orders and directions of top managers—to have a boss.

Technical Skills Technical skills are used the most by first-line supervisors. They must know how to operate production machines, fill out daily reports, schedule workers, and take care of daily activities and technical problems.

Management Functions

Each management function is a key ingredient in the success of the company. All managers are involved in all of the major management functions:

- Planning
- Organizing
- Directing
- Control

Planning Processes

The definition of **planning** is outlining a course of action for the future. A typical planning process **features** several tasks:

- **Situation analysis**—analyzing the company's situation
- **Decision making**—deciding on a course of action
- **Setting goals**—creating targets to implement the plan

Situation Analysis

To analyze a firm's situation, management does an external and an internal examination of the factors that impact the company. This study is known as a *situation analysis*. A company can focus on the four factors of a SWOT analysis: **s**trengths, **w**eaknesses, **o**pportunities, and **t**hreats, which are factors that impact business success.

Outside the Company The world around a company constantly changes. Economic conditions, technological changes, and many other forces present problems and opportunities. Consider a drastic rise in the cost of oil. Airlines, trucking firms, and many other companies must find ways to keep making profits as costs rise.

Inside the Company Some products a company makes sell while others fail. Managers must adjust the product line as a result. The firm may lose a key salesperson with loyal customers. The sales department must decide how to handle the loss.

Top-level executives examine the strengths and weaknesses of their firm and develop plans to correct problems and take advantage of strengths.

GAS GUZZLING A change in one factor, such as oil prices, can have a major impact on many companies. *Can you think of another business, besides shipping, that would be affected by high gas prices?*

Decision Making

Decision making plays a key role in creating good plans. Company leaders must decide what to do. Based on a situation analysis, company leaders can discover the areas where the firm has the best chance of succeeding.

Decision making also involves deciding what *not* to do. For example, company leaders may discover a new technology that will lead to many new products. This situation occurred when digital technologies first emerged. However, not every company can design and sell digital equipment.

Steps of Decision Making

When managers use the decision-making steps, the odds of making a good decision increase. The decision-making process includes six steps:

1. **State the problem in a positive way.** For example: "We are looking for a way to improve sales by 10 percent next year."

2. **Identify key limitations.** Limitations often include not having time, money, technology, or skilled people to make a change.

3. **Generate creative alternatives.** Look for new and innovative ways to solve problems.

4. **Evaluate alternatives.** This is normally done by examining the "pros and cons," or benefits and problems, of each alternative.

5. **Choose a solution and state the reason you chose it.** Solutions are usually combinations of alternatives, such as when a company cuts prices and increases advertising expenditures to increase sales.

6. **State a plan of implementation.** This plan includes who is in charge and what is to be done when, where, and how.

Setting Goals

The third crucial ingredient in an effective planning process is goal setting. A simple list of characteristics that define effective goals is known as *SMART goals*—specific, measurable, achievable, realistic, and time bound. Goals are targets for everyone, from the individual salesperson trying to meet a sales quota to the CEO trying to achieve a profit goal for the company. Planning begins and ends with goals.

Strategic Plan and Strategic Management

Plans are often divided into three categories: 1) short-term, 2) medium-range, and 3) long-term plans. Short-term plans cover one year or less. Medium-range plans are for one, two, or three years. Long-term plans affect a company for three years or more.

A company's long-term plan is also called its **strategic plan**. A strategic plan is made for three situations. Examples of the three types of strategies are displayed in **Figure 9.2**. Notice that some plans emphasize rapid growth. Rapid growth normally takes place when the company's leaders identify a significant opportunity. Many years ago, the management team at Bic® discovered a trend: People liked disposable products. Bic had been selling only ballpoint pens. To take advantage of the trend, the company expanded by adding razors, lighters, and other disposable items. The company grew quickly as a result. This form of growth is based on product diversification.

Sometimes the strategic direction of a company is best served by slower growth. When a company adds customers or becomes more efficient, it grows in sales, profits, or both. When a company is in trouble, it might use decline strategies. The company eliminates either locations, products, employees, or an entire section of the company.

Internationalization Strategy

Starting up an internationalization project is a medium-to rapid-growth strategy. For example, a company is looking for new markets to greatly increase its sales. It must analyze the external market.

Figure 9.2

Types of Strategies

GROWING OR SHRINKING
Most companies use one of these types of strategies.
When is a decline strategy the best option for a company?

Decline	Slow Growth	Rapid Growth
Closing locations	Adding new customers	Product diversification, or adding new products or services
Leaving entire market areas	Increasing profits by becoming more efficient (includes outsourcing)	
Eliminating employees		Merging with or taking over another company
Selling fewer products or services		Joint venture with another company

The Flavor of UVAN

In 1990, World Bank experts verified Aga Sekalala's theory that growing the vanilla bean in Uganda could be a viable business. With their support, he gained funding for his company UVAN. Sekalala then opened a vanilla-processing plant to make one of the world's most popular flavorings. The plant is on a dusty road in Gayaza, a small town outside of Kampala, Uganda. There, locals dry and steam vanilla for export to America, the world's biggest buyer of vanilla.

The vanilla bean, grown in Uganda prior to political unrest, is a difficult crop to manage. The finicky bean must be pollinated and picked by hand, making it more appropriate for a family of farmers to manage, instead of a large agribusiness. UVAN provides information to farmers, secures loans for them, and then processes their beans. In addition, the company assists farmers with school fees, taxes, and other expenses. The finished product is sold to businesses, such as soft drink manufacturers and ice cream companies.

Because there is a low supply of vanilla globally and no quality artificial substitute, the demand for the product is high. Vanilla exporters Malaysia, Madagascar, and Indonesia were hit with storms that destroyed crops during the 1990s and early 2000s. The Ugandans have been ready to fill the demand in the world marketplace.

THINK GLOBALLY *Why would local farmers associate with a company such as UVAN?*

 To learn more about the country of origin for this global business, go to the International Business Online Learning Center through **glencoe.com**.

Other Strategies

There is one other way to think about strategies. Most companies will compete by using one of two strategies:

1. Cost and price
2. Differentiation

As You Read

Relate Have you ever purchased one product over another based solely on price?

Cost-and-Price Strategies When a company competes based on cost and price, its goal is to find efficient ways to produce and deliver goods. The end price is then lower. In the world of retailing, Wal-Mart® is a company that competes with low costs and low prices. As Wal-Mart expands into new nations, its overall strategic approach based on cost and price remains a key selling point.

Differentiation Strategies A company may compete based on quality. **Differentiation** is a strategy of developing and delivering products that are different and better than others in the same industry. For example, Saks Fifth Avenue competes by using a differentiation strategy in retail sales—it carries high-end luxury items. Many U.S. firms enter new international markets with products that are simply better. There is also a middle ground. Japanese companies such as Toyota and Sony have been successful by selling products that offer a reasonable price plus quality.

Outsourcing

Some U.S. companies outsource jobs to foreign workers who will work for lower pay than their American counterparts. Moving manufacturing jobs overseas allows companies to close their expensive U.S. factories. Recently, companies have also started to move their skilled work offshore. For example, Penske Truck Leasing outsources its data-processing jobs to Genpact's Mexican and Indian call centers. Some critics argue that outsourcing "steals" jobs from American workers, but reducing cost increases productivity and efficiency and results in lower prices for the consumer. *Do you think it is ethical to lay off U.S. workers as a result of outsourcing? Why or why not?*

Organizing Processes

There are two similar terms in business: *organization* and *organizing*. They are different things. An organization is a group of people working together for a common cause or goal. Organizations can be profit-seeking, nonprofit, or governmental. An easy way to decide if a group of people has created an organization is to look for two things:

1. A leader
2. Separate tasks for individual members

Organizing is a process that brings together people and materials or technology in an organization to make a product. Organizing is a managerial activity. An organization is a group of people doing certain activities. Organizing has three distinct parts:

- Job design
- Departmentalization
- Creation of authority relationships for the organization

Reading Check **Analyze** What is the difference between organization and organizing?

Job Design

Job design is usually assigned to the human resources (HR) department. HR staff writes job descriptions that tell each worker what to do and what not to do as part of the job.

Departmentalization

The term *departmentalization* may sound complicated. However, it is not a difficult concept to understand. Departmentalization, or organization, is simply the process of placing jobs and workers into departments. Departments can be organized in several different ways.

Departmentalization by Function The most common and simple form of departmentalization uses job functions to create departments. One set of workers puts the product together. They all work in the production department. Two groups of workers sell the product. They form the sales department and marketing department. Another group takes care of the money in the accounting department.

A small company usually sells or delivers only one major product. Examples include a family-owned restaurant, a small-town newspaper, a dry-cleaning store, or a single-unit insurance agency. Small companies use departmentalization by function. Departmentalization by function would rarely be used in an international company.

Departmentalization by Product As companies grow, they find new customers and create new sales by adding additional goods or services. This type of strategic plan is called "product diversification." The strategy may require a change in company structure. The new organizational form would be "departmentalization by product."

When the management team at Bic decided to sell other disposable items, they began producing razors and lighters. They also began departmentalizing by product. Some tasks remained the same, such as accounting and human resources, but others became part of new departments. For example, a pen-making production department made pens, while a razor sales department focused on selling razors.

Departmentalization by Geographic Area If you have traveled around the United States, you have probably noticed that one Sears store looks quite a bit like all the other Sears stores. Every McDonald's and Arby's is very similar to units in other towns. All over the country, Bank of America branches resemble one another.

This structure is called "departmentalization by geographic area." The company is divided up by regions. Managers carry titles such as zone manager, regional manager, or district manager.

Matrix Organizations The most unique form of departmentalization is a matrix organization, or two-boss system. A matrix organization divides the management team into two groups: those who manage products and those who manage functions or activities. Then every single person or group answers to one of each—a product manager and a functional boss.

The matrix organization is best suited to project-type companies around the world. Once the project is complete, the unit dissolves, and people are reassigned. When the departments have been created, the final step is to put someone in charge.

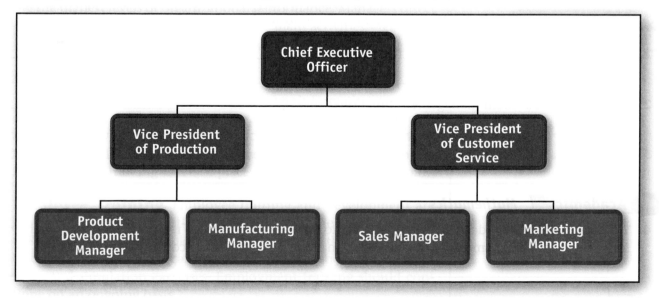

Figure 9.3

Organization by Function

HIERARCHY Organizational charts offer a visual representation of a company's structure. *Who might be subordinate to the sales manager? How would you illustrate this?*

- Chief Executive Officer
  - Vice President of Production
    - Product Development Manager
    - Manufacturing Manager
  - Vice President of Customer Service
    - Sales Manager
    - Marketing Manager

BUILDING REAL-WORLD SKILLS

12. Budgeting for Benefits Packages
One of the major devices used in planning is budgeting. The amounts assigned to the different elements of a corporation's budget provide a means of control. One of the primary elements in such a budget is labor costs. In the United States and other nations, workers often receive an hourly wage and benefits.

Research and Share

a. Find examples of the benefits packages offered to auto workers in Sweden, the United States, Japan, and Mexico. List the types of benefits these workers receive.

b. Rank the packages from best to worst. Share your conclusions with the class.

13. Performance Evaluations
In many organizations the quality control and human relations departments overlap where employee performance evaluations are concerned. The use of various types of evaluations provides a measure of control over the quality of employees.

Research and Write

a. Research these types of employee performance evaluations.

b. Prepare a short paper expressing your opinion of the relative worth of each evaluation measure.

BUILDING ACADEMIC SKILLS

ELA English Language Arts

14. One function of the Human Resources (HR) department is to write job descriptions. Write a realistic job description of your ideal job. Then explain how you plan to prepare yourself to qualify for the position.

MATH Mathematics

15. A large span of control may reduce overall effectiveness of an organization. A manager should have only four to seven people to supervise. On an assembly line, ten people per one supervisor is the limit. Consider, an entire company is comprised of one Chief Executive Officer (CEO) and five layers of employees under her. Each manager (including the CEO) supervises five people. How many employees does the company have?

Computation and Estimation To solve this problem, you need to understand the principles of multiplication and addition.

SOC Social Studies/Sociology

16. One interesting theory focusing on organizational behavior is expressed in a book entitled *The Peter Principle*. Research what the author, Dr. Laurence J. Peter, means by this principle. Write a definition of it and provide a hypothetical example of the theory in a company. Discuss its application in today's world.

SOC Social Studies/World Languages

17. Many multinational companies must decide which language(s) to use for meetings and correspondence. Instead of unifying the company, the choice of one language or two, to the exclusion of others, may produce problems. Research the factors that should be considered in such a decision. Prepare a recommendation for the class about how a corporate language(s) should be chosen.

COMPETITIVE EVENT PREP

Promoting Quality Offshore

18. **Situation** Your company wants to improve the quality of its digital games coming out of its offshore plant in Malaysia. While the labor costs are advantageous, the product failure rate is unacceptable. You believe your company should apply Dr. W. Edwards Deming's philosophy of building in quality.

    Activity Evaluate the culture and technological capacity of Malaysia. Research Deming's 14 principles and relate the history of his involvement in Japanese production to possible issues in Malaysia. Design a plan to promote quality.

    Evaluation You will be evaluated on how well you meet the following objectives:

    a. Correctly define related elements of Deming's work.

    b. Prepare a plan of action for your company.

    c. Consider the potential for other companies to develop a competitive strategy similar to your plan.

BusinessWeek online

19. **Newsclip: A Game Plan for Global Growth** Many companies are "going global." But increasing sales in China and India may not be enough. Companies must match their organizational strategy to their long-term goals.

    @ Go to the International Business Online Learning Center through **glencoe.com** to read an article about this topic. Then write a paragraph that describes how organizational strategy impacts a company's ability to compete overseas.

Internet Travels

North Korea

Using the Internet, find a map of North Korea. Note especially its size and resources. Answer the following questions about North Korea on a separate sheet of paper.

➤ Research North Korea's type of government and economy.

➤ Identify the managerial style that is typical in North Korean government and industry.

@ For resources to help you do this exercise, go to the International Business Online Learning Center through **glencoe.com**.

Standardized Test Practice

20. Read the paragraph below, and then select the best answer to the question that follows.

    In general, top managers are responsible for setting goals and planning for the future. Middle managers carry out the decisions and plans made by top management. These managers are normally associated with production, human resources, accounting, or sales. First-line supervisors take care of daily operations. They hold titles such as office manager, crew chief, head server....

    Which of the following statements is not correct?
    ○ The goals for the company are set by top management.
    ○ A middle manager may be involved with human resources.
    ○ An office manager is a part of a management team.
    ○ All of the above are correct.

Test-Taking Tip As you read, pick out the main idea and key terms. This will help you answer questions about the paragraph you just read.

Chapter 10

Production and Quality Control

Chapter Objectives

When you have completed this chapter, you will be able to:

Section 10.1

- Discuss the importance of quality and value in production systems.
- Explain how businesses choose which goods and services to make and export.

Section 10.2

- Identify the elements of a quality production or manufacturing system.
- Identify the systems used for the process of quality control.
- Describe the latest programs designed to improve quality.

▶ STARBUCKS

Starbucks Corporation is a publicly owned corporation whose shares are traded on the stock exchanges. When you research this company through Standard & Poor's, you will find investment information such as this:

Index:	S&P Global 1200
Sector:	Consumer Discretionary
Company:	Starbucks Corporation
Symbol:	SBUX
Country:	U.S.A.
Price:	(varies)

Global Profile Starbucks is the world's number-one specialty coffee retailer with locations in more than 30 countries. Shops offer coffee drinks, food, exotic coffee beans, coffee accessories, teas, and music CDs. As an expanding music outlet that also provides CD burning services, the stores sell more than 3.5 million CDs annually.

Business Report Starbucks operates some 11,000 coffee shops, employing more than 96,700 people worldwide. As a franchiser, Starbucks operates about 4,200 stores. Other franchises include Seattle's Best Coffee and Torrefazione in the United States. The company sales exceeded $6,369,000,000 for 2005. Despite competition, analysts strongly favor Starbucks stock over the long term.

English Language Arts/Writing

Starbucks coffee first percolated in a small Seattle coffee house in 1971. Two decades later, the Starbucks brand went global. Noted as a "culture-defining brand" in the United States, its stores readily adapt to the cultures in Canada, England, Australia, Singapore, Germany, China, Chile, Ireland, and Thailand. *Research and write a one-page paper identifying possible quality standards set by Starbucks that have led to international success.*

To do this activity, go to the International Business Online Learning Center through **glencoe.com**.

Production Processes

WHAT YOU'LL LEARN

- To discuss the importance of quality and value in production systems
- To explain how businesses choose which goods and services to make and export

WHY IT'S IMPORTANT

One key to success in international business is developing quality products and services that meet the needs of foreign customers. They also must be sold at a good price.

KEY TERMS

- quality
- value
- standardization
- adaptation
- sourcing

Academic Vocabulary

You will find these words in your reading and on your tests. Make sure you know their meanings.

- assess
- volume
- automate

Reading Guide

Before You Read

What is the difference between quality and value?

MAIN IDEA

Businesses must carefully consider various factors before deciding to export a product or produce it in another country.

GRAPHIC ORGANIZER

Draw this table. As you read, list characteristics of high quality, low quality, high value, and low value.

	Quality	Value
High		
Low		

Production Management

Have you ever heard of a "widget"? A widget is a hypothetical product made by a hypothetical company. A widget represents a good or a service. In this chapter, you will be looking at widgets. The essence of business is producing a "widget" that someone else is willing to buy. The production process is a crucial part of every company's operations.

Since the 1980s, two words have been regularly associated with production—quality and value. **Quality** is the level of excellence present in a product. A low-quality product has a low level of excellence. It is poorly made and may break easily. A high-quality product has a high level of excellence. It is useful, helpful, or in some way contributes to the buyer's well-being. A high-quality product is one that will not easily break or become damaged. **Value** is the degree of quality as compared to the price or cost of a product. High value means you can buy good quality at a reasonable price. Low value means you are paying too much for the quality of a product.

Deciding What to Produce

The first challenge in the area of production is to decide about the design of a product. The choice is whether to use standardization or adaptation. **Standardization** is the practice of making a product the same, without modification, for all markets. A ballpoint pen can be standardized. Many component parts, such as ball bearings, screws, and sophisticated parts such as Pentium® processors for computers are standardized.

Adaptation is the process of adjusting or modifying a product to fit the needs of a particular market, country, or region. Managers must select the goods and services that will be appropriate candidates for exporting and/or producing in another country.

When making the decision to enter a foreign market with a new product, company managers consider three types of factors:

- Country factors
- Technological factors
- Product factors

✓ **Reading Check** **Recall** What does the term *adaptation* mean?

Country Factors

Managers must ensure that products appeal to the target country. **Figure 10.1** on page 232 illustrates the six main country factors. Culture is one country factor. Customs, religious practices, and mores and folkways are all aspects of a country's culture. People in the United States enjoy the convenience and speed of ready-to-eat food products and fast-food restaurants. The same is not true around the world. In some cultures, food preparation and consumption customs have a different meaning and level of importance to family life.

Trade barriers are an important country factor. A product cannot be exported successfully if there are quotas, tariffs, and other governmental efforts to keep competition out.

Location is also a vital factor. Countries located away from trade routes face disadvantages in exporting. Both importers and exporters need access to quality transportation systems such as rail, roads, or rivers.

The exchange rate is a crucial factor. A product must be sold at a price that results in profits. A country's unstable currency can be a major warning signal not to try to export the product to that country.

Managers also study a country's political and legal system. They consider issues including its liability laws, labor laws, and the tax system before deciding to sell a product in another country. A product must succeed in the political environment where it is being made and/or sold.

National resources are an especially important country factor. To make an item, a country and a company must have, or be able to acquire, key inputs. These inputs include three resources: natural resources, human resources, and capital resources. Inputs are the factors of production that combine to produce output of goods and services.

How Do You Say?

Q: In Japanese, how do you say: "Happy birthday!"

A: めでとう! 誕生日お (pronounced: Ōtăn-jō-bā ōmādātō!)

ⓠ To learn this phrase in other languages, go to the International Business Online Learning Center through **glencoe.com**.

Figure 10.1

Country Factors

WHERE TO EXPORT A company's decision to export its product to another country and/or make it there depends on many factors within the country. *What natural resources affect the decision to produce a good in another country?*

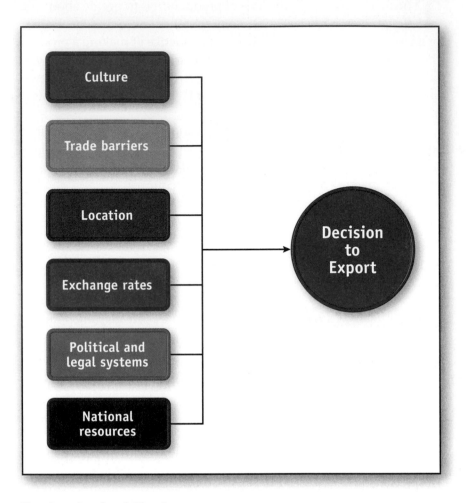

Technological Factors

Technology is a key factor in the decision-making process. When making export decisions or considering whether to open a plant overseas, managers study these factors that are related to technology:

- Fixed costs
- The minimum efficient scale
- The availability of flexible manufacturing technology

Fixed Costs Fixed costs are the actual costs of building and running the production plant, equipment, computers, and other parts of a technology system. These costs do not vary from year to year. Sometimes fixed costs are high. A company that manufactures cars, refrigerators, or other durable goods normally has high fixed costs. In those cases, it is more likely that the item will be produced in the home country and shipped elsewhere. If fixed costs are low, then the entire manufacturing and selling operation can be set up in another country.

The Minimum Efficient Scale The minimum efficient scale is a measure of the cost of each unit, or item, produced by a manufacturing operation. As a company produces more items in the same plant, the production cost for each one is reduced.

There are two reasons for this reduction. First, each item is "charged" with a percentage of the fixed costs as part of the price for that item. If the fixed costs in a plant are $100,000 per year, and the plant produces 100,000 units during the year, the fixed cost per unit is $1 each. If the plant produces 200,000 units in the next year and fixed costs do not increase, the fixed cost per unit drops to 50 cents each.

The second reason for reduced production costs is that, as a producer makes more goods, the producer is able to buy raw materials at a lower price per unit. This is because raw materials cost less as you buy more. For example, a raw materials company may charge $1,000 for 1,000 pounds of an item, but only $1,700 if 2,000 pounds are purchased. This means the cost per unit of the raw material will be lower. Lower costs lead to lower prices.

Flexible Manufacturing Technology The availability of a flexible manufacturing technology influences exporting decisions. A company that can easily adapt production of a good for sale in another country has flexible manufacturing technology. So, the company is more likely to export to the new country.

Product Factors

There are two product factors that company leaders may consider before exporting an item:

- Value-to-weight ratio
- Degree of acceptance

Value-to-weight ratio compares the price of the item to the cost of shipping that item. Items that are heavier have a lower value-to-weight ratio because it costs more to ship them. Cell phones, makeup products such as lipstick, and component parts often have higher value-to-weight ratios because they are light and sell for relatively higher prices. Higher ratios mean lower shipping costs.

The second product factor to consider is the degree of acceptance by consumers in a country. A product that has low levels of acceptance in several countries is less likely to be a choice for future export. Products that have high or "universal" acceptance are better candidates to be shipped to other nations. Food products, construction items such as nails and screws, and many raw materials have the highest degree of acceptance.

Managers **assess** country factors, technological factors, and product factors in order to make an informed decision about whether an item is a good candidate for exporting. There are other considerations that may also impact the decision.

Labels and Packaging

The final set of considerations about a new product does not relate to the product itself. A company must consider the packaging and labels that cover the product. Managers need to understand the legal, cultural, and practical factors involved with product labels and packaging.

ETHICS & ISSUES

Truth in Labeling?

Misleading labels and packages cause major problems for importers and consumers around the world. Sometimes the label does not accurately state what is contained in the package. For example, a label might indicate the package contains "pure" vitamin E gel capsules or 100 percent organic coffee when those claims are not entirely true. Recently, some big food manufacturers asked the U.S. Congress to allow them to label certain products "organic" even when they contain non-organic ingredients. Using misleading packages and labels may lead to a short-term gain in profit. Sooner or later, however, importers and customers look for producers who deliver what they promised. *Have you ever been misled by a package or label? What was it? Did this affect your opinion of the company that made that product?*

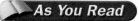 **As You Read**

Relate Do you read package labels? If so, what do you look for and why?

WHAT IS IT? A product must have the right package and label for the country where it will be shipped. *Do you think labels in all countries include the same information? Why or why not?*

Legal Factors

The legal factors concern what can and cannot be printed on a package or label. Most countries insist on some description of the product contained in a package. This includes statements about its **volume**, weight, contents, and, in some cases, the quality of the product. Laws also describe what cannot be printed on a package or label. Depending on the country, this may include false product claims or certain images.

Cultural Factors

The label should also match the culture of a country. Important characteristics include colors, symbols, and brand names. The label should make its contents clear, using language and art that are appropriate for the culture.

Practical Factors

Practical factors also affect packaging around the world. The package usually identifies what is inside. A package should protect its contents. It should withstand refrigeration, freezing, or heat. It should not easily tear or lose its label.

When the company has met all of the packaging and labeling requirements, it can move forward with the production process. When certain goods and services meet requirements, preparations begin for shipping the products out of the country.

Producing Goods and Services

The next step is to design an effective production process. Both goods and services have some physical features. The physical feature of a good is the product itself, such as a skateboard or CD. A service has some physical elements too, such as sales brochures, paperwork, and contracts. Even an Internet service such as Google® has physical elements that might include the computer systems that deliver the information.

Nissan's Global Ride

Nissan made the first mass-produced vehicles in Japan, which were also among the first Japanese vehicles to enter the American automobile market. Originally calling its brand "Datsun," the company started out with compact passenger vehicles. Then it made a name for itself with sports cars, such as the 2000 Roadster, and the Patrol, an early utility vehicle. The Japanese automaker opened its first plant in North America in 1966, and in 1968 it introduced its first model aimed at the American market. By 1973, the millionth Datsun sold in America.

With sales boosted by the energy crisis, the company continued to prosper in the 1970s with its fuel-efficient imports. Although the Datsun name was changed by 1984, after the company rededicated its brand as "Nissan," the manufacturer remained strong. With its popular trucks, luxury cars, famed racing division, and award-winning design team, Nissan is the second-largest Japanese auto manufacturer with a worldwide presence.

THINK GLOBALLY *What are some advantages of Nissan manufacturing its cars in the United States?*

To learn more about the country of origin for this global business, go to the International Business Online Learning Center through **glencoe.com**.

The goal of production is to set up a system through which a good or service is delivered with the best possible quality at the lowest possible cost. It applies to any physical good, from a small screwdriver to heavy industrial equipment, and to any service, such as a credit card or a travel reservation service.

The Make-or-Buy Decision

One important decision a company must make in the area of production is the make-or-buy decision. This decision relates to sourcing. **Sourcing** is the process of locating and acquiring component parts for a final product. The company must decide whether to make or to buy its products' component parts.

Make-Sourcing

A make-sourcing decision means that a company will produce all the components internally. Companies that produce parts for their own manufacturing processes are known as *vertically integrated* firms. A company can limit dependence on other companies or countries if it produces its own parts. A company is also better able to protect its patents and technology. The company does not have to share secrets with other companies in order to manufacture its goods.

Make-sourcing also improves production scheduling. A company can schedule its own production of components for a continuous manufacturing operation. There is less worry about late deliveries from another company, transportation strikes, or competitors buying key materials from a supplier.

Buy-Sourcing or Outsourcing

Buying component parts from other companies is buy-sourcing, or outsourcing. Outsourcing is politically unpopular in many countries. Outsourcing can create trade imbalances. It does, however, provide some advantages for companies.

One advantage of buying components from other countries or companies is increased flexibility. If a country that supplies items or services suddenly has a change in exchange rates, the manufacturer can go to another country where the price is lower. Many times outsourcing leads to the lowest cost for a component, even lower than the manufacturer can create by itself. Buy-sourcing also allows a company to create alliances with other companies and countries. When a company shares production across several companies and nations, its products can compete successfully.

Along with reaching a make-or-buy decision, a company's leadership team must resolve several other issues regarding how products will be produced.

Production Methods

When you prepare to manufacture a product, either domestically or in a foreign country, there are four main elements to consider. First, you must select the location of the plant. It should be near transportation routes and close to a population base large enough to provide the necessary employees. The second element to consider is the plant layout. The actual facility must be designed to make the product efficiently and safely. The third element is called "materials handling." This means a company should have easy access to the raw materials to make products. The company should also be able to maintain a warehouse to store goods. Then finished goods should be shipped safely so that a minimum of the inventory is damaged, stolen, or lost. The fourth element is the human aspect. The labor force must include people with enough skill and education to work effectively in the plant.

The method of production should match the economic and cultural factors present in the country where the products are manufactured. There are three basic methods for producing goods:

- Manual production
- Automated production
- Computerized production

Manual Production

People perform manual labor when they use their hands, bodies, and basic tools. Manual labor is the basis of manual production. Manual production is most used in countries with less-developed economies, an abundance of workers, and jobs that can be done only by hand. Some types of mining and farming can be performed using only manual labor. Making crafts, such as jewelry and furniture, is also suited to manual work. Even in developed countries, there are manual labor jobs such as plumbing and food service.

Automated Production

In the 1900s, many manufacturers used an assembly-line process, which was an early type of automated production. Henry Ford and the Ford Motor Company implemented this in the early 20th century. On an assembly line, each worker adds a small part to the overall product as it moves along an automated conveyor. Today manufacturers **automate** the production process as machines do the bulk of the work. Machines perform many jobs that used to be done by manual labor, including harvesting some agricultural crops. The result is more rapid production and lower-cost products. Automated production is used by many companies around the world.

NON-HUMAN RESOURCES
Computerized robotics has dramatically changed many manufacturing operations. *What types of products are best manufactured using robotics?*

Computerized Production

In developed countries, many firms are able to create products using computerized production systems. They are the most sophisticated kind of system, since computers can control machines and assist workers in the manufacture of goods. Computerized production systems can help design a product, produce a product, or assist in manufacturing the product in some other way.

There are many types of computerized production systems:

- Computer-assisted design (CAD)
- Computer-aided manufacturing (CAM)
- Computer-aided engineering (CAE)
- Robotics
- Computer-integrated manufacturing (CIM)
- Automated warehouses

Computer-Assisted Design (CAD) Computer-assisted design programs help to create products or production facilities. A CAD program may be used to design a new car. Using the computer, the car designer can move parts around to make sure they will all fit in the engine compartment and body of the car. CAD programs are also used to set up production facilities. An architect can move virtual rooms and walls around to create the best possible production-site design.

Computer-Aided Manufacturing (CAM) Computer-aided manufacturing is a software process that can convert a product drawing into code so that a machine can manufacture the actual product. A CAM program makes it easier to design a plant to build airplanes, a power plant, or any other large, complex product.

Computer-Aided Engineering (CAE) Computer-aided engineering is the use of computers to help with all phases of engineering design work. It enables engineers to analyze complex projects on a computer. Engineers can complete projects such as the design of a high-rise building or bridge by using CAE software.

Robotics Robotic programs use mechanical robots to assist in the production of goods. They have the advantage of being precise while doing repetitive work, such as counting. Robotics are used extensively in building computer components, and were initially used in the automobile industry.

Computer-Integrated Manufacturing (CIM) Computer-integrated manufacturing programs are used for routine production processes. The assembly of CD players, televisions, washing machines, and even pre-fabricated houses is best done with CIM.

Automated Warehouses An automated warehouse takes advantage of computers, software, and robots to store and ship finished products. A company is able to keep track of inventory and ship it in a timely fashion.

New Production

Computer-based programs and other technologies, such as inventory control chips, bar coding, and radio frequency identification, lead to better, more sophisticated production. They result in products with better value because they hold down the costs of production. The quality of products is also higher.

Production begins with deciding what to produce and how to produce those goods and services. It is only complete when managers define the level of quality required to be successful. Quality control is this key element described in the next section.

Quick Check 10.1

After You Read Respond to what you have read by answering these questions.

1. What is the difference between standardization and adaptation? _____

_____

2. What factors do managers consider before exporting a new product? _____

_____

3. What are the three most common methods of production? _____

_____

 Academics / *Social Studies*

4. Explain the considerations involved in creating labels and packaging.

_____

_____

Quality Control

Reading Guide

Before You Read

What is your definition of the term *added value*?

MAIN IDEA

Companies need systems to ensure products are well made.

GRAPHIC ORGANIZER

Draw this graphic organizer. As you read this section, write in examples of inputs and outputs.

Inputs		Outputs
_____		_____
_____	⟶	_____
_____		_____

WHAT YOU'LL LEARN

- To identify the elements of a quality production or manufacturing system
- To identify the systems used for the process of quality control
- To describe the latest programs designed to improve quality

WHY IT'S IMPORTANT

The world marketplace is crowded with competition. Successful companies deliver quality. Effective quality control systems are an absolute necessity.

KEY TERMS

- International Organization for Standardization (ISO)
- just-in-time (JIT)
- total quality management (TQM)
- quality circles
- process reengineering
- Six Sigma®

Academic Vocabulary

You will find these words in your reading and on your tests. Make sure you know their meanings.

- enhance
- method
- sequence

Quality Control and Adding Value

The key aspect of any production process is finding ways to add value. The essence of quality control is finding ways to measure success. Managers look for ways to add value and measure success by considering the four parts of a production system: acquiring inputs, the transformation function, delivering outputs (logistics), and the feedback system.

Inputs

Inputs are things that enter a process from the outside. Besides money, the most common inputs into a business are raw materials and employees. A company adds value by acquiring quality inputs.

Raw Materials When a company discovers it has produced defective items, raw materials may be the cause. This is part of the quality control process. For example, if a clothing manufacturer discovers too many shirts have flaws, the cloth may be defective. Using a better quality cloth would add value.

Employees The human resources (HR) department measures rates of absenteeism, tardiness, turnover, and accidents among employees. If the wrong people have been hired, these rates may rise. Effective recruitment of new workers can add value to a company's operations.

Culture Corner

Singapore: Lion and Dragon

Think About It Why would quality control be especially important for new companies?

Two centuries ago Singapore (meaning "Lion City") was a sleepy outpost inhabited by fishermen and pirates. Today, with a multiethnic, multireligious population of more than four million, the small nation is one of Asia's "economic dragons." Located north of Australia at the southernmost point of Asia on the sea-lanes that connect Asia with the Americas, the Republic of Singapore is the world's busiest seaport. This country boasts a per capita GDP equal to that of the four largest western European countries.

Its prosperity and international trading activity contribute to the growth of businesses there.

Companies that produce products for the world include Singapore Air, Tiger Airways, several electronics firms, shipping companies, and financial services businesses.

Meeting and Greeting Shake hands firmly and again when you leave. You may also bow slightly. Exchange business cards with both hands after you are introduced.

Business Etiquette Be on time for business meetings. Singaporeans are fast-paced.

Business Dress Men wear white shirts, a tie and slacks; jackets are not required. Women wear skirts and blouses with sleeves, or pantsuits.

English Language Arts/Writing

In what ways can an airline company add value?

Transformation Process

The transformation process is the act of changing an input into an output by adding value to it. Outputs are goods, services, and information that a company provides to its customers or clients. Efficient production; effective sales, marketing, and advertising programs; and innovative research and development (R & D) efforts can create new value. A production department transforms raw materials into finished goods and services. The R & D department transforms ideas into potential new products or product improvements. A transformation process provides the opportunity to **enhance**, or add value.

Outputs

Outputs add value to the lives and activities of customers. They also add value to the company when they are sold at a profit. The delivery of outputs, or goods and services, is part of a production system.

Feedback Systems

Feedback systems measure company performance. Feedback is both formal and informal. Formal feedback includes interviews, customer surveys, reports, statistics, and comparisons of actual performance to previously set standards.

Informal feedback includes comments and complaints from customers as well as suggestions by sales representatives. Managers try to find out how customers view their products. They also compare competitors' products. Formal and informal feedback help a company develop solid quality control systems.

Reading Check **Recall** What is formal feedback and informal feedback?

Quality Control Systems for Individual Departments

There are many strategies and systems used by companies to control quality with useful production standards. Various systems are used for individual departments.

Acceptance Sampling and Statistical Process Control

To check a set of products, "acceptance sampling" is a **method** used to test a sample from a production run, such as a set of music CDs. If the sample set has no defects, the entire production run is accepted and shipped. "Statistical process controls" show when a process is moving off course by using statistical tools to identify problems.

ISO Standards

A production department can set quality goals by adopting appropriate ISO standards. In 1946, delegates from 25 countries created the **International Organization for Standardization (ISO)**, the world's largest developer of quality control standards. It is a non-governmental organization. The ISO facilitates international commerce and sets common, unified standards for industrial production systems. The ISO standards are part of quality control systems for companies in about 150 countries.

As You Read

Question What is the purpose of the ISO?

Quality and Safety When a company agrees to meet ISO standards, it agrees to create products that have a common quality standard. This helps suppliers, customers, governmental regulators, and interest groups to be sure a product has consistent quality, no matter where it is manufactured. The ISO 14000 standards focus on reducing hazards to the environment due to byproducts of production processes. Standard ISO symbols also provide danger warnings.

Standard Specifications The ISO standards set precise product specifications, such as the size of a screw thread and the measurement system used in a medical device. Measurement sizes and grades of various raw materials (such as iron ore or aluminum) are universal. This consistency makes it possible for individuals and companies to buy goods from international companies with confidence.

Just-in-Time (JIT)

Inventory consists of a company's current assets, such as raw materials waiting to be processed and finished goods ready to be shipped. It is expensive to store inventory. A company has to pay for a warehouse and for financing the items. Companies use **just-in-time (JIT)**, an inventory system used to make sure raw materials arrive at the plant just when the manufacturer needs them, thus avoiding storage costs. Retailers use JIT for finished goods. Shipping is scheduled so products arrive at the retail outlet when they will be sold.

The Japanese use a type of just-in-time inventory control called *kanban*, which means "card" or "sign." The system uses small signs on inventory that signal the need for an item. The goal is to keep goods moving on schedule.

Companywide Quality Programs

After World War II ended in 1946, American statistics expert W. Edwards Deming (1900–1993) moved to Japan to help that country improve the quality of its goods and services. Deming developed and influenced others to develop a number of programs designed to improve quality in business production:

- Total quality management (TQM)
- Quality circles
- Kaizen
- Process reengineering
- Six Sigma®

Total Quality Management (TQM)

Total quality management (TQM) is a program in which all of management focuses on quality and quality improvement as the most important company goal. The goal of a TQM program is zero defects so that every item is made correctly.

To make TQM work, employees must be motivated by incentives to find ways to improve quality. TQM relies on a system called "plan-do-check-act," or the PDCA cycle. This system promotes better quality instead of a rejection of defective items after they have been produced. TQM processes apply to every aspect of a company's operation, not just manufacturing.

Quality Circles

A smaller companywide program is the **quality circle**, which is a group of employees who meet regularly to discuss ways to increase quality. Quality circles suggest improvements. Employees who make good suggestions receive rewards.

Kaizen

Kaizen is a Japanese word for "improvement." It is also a business philosophy advocating a companywide focus on efficiency and improvement. The goal is to identify small steps that will improve efficiency and performance. The company makes a small change, reviews results, and then adjusts further. Toyota® is known for using kaizen.

Process Reengineering

In contrast to the kaizen approach, **process reengineering** is a program to improve a business through major changes to the production process. The goal is to create a new process that is more efficient and produces better quality products. Process reengineering uses computer models and systems to design changes.

Six Sigma

The **Six Sigma** approach is a quality management program designed to find ways to make products efficiently and without mistakes or variations. It was developed by Motorola® in 1986. The Six Sigma level means a company seeks to have fewer than 3.4 defects in every one million products, which is almost perfect production. A company reaches this goal through a **sequence** of five steps: Define, measure, analyze, improve, and control.

RETAIL BUYER

Retail trends come and go very quickly. From hula hoops to Rubik's Cubes® to Furbys®, the retail world has seen one hit after another. Retail buyers are responsible for researching and predicting the next big thing. In retail firms, buyers purchase goods from wholesale firms or from manufacturers for resale to the public. They determine which products their company will sell. It is up to the retail buyer to recognize trends and act on them before they are yesterday's news.

Retail buyers truly have an international job. They must negotiate with wholesale firms and manufacturers around the world. The job is even more complicated when a retail buyer works for a multinational company because he or she must understand world cultures in order to predict what products will sell in those cultures. Retail buyers frequently travel internationally.

Buyers can influence the growth of a trend by making certain products more widely available or by introducing the product to new markets. Retail buyers also help their companies "ride the coattail" of an existing trend by buying related products—for example, the Apple iPod generated an entire iPod accessory industry.

Skills and Training

Retail buyers need sound leadership, decision-making, communication, and negotiation skills. A high school diploma, training, and experience are essential for success, but a bachelor's degree is not always required.

English Language Arts/Writing

Why might retail buyers need to be aware of a manufacturing company's quality control system?

@ To learn more about retail buyers and their career paths, go to the International Business Online Learning Center through **glencoe.com**.

Career Data

Education: High school diploma, associate's degree, or bachelor's degree

Skills: Computer, negotiation, bilingual or multilingual, and mathematical skills

Outlook: Growth slower than average in the next ten years

Management Functions and Quality

In all quality control approaches, every employee becomes responsible for identifying and implementing new ways to improve the quality of a company's performance. In addition, every management function plays a part in creating quality. Effective management leads to better quality.

Efficiency and Effectiveness

Efficiency is the ability to do things well without wasting raw materials, time, or energy. Efficient manufacturing is production with few mistakes or defects. Efficiency and effectiveness are both tied to quality management. Effectiveness produces results that are successful. A company can make a product efficiently, but that product is only effective if people buy it and use it. Efficiency is doing things the right way. Effectiveness is doing the right things. To succeed in both areas, a company must choose the right products to make and export, produce those products efficiently, and make sure they reach the right markets.

Competitive Advantage

A variety of quality control methods are available, from methods designed for a production department to systems that include an entire company. Product and quality control processes are vital elements in the success of an international operation. The efficient and effective design of the production process gives a company a major advantage in meeting and beating the competition.

Quick Check 10.2

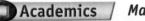 **After You Read** Respond to what you have read by answering these questions.

1. What are the four parts of a production system? _____

_____

2. What quality control systems can be used in individual departments? _____

_____

3. How do the terms *efficiency* and *effectiveness* relate to quality control? _____

_____

Academics / Mathematics

4. According to the Six Sigma approach, calculate how many defects a company would be allowed in 17.5 million products.

_____

_____

Portfolio Worksheet

Adapting a Product

Pick a consumer product originating in or unique to the United States domestic market. Study the features of the product, including design, packaging, and advertising. Now choose another country in which you feel you could market that product. Research the country. List the changes you would need to make to the product, if any, in order to market it successfully in the new country. Explain why the changes are needed or not needed.

New location: _____

Product features: _____

_____

_____

_____

Changes necessary to market product in new location: _____

_____

_____

_____

_____

_____

_____

_____

_____

_____

_____

_____

_____

_____

ACADEMICS APPLIED Check off the academic knowledge you used to do this activity:

☐ English Language Arts   ☐ Mathematics   ☐ Social Studies   ☐ Science

ACADEMIC AND CAREER PLAN Add this page to your Academic and Career Plan Portfolio.

CHAPTER SUMMARY

Section 10.1 **Production Processes**

quality (p. 230)
value (p. 230)
standardization (p. 231)
adaptation (p. 231)
sourcing (p. 235)

- Since the 1980s, quality and value have been associated with production. Quality is the level of excellence present in a product. Value is the degree of quality compared to the price or cost of a product.

- The decision of which good and service to make or export depends on several factors: country, technological, and product factors. A company must also choose whether to standardize or adapt a product for a market in another country.

Section 10.2 **Quality Control**

International Organization for Standardization (ISO) (p. 241)
just-in-time (JIT) (p. 241)
total quality management (TQM) (p. 242)
quality circles (p. 242)
process reengineering (p. 242)
Six Sigma (p. 242)

- Elements considered for a high-quality manufacturing system include: inputs, which are raw material and employees; transformation; outputs, which are the products themselves; and feedback systems.

- Quality control systems use standards. Some systems include acceptance sampling, statistical process control, ISO standards adoption, and just-in-time (JIT) inventory systems.

- Companies can improve quality in any type of production by using various programs, such as total quality management (TQM), quality circles, kaizen, process reengineering, or Six Sigma.

CONCEPTS REVIEW

1. **Distinguish** value from quality.

2. **List** four of the country factors that companies consider when deciding what to export.

3. **Describe** each of the technological factors that affect the decision about what to export.

4. **Discuss** how managers seek to add value to and measure success in their products.

5. **Explain** why a system of quality control must carefully identify how quality is measured.

6. **Compare and contrast** the use of acceptance sampling and the use of statistical process controls.

KEY TERMS REVIEW

7. Match each term to its definition.

_____ quality

_____ value

_____ standardization

_____ adaptation

_____ sourcing

_____ International Organization for Standardization (ISO)

_____ just-in-time

_____ total quality management

_____ quality circles

_____ process reengineering

_____ Six Sigma

a. the practice of making a product the same, without modification, for all markets

b. the degree of quality as compared to the price or cost of a product

c. the level of excellence present in a product

d. the world's largest developer of quality control standards

e. an inventory system used to make sure raw materials arrive at the plant just when the manufacturer needs them

f. a program in which all of management focuses on quality and quality improvement as the most important company goal

g. a program to improve a business through major changes to the production process

h. a quality management program designed to find ways to make products efficiently and without mistakes or variations

i. the process of adjusting or modifying a product to fit the needs of a particular market, country, or region

j. the process of locating and acquiring component parts for a final product

k. a group of employees who meet regularly to discuss ways to increase quality

Academic Vocabulary

8. On a separate sheet of paper, write a sentence or two related to production and quality control using at least three of the academic terms you learned in the section openers:

- assess
- volume
- automate
- enhance
- method
- sequence

Critical Thinking

9. "Trading down" involves reducing the quality of a product without reducing the price. Evaluate this strategy.

Discussion Starter

10. Often a product has to be modified for a different culture. Yet some American products, such as music and sports products, succeed without modification. Research and discuss why.

Point of View

11. Which is more difficult to implement, a new kaizen program or a process reengineering program? Why?

BUILDING REAL-WORLD SKILLS

12. Currency Exchange Rates Former Chairman of the Federal Reserve Board Alan Greenspan once said that forecasting currency exchange rates "has a success rate no better than that of forecasting the outcome of a coin toss." The daily volatility of currency exchange rates and the potential for a financial crash make international business deals with small profit margins nearly impossible.

Research and Share

a. Research the value of the dollar against either the euro, yen, pound, or Swiss franc over the last year.

b. Choose a foreign currency. Consider how the exchange-rate fluctuations would affect your bargaining in a business deal with a company in a country using the currency you chose.

13. Entrepreneurial Skills Whether a person is a natural or trained by experience, certain skills are necessary for an entrepreneur to succeed.

Research and Write

a. Research the types of skills associated with entrepreneurial success.

b. Rank these skills in order of importance. Justify your ranking in a paragraph.

BUILDING ACADEMIC SKILLS

ELA English Language Arts

14. Implementing employee suggestions is one of two keys necessary to making quality circles work. Write a one-page essay explaining how you would reward such employees.

MATH Mathematics

15. You retired in 2002 to Italy. Your income is $3,000 per month in U.S. dollars. In 2002, when $.82 bought one euro, you had 3,659 euros to spend each month. Now, the dollar buys 0.83 euros. How many euros do you have each month for living expenses? How much monthly income have you lost in four years due to currency fluctuation?

Computation and Estimation To solve this problem, you need to use the principles of ratios and subtraction.

SOC Social Studies

16. In his classic book *Up the Organization: How to Stop the Corporation from Stifling People and Strangling Profits,* author Robert Townsend describes an interesting version of the quality circle idea. Go to the library or research this book online. Write a short report summarizing your findings.

SOC Social Studies/History

17. Packaging is vital to product marketing. Where would we be without bottles for soda? Without cardboard boxes for cereals? Research the history and factors that affected the development of one type of packaging. Report your discoveries to the class.

To Import or Not to Import

18. Situation You have been placed in charge of a task force to decide whether to import the wood trim parts for furniture that your company makes in the United States. The cost to produce the parts in the United States is approximately double the costs of foreign parts. Your sales volume is $1,000,000 per year; but you believe your potential sales will be double that if you can reduce the selling price. Your material costs are 38 percent of the selling price, and your operating costs are 20 percent.

Activities Evaluate the potential increase in inventory costs over the reduction of your cost of goods sold. Consider financial statistics over the past ten years to estimate cost.

Evaluation You will be evaluated on how well your report meets the following objectives:

a. Develop a financial statement under both scenarios.

b. Make a decision about export versus domestic production, and defend your position.

c. Describe any other considerations.

BusinessWeek online

19. Newsclip: Starbucks: Selling the American Bean
Today U.S. companies must decide whether to standardize or adapt their products for foreign markets. Starbucks has found the perfect blend.

@ Go to the International Business Online Learning Center through **glencoe.com** to read an article about this topic. Then write a paragraph that compares and contrasts the benefits of standardization versus adaptation.

Standardized Test Practice

20. Choose the best answer to the following multiple-choice question.

Which of the following statements is most correct?
○ The types of methods for producing goods include manual and automated production.
○ The type of production used reflects many factors.
○ There may be more than three methods of production.
○ Manual, automated, and computerized production are three methods for producing goods.

Internet Travels

Antarctica
Using the Internet, find a map of Antarctica. Study its positioning. Research and answer the following questions about life in Antarctica on a separate sheet of paper.

➤ Do any people inhabit or spend time in Antarctica?

➤ What special considerations have to be given to products taken to such a region and what needs would those products fill? Give specific examples.

@ For resources to help you do this exercise, go to the International Business Online Learning Center through **glencoe.com**.

Test-Taking Tip Eliminate unlikely answers first. By eliminating two alternatives, you will greatly increase the probability of choosing the correct answer.

Global Social Entrepreneurship

Success Model: NEWMAN'S OWN
Country of Origin: UNITED STATES
Business: FOOD PRODUCTS

While most businesses judge success by production or profit, Newman's Own measures it by how much money it gives away. The company is a for-profit venture, but founder Paul Newman has used a portion of profits to give away more than $200 million to charities. Among many charities, Newman's Own has funded the rustic Hole-in-the-Wall Camps, located in the United States and abroad. Children with cancer and other life-threatening illnesses "find camaraderie, joy, and the renewed sense of being a kid" in the great outdoors, equipped with swimming pools, horseback riding, sports, crafts, and tee-pees.

The Newman's Own brand and business began when the Oscar-winning actor and his friend A.E. Hotcher decided to package and sell the salad dressing they would give away as holiday gifts. Newman's popularity, the tasty, all-natural products, and the charitable contributions from the profits, have led to the success of this multimillion dollar business. Today Newman's Own sells popcorn, pasta sauce, salsa, salad dressing, and a complete line of organic products. In addition to the United States, Newman's Own products are sold in 15 countries around the world.

● Situation

Ever since you graduated from high school, you have dreamed of starting a business that would help others. The idea of creating something from the ground up excites you, and you think you are ready to give it a try. So, after saving $15,000 over the last three years, you have decided to begin planning for your entry into the world of entrepreneurship. You know there are rewards as well as risks in being your own boss. But you want the opportunity to be creative, the freedom to do something you enjoy, and the ability to set your own schedule. You are also willing to work hard.

● Assignment

✓ Choose a business that might benefit people or the environment.
✓ Think of a good or service to offer.
✓ Design a logo and a package for your good or service.
✓ Create a basic business plan.

● Resources

SKILLS NEEDED

✓ *Academic Skills:* reading, writing, math, and social studies
✓ *Basic Skills:* speaking, listening, thinking, problem-solving, and interpersonal skills
✓ *Technology Skills:* word-processing, graphics, presentation, and Internet skills

TOOLS NEEDED

✓ Newspapers and magazines, such as *FastCompany, Entrepreneur, BusinessWeek,* and *U.S. News and World Report*
✓ Access to the Internet and library
✓ Paper, pens, pencils, and markers
✓ Magazines you can cut up, construction paper, ribbon, and miscellaneous supplies
✓ Word-processing, spreadsheet, graphics, and presentation software

● Procedures

STEP 1 | REAL-WORLD RESEARCH

Develop your business concept by researching:

- The good or service you want to provide
- The customer for your product
- The benefit you are providing
- Your competition
- Start-up resources you will need

STEP 2 | COMMUNITY RESEARCH

Interview two entrepreneurs (if possible, international) from your community. Find out the process they used to start their businesses. Ask about resources available for people who want to start their own business.

STEP 3 | INTERNET RESEARCH

Using the Internet, do research to find examples of business plans.

STEP 4 | WRITE IT

Write a business plan (2–3 pages) and include:

- Name of business and the good or service
- Description of the product benefit
- Management strategy with your qualifications and those of team members
- Market research on customers/competition
- Financial plan with start-up costs

STEP 5 | CREATE IT

Be creative and design the following:

- A logo that represents you and your company. Use software if possible.
- A mock-up of the packaging for your good or service.

STEP 6 | OUTLINE IT

Create a basic business plan using this outline:

Business Plan Outline	
I.	Cover page, title page, and table of contents
II.	Executive summary
III.	Mission statement
IV.	Company description
V.	Product and service plan
VI.	Management team plan
VII.	Industry overview
VIII.	Market analysis
IX.	Competitive analysis
X.	Marketing plan
XI.	Operational plan
XII.	Organizational plan
XIII.	Financial plan
XIV.	Growth plan
XV.	Contingency plan
XVI.	Supporting documents

● Report

Prepare a report of your findings using the following tools, if available:

- *Word-processing program:* Prepare a 3-page report about your research; include business plan.
- *Spreadsheet program:* Prepare a data sheet listing your start-up costs.
- *Presentation program:* Prepare a ten-slide presentation.

● Evaluation

Present your report to the class and/or hand it in to your teacher. Use this chart to assess yourself before and after your presentation:

PRESENTATION SELF-CHECK RUBRIC	1 Needs Work	2 Average Quality	3 Good Quality	4 Excellent Quality	Totals
Business plan					
Logo and packaging					
Continuity of voice					
Eye contact with audience					
				TOTAL =	

0–6 Needs Work; **7–10** Average Quality; **11–14** Good Quality; **15–16** Excellent Quality

● Academic and Career Portfolio

Add this report to your Academic and Career Portfolio.

UNIT 4

INTERNATIONAL MARKETING AND FINANCE

凯越人生,智慧引路

In This Unit . . .

❝Any communication or marketing professional needs cross-cultural research and communication skills to be able to succeed in the future.❞

Marye Tharp
Marketing Educator

252

A Billion Tough Sells

Zhang Guangming's car-buying synapses have been in overdrive for months. He has spent hours poring over Chinese car-buff magazines, surfing Web sites, and trekking out to dealerships across Beijing. Finally, Zhang settled on either a Volkswagen Bora or a Hyundai Sonata sedan. But with competition forcing dealers to slash prices, he's not sure whether to buy now or wait. "I am looking for the best performance, and style is important."

So make that an economy sedan with high-end performance and bodacious styling. While 84 percent of new-car sales in China are to first-time buyers, those folks are anything but naive.

For Toyota and its rivals, cracking the code on Chinese buying habits is crucial. Idiosyncrasies call for some innovative tactics. General Motors Corp. advertises heavily on MTV to attract younger customers in a market where the median age of car buyers is 35. GM displayed its Chevy Epica sedan at last year's MTV music awards show in China, and MTV has lined up Chinese pop stars for GM promotions.

Chinese brands are jumping in with their own marketing gimmicks. Geely Automobile Holdings Ltd. sponsors owners' clubs, which help build brand loyalty. Last year a pair of company engineers joined Geely drivers on a 300-mile journey from Beijing to Inner Mongolia to teach owners how to handle their cars. "The most effective marketing is to treat your existing customers very well," [Geely executive] Ang says.

English Language Arts/Writing

1. How are automakers promoting their cars in China?
2. How might Chinese and American customers differ?

@ To read the complete *BusinessWeek* article, go to the International Business Online Learning Center through **glencoe.com**.

UNIT THEMATIC PROJECT PREVIEW

Marketing Entertainment Electronics

Electronic entertainment products are popular everywhere around the globe. Because so many companies are competing for customers, marketers must do research and develop creative marketing strategies. Imagine you are a marketing director creating a plan for a new super-mini MP3.

Pre-Project Checklist

❑ Gather newspaper and magazine ads for MP3 players and note differences and similarities.

❑ Go to stores to research MP3 players and features.

❑ Ask salespeople or store managers if these sell in other countries, and which ones.

❑ Use the Internet to find stores that sell MP3 players in Mexico and Canada.

Chapter 11

Marketing and Promotion

Chapter Objectives

When you have completed this chapter, you will be able to:

Section 11.1

- Explain the four Ps of marketing, or the marketing mix.
- Define market segmentation and product differentiation.
- Identify the characteristics of consumer, organizational, and governmental markets.

Section 11.2

- Describe the elements of the promotional mix.
- Discuss effective ways to contact international customers.
- Identify public relations activities for a business's international promotional mix.

VIACOM

Viacom is a publicly owned corporation whose shares are traded on the stock exchanges. When you research this company through Standard & Poor's, you will find investment information such as this:

Index:	S&P Global 1200 and S&P 500
Sector:	Consumer Discretionary
Company:	Viacom Incorporated
Symbol:	VIA and VIA.B
Country:	U.S.A.
Price:	(varies)

Global Profile Viacom owns and operates cable networks and entertainment brands, including more than 120 global television networks. MTV Music Television, MTV2, MTV U, Nickelodeon, Nick at Nite, TV Land, VH1, Spike TV, Country Music Television, and Comedy Central are Viacom networks. Cable-program services include BET, BET Jazz, BET Gospel, and BET Hip Hop. Through Paramount Pictures, Viacom produces, finances, and distributes feature motion pictures and DVDs. It also runs a music publishing business.

Business Report With sales of more than $9.6 billion worldwide, it is a leading provider of content and programming in the world today. Its numerous networks and brands provide a strong, diversified base for investors.

English Language Arts/Writing

The Famous Players Film Corp. of 1912 grew into the media empire Viacom. As part of Viacom, MTV showcases music videos and creates original television programming. Some global networks include MTV Australia, MTV Brazil, and MTV Taiwan, as shown here, plus the newer networks MTV Chi (for Chinese-Americans) and MTV Desi (for Americans of Indian descent). *Write a paragraph about factors to consider for promoting MTV in other countries.*

To do this activity, go to the International Business Online Learning Center through **glencoe.com**.

Marketing Strategies

WHAT YOU'LL LEARN

- To explain the four Ps of marketing, or the marketing mix
- To define market segmentation and product differentiation
- To identify the characteristics of consumer, organizational, and governmental markets

WHY IT'S IMPORTANT

To compete successfully in international markets, you must understand marketing, identify target markets, create products people want, and effectively promote them.

KEY TERMS

- marketing
- market
- market segmentation
- demographics
- product differentiation
- organizational market

Academic Vocabulary

You will find these words in your reading and on your tests. Make sure you know their meanings.

- statistic
- target
- predict

Reading Guide

Before You Read

Do you think marketing begins with the product or the customer?

MAIN IDEA

When people find the products they need, they become satisfied consumers, and businesses thrive.

GRAPHIC ORGANIZER

Draw this pie chart. As you read this section, fill in seven different characteristics used for different demographic statistics.

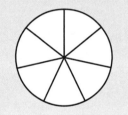

Meeting Consumer Needs

What do you want? What do you need? Marketers may have the answers. That is because **marketing** is the process of planning, pricing, promoting, selling, and distributing products to satisfy customers' needs and wants. Marketing is a field that includes a wide variety of activities. The four basic strategies of marketing are known as the *marketing mix* or *four Ps of marketing:*

- Product
- Price
- Place
- Promotion

What Is a Market?

The first part of the marketing process is discovering consumer wants and needs and identifying specific markets. A **market** is a set of people who share similar wants or needs and who are capable of buying products. Companies sell products in three major types of markets:

1. Consumer markets
2. Organizational markets
3. Governmental markets

Consumer Markets

Consumer markets are made up of individuals and households of people who purchase goods and services. These people are also called "end-users." Marketers use a wide variety of marketing tactics to reach end-users.

One key marketing activity is finding end-users of a product by identifying various market segments. **Market segmentation** is the process of analyzing and classifying customers in a market to create a smaller, more precise market. A successful business reaches consumers in one or more market segments. There are three main types of characteristics that identify market segments of consumers:

1. Demographics
2. Geographic characteristics
3. Psychographics

Demographics

Demographics are **statistics** that describe a population in terms of personal characteristics such as age, gender, income, marital status, ethnicity, education, and occupation. People with common characteristics often want similar things. For example, males between the ages of 7 and 27 may want the best pair of athletic shoes. Many married people with children want good life insurance policies for themselves and their families. By analyzing demographics, a marketing team can discover the wants and needs of a market segment. The most common demographic categories are age and gender.

Demographics by Age Consumers in market segments based on age have common needs and wants that can be met with various goods or services. Divisions by age include these groups:

- Children
- Teenagers
- Young adults
- Middle-aged adults
- Senior citizens

A common term associated with age segmentation is *generational cohorts*—sets of people born at about the same time. Generational cohorts have common interests in music, entertainment, clothing, and services. Baby boomers and Generations X and Y are examples of generational cohorts. Baby boomers were born between 1946 and 1964. Generation X is composed of the children of baby boomers. Generation Y includes people born between 1976 and 2001.

Demographics by Gender Gender is another category that marketers use to identify market segments. Women usually buy specific products, as do men. They wear clothing designed for them. Businesses can combine age with gender to **target** even more specific groups, such as females and males, ages 18 to 35 years.

ETHICS & ISSUES

The Real Things?

A strong brand name can communicate around the world. Unfortunately, in many countries, there are no copyright laws or protections for brand names to stop counterfeiting—or laws are ignored. Consequently, in street markets and other shopping areas, brand names such as Nike, Apple Computers, and Microsoft are routinely pirated and used on "knock-off" products. The buyer does not know the quality level of these goods. In the United States, licensing laws are quite strong. Even names that closely resemble powerful brand names cannot be used. The same is true in most of Europe. *Is it ethical or fair to "steal" a brand name? What should be the policy of the United States government toward countries that allow this type of piracy?*

As You Read

Relate How would you label the demographic group to which you and your friends might belong?

Demographics by Income Another important type of market segment is based on income. Many consumers buy goods and services according to their income levels. Marketing experts target products to each of these groups in different ways.

Other Demographics There are other demographic characteristics that businesses use to identify and **predict** potential customers—race, religion, or nationality. For example, some food products may appeal more to customers of Hispanic heritage. People from various Asian countries may prefer other foods. During December in countries such as the United States and Canada, many ads portray people celebrating Christmas or Hanukkah. These ads for specific products appeal to certain market segments.

Geographic Characteristics

Another type of characteristic that identifies market segments is the location where people live. A neighborhood, city, state, or region of a country can be a target market area. International businesses can focus on even larger geographic areas as markets, such as the countries in Central America or countries around the Pacific Rim.

Psychographics

Marketers may find it difficult to identify people who share common psychological or sociological characteristics, but most agree it is worth the effort. To identify these consumers, marketers use psychographics, which are studies of consumers based on social and psychological characteristics, such as attitudes, interests, and opinions. People may have a psychological identity, such as family-oriented, conservative, or liberal. Sociology is the study of people in groups. Sociological categories include the family unit, such as single-parent families or two-parent families. People from different social groups also buy products in different ways. Psychographic markets can relate to hobbies or work groups. "Soccer Moms," suburban mothers who take their children to play soccer or similar recreational activities, are one market segment. Another psychographic group might be people who enjoy Xtreme sports.

In addition, some people choose products or services on the basis of product benefits. For example, some consumers make purchases because they are trying to stay healthy. This group may buy vitamin supplements or low-fat foods.

Product Differentiation

Another marketing approach to selling goods and services is **product differentiation**, an advertising approach whereby a company suggests its product is different from and better than similar products offered by competitors. This approach is used for products sold to a wide population rather than to select segments. For example, Pepsi® may claim it has a better taste than Coke. Apple's ads may boast its iPod® digital music players have more features for the price than competitors' players.

The Organizational Market

A company may be more interested in selling goods or services to other businesses rather than to individual consumers. The **organizational market**, or business market, is a group of companies that buy and resell goods, and companies that use these goods to create other products. Two basic types of companies are part of the organizational market:

1. Wholesale distributors
2. Retail outlets

Wholesale distributors sell products to retailers. A wholesale company that buys goods and resells them to retailers is called a "merchant middleman." When a company simply represents goods without ever owning them, that company is called an "agent middleman." Retail outlets, or stores, are almost always "merchants." Occasionally, a retail store may operate as an agent by offering consignments for sale.

Reading Check **Recall** What are organizational markets?

The Commercial Market

A large sector of the organizational market consists of companies that buy goods and services to make products. These companies are within the commercial market. When Intel sells Pentium processors to IBM, the transaction is taking place in the commercial market. The same is true when General Motors buys steel and aluminum from another company to produce its cars and trucks. Businesses that sell goods to other businesses in the commercial sector of the organizational market are involved in business-to-business marketing.

Governmental Markets

Some companies specialize in selling items to various government markets. These include city, state, and national governments that buy goods and services. For example, many computers are sold to U.S. governmental agencies such as the Pentagon, the Social Security Administration, and city police departments.

The process of marketing to governmental buyers is different than the processes for consumer marketing and organizational marketing. Governments usually have complicated bidding processes. Products must fit exact government specifications before a company can make a bid, which is usually called a "request for proposal," or RFP.

A business that markets goods or services to governments in other nations will find the experience challenging. The first step is to understand how those governments purchase products. If it seems feasible, a company can develop marketing programs for them.

Steps of an International Marketing Plan

Creating a marketing program takes time, effort, and patience. Company leaders must integrate marketing programs with other aspects of operations, such as production, accounting, quality control, and even plant maintenance. The steps of a marketing plan for a business entering an international market are listed in **Figure 11.1**.

Figure 11.1

International Marketing Plan

TARGETING THE GLOBAL CUSTOMER International marketing requires step-by-step preparation.
In what ways might international marketing differ from domestic marketing?

Step 1	Set company goals for sales, market share, and production levels.
Step 2	Define the target market and customers. Use demographics, geographic characteristics, and psychographics; identify business-to-business customers.
Step 3	Make a list of competitors and potential competitors.
Step 4	Identify any social, legal, economic, or technological challenges in the foreign country.
Step 5	Prepare financial information, such as how to fund the expansion and when to expect a profit.
Step 6	Identify how nationality will apply to prospective staff (expatriates, local nationals, third-country nationals).
Step 7	Set a timeline and create a plan of implementation.
Step 8	Follow up to see if the goals set in Step 1 have been reached.

The International Marketplace

The fastest-growing marketplace for many companies is beyond the company's national borders. Many firms around the world are now interested in selling to end-users, middlemen, manufacturers, and governments in other countries.

To successfully expand into the international marketplace, a company must first examine the social, cultural, technological, geographic, and legal factors that influence consumer buying behavior in a particular country. The company's products must mesh with the local culture. They must be appropriate for a region's traditions, customs, and religious practices. Something as simple as the time of day that people prepare and consume meals can affect marketing.

Geographic factors can have a big impact on an international operation. Useful transportation must be available to provide access to local markets. Climates also vary. Products must be suited to local conditions, whether regions are hot and dry or cold and wet.

A product must meet all of a country's legal requirements. Company leaders also must review the country's legal system and form of government.

Products sold in other countries must be compatible with local technologies. The goods and services to be marketed should be compatible with the methods of communication (telephone versus Internet), the type of electrical current (AC versus DC), and the degree of technological sophistication in the country. A population that has limited education may not be ready to use complicated technologies.

The same principles that drive domestic marketing also apply to international markets. Company leaders must first discover markets that have wants and needs, as well as people who can spend money. Then the company must be able to meet those wants and needs with an appropriate good or service. The marketing mix may change depending on the country, but each of the four Ps plays a role in the international marketplace.

OUR MULTICULTURAL WORKPLACE

Think Globally

When the four Ps of marketing (product, price, place, and promotion) are standardized across cultures, companies can achieve efficiency and reduce costs. However, marketers must recognize different cultures' religions, beliefs, and customs—and most importantly, not offend the market. For an Islamic market, it would be inappropriate to market bikinis in magazines targeted for that demographic group. *Select a popular U.S. product or commercial. Describe how it would need to be modified, based on cultural influences, for three markets of your choice.*

Quick Check 11.1

After You Read Respond to what you have read by answering these questions.

1. What are the three main types of markets? _____

_____

2. What are the four common market segments? _____

_____

3. What types of companies are found in organizational markets? _____

_____

Academics / Social Studies

4. Explain why marketers use segmentation to sell products.

_____

_____

Promotion

WHAT YOU'LL LEARN

- To describe the elements of the promotional mix
- To discuss effective ways to contact international customers
- To identify public relations activities for a business's international promotional mix

WHY IT'S IMPORTANT

Promotional programs are key ingredients in developing effective international business operations.

KEY TERMS

- promotional mix
- personal selling
- trade promotions
- consumer promotions
- public relations

Academic Vocabulary

You will find these words in your reading and on your tests. Make sure you know their meanings.

- constant
- survey
- database

Reading Guide

Before You Read

How might public relations be used for crisis management?

MAIN IDEA

Marketers must adapt promotional methods to the cultural expectations of their international customers.

GRAPHIC ORGANIZER

Draw a diagram similar to this one. As you read this section, write in the components of the promotional mix and sub-components of each one.

The Promotional Mix

You learned that marketing is discovering consumer wants and needs, creating the product, and then pricing, promoting, and delivering the product. Just as there is a mix of the four Ps of marketing (product, price, place, and promotion), there is a mix of different kinds of promotional activities. The **promotional mix** is any combination of the four components of promotion: advertising, personal selling, sales promotion, and public relations and publicity. These components are part of a company's marketing plan.

Advertising

Advertising is a form of nonpersonal promotion through which companies pay to promote ideas, goods, or services in a variety of media outlets. It reaches people with a personal message through an impersonal medium, such as a television set or computer screen.

An advertiser can choose an approach from all of the different media, prepare clever and convincing ads, and use celebrities who serve as spokespersons. There are two main tasks associated with advertising that are **constant**. The first is preparing the message. The second is selecting the right media to deliver the message. Both must be coordinated to get the word out to potential customers.

Advertising Messages

Some companies have internal departments that create advertisements. Others hire outside companies to design advertising campaigns. Both approaches utilize several elements:

- Advertising objectives
- Message theme
- Target audience
- Support for the theme

Advertising Objectives The most common advertising objectives are to inform, to persuade, or to remind. If a product is new to a market, advertisers inform customers that the new item exists. When there are several choices, advertisers try to persuade customers to pick a specific brand. When a product has a long history, marketers remind consumers about the product so they will continue to buy it.

✔ **Reading Check** **Analyze** What is the purpose of advertising?

The Target Audience The target audience is the target market, the group of people identified as those most likely to become customers. These are the people advertisers hope to reach through their ads.

The Message Theme The theme of the advertising message communicates the advertising objective to the target audience. The theme of a cell phone advertisement targeting families with teenagers may remind the target audience that all members of the family can stay in touch by cell phone for one low monthly price.

Culture Corner

An Island in Dubai

Think About It Why might descriptions—biggest, highest, longest—be used in advertisements?

Part of the United Arab Emirates (UAE), Dubai is the site of the world's tallest building and the world's largest mall, which includes a three-story aquarium with glass tunnels for visitors. One of the country's most ambitious projects is a collection of man-made islands called "The World." Builders have poured tons of sand and rock into the Persian Gulf to create 250–300 islands shaped to look like the map of the world. Each island, ranging from 5 to 20 acres in size, is named for a country, province, or major world city. Ready for builders, each site will feature a private home, an estate, a resort, or a community. There is one stipulation for developers: The design should fit the geographical name of the island. A Scottish castle would look out of place on an island named for Africa.

Meeting and Greeting The Arabic custom involves touching the right palm to your heart after each handshake. Greet a man as *Sayed* (Mr.) and a woman as *Sayeda* (Mrs.), followed by his or her first name. Visitors should not offer their hand to an Arabic woman unless she extends her hand first.

Business Etiquette Informal chatting precedes business at meetings. Alcohol is forbidden; tea and coffee are popular. No meetings occur on Friday.

Business Dress Wear conservative clothing, despite heat and humidity.

English Language Arts/Writing

Write advertising copy for a travel magazine ad for a resort in Dubai.

Theme Support One of several types of appeals can support and promote the advertising theme. Most common advertising appeals use emotions, fear, humor, romance, music, rational thinking, or scarcity to promote products. Examples of each of these appeals are shown in **Figure 11.2**.

Promoting Services

When a company is selling services, it must adapt and adjust the marketing mix, using the right combination of components. It is crucial for the company to choose the right service name, or brand name. The brand name must help customers remember the company. Prices of the services being offered must be competitive. When a business enters a new international market, marketers **survey** what other companies are charging for the same services they are offering.

Promotional programs for services must feature their intangible benefits. This is especially important if a service is being offered for the first time in a country. Prospective local customers must be convinced that a service will be valuable, especially if they have not previously relied upon it.

International Advertisements

International advertisers adjust their messages to match the cultures to which they are communicated. The company must make the choice between standardization or adaptation. A standardized message is one that stays the same in all countries, wherever an ad appears. Very few products can be advertised in a standardized fashion. Most often, marketing specialists adapt messages to local situations. Businesses also make the same type of decision when developing a new product itself.

Consider a fear-based message. In the United States, it is possible to fear being a social outcast because of perceived problems such as body odor. However, in some other countries, body odor is not considered offensive. In addition, the musical background in an advertisement may vary depending on the culture. An ad may feature songs or music typical of the particular culture. Also, humor varies—what is funny in one culture may not be funny in another culture.

INTERNATIONAL ADS
Pringles translates its slogan into Italian—"Once you pop, you can't stop!" This advertisement might appear in a print magazine or on the Internet. *What advertising medium do you think is most effective for reaching American teens?*

Figure 11.2

Advertising Appeal

Appeal	Example
Fear	Fear of financial problems for your family if you die; used to sell life insurance
Humor	Attention to a product by showing how it solves a problem in an amusing way; or how not using it causes a problem in an amusing way
Romance	Depicting perfume to attract a romantic partner
Music	Supporting the advertising message with a jingle or song
Rational thinking	Explaining why one investment company is better than others because it is well managed
Emotions	Showing a product that has health benefits makes you a better mother or father
Scarcity	Buy now. The product will be gone soon.

REACHING AN AUDIENCE These appeals can be used to reach consumers. *Can you think of an ad that uses at least one of these approaches? Explain.*

Media Selection

Marketers must select the right media for presenting an advertising message. An advertising campaign may feature a primary medium and one or more support media. These media should match the message, the audience, and each other. There are several media:

- Television
- Radio
- Magazines
- Newspapers
- Outdoor, including billboards
- Internet
- Specialty advertising

Television Television is a global medium that has both visual and sound elements that allow viewers to see and hear a message. Television advertisements are regulated in different ways. Some TV stations are government-owned and controlled. Preparing television advertisements can be costly, and buying time for ads is usually expensive.

Radio Radio advertisements rely on the listener's imagination to make an impression. People listen to the radio on the road, at the beach, and at home. People like different radio formats: talk, hip-hop, rock, soft rock, reggae, or classical music. This diversity makes it difficult to get a general message out to a wide audience. However, target audiences are readymade for specific product advertisements.

Magazines People take time to read magazines when they are relaxing and usually keep them for a period of time so that they have a longer "shelf life" than newspapers. Companies can advertise products in magazines, which have precise target markets—running shoes in runners' magazines, hotels in travel magazines, or wedding attire in bridal magazines. Magazines offer high-quality color photos and are relatively inexpensive for advertisements. However, magazines may require as much as four months for ad preparation.

Growing Roots

Having met at summer camp in Canada as children, Michael Budman and Don Green had a long-standing friendship and interest in the outdoors. In 1973, the two came up with an idea to start a business that would require only six months of work per year and allow time for relaxing during the remainder of the year. They introduced their first Roots product, the "negative heel" leather shoe. The success of this product and its popular sweatshirts, imprinted with a Canadian beaver, helped Roots make a name for itself in rugged, comfortable outerwear.

Later the company gained international exposure through promotional activities by sponsoring Team Canada in the 1998 Winter Olympics at Nagano, Japan. Roots continued its sponsorship of athletes in the 2000 Summer Games at Sydney, Australia, and the 2004 Olympics at Athens, Greece. While outfitting American Olympic athletes in the 2002 Olympics at Salt Lake City, Utah, Roots sold more than a million Team USA berets.

In spite of some struggles with getting the Roots Air airline company off the ground, the Roots product line has persevered and flourished, with more than 150 stores in Canada, the United States, and Taiwan—as well as a Roots Direct online store.

THINK GLOBALLY *What were some promotional strategies used by Roots?*

@ To learn more about the country of origin for this global business, go to the International Business Online Learning Center through **glencoe.com**.

Newspapers Newspapers have a local audience. Smaller companies can target consumers in their own communities with newspaper ads and promotional devices such as coupons. However, newspapers have a shorter "shelf life" than magazines.

Outdoor Ads Outdoor advertisements, which include billboards, can be placed by the side of a road or on a building, or they can be mobile on a bus or taxi. The message on a billboard must be short, since people see it briefly. However, a billboard on a busy commuter route will be seen over and over by drivers or passengers who take that route daily or weekly.

Internet Ads The Internet has a worldwide reach. Ads can be created, and then updated or replaced quickly and inexpensively. However, with so many Web sites on the Internet, it is difficult to make sure a message reaches the target audience.

Specialty Advertising Specialty advertising encompasses all other ways to advertise. Mall kiosk ads, leaflets and brochures, ads on T-shirts and caps, trailers in movie theaters, *Yellow Pages* ads, and ads on carry-home bags are examples. Large companies might also sponsor arenas and other venues as a form of advertising.

The Media Mix

The media mix is the combination of media that an advertiser chooses for a campaign. It must be adjusted to local conditions in international markets. Many nations do not have cable or satellite television channels. In Europe, consumers tend to read magazines. Ads on television and the Internet have the greatest reach in America.

Methods of buying advertising time also vary by the country involved. Sometimes a business may hire a media-buying company. Other companies might purchase ad time or space for themselves.

Advertisers must adjust ads to the language and culture of the target audience. An international advertiser may hire a cultural assimilator to review an ad to make sure the message presented is the message the company intends. In Mexico, the Chevy model Nova might be heard as "No va," which means "don't go" in Spanish. Advertisers must be aware of how cultures view the messages and the media.

Personal Selling

Personal selling is sometimes called the "last three feet of marketing," because a salesperson might stand about three feet away from the customer. **Personal selling** is any form of direct contact between a salesperson and a customer. Personal selling includes all of the contacts sales representatives make with the company's customers. Sometimes the customer shops in a retail store. Other times the customer is a buyer who purchases goods for a business.

Prospecting

When making sales to other businesses, the sales representative must first do prospecting. Prospecting is the process of identifying potential customers, or prospects. Prospects are found using the *Yellow Pages,* referrals from customers, or **databases**. Sales representatives might also send mail or e-mails to organizations and wait for a response. Prospecting can be especially difficult when the salesperson is in a new country or a new region of a country. Sales representatives might also prospect by making cold calls, or unannounced visits. However, cold calls are expensive and do not often yield results.

Steps of Making a Sale

Selling techniques must be adapted to the culture in which sales take place. Communication must make the international customer comfortable. In several far eastern countries, a bow replaces a handshake. In the Middle East, people stand close together as they speak. Gestures, eye contact, and other forms of communication are concerns when doing business in other cultures.

There are seven steps in any personal selling situation:

1. Approach.
2. Determine needs.
3. Present the product.
4. Overcome objections.
5. Close the sale.
6. Perform suggestion selling.
7. Follow up.

Approach The approach establishes a relationship with the customer in a company. Retail salespeople avoid questions that lead to yes/no answers, such as "May I help you?" Instead, a friendly, more creative approach may be effective: "That color looks nice on you," or, "Let me tell you why my company offers better liability insurance."

Determine Needs A good salesperson can determine needs by asking and learning about a customer's preferences. With this information, the salesperson can present the right product to the customer.

Present the Product The salesperson tells the customer why a product is different from and better than others. A presentation should describe a product difference or advantage.

Overcome Objections The salesperson answers questions and addresses objections. The customer must feel confident with the choice before the salesperson can close the deal.

Close the Sale A sale is completed when the seller writes an order or places it online, or when a retail customer offers payment to make a purchase. In a retail store, the salesperson puts the item into a carry-out bag. When a seller closes a sale with another company, the seller provides information about when the items will be shipped and terms of payment or credit.

Perform Suggestion Selling After the sale, the salesperson can suggest other purchases that will complement the original product.

Follow Up The salesperson provides assurance to calm any uncertainty a customer may experience. In sales to businesses, the reassurance may come in the form of a follow-up phone call or thank-you letter that offers to help if problems arise.

Trade Promotions

Promotional programs may include trade promotions as well as consumer promotions. **Trade promotions** are the tactics used to sell goods and services to other businesses. A company offers something attractive to wholesale distributors and retail stores to encourage purchases. There are many effective trade promotional programs:

- Trade allowances
- Trade contests
- Trade incentives
- Trade shows
- Training programs
- Vendor support programs
- Specialty advertising
- Point-of-purchase advertising

Trade Allowances

Trade allowances are financial incentives the seller offers to wholesalers and retailers. Trade allowances may take the form of a discount, rebate, or an agreement to pay the shipping costs for a load of merchandise. Shipping to another country is a major expense. A shipping discount can help close an international sale.

Trade Contests

Retail salespeople, store managers, and others can receive prizes for selling a vendor's merchandise through trade contests. A prize may be a television, computer, or a vacation. The contest should be acceptable to the culture. Employees in some countries may view a contest as a bribe or a sign of disloyalty to their employer.

Trade Incentives

Companies give trade incentives, or discounts, to retail outlets in exchange for their agreement to make a particular purchase. Sellers most often give trade incentives when the retailer orders a large quantity, such as a pallet full of merchandise or a truckload of a product. Trade incentives can involve cutting the price by paying for shipping.

Trade Shows

Marketing professionals use trade shows as a promotional tool. Trade shows feature products from around the world and are common in many industries. A chief advantage of this trade promotion is that the people attending the trade show are interested customers. A manufacturer can see a variety of prospective buyers in a few days. The main disadvantage is that the company is positioned next to the competition, each in individual booths.

Training Programs

Training programs are a unique way to reach retail stores. A manufacturer such as Amana, which makes washers and dryers, provides training to salespeople in the retail outlet, an appliance store. Doing so gives Amana an advantage over competing brands because the company is teaching the salespeople how to sell only Amana products.

Training programs are especially valuable when a new product is being offered in another country. When salespeople better understand a product and how to sell it, they are more likely to sell it.

Vendor Support Programs

Vendor support programs are designed to build relationships with retail stores and other businesses. The two most common programs are "billback" programs and "cooperative advertising." In a billback program, a manufacturing company pays for product displays, advertisements, or price cuts. The retailer can bill the manufacturer for the costs of display and advertisement.

Cooperative (co-op) advertising occurs when a retailer and a manufacturer share the costs of an advertisement. When the Intel logo is featured in an ad for Dell Computers, the companies share ad costs.

Specialty Advertising

Specialty advertising or "giveaways" include small gifts that companies give to customers. A pen, key chain, coffee cup, calendar, or some other small item carrying the name of the company helps remind the customer about the firm's products. In many cultures, the giving of gifts creates a sense of obligation, known as *reciprocation,* which means "to return the favor." A gift may lead to more purchases.

How Do You Say?

Q: In Arabic, how do you say: "My name is _____"?

A: _____ إسمي
(pronounced: _____
ĭss mē.)

To learn this phrase in other languages, go to the International Business Online Learning Center through **glencoe.com**.

Point-of-Purchase Advertising (POP)

Point-of-purchase advertising (POP) may use a display device depicting its product. A POP ad might be a life-size, cardboard stand-up image of a model or celebrity in a store. Some POP ads are small and designed to hold merchandise, such as a Lay's® potato-chip display holder in a 7-Eleven® store. Lay's pays for the POP display.

Consumer Promotions

Another promotional program involves **consumer promotions**, which are tactics used to sell products to end-users, or consumers. Consumer promotions items can include coupons, premiums, contests and sweepstakes, refunds and rebates, free samples, price-off deals, and bonus packs. International companies take advantage of all of these promotions. They adapt the promotion to the country.

As You Read

Question When you shop at a retail store, what types of discounts are available?

Coupons

Coupons are used widely in some countries, such as the United States, but not at all in some countries. Coupons are very popular in Belgium and England but are hardly used in Italy and Spain. A coupon is a certificate that pays part of the price for products, such as groceries, fast food, or other products.

Premiums

Premiums are small gifts. The prize in a Cracker Jack® box is a premium. A toy in a McDonald's® Happy Meal® is also a premium. In Japan people are becoming accustomed to the idea of free gifts, or premiums, such as "buy one, get one free."

Contests and Sweepstakes

Contests and sweepstakes generate interest in products in many nations. A participant must fill out a form to enter. The contest involves a judged activity, such as answering a question or writing an essay. The winner receives a prize.

Refunds and Rebates

Any time you get money back for making a purchase, regardless of the product, you are receiving a refund or a rebate. Small discounts are refunds. Larger amounts of money over $10 are rebates.

Free Samples

Free samples attract customers to a new product or one with sagging sales. They are given out around the world. A taste of food in a grocery store or a free small bottle of shampoo are examples of free samples.

Price-Off Deals

A price-off deal is a discount printed on the label of a product. A bottle of aspirin with a label that says "25 cents off" is one example. Another example is getting 50 percent more for the same price.

Bonus Packs

Bonus packs give customers the impression they are getting more for their money. A 3-pak might include a fourth item at no extra charge.

MARKETING MANAGER

Marketing managers develop domestic and international marketing strategies for selling products to consumer, organizational, and governmental markets. A multinational company must consider many factors when developing a marketing strategy for a foreign market.

Job Description

Marketing managers estimate demand, identify potential markets, monitor trends, develop pricing strategies, oversee product development, and serve customer needs. They collaborate with their subordinates and with colleagues in product development, sales, promotion, and advertising.

To help their company successfully compete in a world market, marketing managers must study the demographics, geographical area, and psychographic traits of the market's consumers. They must consider social, religious, cultural, technological, geographic, and legal factors. Learning about the target market often requires international travel.

Skills and Training

Potential marketing managers must be creative, highly motivated, persuasive, flexible, and decisive. Strong communication skills are necessary and it is helpful to be fluent in two or more languages. Marketing managers also need diplomacy, good judgment, and exceptional interpersonal skills.

Marketing managers may start out as product development managers or market research managers. A bachelor's degree is desirable, but not necessarily required. Large companies offer training programs.

English Language Arts/Writing

List the categories marketers use to identify a target market segment.

@ To learn more about marketing managers and their career paths, go to the International Business Online Learning Center through **glencoe.com**.

Career Data

Education: High school diploma, associate's degree, or bachelor's degree

Skills: Bilingual or multilingual, computer, and communication skills

Outlook: Growth faster than average in the next ten years

Public Relations and Publicity

Other components of the promotional mix are public relations and publicity—any non-paid message that communicates information about a company or its products. Both focus on improving or enhancing a company's image.

Public Relations Programs

Public relations is a program of activities that help an organization influence a target audience. Press releases, charitable activities, unsolicited feature stories about the company in magazines and newspapers, company magazines and newsletters, and newspapers are part of a public relations program.

The goals of public relations programs are to provide positive messages and images, and to avert negative publicity about a product or the company through "crisis management." For example, a negative story appearing on TV or in newspapers can adversely affect sales.

Sponsorship Programs

Sponsorship programs are promotional programs in which a company pays money to sponsor a person or a group participating in an activity. Small businesses provide funds for local children's baseball or soccer teams as a form of sponsorship. In Europe, sponsorships of professional soccer teams provide free publicity for companies.

Closely related to sponsorships is "event marketing," a program in which a company sponsors an event, such as a rodeo or music concert. "Lifestyle marketing" occurs at county fairs and places related to consumers' lifestyles.

An effective promotional program relies on all components of the promotional mix—advertising, personal selling, sales promotion, and public relations and publicity. This approach gives a business the best chance to successfully enter any market, domestic or international.

Quick Check 11.2

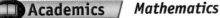 **After You Read** Respond to what you have read by answering these questions.

1. What are the elements of the promotional mix? _____

_____

2. What are some of the media that advertisers can use to reach consumers? _____

_____

3. What is the main difference between trade promotions and consumer promotions? _____

_____

Academics / Mathematics

4. You bought a snowboard for 25 percent off. You then received a point-of-sale rebate of $20 before taxes. Sales tax is 7.5 percent. How much did you pay if the snowboard originally cost $200?

_____

_____

Portfolio Worksheet

Promotional Mix

You have accepted a marketing executive's job with a company known for its marketing expertise. To prepare for your new position, you attend in-house training sessions. The course teaches the company's methods of marketing. The first exercise requires you to develop a promotional mix with you as the target market. Develop a promotional mix and explain to the class why it would be effective.

_____

_____

_____

_____

_____

_____

_____

_____

_____

_____

_____

_____

_____

_____

_____

_____

_____

_____

ACADEMICS APPLIED Check off the academic knowledge you used to do this activity:

☐ English Language Arts　☐ Mathematics　☐ Social Studies　☐ Science

ACADEMIC AND CAREER PLAN Add this page to your Academic and Career Plan Portfolio.

CHAPTER SUMMARY

Section 11.1 Marketing Strategies

marketing (p. 256)

market (p. 256)

market segmentation
(p. 257)

demographics (p. 257)

product differentiation
(p. 258)

organizational market
(p. 259)

- The four Ps of marketing, or the marketing mix, is comprised of four marketing strategies: product, price, place, and promotion.

- Market segmentation is the process of analyzing and classifying customers in a market to create a smaller, more precise market. Market segments are identified by demographics, geographic characteristics, and psychographics. Product differentiation suggests a product is different from and better than similar products.

- A market is a set of people who share similar wants or needs and who are capable of buying products. A consumer market is made up of individuals and households of people who purchase goods and services. The organizational market includes companies that buy and resell goods, and companies that use goods to create other products. A governmental market includes city, state, and national governments.

Section 11.2 Promotion

promotional mix
(p. 262)

personal selling
(p. 267)

trade promotions
(p. 268)

consumer promotions
(p. 270)

public relations (p. 272)

- The promotional mix is a combination of the four components of promotion: advertising, personal selling, sales promotion, and public relations and publicity activities.

- Advertising messages are effective for contacting international customers. Messages can be adjusted to match cultures in any medium, including TV, radio, magazines, newspapers, outdoor advertising, the Internet, or specialty advertising. Personal selling and promotions activities are also ways to contact customers.

- Public relations is a program of messages that businesses use to publicize their products through non-advertising media, such as press releases, charitable activities, unsolicited feature stories in magazines or newspapers, and sponsorship programs.

CONCEPTS REVIEW

1. **Identify** the four Ps that make up the marketing mix.

2. **Define** the term *demographics*.

3. **List** three types of demographics used to segment a market.

4. **Distinguish** between advertising and personal selling.

5. **Explain** why most international advertising is adapted to the culture for which it is displayed.

6. **Compare** public relations to other types of promotions.

KEY TERMS REVIEW

7. Match each term to its definition.

_____ marketing

_____ market

_____ market segmentation

_____ demographics

_____ product differentiation

_____ organizational market

_____ promotional mix

_____ personal selling

_____ trade promotions

_____ consumer promotions

_____ public relations

a. the process of analyzing and classifying customers in a market to create a smaller, more precise market segment

b. an advertising approach whereby a company suggests its product is different from and better than similar products offered by competitors

c. the process of planning, pricing, promoting, selling and distributing products to satisfy customers' needs and wants

d. any combination of the four components of promotion: advertising, personal selling, sales promotion, and public relations and publicity

e. a program of activities that help an organization influence a target audience

f. tactics used to sell products to end-users, or consumers

g. any form of direct contact between a salesperson and a customer

h. tactics used to sell goods and services to other businesses

i. group of companies that buy and resell goods, and companies that use these goods to create other products

j. a set of people who share similar wants and needs and who are capable of buying products

k. statistics that describe a population in terms of personal characteristics such as age, gender, income, marital status, ethnicity, education, and occupation

Academic Vocabulary

8. On a sheet of paper, write a sentence or two related to market planning and strategy using at least three academic terms:

- statistic
- target
- predict
- constant
- survey
- database

Critical Thinking

9. Prepare a paper that discusses products purchased by people your age and why marketers target your age group.

Discussion Starter

10. Research and discuss whether you would appoint a woman to represent your company in Asian trade promotions.

Point of View

11. You are a marketing executive for a company that markets a line of baby products. Research and decide upon the best media for advertising.

BUILDING REAL-WORLD SKILLS

12. Reading Arabic Mistakes in communication between cultures often begin with presumptions. One presumption involves the direction in which written text is read. Arabic is read right to left.

Research and Share

a. What problems, especially in mass marketing, do you think might stem from such a difference?

b. How would you prevent such problems from occurring?

13. Personal Marketing All of us are "products." We go to school and seek experience in order to create our "product" that will be valued by prospective employers. We also emphasize our own product differentiation. We try to advertise ourselves in positive ways by creating a professional image that speaks of success.

Research and Write

a. Identify sources that provide information on how to create a professional image.

b. Make a list of useful suggestions to share.

BUILDING ACADEMIC SKILLS

 English Language Arts

14. In American advertising, fear of being a social outcast serves as the motivator for many advertising messages. Write a short essay that pinpoints some of your fears. Note in the essay some advertising campaigns that might use such fears to sell specific products.

Mathematics

15. When you hear the words *Super Bowl*, do you think of football or expensive commercials? In 2006, a 30-second ad spot for the professional football championship game cost a record $2.6 million. That is up from $1.6 million in 1999. How much has the cost for that 30-second commercial spot gone up on average each of those seven years?

Computation and Estimation To solve this problem, you need to understand the principles of subtraction and averaging.

 Social Studies/History

16. In 1850, P. T. Barnum introduced an unknown singer, Jenny Lind the "Swedish Nightingale," to America through numerous newspaper ads, handbills, and posters. The ad campaign was so effective that 30,000 New Yorkers met her ship at the dock when it arrived from Sweden. Like its beginnings, American advertising has remained colorful and influential. Research its history. Draft a short report on the events you think are most significant.

Science/Psychology

17. The melding of technology and psychological theory produced subliminal advertising. Such advertising allegedly produces results by exposing consumers to products without people being aware. From political ads to commercial ads, the presence and effectiveness of this advertising have been argued for decades. Research this debate. Prepare a short oral report for the class on the issue.

COMPETITIVE EVENT PREP

Cross-Cultural Salsa

18. Situation As an executive vice president of marketing for a salsa company, you must determine when and how to enter the prepackaged salsa market in Thailand. Your company has been in business in the United States for more than 30 years, and you have locations in Europe, Japan, and China.

Activities Determine the influence that Thai culture will have on your product and the salsa-related products you should offer. Develop a plan to identify your target demographic group and design an advertising campaign that will appeal to it. Identify your direct and indirect competition and evaluate your promotional approach. Consider other country issues you think are pertinent.

Evaluation You will be evaluated on how well you meet the following objectives:

a. Define the relevant cultural issues.

b. Select and evaluate the target market.

c. Compare and contrast the indirect and direct competition that exists.

d. Relate your activities to the four Ps of marketing.

BusinessWeek online

19. Newsclip: Global Packaging: The Reality It turns out that most "global brands" are really not so global after all. Even powerful multinational companies such as McDonald's and Colgate must tailor their products to a local target market.

@ Go to the International Business Online Learning Center through **glencoe.com** to read an article about this topic. Then write a paragraph that explains why a company might want to use different marketing strategies in different countries.

Standardized Test Practice

20. Find a map of Norway on the Internet or look at Appendix 1. Choose the best answer to the following multiple-choice question.

Using the map scale, what is the approximate distance from the northernmost to the southernmost point of Norway?
- ○ 1800 km
- ○ 1800 mi
- ○ 1200 km
- ○ 3000 mi

Internet Travels

Norway

Using the Internet, examine a map of Norway. Notice especially its geographical position. Research and answer the following questions about Norway on a separate sheet of paper.

➤ What are the significant demographics of the population?

➤ What forms of media would be most useful in advertising products in Norway?

@ For resources to help you do this exercise, go to the International Business Online Learning Center through **glencoe.com**.

Test-Taking Tip Examine the map key carefully. Identify which scale you want to use. If it is difficult to judge the distances visually, use some scrap paper to draw and estimate.

Chapter 12

Products, Pricing, and Distribution

Section 12.1
Product and Pricing Strategies

Section 12.2
Distribution Programs

Chapter Objectives
When you have completed this chapter, you will be able to:

Section 12.1
- Discuss methods of developing products that will succeed in the marketplace.
- Explain the process of setting prices to recover costs, meet demand, and challenge competition.

Section 12.2
- Define channels of distribution.
- Discuss choosing a mode of transportation to move goods to customers.

CASE STUDY

▶ **MATTEL**®

Mattel is a publicly owned corporation whose shares are traded on the stock exchanges. When you research this company through Standard & Poor's, you will find investment information such as this:

Index:	S&P Global 1200 and S&P 500
Sector:	Consumer Discretionary
Company:	Mattel, Incorporated
Symbol:	MAT
Country:	U.S.A.
Price:	(varies)

Global Profile In 1945, Mattel was founded in a Southern California garage by Ruth and Eliot Handler and Harold "Matt" Matson. Today Mattel designs, manufactures, and markets toys domestically and internationally. The group's best selling brands include Barbie®, American Girl®, Hot Wheels®, and Fisher-Price®. Within each brand division, Mattel produces toys and other products such as clothing.

Business Report Mattel is expanding into China's growing market of consumers who have some brand recognition of toys such as Barbie. Mattel is also working to reinvigorate the Barbie brand by launching non-toy products such as a girls' clothing collection called "Barbie loves Benetton." With global sales of more than $5.2 billion, analysts view Mattel, Inc., as a solid performer.

English Language Arts/Writing

As youth culture developed, Mattel's product lines expanded. The company has invented product franchises and also licensed figures and themes from television shows, films, and professional sports. In 1996, Mattel obtained a license to be the exclusive maker of toys related to the Nickelodeon television network, including SpongeBob SquarePants™. *Write a paragraph describing a new toy and how to develop it.*

@ To do this activity, go to the International Business Online Learning Center through **glencoe.com.**

Product and Pricing Strategies

WHAT YOU'LL LEARN

- To discuss methods of developing products that will succeed in the marketplace
- To explain the process of setting prices to recover costs, meet demand, and challenge competition

WHY IT'S IMPORTANT

Effective marketing requires matching the right product with the right consumers. Setting the right price for a product affords the best chance of success.

KEY TERMS

- skimming pricing
- penetration pricing

Academic Vocabulary

You will find these words in your reading and on your tests. Make sure you know their meanings.

- distribute
- income
- acquire

Reading Guide

Before You Read

When retail stores sell products on sale, what are some types of sales?

MAIN IDEA

A business must do careful research and planning when developing products and determining their prices.

GRAPHIC ORGANIZER

Draw this diagram. As you read, write in the steps of product development.

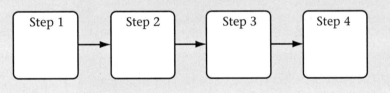

Product Development

Step 1 → Step 2 → Step 3 → Step 4

Types of Products

A business can sell many types of products, which may include both goods and services. Most products go through a product life cycle, during which time an item either peaks and declines or declines and revives as customer interest renews. The typical phases of a product life cycle include: introduction, growth, maturity, and decline. **Figure 12.1** lists three categories of products: consumer goods, industrial goods, and services. Goods are targeted to consumers, or end-users, and to businesses.

Types of Goods

Convenience consumer goods are items that are small, easy to **distribute**, have a low price, and are purchased frequently. Many large U.S. companies sell convenience goods in other nations. For example, Coca-Cola is a popular product in France.

Shopping goods tend to have higher prices than convenience goods. Consumers use a complex selection process when purchasing shopping goods such as computers.

Specialty goods are products that have unique brands and characteristics. Starbucks coffee is a specialty good because of its branding. Birkenstock shoes have distinctive styling.

Durable goods are products that are expected to last more than a year. In contrast, *nondurable goods* do not last long. Consumers purchase and use them in less than a year.

Industrial goods are sold in organizational or business-to-business (B2B) markets. Industrial goods are ideal candidates for export. Many companies export *renewable goods* and *nonrenewable extractive goods*. Renewable goods, such as agricultural products, can be regenerated or re-grown. Nonrenewable extractive goods, such as diamonds, are taken from the ground and cannot be replaced.

Types of Services

For many years, the fastest-growing segment of the U.S. economy has been services. Services are intangible benefits provided by a business to its customers. Advertisements for services highlight the benefits of using the service. Services such as hairdressing and banking services are difficult to mass produce. Services are temporary and cannot be stored or counted in an inventory. An unsold seat on an airplane flight cannot be stored for later use.

Product Development

A company identifies a target market, and then develops products to meet the needs of people in the target market. Product development is a complex task and takes time. Marketers develop products in several stages:

- Generating ideas
- Evaluating ideas
- Developing the product
- Introducing the final product to the marketplace

Figure 12.1

Types of Products

YOUR SHOPPING CART Goods and services are sold to consumers, businesses, and governments. *Do you buy or use more of one type of product? If so, which one?*

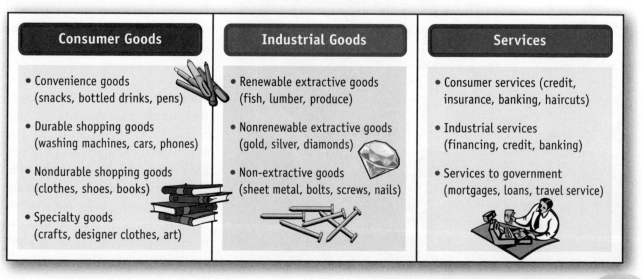

Consumer Goods	Industrial Goods	Services
• Convenience goods (snacks, bottled drinks, pens)	• Renewable extractive goods (fish, lumber, produce)	• Consumer services (credit, insurance, banking, haircuts)
• Durable shopping goods (washing machines, cars, phones)	• Nonrenewable extractive goods (gold, silver, diamonds)	• Industrial services (financing, credit, banking)
• Nondurable shopping goods (clothes, shoes, books)	• Non-extractive goods (sheet metal, bolts, screws, nails)	• Services to government (mortgages, loans, travel service)
• Specialty goods (crafts, designer clothes, art)		

Generating Ideas

Product developers generate ideas in order to identify potential new goods or services that will meet a specific need of a target market. Ideas can come from customers, middlemen, suppliers, employees, and even people outside of the company. When a company is developing a product to be sold in international markets, the marketing team must consider social, cultural, and political factors.

A culture's decision-making style affects how products are developed. In some countries a leader makes a decision and expects others to follow. In other countries it is crucial to obtain a consensus, or general agreement, before moving forward.

Political factors influence product development on two levels. Company politics refers to the way employees use tactics and strategies to gain power in workplace decisions. A staff member may push for one product to be developed over another. Governmental politics refers to policies of nations, such as their tax laws and regulations that affect business practices.

Evaluating Ideas

Companies use market research to evaluate new product ideas. You can use market research to find out if a need for a product exists, how much money people would be willing to spend to meet the need, and how many people would buy the product.

Quantitative Primary Research: Surveys Primary research involves acquiring data directly from consumers. The most common method is a survey, which is a series of questions designed to obtain consumer opinions. Consumers may fill out surveys in person at stores, by mail, over the phone, or through the Internet.

Qualitative Primary Research: Focus Groups Qualitative primary research requires the study of in-depth discussions by a small number of people. One of the best methods is a focus group. In a focus group, a facilitator asks for feedback about a product from a selected group.

Observational Primary Research Observational primary research allows marketers to observe people shopping to see how they respond to various tactics.

Experimental Primary Research Experimental primary research involves conducting an experiment using small sets of people or regions. This is also called "test market research." A company sells a good or service for a period of time to see if people will buy it. For example, McDonald's test-marketed salads on its menu.

PRIMARY RESEARCH When a survey is taken in a mall, the procedure is called a "mall intercept." *Have you ever participated in a marketing survey?*

Click on the Art of Peru

Think About It What types of goods do you think the country of Peru produces?

Half the population of Peru lives on the coast—and most people live in the capital city Lima. However, many indigenous groups also live in the Andes mountains to the east. Today indigenous artists can sell their handicrafts over the Internet through partnerships with companies that post photographs of their work online. Businesses such as Novica enable artisans worldwide to sell their work directly to individual buyers. Peruvian weaver Isidoro Rojas makes alpaca sweaters and tapestries. His life has changed by working with an online distributor. Rojas no longer spends five hours traveling from his mountain pueblo to sell his tapestries to merchants in Lima. Instead, his crafts are on the Internet for potential customers to see and buy.

Meeting and Greeting When doing business in Peru, shake hands when you meet and when you leave. Exchange business cards. It is rude to back away if Peruvians are standing close when speaking. Spanish is the language of commerce, while Quechua is the most common native language.

Business Etiquette Meetings may start on time or after a half-hour of socializing.

Business Dress Men wear formal suits, and women wear suits or dresses. Business casual and indigenous Peruvian clothing are not appropriate attire.

English Language Arts/Writing

Describe the advantages and disadvantages of an Internet site that distributes products from around the world.

Secondary Data Research Secondary data research uses information gathered by other researchers instead of new research. Sources of secondary data include databases in the library and online, government reports, reference materials and books, and information purchased from data collection companies. Secondary data may help a company determine population distribution and average income of the target market. For example, the CIA publishes data about countries on its Web site. Market research can also be used to develop a product's name and price, and to determine advertising strategies.

Developing the Product

When developing a product, a company must decide to use a standardized approach or to adapt products to individual countries. Standardization is the practice of selling the same product without modification in all markets. Many convenience goods are standardized.

Companies often adapt shopping goods for international sales. Adaptation is the modification of a product or service to fit local conditions before export. Services such as insurance and health care must be adapted to local laws and customs. Many food products are also adapted to local tastes. For example, KFC offers rice in its restaurants in China.

Introducing the Final Product

A product is produced in several stages. After an item is designed and manufactured, designers must create the packaging, labels, warranties, logos, and brand names, and then introduce the product to the marketplace.

> **As You Read**
>
> **Question** Why is primary research more costly than secondary research?

Economic Conditions

As you learned in Chapter 6, economic conditions have an impact on prices. During recessions, many buyers are more aware of prices, and lower-priced goods have an advantage.

International Business Environment

The international business environment includes all of the factors that can affect prices, including trade agreements, tariffs, taxes, import restrictions, and political unrest. These factors must be reviewed before a company decides to enter a market or to set prices.

Pricing Strategies

When a company introduces a new product, it can use two pricing strategies—skimming pricing or penetration pricing.

Skimming pricing is the practice of setting the price of a new or prestige product as high as possible. The goal is to generate revenue quickly to pay for all of the costs of developing the product. A company uses skimming when the competition will not soon enter the market. The product may be so unique that the competition cannot easily copy it. Examples of such products are iPods and electronic games.

Penetration pricing is the practice of setting the price for a product as low as possible to quickly enter a market. The competition will find it hard to get a product, such as a soft drink, into the marketplace, because it will also have to charge a low price. "Dumping" is an extreme form of penetration pricing.

Price Discounts

Sometimes a company reduces set prices. Discounts are price reductions designed to encourage new customers to buy a good or service. Businesses might also offer discounts in exchange for customer loyalty to a product or brand. The basic types of discounts are off-season, cash payment, quantity-based, trade discounts, and shipping discounts.

Off-Season Discounts

Companies may offer off-season discounts at the end of a cycle, or season. For example, businesses in the travel industry—airlines, hotels, and cruise ships—give seasonal discounts. If you are willing to travel when most people stay home, you might receive lower air fares and cheaper hotel rooms.

Cash Payment Discounts

Though not often used, businesses may offer cash payment discounts to customers who pay quickly, with cash, instead of using credit. When selling to another business, a company may offer a discount such as "2/10 net 20." This means that the seller will take 2 percent off the price if the customer pays for the goods within ten days. Otherwise, the total bill is due in 20 days.

Quantity-Based Discounts

Quantity-based discounts can be given to both individuals and organizational customers. Larger containers usually result in a lower price per unit. These quantity discounts are found on retail shelves every day.

Organizational, or business, customers may receive a lower price per unit when they buy a large quantity of items. The seller can give the discount for single purchases of the product, or the discounts can accumulate over time. For example, when a business purchases a service such as newspaper advertising, the newspaper may charge a discounted price based on the amount of advertising space the business purchases over a month.

Trade Discounts

Trade discounts are price breaks a company gives to businesses that carry its products. Their purpose is to entice the organizational buyer to purchase a large quantity of the product. For example, if Pepsi offers a trade discount on a product sold to retail grocery stores, the product is considered "on-deal." When the discount is not given, the product is called "off-deal."

Shipping Discounts

When a company offers to pay the shipping costs for an order of its products, it is providing a shipping discount. Though not free, shipping discounts can be given to individual consumers and to organizational customers.

Discounting is an important part of a pricing program. A business cannot allow another company to steal its customers because the competitor is willing to cut prices.

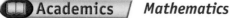

Quick Check 12.1

After You Read Respond to what you have read by answering these questions.

1. Name the main types of products. _____

_____

2. What are the steps of product development? _____

_____

3. What three factors help marketers set the price? _____

_____

Academics / Mathematics

4. If the seller offers you a 2/10 net 20 discount on a $25,000 purchase, how much will you pay if you pay within ten days?

_____

_____

Distribution Programs

WHAT YOU'LL LEARN

- To define channels of distribution
- To discuss choosing a mode of transportation to move goods to customers

WHY IT'S IMPORTANT

Shipping and handling are essential activities in international business. Customers who receive products on time and in good condition usually remain loyal.

KEY TERMS

- channel of distribution
- indirect channel of distribution
- direct channel of distribution
- direct marketing

Academic Vocabulary

You will find these words in your reading and on your tests. Make sure you know their meanings.

- range
- transfer
- adjust

Reading Guide

Before You Read

Can you name some methods of transportation used to deliver goods to consumers?

MAIN IDEA

When marketing and delivering items internationally, successful businesses must navigate national boundaries so their products reach their customers.

GRAPHIC ORGANIZER

Draw this diagram. As you read, write three methods of distribution using this diagram.

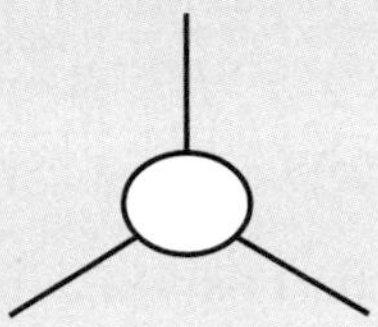

Methods of Distribution

After a company develops, prices, and also promotes a product, company marketers arrange for the final element of the marketing mix—place, or distributing the product to the customer.

Marketers first choose between three basic options for distribution: intensive distribution, selective distribution, or exclusive distribution.

Intensive Distribution

Intensive distribution is the placement of products for sale in every possible place. Typically, convenience goods such as candy, coffee, and gasoline are intensively distributed. Some locations where these goods are sold may not even return a good profit, but the goal is to make the product as convenient and widely available as possible.

Selective Distribution

Selective distribution is the practice of placing items for sale only in carefully chosen retail outlets. Companies are careful not to license too many retailers in a certain **range** because competition will drive down profits.

Exclusive Distribution

A company uses exclusive distribution when its products are for sale in only one retail outlet per market area. The purpose is to give the product an elite status. Exclusive distribution is often used for high-priced durable goods.

As You Read

Question What are the benefits of exclusive distribution?

Channels of Distribution

A **channel of distribution** is the path a product takes from the producer to the consumer. It is a chain of intermediaries that take a product from production to consumption. Distribution channels differ for end-users, or consumers, and for organizational markets, or businesses. (See **Figure 12.3**.)

Consumer Markets

The consumer service market uses one or more versions of the channel of distribution. These channels and intermediaries make up a traditional marketing channel:

Producer → Wholesaler → Retailer → Consumer

An **indirect channel of distribution** is a path that uses consumer agents or merchant middlemen to distribute products from producer to consumer. A wholesaler that represents goods but does not sell them is an agent wholesaler. Merchant wholesalers buy goods and resell them. The same is true for agent retailers and merchant retailers.

Figure 12.3

Channels of Distribution

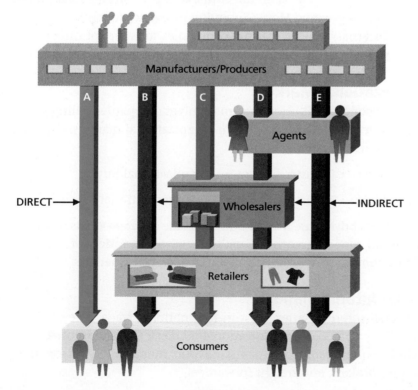

PATHS TO THE CONSUMER
Many different paths lead to a product's final destination—the consumer. *What type of channel is used for a store brand?*

DIRECT MARKETING The Home Shopping Network (HSN) is a direct distribution channel in the United States. *How would you adapt HSN for a Japanese audience? An Italian audience?*

Direct Marketing

A **direct channel of distribution** is a path used to sell products directly to customers without the use of wholesalers or retailers. **Direct marketing** is the practice of contacting buyers directly. A company contacts buyers in several ways:

- Catalogs (via postal mail)
- E-mail (via the Internet)
- Television and radio

Catalogs and Mail Paper catalogs sent to consumers by postal mail are a popular form of direct marketing. Consumers read catalogs during leisure time and can purchase items using the telephone, e-mail, online order forms, or the postal system.

E-Mail Successful e-mail marketing programs are usually part of a larger marketing approach. Examples include customer relationship management (CRM) programs, frequency programs such as frequent flyer miles, or e-commerce programs. Many e-tailers send e-mails announcing sales or products. Most consumers do not welcome mass e-mail, which can be considered "spam" or "junk mail."

Television and Radio Television and radio ads offer direct response methods, such as calling a toll-free number to order goods. The most elaborate forms of television direct marketing are infomercials, often aired late at night, and Home Shopping Network programs.

For international marketing, companies must adapt direct marketing programs to specific countries, their languages, and customs.

Organizational Markets

The second distribution system involves companies selling goods and services to other businesses. In organizational markets, there are two main distribution channels:

Producer → Industrial Agent → Organizational Buyer

Producer → Industrial Merchant → Organizational Buyer

Business buyers use merchandise to make other products. Iron ore, aluminum, wood, sheet metal, nails, screws, and a variety of goods are sold in domestic and international organizational markets.

Global Intermediaries

Global intermediaries assist in international trade. They operate in both consumer and organizational markets. Global intermediaries include export trading companies, export management companies, customs brokers, and freight forwarders.

Riding Reef's Wave

Fernando and Santiago Aguerre have been in business together since they were children in Argentina. As teens, they fixed surfboards, made jewelry, and eventually opened a surf shop. In 1981, Santiago moved to San Diego. Then, after graduating from law school, Fernando joined his brother Santiago in Southern California. Naturally, their thoughts turned to starting another business.

As beachgoers, they recognized a need for quality sandals. So, while traveling in Brazil, they met with a footwear maker who serviced the shop they ran in Argentina. With $4,000, they started a line of middle- to high-end sandals sold through action-sports and beach-lifestyle shops around the world. Reef carefully cultivated core customers, instead of selling to average consumers at sporting goods outlets and stores in malls. Reef's catalog then expanded to include women's footwear, shoes, and accessories. In 2005, the Aguerre brothers sold Reef for more than $100 million to VF Corp—but they remain on board as consultants riding the wave of this international business.

THE FANNING

THINK GLOBALLY *What factors might affect selling Reef's products on a global scale?*

To learn more about the country of origin for this global business, go to the International Business Online Learning Center through **glencoe.com**.

Export Trading Companies Export trading companies buy goods from producers and resell them to companies that they operate. Trading companies work with department stores, grocery stores, car dealerships, and other retail operations. They also buy raw materials on behalf of local manufacturers.

Export Management Companies Export management companies represent specific products in world markets. They provide all of the distribution services, including preparation of the necessary documents. Export management companies tend to work with established customers and assist producers with selling their products to end-users and organizational buyers.

Customs Brokers Customs brokers specialize in moving products through the customs process. They need a license to clear the inspection process and duties-payment system efficiently.

Freight Forwarders Freight forwarders help **transfer** a physical product to its final destination. A freight forwarder can combine small shipments from several companies into one larger shipment. The result is lower shipping rates for the companies.

Physical Distribution and Shipment

Delivering the actual good or service requires distribution and shipment. The seller chooses the proper mode of transportation—trucking and motor carriers, airline carriers, railroads, sea carriers by water routes, pipelines, or combination methods.

- **Trucking and motor carriers**—This is an excellent choice if the sender and receiver are connected by roads. However, inspections at international border crossings can delay shipping.

- **Airline carriers**—This mode offers quick, though more expensive, service for packages, mail, and perishable goods, such as food and flowers.

- **Railroads**—Trains carry large goods and bulk goods to organizational buyers. They transport many products, including wheat and flour, lumber, iron, and steel, and automobiles. Rail delivery functions only where there are tracks leading to key destination areas.

- **Sea carriers by water routes**—Oceans, rivers, lakes, and canals are water routes. Ships and barges can inexpensively carry many items that trucks or trains deliver on land routes.

- **Pipelines**—Liquids such as natural gas and oil can be transported via pipelines. Many international pipelines exist around the world to quickly deliver huge volumes of product at low cost.

- **Combination methods**—Another option for distribution involves "intermodal delivery"—using two or more transportation methods. A rail system combined with a delivery truck, or a tractor with trailers, may be used for "piggyback delivery."

Shipment Packages and Labels

Packaging and labels for international shipments must meet stringent requirements. A package must be strong enough to protect the contents for a long trip. It must be moisture-proof and as tamper-proof and theft-proof as possible. The package should also be lightweight in order to minimize shipping costs.

Companies adapt labels for the world market. Labels must communicate the right message in the right language with all required information in order to avoid delays when officials at border checkpoints inspect shipments. Some international symbols on labels include *Fragile, Keep Cold, Wash in Cold Water,* and *Flammable.*

Shipping Documents

Shipping documents accompany goods across national borders. They must meet the logistical and legal requirements of international trade. Accurate shipping documents can help keep products from being unnecessarily detained at international borders. In addition to the certificate of origin and the bill of lading, which includes a product description and weight, there are other shipping documents:

- **Export declaration**—This document is required on shipments with a value of $500 or more. The export declaration is a copy of the bill of lading plus the names of the carrier company and the exporting vessel that are transporting the shipment.

- **Destination control statement**—This document verifies the contents of goods and the final destination.

- **Insurance certificate**—This important document states the amount of insurance provided for goods being shipped. It names the insurance company and the exporting company.

INDUSTRIAL PRODUCTION MANAGER

The industrial production manager's job has become more complex over the past decades. Running a warehouse involves managing employees, handling a set number of products, monitoring their inventory, placing orders for replacements, and ensuring that products being shipped out go to the right place. However, international business has changed the role of the industrial production manager. Warehouse orders are often shipped to destinations all over the globe, which means they have to be packed and labeled in certain ways.

Overseeing the logistics of a shipping and warehousing operation means making sure that each step in the process makes logical sense, and wastes as little time and resources as possible. This means creating separate processes—and perhaps, separate sections of the warehouse—for different destinations. Industrial production managers split their time between the warehouse and the office. They are always on call and may work more than 40 hours a week.

Skills and Training

Industrial production managers have computer, leadership, and stress-management skills. They need good mathematical skills in order to manage their budget and schedule. Strong communication skills are necessary for managing other employees and handling shipping documents.

Some companies require industrial production managers to have a bachelor's degree, while others provide training to those with a high school diploma or associate's degree.

English Language Arts/Writing

What role do industrial production managers play in the distribution channel?

@ To learn more about industrial production managers and their career paths, go to the International Business Online Learning Center through **glencoe.com**.

Career Data

Education: High school diploma, associate's degree, or bachelor's degree

Skills: Technical, computer, mathematics, and communication skills

Outlook: Growth slower than average in the next ten years

The Right Place and Time

Sourcing, transportation, and safety in moving products to market are becoming increasingly more complex because of the variety of transportation choices, increasing threats, and added security measures of a global marketplace. The method and efficiency of distribution can determine the success or failure of a product line. If an American car assembly plant is waiting for parts from a Japanese manufacturer, production could be shut down until the parts arrive. *Research and write about why employees' cultural diversity would be advantageous in companies such as FedEx and UPS.*

The Global Marketing Mix

Chapter 11 and Chapter 12 explain how the components of the marketing mix (product, price, place, and promotion) combine to create an effective marketing program. This mix applies in both domestic and global markets.

Promotional programs include a mix of advertising, personal selling, consumer and trade promotions, and public relations and publicity. These efforts must adapt to local customs, cultures, and languages.

Companies must either standardize or adapt their products for international distribution. Producers must **adjust** brands, packages, and labels to the local culture and legal requirements of the countries where they are marketing their products. Production methods must also be adapted.

Prices must reflect costs, demand, and competitive challenges of the countries involved. Producing companies tailor their discount programs to fit the needs of the international trading partner.

Companies also choose intensive, selective, or exclusive distribution programs to get their products to customers. For this, they must choose the best transportation method for a product to be placed in the global marketplace.

Reading Check **Analyze** Describe the marketing mix and how "product" relates to distribution.

International Marketing

Marketing is an extremely important part of any successful business operation. Making the needed adjustments can help a business find new customers on a global scale, and then expand sales.

Quick Check 12.2

After You Read Respond to what you have read by answering these questions.

1. Name the two main channels of distribution used to reach end-user consumer customers. _____

_____

2. Name the major forms of transportation that can be used to deliver products. _____

_____

3. Name all of the elements in the marketing mix. _____

_____

Academics / Social Studies/Geography

4. If a freight forwarder plans to transport 500 compact cars from Boston to London, what shipment method will the freight forwarder most likely choose? Explain why.

_____

_____

Development of Goods and Services

As part of an in-house training program, your employer wants ideas for new products. You must develop one new good and one new service idea for the company. Describe the company and the ideas as well as the steps of your product development.

_____

_____

_____

_____

_____

_____

_____

_____

_____

_____

_____

_____

_____

_____

_____

_____

_____

_____

_____

_____

_____

ACADEMICS APPLIED Check off the academic knowledge you used to do this activity:

☐ English Language Arts   ☐ Mathematics   ☐ Social Studies   ☐ Science

ACADEMIC AND CAREER PLAN Add this page to your Academic and Career Plan Portfolio.

(tl) Ulf Wallin/Getty Images; (tr) Royalty-free/David De Lossy/Getty Images; (b) Royalty-free/Getty Images

CHAPTER SUMMARY

Section 12.1 Product and Pricing Strategies

skimming pricing
(p. 286)

penetration pricing
(p. 286)

- Product development is a complex task. A product must meet the needs of people in the target market. There are several stages of product development: generating ideas, evaluating ideas, developing the product, and introducing the final product to the marketplace. Companies often adapt products for international markets.

- Setting prices in international markets is a challenge. Businesses must consider the effects of monetary exchange rates, economic conditions, and the overall global business environment. Companies may use pricing strategies, such as skimming pricing or penetration pricing, to gain an advantage in the marketplace. Various price discounts also encourage consumers to purchase products.

Section 12.2 Distribution Programs

channel of distribution
(p. 289)

indirect channel of
distribution (p. 289)

direct channel of
distribution (p. 290)

direct marketing
(p. 290)

- The channel of distribution is the path a product takes from the producer to the consumer. Within that path, there is an indirect channel of distribution, which is the path that uses consumer agents or merchant middlemen to distribute products from producer to consumer. Another path is a direct channel of distribution, which is the path used to sell products directly to customers.

- Delivering products requires physical distribution, which involves moving a product from producer to consumer. Different modes of transportation include trucking and motor carriers, airline carriers, railroads, sea carriers by water routes, pipelines, and combination methods.

CONCEPTS REVIEW

1. **List** the stages of product development.

2. **Identify** the three factors that must be considered in evaluating a target market.

3. **Explain** how monetary exchange rates may affect pricing decisions in international marketing.

4. **Describe** the international business environment.

5. **Distinguish** between a direct and an indirect channel of distribution.

6. **Explain** the three basic distribution options.

KEY TERMS REVIEW

7. Match each term to its definition.

_____ skimming pricing

_____ penetration pricing

_____ channel of distribution

_____ indirect channel of distribution

_____ direct channel of distribution

_____ direct marketing

a. the practice of setting the price of a new or prestige product as high as possible

b. the practice of setting the price for a product as low as possible to quickly enter a market

c. a path that uses consumer agents or merchant middlemen to distribute products from producer to consumer

d. the practice of contacting buyers directly

e. a path used to sell products directly to customers without the use of wholesalers or retailers

f. the path a product takes from the producer to the consumer

Academic Vocabulary

8. On a separate sheet of paper, write a sentence or two related to products, pricing, and distribution using at least three of the academic terms you learned in the section openers:
- distribute
- income
- acquire
- range
- transfer
- adjust

Critical Thinking

9. Customs brokers and freight forwarders offer companies assistance with international trade. Write a paragraph about whether the use of such assistance in selling goods in foreign markets is justified.

Discussion Starter

10. Focus groups bring out potential user reactions to products in a cost-effective way. However, they reflect only what subjects in the group say they would do rather than what they would actually do. Focus groups are expensive. Research the use of focus groups. Discuss whether they are worth the expense.

Point of View

11. Certain dimensions and heat patterns on faces can be used to identify people. Today facial mapping and thermography, coupled with a database of driver's license pictures, can identify up to 17 individuals per second. Marketers in the United States want to match the identifications with a consumer's disposable income and spending patterns. Write a short paragraph expressing your opinion of such a practice.

BUILDING REAL-WORLD SKILLS

The GLOBAL WORKPLACE

12. Haggling over Prices You walk into a store in a middle-eastern country to buy a scarf displayed in its window. The friendly shopkeeper smiles and nods as you pick up the scarf. You take the exact marked price in change out of your coin purse and put it on the counter. The shopkeeper scowls at you as he counts the money. As you leave the store, he throws his hands up. Mystified by his behavior, you explain what happened to a friend. She explains that he was insulted because you did not haggle over the price.

Research and Share

a. Research the tradition of bargaining.

b. Present your findings to the class, and explain why the shopkeeper was insulted.

The U.S. WORKPLACE

13. Beware of Competitors Intelligence information about a competitor's prices, products, and distribution plan may make or break a company. Commercial spying reached new heights with the launching of private spy satellites available to anyone with a credit card. Even governments spy on behalf of their country's companies. The U.S. government regularly tracks bribery attempts by foreign firms in competition with American firms for contracts.

Research and Write

a. Research current commercial spying.

b. Write a one-page paper about whether you would recommend such a tactic.

BUILDING ACADEMIC SKILLS

ELA English Language Arts

14. Write a short essay that predicts the global impact that increased standardization may have.

MATH Mathematics

15. A Japanese car company is considering building a production facility in Brazil. The fixed costs for plant and equipment are estimated at 1.5 billion in U.S. dollars. However, the plant is expected to produce more than 200,000 vehicles during its life. The variable cost for each vehicle is projected at $2,500. If the cars were sold at an average price equal to double their total costs, what is the average sales price?

Computation and Estimation To solve this problem, you need to understand and apply the principles of division and averaging.

SOC Social Studies/Sociology

16. The kind of products marketed in a country by international firms depends on many factors, such as the amount of time for relaxation and other activities. This is dependent on the number of hours in the typical work week. Research the typical work week in a country of your choice, other than the United States. Report on the advisability of marketing labor-saving devices and hobby items in that country.

SOC Social Studies/Economics

17. New product introductions, especially of electronic goods, often utilize a skimming pricing strategy. Research the use of this technique for cost recovery. Report to the class about why this approach is advisable for electronics.

COMPETITIVE EVENT PREP

Creating High-End Appeal

18. Situation You are the marketing director for Ferrari. Your job is to create a profile of the type of customer who would purchase your sports car in the United States. You must then create a design that will appeal to that customer.

Activity Start by creating a profile of the car itself. What are the best features of a Ferrari? What image does the company use to sell its cars in the United States as well as abroad? Identify the age, income level, geographic area, and psychographic characteristics of current Ferrari customers, and then determine which product and price changes could be made to appeal to a wider market.

Evaluation You will be evaluated on how well you meet the following objectives:

a. Prepare a list of the most unique and desired characteristics of the Ferrari.

b. Identify and define the target market in America.

c. Modify the product design to attract a wider market. Explain each change and its appeal.

d. Write a script for a TV commercial or ad copy for a magazine advertisement to sell the new product design. Explain where and when you would place these ads.

Internet Travels

Vietnam

Using the Internet, find a map of Vietnam. Study its geographical position. Answer the following questions about Vietnam on a separate sheet of paper.

➤ Research the form of government of Vietnam.

➤ Would you expect gaining access to the Vietnamese market to be relatively easy or relatively difficult? Explain your answer.

@ For resources to help you do this exercise, go to the International Business Online Learning Center through **glencoe.com**.

BusinessWeek online

19. Newsclip: FedEx Companies whose products are manufactured in China are turning to third-party carriers such as FedEx for fast, cost-saving shipping.

@ Go to the International Business Online Learning Center through **glencoe.com** to read an article about this topic. Then write a paragraph that explains how FedEx can help cut warehousing costs.

Standardized Test Practice

20. Choose the best answer to the following multiple-choice question.

You are a Panamanian manufacturer of integrated circuit boards who needs to rush product samples to a buyer in Los Angeles, California. Which transportation mode would be the most cost-efficient?

○ Container ship
○ Motor carrier
○ Air carrier
○ Railroad

Test-Taking Tip This question requires you to make inferences based on generalizations. Note details in the question that provide the basis for choosing the correct answer or eliminating the wrong ones.

Accounting and Financing Practices

Chapter Objectives

When you have completed this chapter, you will be able to:

Section 13.1

- Explain how to assess profits and assets using standard accounting documents.
- Identify ways in which currency exchanges and inflation rates affect accounting statements.
- Discuss financial laws and accounting standards.

Section 13.2

- Identify the four Cs of the negotiation process.
- Describe the three primary sources of capital.
- Differentiate between common and preferred stock.
- Explain funding with bonds, bank loans, and governmental funding.

▶ BANK OF AMERICA

Bank of America is a publicly owned corporation whose shares are traded on the stock exchanges. When you research this company through Standard & Poor's, you will find investment information such as this:

Index:	S&P Global 1200
Sector:	Financials
Company:	Bank of America Corporation
Symbol:	BAC
Country:	U.S.A.
Price:	(varies)

Global Profile The origins of Bank of America can be traced to San Francisco's Bank of Italy, founded by A.P. Giannini in 1904. Bank of America provides banking and non-banking financial services and products. Services include deposit products, lending loans, investment banking, capital markets, and leasing and financial advisory services. Individuals, small businesses, middle market companies, financial institutions, and government entities are all customers of Bank of America.

Business Report Bank of America employs more than 77,000 full-time workers in 29 states and the District of Columbia. Through its network of 5,800 banking centers and 16,700 ATMs located in 37 countries throughout North America, Asia, Europe, the Middle East, Africa, and South America, the corporation maintains a global presence. With more than $82.5 billion in sales globally, Bank of America stock is part of many investment portfolios.

📝 *English Language Arts/Writing*

Bank of America has operated in Central America and South America since 1917, when it opened an office in Argentina for wool merchants. Known as *BankBoston* in Argentina, Brazil, Chile, and Uruguay, the bank serves individuals and businesses. *Why might a South American company use an American bank?*

@ To do this activity, go to the International Business Online Learning Center through **glencoe.com**.

Accounting Practices

WHAT YOU'LL LEARN

- To explain how to assess profits and assets using standard accounting documents
- To identify ways in which currency exchanges and inflation rates affect accounting statements
- To discuss financial laws and accounting standards

WHY IT'S IMPORTANT

Businesses must know how to use accounting systems around the world.

KEY TERMS

- accounting
- income statement
- balance sheet
- inflation
- cost accounting
- audit
- accounting cycle
- International Accounting Standards Board (IASB)

Academic Vocabulary

You will find these words in your reading and on your tests. Make sure you know their meanings.

- estimate
- appreciate
- journal

Reading Guide

Before You Read

What are assets? What assets do you own?

MAIN IDEA
Knowing the accounting rules that international trading partners must follow can help a business avoid costly errors.

GRAPHIC ORGANIZER
Draw this table. As you read, write in the complete phrase or name represented by each of the following acronyms.

Acronym	Phrase
IASB	
FASB	
GAAP	

Accounting Basics

Are you good with numbers? International businesspeople need math skills to understand accounting and financial statements. This chapter discusses the basics of accounting and finance.

International Accounting

Records and reports help businesses operate efficiently and profitably. **Accounting** is the systematic process of recording and reporting the financial position of a business. There are two basic financial reports used by accountants to study the financial well-being of a company:

1. The income statement
2. The balance sheet

Preparing these documents for a business in a single country such as the United States is relatively simple. On the other hand, when they are used for a business in more than one country, the preparation process can be more complicated.

Figure 13.1 illustrates a typical **income statement**, which is a report of a business's net income or net loss for an accounting period. An accounting period may be a month, a quarter, or a year. The beginning of the report is a statement about sales called "Revenue." Revenue is income for a business. The bottom line on the statement lists "Net Income," which is the actual profit that a company has earned after paying costs and operating expenses. This statement is also called a "profit and loss statement." The income statement is used for tax purposes. It also provides information to owners or shareholders as well as for banks or lenders.

Figure 13.2 on page 304 illustrates a typical **balance sheet**, which is a report of the balances of all assets, liabilities, and owner's equity at the end of an accounting period. It lists two categories—*assets*, or what a business owns such as inventory and equipment, and *liabilities*, what a business owes. The total liabilities are subtracted from the total assets to find the amount of equity, which is what the company owns after paying all expenses and debts. This calculation is expressed as a formula:

$$\text{Assets} - \text{Liabilities} = \text{Equity}$$

Figure 13.1

Income Statement

PLUS AND MINUS An income statement is used to report profits to both the government and to company owners. *What might the term* bottom line *mean?*

City Pets
Income Statement
For the Year Ended December 31, 20--

Revenue:		
Sales		292,619
Cost of Merchandise Sold:		
Merchandise on Hand Jan. 1	83,744	
Plus Merchandise Purchased	205,813	
Merchandise Available for Sale	289,557	
Minus Merchandise Still on Hand	93,281	
Total Cost of Merchandise Sold:		196,276
Gross Profit on Sales		96,343
Operating Expenses:		
Advertising Expense	2,734	
Insurance Expense	487	
Maintenance Expense	3,551	
Miscellaneous Expense	762	
Rent Expense	18,500	
Salaries Expense	26,931	
Supplies Expense	1,024	
Utilities Expense	4,107	
Total Operating Expenses:		58,096
Net Income		38,247

Figure 13.2

Balance Sheet

IN BALANCE The balance sheet states what you owe and what you own. *What is the amount of assets owned by City Pets? Of equity?*

City Pets
Balance Sheet
December 31, 20--

ASSETS

Cash in Bank	35,372	
Accounts Receivable	14,201	
Merchandise Inventory	93,281	
Supplies	8,285	
Office Equipment	12,187	
Display Equipment	47,883	
TOTAL ASSETS		211,209

LIABILITIES

Accounts Payable	42,722	
Sales Tax Payable	3,621	
Payroll Taxes Payable	2,749	
TOTAL LIABILITIES		49,092

OWNER'S EQUITY

Jake Akimoto, Capital	162,117
TOTAL LIABILITIES + OWNER'S EQUITY	211,209

When a company operates in more than one country, several factors affect the income statement and the balance sheet:

- Currency conversion and the exchange rate
- Inflation
- Accounting standards
- Auditing standards
- Disclosure

Currency Conversion and Exchange Rates

Consider a company that has branches in Japan, Korea, and Brazil. The currencies used in these three countries are the *yen, won,* and *real,* respectively. The traditional way of recording money on financial statements is to convert all money into the currency used in the home country. If the home country is the United States, the yen, won, and real amounts would be converted to U.S. dollars.

In addition, as described in Chapter 7, there are several types of exchange rates. The hard currency rate is the most common. Some countries, such as China, have exchange rate controls—the rate is determined by the government. Exchange rates can change daily. An **estimate** of the exchange rate is not sufficient for reports. So, many companies rely on exchange rates provided by the International Monetary Fund, the World Bank, Eurocurrencies, and other organizations.

Inflation

When business transactions occur between companies that are in different countries, accountants must be aware of inflation rates for each country. **Inflation** is the rise in the level of prices for goods and services over time. The inflation rate is not the same in every country.

Accountants need to know how much things cost in order to prepare balance sheets and income statements. Inflation affects those costs. **Cost accounting** is a method of accounting that adjusts the cost of goods to reflect a country's inflation rate. This method gives a more accurate estimate of the real cost of replacing items.

As You Read

Predict Why is accounting called the "language of business"?

Accounting Standards

Accounting standards are the rules an accountant must follow to prepare financial statements. They determine how an accounting department presents financial information. The problem for international companies is that accounting standards are not the same in every country. The standards vary due to several financial factors:

- Replacement costs
- Lease payments as tax deduction
- Depreciation

Replacement Costs When a company buys new computers, what is the replacement cost for the computers? How should the computers be valued? The *current cost* (what it would cost to replace an item) versus the *historic cost* (the purchase price) affect value. In the case of computers, many computers are cheaper to buy now than they were three years ago. Accountants must know the country's laws regarding the value of assets. In the Netherlands the current cost is the value. In Japan the historic cost is the value.

Lease Payments A lease payment is similar to rent. For example, instead of purchasing an item, a business leases an item, such as a building, computer, or automobile. The business makes monthly payments in exchange for being able to use the item. The lease is a contract that spells out all of the terms, such as how much the business will pay each month, the length of time of the lease, and what happens when the lease ends. Some leases state a purchase price for the item so the business can either buy the item at that price or create a new lease for a new or upgraded item.

In the United States, lease payments on business items are tax-deductible. This means the yearly cost of renting a building or a computer can reduce the amount of taxes a company pays. Different countries treat lease payments in different ways. The tax considerations for lease payments in France vary greatly from those in the United Kingdom.

RENTED PROPERTY Many businesses lease space in the United States and abroad. *Is leased space a business asset? Why or why not?*

A World Bank: HSBC

The Hong Kong and Shanghai Banking Corporation Limited (HSBC) was formed in 1865 to foster trade between China and Europe. It was founded by Thomas Sutherland, an employee of Peninsular and Oriental Steam Navigation Company. He recognized the need for banks while working in Asia. After opening branches in Hong Kong and Shanghai, the bank expanded to Japan and Thailand, where it helped to print money, or currency. The bank shut its doors in many parts of Asia during World War II but continued to operate out of its London office.

In 1946, HSBC returned its operations to Hong Kong, and proceeded to bankroll the recovery of that British colony and do business in Malaysia, India, and other countries.

In the 1980s and 1990s, HSBC expanded in the United States and Europe. With more than 98,000 offices in Europe, the Asia-Pacific region, the Americas, the Middle East, and Africa, HSBC is now among the world's largest financial institutions—but calls itself "The world's local bank."

THINK GLOBALLY *What are some challenges of handling finance between countries?*

@ To learn more about the country of origin for this global business, go to the International Business Online Learning Center through **glencoe.com**.

Depreciation Depreciation of a business asset means that the value of the item decreases over time due to use and/or age. For example, if a company has a fleet of company cars, those cars lose value each year. A 2005 Honda Element is worth less today than when it was purchased. Depreciation is the amount that represents the loss. On the other hand, if a business asset **appreciates**, its value increases over time.

In the United States, the amount of depreciation during a year is tax-deductible, which is an advantage. A company can spread the costs of an asset over several accounting periods. Individual countries have different laws regarding whether depreciation can be called a company expense on an income statement. Depreciation also appears in different ways on the balance sheet. In Germany, depreciation is shown as a liability. In Great Britain and the United States, depreciation is deducted from the value of an asset to calculate its current worth.

Auditing Standards

To ensure that a company completes tax statements, shareholder statements, and other documents fairly and legally, an outside observer can perform an audit. An **audit** is a review of a company's accounting statements by an independent observer, or auditor. Many firms also conduct internal audits. An employee who is not directly involved in preparing accounting statements can perform the audit.

Auditing standards are the rules governing observers who conduct audits. These rules vary according to a nation's laws. Anyone who performs audits must use methods set by the local government.

✔ **Reading Check** **Analyze** Why do companies conduct both internal and external audits?

Disclosure

Disclosure is the act of revealing business and financial information to the public. Laws vary widely in different countries regarding disclosure. It is important for an accountant to know what a company must disclose when preparing balance sheets, income summaries, and other financial documents.

In some countries, financial records are easy to access. The law requires companies to openly report their accounting statements. For example, the United States enacted the Accounting Reform and Investor Protection Act of 2002, or Sarbanes-Oxley Act. The purpose of this act is to improve the accuracy of financial statements and to ensure full disclosure of information. In countries that require higher levels of disclosure, it easier to check whether a company is acting ethically and legally. In other countries, such as some Asian countries, financial records are often kept secret, especially by companies owned by individual families or the government.

The Accounting Cycle

During an accounting period, a business records all financial transactions. The **accounting cycle** includes the activities, or steps, that help a business keep its accounting records in an orderly manner. **Figure 13.3** illustrates the steps of the accounting cycle. Accountants record business transactions in a **journal** to comply with international accounting practices.

Figure 13.3

The Accounting Cycle

STEP-BY-STEP PROGRAM Accountants use these steps to create reports and keep company records in order. *What might be one advantage of using the accounting cycle?*

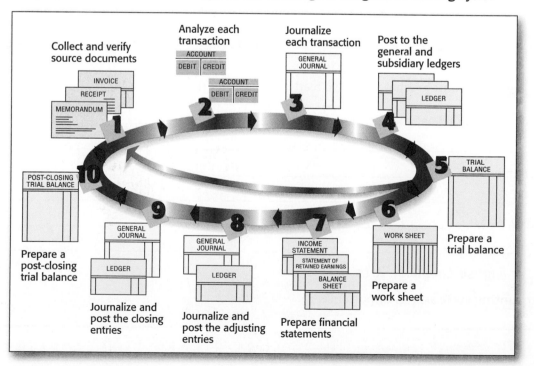

International Accounting Practices

Two organizations have helped to create uniform accounting practices worldwide. The International Accounting Standards Committee (IASC) was established in 1973. In 2001, it was replaced by the **International Accounting Standards Board (IASB)**, an organization that creates accounting standards that businesses use around the world. Many nations recognize and use IASB standards. However, IASB standards have not had much impact on U.S. companies because most of the standards are consistent with standards set by the U.S. Financial Accounting Standards Board (FASB).

GAAP

In the United States, accountants use the *generally accepted accounting principles (GAAP)*. GAAP is a standard set of guidelines used in recording and reporting financial changes. With all businesses using the same system, anyone examining a company's records can understand its financial reports.

However, GAAP standards and IASB standards are not exactly the same. For example, IASB standards require that "goodwill" is reported. Goodwill is an estimate of a company's value that includes intangible things such as a name and customer loyalty. It appears on balance sheets when a company is sold. With such variations, it is important for businesspeople to understand global accounting standards.

The Language of Business

When a company has operations in another country, the job of accounting becomes more complicated. Some people call accounting the "language of business." In a sense, an international accountant must become fluent in a new "language of business." Accountants must adjust the value of money and the accounting methods when preparing an income statement or a balance sheet.

Quick Check 13.1

After You Read Respond to what you have read by answering these questions.

1. What does a balance sheet reveal about company assets? _____

_____

2. What is an exchange rate? _____

_____

3. What is an audit? _____

_____

Academics *English Language Arts*

4. Explain the accounting cycle and its importance.

_____

_____

Financing Practices

Reading Guide

Before You Read

If you were a seller in a "buyer's market," do you think you would be able to bargain for a lower price? Why or why not?

MAIN IDEA

A country's lending practices and a business owner's ability to negotiate determine the best way to raise money for an international business.

GRAPHIC ORGANIZER

Draw this flow chart. As you read, write in the three primary sources of capital.

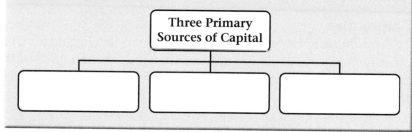

Three Primary Sources of Capital

WHAT YOU'LL LEARN

- To identify the four Cs of the negotiation process
- To describe the three primary sources of capital
- To differentiate between common and preferred stock
- To explain funding with bonds, bank loans, and governmental funding

WHY IT'S IMPORTANT

Effective companies manage money well. Managing money includes raising capital, bargaining, and finding money at reasonable rates.

KEY TERMS

- bargaining power
- common stock
- preferred stock
- bond

Academic Vocabulary

You will find these words in your reading and on your tests. Make sure you know their meanings.

- purchase
- percent
- equate

Types of Financing Practices

You have learned about accounting practices. You were also introduced to the documents needed for closing a sale and shipping goods. This section focuses on how to finance international operations. You will learn about negotiation processes, which vary widely around the world. Companies negotiate price, delivery options, financing, and payment. The section also discusses how companies can raise money for international expansion.

Negotiation Processes

How do you close a deal? The answer to that question may be very different depending on where you live. Negotiation is part of nearly every international business transaction. Negotiation processes include four components, also known as the *four Cs*:

1. Common interests
2. Conflicting interests
3. Criteria
4. Compromise

As You Read

Relate Have you ever had to make a compromise? What was it?

Common Interests

Common interests can build strong bonds when a buying company negotiates with a selling company. Both parties may share similar goals. The buying company must be able to purchase goods from a reliable, trustworthy company. By establishing common interests, companies can develop an understanding and atmosphere of trust.

Conflicting Interests

Each side should reveal any conflicts with national or governmental interests. For example, the exporting of jobs conflicts with the national interests of many countries. Most countries want to encourage employment for their own residents.

Dependence is a form of conflicting interest. Dependence can occur when a company relies on just one other firm in another country. It is not in a company's best interests to be 100 or even 90 **percent** dependent on one supplier, especially if the supplier goes out of business, raises prices, or cannot deliver goods.

Criteria

Criteria are the objectives of both sides in the negotiations. The buyer company wants a certain price to achieve certain profit goals. The seller is interested in receiving a good price and selling as many units as possible.

Compromise

Compromise is the "give and take" that occurs in a negotiation, or bargaining session. Each party must usually give up some interest in order to reach a middle ground and arrive at an agreement. Both sides know what concessions they are willing and not willing to make.

Bargaining Power

A firm's willingness to compromise is affected by its level of bargaining power. **Bargaining power** is a company's ability to achieve its goals without compromise. A firm with no bargaining power must always concede or compromise. A company with high bargaining power can dictate terms. Bargaining power depends on relative value, available alternatives, and the time horizon.

Relative Value

Relative value is a key component of bargaining power. If a buying company highly values what the other company is selling, the buying company has a weaker bargaining position. On the other hand, if the buyer can "take it or leave it," **preceding** the sale the buyer has a stronger bargaining position.

Available Alternatives

Having alternatives can allow a company to walk away from the bargaining table. When a buyer knows there are plenty of suppliers, the buyer has a stronger bargaining position. This situation is known as a *buyer's market*. If the seller has many potential buyers, he or she has the stronger position. That situation is a *seller's market*.

The Time Horizon

Time is another factor in the negotiation process. The time horizon is viewed as either short term or long term. If one company has a short-term time horizon, it is in a hurry to finalize a deal—and has less bargaining power. Having patience and a long-term time horizon is almost always a bargaining asset.

Culture and Negotiations

Culture affects negotiations in different countries. Some of the key cultural issues that affect bargaining include punctuality, eye contact and directness, who speaks first, disagreement and agreement, and honor systems.

Punctuality

Being on time is a high priority in some cultures, including the United States. To arrive late is to be rude. In many other countries, however, people adhere to different standards of punctuality. People may arrive at a meeting or event later than the designated time.

Eye Contact and Directness

In many western cultures, eye contact and directness are expected in negotiations. Failure to make eye contact may suggest the person is hiding something. In other cultures, however, looking at someone directly is not acceptable and is considered aggressive or disrespectful.

Who Speaks First

Another cultural difference relates to customs about who speaks first in a meeting. Find out if you should speak after being spoken to, or if you should talk first at a negotiation meeting.

Disagreement and Agreement

Methods of disagreeing and agreeing in an international business meeting also reflect the cultures of the participants. In the United States, someone might say, "No, it is out of the question." People from another country may view such a direct statement as confrontational. In Japan a negotiator will avoid looking you in the eye and may say, "I am very sorry, but that could be very difficult." You can **equate** this response with "No." The same holds true for saying, "I agree." In some cultures, a direct response is best. In others, too much agreement is a sign of weakness.

▼ **EVERYDAY NEGOTIATIONS**
The four Cs of negotiation are keys to effective bargaining. *What types of companies have the most bargaining power in today's world marketplace?*

Culture Corner

Fun in South Korea

Think About It A 19th-century accountant advised, "Never call an accountant a credit to his profession; a good accountant is a debit to his profession." What does this mean?

Disney is not the only company to create a wonderful world of magic. Seoul, South Korea's capital, has Lotte World. Lotte World features the world's largest indoor theme park, an outdoor amusement park, a Korean folk museum, a sports center, and a luxury hotel—all connected by monorail. Opened in 1989, Lotte World has something to entertain the entire family. Sail with Sinbad, relax in a sauna, loop and spiral on the French Revolution, or ride the Gyro Drop.

To make sure its 8 million annual visitors stay happy, Lotte World has taken its cue from the world of finance. Employees carry pocket computers to track sales and other park operations in real time.

Meeting and Greeting A bow and a handshake are common between men. Address Koreans with their professional title followed by their family name. Korean names place the family name first.

Business Etiquette Be on time. Exchange business cards using both hands. Do not ask yes or no questions as Koreans will avoid saying "no."

Business Dress Dress conservatively. Men wear a formal suit and tie. Women wear dresses or skirts and avoid bright colors.

English Language Arts/Writing

What are the advantages of knowing a company's financial status hour to hour?

Honor Systems

The concept of honor plays an important role in many cultures. For example, in Asian countries, never "show someone up." Tactfully allowing the other side to "save face" when that side must compromise can create a valuable ally in the future. The goal is to get the best possible deal while keeping good relations.

Negotiators must use the four Cs while being aware of cultural differences. Doing so provides the best chance of achieving bargaining objectives.

Obtaining Funding

It takes money for a business to become global. The particular country where a business is operating affects choosing the source of capital. A business has three primary sources of capital to fund activities:

- Private investors
- Banks
- The government

Private Investors

In the United States and Great Britain, businesses raise a great deal of capital through private investors. These investors buy various kinds of stocks and bonds, which give companies capital. In exchange, the companies give the investors returns, or profits, on their stock or bond investments. The two types of stock sold in the United States are common stock and preferred stock.

Common Stock A share of **common stock** is a unit of ownership of a company that entitles the owner, or stockholder, to voting privileges. If a company has 1,000 shares of common stock held by private investors, and one investor owns 100 shares, that investor owns 10 percent of the company. Each share of common stock carries one vote. Stockholders elect the company's board of directors. The board then chooses the company's president and chief executive officer (CEO).

A share represents a portion of the company's profits. When a company makes a profit, it reports the amount to investors as *earnings per share*. The earnings are paid to the stockholders, or shareholders, in one of two ways. First, the company can pay earnings as dividends. Dividends are distributions of money, stock, or other property that a corporation pays to stockholders. Second, the company may reinvest the earnings back into the company. Reinvested earnings are recorded as *retained earnings*. When a company retains profits, stockholders can expect the value of their shares to rise. If they sell their stock, they receive a higher price.

Investors can buy and sell shares of stock through various stock markets, including the New York Stock Exchange and NASDAQ in the United States. In addition, there are many other stock markets around the world, such as the exchanges in London, England, and in Tokyo, Japan.

A privately held company is one in which a person or a family holds all of the shares of common stock. A company may make a public offering of its stock. This means the owner(s) is offering company stock by selling it to new investors in order to raise capital. The greatest advantage of selling shares of common stock is that the company collects money it does not have to repay, as it would for a loan. Also, a company that "goes public" by selling common stock has more prestige.

The disadvantage of selling stock to the public is that each new share of stock dilutes ownership. With more owners, each one owns a smaller share of the company. Another disadvantage is that dividends paid to stockholders are not tax-deductible for the company.

Preferred Stock Preferred stock is not widely bought and sold in many countries. **Preferred stock** is a type of stock that gives the stockholder the advantage of receiving cash dividends before common stockholders receive cash dividends. Dividends must be paid to preferred stockholders each year. However, a share of preferred stock does not entitle the stockholder to a vote. In that sense, it is not a share of ownership.

WORLD-CLASS STOCK MARKET Investors buy and sell common stock through stock exchanges around the world, such as this one, the New York Stock Exchange, located in the United States. *What is the name of the other major stock exchange in the United States?*

Bonds Private investors can make "loans" to companies in the form of bonds. A **bond** is a corporation's written pledge to repay a specific amount of money, along with interest. The bond guarantees a rate of interest that the company will pay the investor. For example, a $100 bond with a 5 percent interest rate results in a payment of $5 to the bondholder each year. A bond also guarantees a maturity date. This means that on a certain date in the future, the bondholder will receive the original amount he or she loaned to the company, along with any final interest payment.

Bonds have several advantages for companies. First, there are no new owners. Second, interest paid to bondholders is tax-deductible for the company. Third, as the company's sales and profits grow, it becomes easier for the company to make the required interest payments to bondholders.

The negative side of bonds is they carry risk. If a company cannot repay the interest and principal on the "loan," the bondholders can sue the company. A successful lawsuit may force the company into bankruptcy, which is a legal proceeding in which some or all company assets are distributed among creditors. This could destroy the company.

Sometimes a company sells bonds called "convertible bonds." These are bonds that a company can convert into common stock, at a price that is spelled out on the bond.

Investors who buy stocks and bonds usually do not want to be involved in the day-to-day operations of the company. They simply want a good return on their money. Financial advisors help many private investors buy stocks and bonds that help them reach their financial goals.

Reading Check   **Analyze** If you ran a company that needed to raise capital, would you prefer to offer common stock or bonds? Why?

Bank Loans

Bank loans have some of the same characteristics as bonds. They require a company to pay interest. A major difference is that a bank loan may require annual repayments rather than a lump sum payment at the end. These annual payments to the bank are called "installments." In addition, a company usually must secure the loan with some of its tangible assets.

It is important for a company to know what source of funding is available in the particular country where it does business. In countries where bank loans are the largest source of capital, the system is somewhat different. In these countries, bank employees or officials are on the boards of directors of the companies that receive loans. This close involvement provides the bank with information about a company's operations. Switzerland, Germany, and Japan are countries where a few very large banks provide loans of capital for most companies in the country. In these countries, private investors are less common than in the United States.

ACCOUNTANT

If you are good with numbers, and, if you enjoy working with them, a career as an accountant may be a good match for you.

Accountants do work with numbers, but there is more involved than mathematics. Good accountants can take numbers and use them to paint a picture of how a business is doing. Which areas are strongest? Which ones are weakest? What are the prime opportunities for growth?

Accountants working for international firms contribute to strategic planning. They need to keep their eyes on the financial trends in each of the companies where business takes place, and watch for ways those trends affect the bottom line. This may require international travel.

Besides all of the adjustments that are made to the value of money, international accountants face other challenges. Accounting standards, auditing standards, and levels of disclosure all require special attention.

Skills and Training

Accountants have excellent mathematical, analytical, and computer skills. They must also have high ethical standards. Strong communication skills are necessary for writing reports and working with others.

A bachelor's degree is required. An accountant working in international business will most likely need to pass the CPA exam to become a certified public accountant.

✏️ English Language Arts/Writing

Why do multinational companies employ accountants to perform internal audits?

@ To learn more about accountants and their career paths, go to the International Business Online Learning Center through **glencoe.com**.

Career Data

Education: Bachelor's degree

Skills: Mathematical, computer, analytical, and communication skills

Outlook: Growth faster than average in the next ten years

Government Capital

In some countries, such as France and Sweden, the federal government provides the most capital for businesses. A government usually gives capital to companies that represent the country's "national interests." The repayment program and tax requirements are spelled out for the company in government documents. Governments can either lend or grant money to businesses. The United States government has lent money to individual companies. Chrysler and Lockheed are two corporations that have received government loans. After the events of September 11, 2001, many airline companies received government loans.

Choosing Sources of Capital

Many companies obtain all three forms of financing: private investments, bank loans, and government assistance. A small company may often start out with an individual businessperson investing his or her own personal money to get started. As the small business grows, it may use the other forms of financing.

The Importance of Accounting and Finance

Accounting practices vary widely. It is important to know the differences in accounting systems in other countries. Effective accountants are familiar with currency conversion and know exchange rates set by governments and international organizations. They also know how assets are valued on the books and how depreciation is treated. The company's management team must work with both accounting and financial experts. This is especially crucial when negotiations take place and when the company needs additional capital in order to expand.

Quick Check 13.2

After You Read Respond to what you have read by answering these questions.

1. Name the four Cs of negotiation. _____

_____

2. What determines a company's level of bargaining power? _____

_____

3. What are the three primary sources of capital for an international company? _____

_____

Academics / Mathematics

4. You own 9 percent of a company's 7,500 shares of common stock. How many shares do you own?

_____

_____

Portfolio Worksheet

Finding Funds

After working for several years in your chosen field, you have decided to be your own boss. Describe your dream business. Assume that the average start-up capitalization for a new small business is $250,500. Then based on the information in the chapter, prepare a step-by-step plan for raising this amount of capital for your business.

_____

_____

1. _____

_____

2. _____

_____

3. _____

_____

4. _____

_____

5. _____

_____

6. _____

_____

7. _____

_____

8. _____

_____

9. _____

_____

10. _____

_____

ACADEMICS APPLIED Check off the academic knowledge you used to do this activity:

☐ English Language Arts   ☐ Mathematics   ☐ Social Studies   ☐ Science

ACADEMIC AND CAREER PLAN Add this page to your Academic and Career Plan Portfolio.

(tl) Ulf Wallin/Getty Images; (tr) Royalty-free/David De Lossy/Getty Images; (b) Royalty-free/Getty Images

CHAPTER SUMMARY

Section 13.1 Accounting Practices

accounting (p. 302)

income statement (p. 303)

balance sheet (p. 303)

inflation (p. 304)

cost accounting (p. 305)

audit (p. 306)

accounting cycle (p. 307)

International Accounting Standards Board (p. 308)

- The ability to evaluate standard accounting documents is vital to being able to manage a company. The basic documents include an income statement and balance sheet.

- When a company conducts operations in more than one country, currency exchange rates and other related factors must be considered.

- Accounting standards determine how information must be presented, and they vary from country to country.

Section 13.2 Financing Practices

bargaining power (p. 310)

common stock (p. 313)

preferred stock (p. 313)

bond (p. 314)

- Four components called the four Cs comprise the negotiation process: common interests, conflicting interests, criteria, and compromise.

- When a company needs money to finance new activities, there are three primary sources: private investors, banks, and the government.

- The two basic types of stock sold in the United States are common stock and preferred stock. Common stock is a unit of ownership of a company that entitles the owner, or stockholder, to voting privileges. Preferred stock is a type of stock that gives the stockholder the advantage of receiving cash dividends before common stockholders receive cash dividends; common stockholders do not vote.

- Bank loans, the issuance of bonds, and the acquiring of government-backed capitalization are also sources of capital.

CONCEPTS REVIEW

1. **Identify** accounting documents that help in managing a business.

2. **Name** three factors that may affect accounting documents when a company operates in more than one country.

3. **Describe** the effect of accounting standards on accounting documents.

4. **List** three sources of money for financing new ventures.

5. **Distinguish** between common and preferred stock.

6. **Name** two means of generating capital besides sale of stock.

KEY TERMS REVIEW

7. Match each term to its definition.

_____ accounting

_____ income statement

_____ balance sheet

_____ inflation

_____ cost accounting

_____ audit

_____ accounting cycle

_____ International Accounting Standards Board

_____ bargaining power

_____ common stock

_____ preferred stock

_____ bond

a. a unit of ownership of a company that entitles the owner, or stockholder, to voting privileges

b. the systematic process of recording and reporting the financial position of a business

c. a method of accounting that adjusts the cost of goods to reflect a country's inflation rate

d. a report of a business's net income or net loss for an accounting period

e. an organization that creates accounting standards

f. a review of a company's accounting statements by an independent observer

g. a corporation's written pledge to repay a specific amount of money, along with interest

h. a type of stock that gives the stockholder the advantage of receiving cash dividends before common stockholders receive cash dividends

i. a company's ability to achieve its goals without compromise

j. a report of the balances of all assets, liabilities, and owner's equity at the end of an accounting period

k. the activities, or steps, that help a business keep its accounting records in an orderly manner

l. the rise in the level of prices for goods and services

Academic Vocabulary

8. On a separate sheet of paper, write a sentence or two related to accounting and financing practices using at least three of the academic terms you learned in the section openers:
- estimate
- appreciate
- journal
- precede
- percent
- equate

Critical Thinking

9. What carries more risk for a business, selling shares of common stock or borrowing money through bonds or a bank loan? Why?

Discussion Starter

10. Should disclosure be different for a family-owned company compared to a publicly owned corporation? Explain.

Point of View

11. When bargaining in another country, how you negotiate is more important than the agreement. Do you agree? Why?

BUILDING REAL-WORLD SKILLS

12. Worldwide Accounting Beginning in early 2006, the Securities and Exchange Committee (SEC) of the United States began enforcing new rules. These rules required international companies that issue stock to each have their home country financial statements prepared under International Financial Reporting Standards (IFRS), and then conformed to U.S. standards.

Research and Share

a. Research the history of this change.

b. Explain to the class the significance of the change.

13. Personal Finance and Business In the eyes of U.S. law, a corporation is an artificial person. It is separate and distinct from its owners. Like a person, it makes its own income and pays its own bills. Consequently, many of the rules that work well in personal finance can apply to a business.

Research and Write

a. Research the principles of personal finance.

b. Write a short paper on how these principles apply to running a business.

BUILDING ACADEMIC SKILLS

 English Language Arts

14. The level of disclosure required by a country often reflects the attitude of a country toward its business sector. Do you think all countries should require a high level of disclosure? Write a short essay explaining your opinion.

MATH Mathematics

15. Your friend asks you to help capitalize her new business. She needs *a*. She can get *b* of that amount from her own assets, savings, and investments. You agree to contribute the remaining amount, *c,* if you can recover that amount in dividends over the next four years. She plans to buy all the common stock with *b*, but she offers you preferred stock at a dollar a share. What is the dividend that should be set on the preferred stock to get the amount of your investment back in four years? Show your work.

Algebraic Expressions To solve this problem, you need to understand algebraic symbols and equations.

SOC Social Studies/History

16. In 1494, a Franciscan monk wrote a book on mathematics. The book included chapters on practical applications to business. The monk, Luca Pacioli, insisted that a business needed to use a good system to account for its activities. He wrote about a system that he and others had used. Its accuracy rested on the use of double-entry bookkeeping. Pacioli placed debits on the left side of the ledger because "debit" meant "the left." Credits were on the right side. This system caught on, but Pacioli's book did not. Research and report on the history of accounting.

SOC Social Studies/Sociology

17. The chapter emphasizes the need to be sensitive to various cultural attitudes while bargaining. One wise guideline is to allow the person who is bargaining from the weaker position a way to give in with dignity and "save face." Research this aspect of negotiations. Prepare a list of suggestions on how to preserve others' dignity.

COMPETITIVE EVENT PREP

Expansion Finances

18. **Situation** Your firm has decided to expand its surfwear business into Brazil. You must find Brazilian contacts to help you raise capital to fund a new production facility. It is imperative that you conform to U.S. laws, including the Foreign and Corrupt Practices Act and Sarbanes-Oxley Act.

    Activity Research and understand the laws and their implication. Consider the issues raised by the cultural differences connected to conducting business in Brazil and how these laws might affect your success. Look at ways the corporation might choose to raise capital as well as alternatives, such as owning versus leasing a facility.

    Evaluation You will be evaluated on how well you meet the following objectives.

    a. Summarize the Sarbanes-Oxley Act and its implications.

    b. Summarize the Foreign and Corrupt Practices Act.

    c. Define the issues related to ownership versus lease.

    d. Choose the best possible approach and defend your position.

BusinessWeek | online

19. **Newsclip: Lone Star Germany** A German subsidiary of an American private company has gained a lot of business by acquiring billions of dollars in failed real estate loans. As other banks try to get in on the action, Lone Star Germany tries to hold on to its large piece of the pie.

    @ Go to the International Business Online Learning Center through **glencoe.com** to read an article about this topic. Then write a paragraph that explains how private equity firms such as Lone Star Germany make money by buying failed real estate loans.

Standardized Test Practice

20. Choose the best answer to the following multiple-choice question.

    Which of the following statements is NOT true?
    ○ Common stock is like a loan to a business from an investor.
    ○ Bonds are like a loan to a business from an investor.
    ○ A preferred stockholder does not vote for the board of directors.
    ○ Offering company stock to the public is one way to raise capital.

Internet Travels

Costa Rica

Using the Internet, find a map of Costa Rica. Study its geographical position. Answer the following questions about Costa Rica on a separate sheet of paper.

➤ Research the history and government of Costa Rica.

➤ Would you consider Costa Rica a good location for establishing a large factory intended to supply goods to the international market? Explain your answer.

@ For resources to help you do this exercise, go to the International Business Online Learning Center through **glencoe.com**.

Test-Taking Tip Trust your instincts. Often your first impression is correct. Do not change your answer unless you are certain it is wrong.

Marketing Entertainment Electronics

Success Model: **SAMSUNG**
Country of Origin: **SOUTH KOREA**
Business: **ELECTRONICS, FINANCE, TRADE, AND INSURANCE**

imagine freedom

discover the Z5 digital audio player
with up to 35 hours of playback time and
multiple music providers

the Q1
explore the Q1
ultra mobile pc

the 4-door
convertible refrigerator
join the revolution

The Samsung General Stores were founded in Korea on March 1, 1938, by Byung Chull Lee. For the next 70 years, Samsung conducted business in various industries including textiles, electronics, insurance, aircraft manufacturing, chemicals, and communications. A new era for Samsung began in 1987, when Kun-Hee Lee was appointed Chairman of the corporation. He introduced "New Management," a management process with a focus on people and technology—what he believed to be the real power of Samsung. Kun-Hee Lee emphasizes ethics, respect for customers, and a responsibility to the community while understanding the rapidly changing global economy.

Today Samsung Electronics is the number-one producer of memory chips, LCDs, displays, and CDMA handheld phones, and is accelerating in the digital-audio player market with its Z5 player. Samsung has been in the portable audio business for more than seven years. It has 285 overseas operations in 67 countries. With innovations like the smallest LCD monitor at 1.98" with VGA resolution, Samsung is one of South Korea's most important corporations.

Situation

You have been hired as the marketing director for the international division of an electronics manufacturer. Your responsibilities include developing the marketing plan and strategy for a new miniature MP3 player that your company is releasing. The name of the product is "MicroZZ." It is half the size of the leading player yet can hold twice as much music and video. Your company's goal over the next five years is to increase sales by $20 million by doing business in the international marketplace.

Assignment

✓ Research the competition so that you can develop a pricing strategy for the MicroZZ.
✓ Create your marketing plan for this product to include the four Ps.
✓ Develop a promotional activity to announce the new MicroZZ in Mexico and Canada.

Resources

SKILLS NEEDED

✓ *Academic Skills:* reading, writing, math, and social studies
✓ *Basic Skills:* speaking, listening, thinking, problem-solving, and interpersonal skills
✓ *Technology Skills:* word-processing, keyboarding, spreadsheet, presentation, telecommunications, and Internet skills

TOOLS NEEDED

✓ Newspapers and magazines, such as *BusinessWeek* and *U.S. News and World Report, Advertising Age,* and *Fortune*
✓ Access to the Internet and library
✓ Paper, pens, pencils, and markers
✓ Word-processing, spreadsheet, and presentation software

● Procedures

STEP 1 | REAL-WORLD RESEARCH

Conduct research on two MP3 players currently on the market to determine:
- Popular features
- Price
- Promotion
- Channels of distribution

STEP 2 | COMMUNITY RESEARCH

Interview two marketing professionals in your community and ask them how they develop marketing strategies.

STEP 3 | INTERNET RESEARCH

- Research the demographics and buying patterns of Mexican and Canadian teens.
- Find out which activities teens in Mexico and Canada prefer.
- Review Web sites of electronic companies that market to Mexico and Canada.

STEP 4 | CREATE IT

Create a promotional campaign announcing the release of the MicroZZ in Mexico and Canada and include:
- Brief description of campaign
- Specific media used
- One activity that will generate buzz about the product

STEP 5 | GRAPHIC ORGANIZER

On a separate sheet of paper, create a marketing plan that includes strategies for the marketing mix (four Ps).

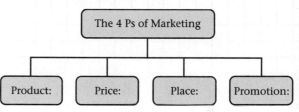

The 4 Ps of Marketing

Product: | Price: | Place: | Promotion:

● Report

Prepare a report of your findings using the following tools, if available:
- *Word-processing program:* Prepare a 2-page report about the marketing strategies used by your interviewees.
- *Spreadsheet program:* Prepare a chart comparing the demographics and teen buying patterns in Mexico and Canada. Create a second chart comparing the competitor's Web sites you researched.
- *Presentation program:* Prepare a ten-slide presentation explaining your marketing and promotional campaign for the MicroZZ.

● Evaluation

Present your report to the class and/or hand it in to your teacher. Use this chart to assess yourself before and after your presentation:

PRESENTATION SELF-CHECK RUBRIC	1 Needs Work	2 Average Quality	3 Good Quality	4 Excellent Quality	Totals
Creativity of marketing plan					
Continuity of overall report					
Voice quality					
Eye contact with audience					
				TOTAL =	

0–6 Needs Work; **7–10** Average Quality; **11–14** Good Quality; **15–16** Excellent Quality

---

● Academic and Career Portfolio

Add this report to your Academic and Career Portfolio.

UNIT 5

YOUR FUTURE IN INTERNATIONAL BUSINESS

> **"**To turn really interesting ideas and fledgling technologies into a company that can continue to innovate for years, it requires a lot of disciplines.**"**
>
> **Steve Jobs
> Co-Founder, CEO,
> Apple Computer**

Speed Demons

Smart companies are creating new products—and whole new businesses—almost overnight. Virgin Group founder Sir Richard Branson got an e-mail out of the blue. Gotham Chopra had a proposal: Branson should team up with Indian entrepreneurs running a comics distribution business and create a new global comics and animation powerhouse—part Marvel Comics, part Pixar. Boom! Bang! Shazam! Virgin Comics was revealed on January 6. Speed is emerging as the ultimate competitive weapon.

The pace is picking up across such industries as retailing, consumer goods, software, electronics, autos, and medical devices. At Nissan, the development of new cars used to take 21 months. Now, the company is shifting to a 10½-month process. Take clothing retailer H&M. Every time it designs a new outfit, the Swedish company can get the plant rolling in hours or days.

The Internet has become ubiquitous, so companies can connect with talent in the blink of an eye. Open-source software can become new software programs or Web sites. Algorithms can [help] spot new trends.

Take the cell-phone business. It takes 12 to 18 months to develop a phone. That's why cell-phone companies are tapping outfits such as Cellon Inc. in California. Cellon has a half-dozen basic designs it can customize. It takes just five months to go to market.

In an era in which once-mighty dinosaurs are struggling to survive, the alternative to "fast and lean" may soon be gone.

English Language Arts/Writing

1. What trend is a competitive weapon?
2. What are some factors enabling this trend?

@ To read the complete *BusinessWeek* article, go to the International Business Online Learning Center through **glencoe.com**.

UNIT THEMATIC PROJECT PREVIEW

International Career Plan Sim

As the world becomes more connected through technological innovations, more opportunities for careers in international businesses develop. Doing real-world research through travel, planning, and preparation are key to developing a great career plan.

Pre-Project Checklist

❑ Find an online career interest inventory.

❑ Look in travel magazines and online to find a country where you might want to work.

❑ Go to your school career center and ask about international business careers.

❑ Visit a business that does global business.

Chapter 14

Human Resource Management

Chapter Objectives

When you have completed this chapter, you will be able to:

Section 14.1

- Explain a strategic approach to managing human resources in domestic and international settings.
- Identify forms of management in various countries.
- Discuss the processes of recruiting, selecting, and training new workers.

Section 14.2

- Describe the impact of local labor conditions on businesses.
- Discuss different types of union-management relationships in global settings.
- Explain how all human resource practices can adapt to international settings.

▶ **BENETTON**

Benetton is a publicly owned corporation whose shares are traded on the stock exchanges. When you research this company through Standard & Poor's, you will find investment information such as this:

Index:	S&P 500 and S&P Global 1200
Sector:	Consumer Discretionary
Company:	Benetton Group SpA
Symbol:	BNG
Country:	Italy
Price:	(varies)

Global Profile Benetton Group SpA was founded by Luciano, Giuliana, Gilberto, and Carlo Benetton in 1965. Benetton is an Italian manufacturer and marketer of fashionable wool, cotton, and denim clothing, shoes, and accessories, such as eyeglass frames, luggage, handbags, hats, belts, perfumes, watches, and sports accessories. Its brands include the casual United Colors of Benetton, Sisley, Playlife leisurewear, and Killer Loop street wear.

Business Report Benetton has more than 5,000 stores managed by independent partners and sells its products in 120 countries (including Russia, pictured here). With sales of more than 1.7 billion euros ($2 billion) annually, the company employs about 7,424 people, from designers to marketers. Benetton is an internationally recognized brand.

English Language Arts/Writing

In the 1980s, Benetton attracted worldwide attention for advertisements created by photographer Oliviero Toscani. His subjects ranged from a newborn baby to a sinking ship, and emphasized diversity and commonalities between races and cultures. The advertising earned attention from customers and accolades from art directors. *How might Benetton's philosophy, implied in ads, affect its hiring decisions?*

@ To do this activity, go to the International Business Online Learning Center through **glencoe.com**.

327

Managing Human Resources

WHAT YOU'LL LEARN

- To explain a strategic approach to managing human resources in domestic and international settings
- To identify forms of management in various countries
- To discuss the processes of recruiting, selecting, and training new workers

WHY IT'S IMPORTANT

People are the heart of every business operation. Successful companies adapt human resource management programs to the needs of people in other countries.

KEY TERMS

- human resource management (HRM)
- strategic human resource management (SHRM)
- ethnocentric management
- polycentric management
- regiocentric management
- geocentric management

Academic Vocabulary

You will find these words in your reading and on your tests. Make sure you know their meanings.

- labor
- alternative
- commission

Reading Guide

Before You Read

What motivates you to be your best?

MAIN IDEA

Human resource managers hire, train, and motivate employees in countries with varying laws and cultures.

GRAPHIC ORGANIZER

Draw this diagram. As you read, list the four main types of Strategic Human Resource Management.

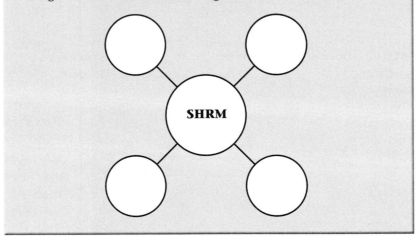

What Is Human Resource Management?

B ecause employees are key to success, human resource management is a crucial ingredient in a successful international business. **Human resource management (HRM)** is the process of finding, selecting, training, evaluating, and helping employees. Almost every company in the United States with more than 100 employees has a human resource (HR) department. Businesses without a dedicated HR department still perform the essential HR functions.

This chapter explains the role of human resource management. The first section of this chapter explains how a strategic human resource management approach helps define and focus a company. Methods for selecting, training, and evaluating employees conclude the first section of this chapter. The second section describes union-management relations. It includes information about global **labor** markets, management styles, and labor unions.

Strategic Human Resource Management

An employee or manager who travels to a host country to live and work is called an "expatriate." In addition, a local citizen working in a company's host country is called a "host-country national." An employee or manager from a completely different country, neither home nor host, is called a "third-country national."

Carefully planned strategies lead to the hiring of home, host, and third-country employees. In the area of HR, this approach to hiring is **strategic human resource management (SHRM)**. A company must decide which form of management to use:

- Ethnocentric management
- Polycentric management
- Regiocentric management
- Geocentric management

Ethnocentric Management

The approach called **ethnocentric management** is the preference of an employer to use its own workers, both at home and abroad. A company may use this approach as a strategy to keep control of its technology and overall operations. A company may also use ethnocentric management when it will be too expensive and time-consuming to train others. Consequently, the majority of employees and managers in another country are expatriates of the home country.

An ethnocentric approach can result in resentment among local workers in the host country. When Japanese automobile manufacturers expanded to the United States, some U.S. residents were unhappy with the Japanese style of leadership. Morale may decline if the company fails to train host-country employees for management roles.

Polycentric Management

Another SHRM approach allows a company to take advantage of the special knowledge and expertise of its local employees. **Polycentric management** is the preference of an employer to use natives of the host country to manage operations there, but home-country residents to manage in the home country.

Home-country managers must work closely and communicate carefully with host-country managers. If they do not, communication and management problems can arise. Host-country managers may come to believe they have limited opportunities to advance to top management. If they find this is true, they may seek work elsewhere.

Regiocentric Management

The approach called **regiocentric management** is the preference of an employer to employ managers from a variety of countries in a region. This method suits companies that have expanded into several other nations and want local leaders to adapt to each country's situation.

The primary challenge of regiocentric management is control. The staff in each country must learn to adapt to the goals and tactics used by the company. Typically, regiocentric managers visit the "home office" on a regular basis.

OUR MULTICULTURAL WORKPLACE

Building a World Community

Human resource managers face many challenges in a multicultural world. Multinational companies recognize that the union of diverse ideas and perspectives is critical in forming creative solutions to worldwide demands. How can companies preserve significant and valuable characteristics in employees from different cultures? For example, companies can have diversity training available for all employees. Some companies with cafeterias offer food from different cultures. *What are some other human resource strategies that companies can use to encourage the appreciation of differences and to build an inclusive corporate culture?*

Geocentric Management

Typically, the geocentric approach is found in multinational companies that have many subsidiary companies located around the world. **Geocentric management** is the preference of an employer to hire only the best managers, regardless of their citizenship.

Leading a geocentric company is much like managing a portfolio of investments. A leader must balance company goals with the diverse conditions of local operations. Careful training and development help managers adjust to local conditions and the larger company.

In general, a company chooses the type of SHRM approach on the basis of its goals for international expansion. Smaller firms are more likely to be ethnocentric. As businesses grow and expand to more nations, they tend to move toward polycentric, regiocentric, and geocentric management styles.

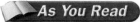

As You Read

Question Is a multinational conglomerate more likely to use an ethnocentric, polycentric, or geocentric management approach?

Finding and Preparing Employees

The most successful businesses are those that do a good job of finding and preparing employees through various activities:

- Recruiting
- Selection
- Orientation
- New employee training

Recruiting

Recruiting is the process by which a company actively looks for qualified people to fill jobs. Human resource managers say that recruiting should be ongoing, systematic, and matched to the needs of the company.

SELECTION PROCESSES An interview is a key part of the selection process. *What might HR managers look for during an interview?*

Ongoing Recruiting is ongoing because a firm needs a constant supply of qualified applicants. Prospective employees sometimes submit résumés even if a company does not advertise. Then, when a job becomes vacant, the company already has a list of people to interview.

Systematic Recruiting is systematic when the HR department methodically utilizes a wide range of possible sources, such as newspapers and Web sites, in order to find potential employees to fill a job vacancy. The contacts and sources that a company uses may be internal, which means within the company, and external, or outside the company.

Figure 14.1

External Recruiting

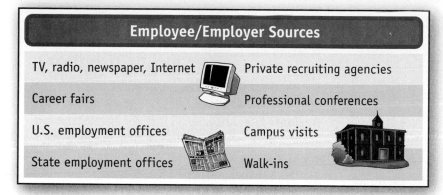

Employee/Employer Sources

TV, radio, newspaper, Internet — Private recruiting agencies

Career fairs — Professional conferences

U.S. employment offices — Campus visits

State employment offices — Walk-ins

FINDING WORKERS
These are places where employers can find potential employees and vice versa. *Which sources might be used for manual labor jobs? High-tech jobs?*

Internal recruiting is the approach of seeking to fill positions by advertising only within the company. When a company is looking for a supervisor or manager, internal employees may apply for a promotion. HR might also ask employees to tell friends about openings.

External recruiting is the approach of going outside the company to find applicants. There are a number of sources that will help a company recruit new employees. **Figure 14.1** lists some of these sources.

Matched to Company Needs Recruiting should be matched to the needs of the company. To recruit the right people, HR should review the job itself prior to seeking candidates. This involves job analysis, job description, and job specification.

Job analysis is the process of making sure there is a clear and complete list of job tasks for a particular position. Job tasks should not overlap with tasks performed in other jobs.

A *job description* is a detailed outline of tasks and duties that are part of a job. Job descriptions are printed in a company manual or handbook or may be listed on a company's Web site.

A *job specification* is a list of qualifications the candidate must have. Typical job specifications include level of education, amount of experience, personality characteristics, and special skills.

Selection

Recruiting is the development of a pool of qualified applicants, but selection is the process of deciding which one to hire. Using the job specification as a guide, the HR manager examines application forms and résumés, and picks candidates. Finalists are chosen after the first interviews. Tests to determine math skills, aptitude, computer skills, or personality type may be administered. The HR manager also checks references and employment history, and may conduct a second interview before making a selection.

HR personnel must follow ethical and legal practices. Discrimination and unfair treatment of applicants should not be allowed.

Orientation

The HR office completes all of the orientation activities before a new employee starts. Orientation includes paperwork, tours, and introductions. A physical exam and drug test might be required.

Culture Corner

Japan's Shrinking Population

Think About It Is it better for a country to have too few people or too many?

While many countries worry about a population explosion, Japan worries about a declining birthrate. Since 1975, the number of babies born each year has steadily decreased. If the birthrate does not increase by 2050, the population could drop to about the same as it was in 1967. Business leaders fear future labor shortages. Who will work in Japan's factories and teach its children?

To solve this problem, the government plans to double current child allowances for couples having their third child. New regulations will influence companies to decrease working hours for both men and women so they will have more time at home. According to Katsuya Saito, a government official,

"The key to higher birthrates is to make it easy for women to work and have a family."

Meeting and Greeting Exchange business cards first. Your business card should indicate your rank. Show respect with a slight bow, handshake, and little eye contact.

Business Etiquette Be on time for meetings. A gift may be expected. Polite conversation precedes the actual meeting; nod to show you are listening. When parting, say that you hope to meet again.

Business Dress The Japanese dress well and conservatively. Men wear dark suits and ties. Women wear dresses or suits and shoes with heels.

English Language Arts/Writing

If you were head of a company that faced a labor shortage, what action would you take?

New Employee Training

New employee training includes on-the-job training and off-the-job training. On-the-job training is a demonstration by an experienced worker who shows the new employee how to do the job. In skilled labor jobs, such as construction or plumbing, an apprenticeship program is a form of training that takes place over a longer period of time.

Off-the-job training includes classroom teaching and films. Some employees may be given books and manuals to study. Employees might also practice doing a job in a simulation setting.

International Employees

Recruitment and orientation of employees are similar around the world. However, there can be significant differences when a company looks for new employees to work in other countries or sets up training programs for workers from other countries.

International Selection

When HR managers select new employees to work internationally, they consider the candidate's cultural sensitivity, adaptability, and language skills. Cultural sensitivity is having an awareness of and enjoying cultural differences. Adaptability is having the emotional maturity to adjust to new settings, new people, and different ways of doing things. Language skills include the ability to speak one or more world languages.

Reading Check **Compare** What is the difference between cultural sensitivity and adaptability?

Training Programs

Expatriate workers must be prepared to work with people from an unfamiliar culture. A company must do everything it can through careful training and counseling to reduce the difficulties of adjusting to a new culture. International training programs typically address several issues:

- **Job-Related Issues**—The same job may be performed differently in another country. For example, a salesperson needs to know if the bargaining process is part of every sale.

- **Company Styles**—While the overall global leadership is the same, a company's operation may be modified for another country to match local conditions.

- **Language Training**—Workers learn a few key phrases (or more) of the unfamiliar language. Ideally, managers are fluent in the host country's language.

- **Cultural Training**—Cultural training addresses religious awareness, eating habits, methods of greeting people, personal space distance, clothing, and manners.

- **Spousal Training**—Some international companies offer training for the expatriate worker's husband or wife. He or she may learn how to find work in another country, navigate local customs, and perform basic tasks such as shopping.

How Do You Say?

Q: In French, how do you say: "May I have the check, please?"

A: L'addition, s'il vous plait. (pronounced: Lă-dēē-sēē-ōn, sēēl-voo plā.)

@ To learn this phrase in other languages, go to the International Business Online Learning Center through **glencoe.com**.

Evaluating and Motivating Employees

Another major part of the HR manager's job is to oversee performance evaluations, or appraisals, and motivational programs. The company needs to know who is doing high-quality work and who is not performing up to standards. Company leaders also expect HR officers to help them design motivational/incentive programs that will enhance employee performance.

✔ Reading Check **Analyze** What is the purpose of performance evaluations and motivational programs?

Performance Appraisal

Typically, employees find out how well they are doing through performance appraisals. Companies benefit from the performance appraisal process because it helps the management team decide who is ready to be promoted or receive merit pay increases. Performance appraisal consists of three main tasks:

- Set challenging, attainable, and fair performance standards.
- Inform employees about how well they reach the standards.
- Find ways to improve performance in the future.

Discipline The discipline system should be a corrective system in which a supervisor notifies a person who violates a rule and shows him or her how to act in the future. The HR department is responsible for discipline, including writing rules, developing a handbook, enforcing rules, and correcting employees.

Workplace Safety Human resource practices regarding workplace safety vary around the world. In the United States and many other nations, a safe workplace is an important part of doing business. The U.S. work safety laws are outlined in the *Occupational Safety and Hazards Act (OSHA).*

Not all countries have adequate safety laws. Some legal systems do not allow workers to sue if injured on the job. Some workers are subjected to high risks and receive low pay in plants called "sweatshops."

Motivation and Compensation Programs

When businesspeople establish a business operation in another country, they must be careful to understand motivational forces in that country. When developing compensation packages, they should understand the roles of money regarding needs and wants, social acceptance, achievement, and religion in motivating employees there.

Motivations Money is an important motivator. Everyone needs money in order to meet their basic needs. Pay is a way of showing position and achievement. In addition, some employees view pay, money, and wealth as a way to compete socially with others. Some workers are motivated by personal recognition and a sense of achievement. On the other hand, many cultures in Asia place a strong emphasis on the role of the team or the group rather than individual status.

Compensation When a culture places a strong emphasis on providing the same benefits to all workers regardless of merit, pay systems are often set up to reward seniority. In more achievement-oriented cultures, such as the United States, pay, bonuses, and other benefits are largely determined by merit and accomplishments. Compensation can include non-cash **alternatives** such as meals and transportation, time off, expatriate bonuses, sales **commissions**, and cost-of-living adjustments for employees in more expensive countries.

Quick Check 14.1

After You Read Respond to what you have read by answering these questions.

1. What are the four forms of international management? _____

_____

2. What tasks are involved in finding and preparing employees? _____

_____

3. What are the three main parts of an employee performance appraisal? _____

_____

Academics / *English Language Arts/Writing*

4. Write a short job specification for a position of your choice.

_____

_____

Union-Management Relations

Reading Guide

Before You Read

What is your definition of a "paternalistic" culture?

MAIN IDEA
Local economic conditions and the role of labor unions in different countries are important considerations for an international business.

GRAPHIC ORGANIZER
Draw this table. As you read, list four rights that are important to unions.

Union Rights	1.
	2.
	3.
	4.

Union-Management Relationships

A labor union is an association of workers that seeks to promote its members' interests. The union movement in the United States has influenced commerce for well over 100 years. Companies large and small around the world come in contact with unions.

Living and Working Conditions

Local labor conditions provide a backdrop for labor relations in any country. Several statistics describe general living and working conditions in a country:

- Gross national income (GNI)
- Purchasing power parity (PPP)
- Per capita income
- Human development index

Gross National Income (GNI)

Gross national income (GNI) represents the total annual income received by residents of a country. It is an overall measure of how much income residents earn in a nation. GNI is sometimes used instead of gross national product (GNP) as a measure of a country's economic well-being.

WHAT YOU'LL LEARN
- To describe the impact of local labor conditions on businesses
- To discuss different types of union-management relationships in global settings
- To explain how all human resource practices can adapt to international settings

WHY IT'S IMPORTANT
Union activities are different in other countries. Successful international business operations adjust to local labor conditions and practices.

KEY TERMS
- human development index (HDI)
- paternalism
- collective bargaining agreement
- affirmative action
- accommodation

Academic Vocabulary

You will find these words in your reading and on your tests. Make sure you know their meanings.
- debate
- interact
- conflict

Per Capita Income

Per capita income is the average number of dollars earned by each individual citizen. A country's per capita income is its overall GNI divided by the number of citizens.

There is **debate** about the value of these statistics. Some critics suggest that the GNI and per capita income figures do not reflect the cost of living (COL)—or what money actually buys. They believe it is better to study GNI and per capita income figures over time.

Purchasing Power Parity (PPP)

An accurate comparison between countries must also consider how much a person can buy with money earned. A number that represents *purchasing power parity* (PPP) is used to adjust for the cost of living. The *purchasing power index* (PPI) reveals that buying power is different than a person's salary. PPP-based data allows a comparison of the buying power of income among countries. (See **Figure 14.2**.)

The Human Development Index (HDI)

Living and working conditions are not explained solely by income. The **human development index (HDI)** is a measure comparing the quality of life in different countries, using three measures: 1) life expectancy at birth, 2) educational attainment, and 3) income, measured by PPI, to cover basic needs.

Other Factors

Trade relationships, isolation, war or political instability, terrorism, and disease can affect the quality of life and work in a country. Innovation and entrepreneurship tend to promote a higher standard of living in a country.

Reading Check **Recall** What statistics describe living and working conditions?

Figure 14.2

Purchasing Power Parity

CONSUMPTION DIFFERENCES Households in developing nations are likely to spend a higher percentage of their income on food and clothing. *How does PPP-based data help companies make business decisions about entering new markets?*

Country	Percentage of Household Consumption					
	Food	Clothing & Footwear	Education	Health Care	Transportation & Communication	Other Consumption
1. United States	13%	9%	6%	4%	8%	60%
2. Denmark	16	6	17	3	5	53
3. Canada	14	5	21	4	9	47
112. Nigeria	51	5	8	2	2	22
113. Sierra Leone	47	9	13	3	8	20
114. Tanzania	67	6	12	4	6	5

Source: "Structure of Consumption in PPP Terms," *World Development Indicators 2000*, pp. 222–23; and *World Development Report 1999–2000*, pp. 230, 231.

Managerial and Leadership Styles

Managerial and leadership styles affect the way union leaders and management **interact**. Individual firms may have leadership programs with characteristics that are different from those found in a culture. Characteristics that might vary include paternalism, delegation of authority, and worker-management antagonism.

Paternalism

Paternalism is a system in which an authority fulfills the needs and regulates the conduct of the people under its control. Managers in paternalistic societies, such as those in Japan and some mid-eastern countries, usually do not consider workers' suggestions.

Delegation of Authority

Managers who delegate authority lead by sharing responsibility. Cultures either emphasize or oppose democratic, or participative, forms of management and leadership. Societies that emphasize freedom and independence tend toward democratic styles.

Worker-Manager Antagonism

It is not uncommon for workers and managers to be in **conflict** with one another. This is an "adversarial" relationship. The nature of the relationship can reveal how the labor force is treated.

Labor Unions

Human resource managers must account for labor unions when designing SHRM programs. In general, the goals of labor unions around the globe are the same. Unions seek better pay, job security, improved benefits, safe working conditions, and equal and fair treatment. Several factors determine the strength of a union: union rights, local economic conditions, and the nature of the work.

Union Rights

One major consideration of unionization is whether unions receive legal protection. Though not enacted globally, in the United States, several laws protect unions. The laws include the *Norris-LaGuardia (Anti-Injunction Act)* of 1932, the *National Labor Relations Act* of 1935, and the *Taft-Hartley Act* of 1947. These laws guarantee certain rights:

- The right to organize and form unions without harassment or intimidation by management
- The right to free speech, including picketing
- The right to strike
- The right to bargain and present grievances

These laws also give management certain rights:

- The right to replace striking workers with new employees
- The right to "lock out" workers as a bargaining tactic
- Protection from mass picketing that blocks a plant entrance
- Protection from secondary strikes and boycotts

TECH Trends

Self-Service Applications

Have you ever applied for a job? If so, you may have walked into an office to fill out a job application, and then sat down in front of a human resource professional who asked you about yourself, your habits, your hobbies, and your interest in the job. Today most big retailers, such as Target and Home Depot, use touchscreen kiosks where potential employees fill out applications on their own. The software pre-screens the applications and removes any that do not meet requirements. Then the actual Human Resource professional calls an applicant and sets up a live interview. *Find and list three large corporations that allow an applicant to fill out a job application online.*

For links to help you do this activity, go to the International Business Online Learning Center through **glencoe.com**.

Global Recruiting: L'Oréal

L'Oréal has been dedicated to the manufacturing, marketing, and selling of cosmetics since it was founded in 1907. With properties such as Ralph Lauren fragrances, Redken hair care, and Vichy skin care, in addition to other cosmetics brands, such as Maybelline, it has entered markets at all levels around the world. Sponsoring a fashion festival in Australia, demonstrating global philanthropy with the international L'Oréal-UNESCO for Women in Science program, and touting Bollywood star Aishwarya Rai as a spokesperson, the company is truly international.

Such forward thinking is also shown by an online business simulation that the company offers, called the e-Strat Challenge, which attracts teams of students from around the world. In 2006, winners came from Turkey, Italy, and Mexico. The program has been so effective that it is now used as a recruiting tool for L'Oréal worldwide.

THINK GLOBALLY *How might recruiting via an online tool help L'Oréal compete globally?*

@ To learn more about the country of origin for this global business, go to the International Business Online Learning Center through **glencoe.com**.

Collective Bargaining Processes U.S. law requires management and labor to "bargain in good faith." They must meet regularly at reasonable times to agree on wages, hours, benefits, and working conditions. A **collective bargaining agreement** is the contract created by a union and management that covers these agreements.

Discrimination Laws A nation's laws reflect its policies toward discrimination. The Equal Employment Opportunity Commission (EEOC) monitors U.S. laws prohibiting employment discrimination based on race, religion, gender, age, national origin, and disability. Such laws do not exist globally.

Affirmative Action Affirmative action is a program designed to increase participation of various underrepresented groups in the workplace and government. Such programs are controversial, even in countries where discrimination is illegal.

Local Economic Conditions

Local economic conditions strongly influence unions. A nation with widespread unemployment is less likely to have powerful unions.

The Nature of Work

Traditionally, unions have represented workers involved in manual labor. Service providers and professional employees are much less likely to be unionized. Supervisors are not usually in unions.

HUMAN RESOURCES MANAGER

A business lives or dies by the strength of its employees. As a result, one of the most important people in any company is the HR, or human resource, manager—the one who hires new employees, monitors existing ones, and makes sure that the work climate is a happy and positive one. HR professionals conduct interviews, identify personal strengths and weaknesses, and allow people to work in areas where their abilities are the strongest.

Job Description

HR professionals must be familiar with occupational safety and health, equal employment opportunity, wages, health care, pensions, and family leave policies. They must also be able to coordinate training and labor relations. Human resource professionals sometimes specialize in one of the following areas: recruitment, employee benefits, training and development, industrial relations, or labor relations.

International firms often recruit "on the ground"—that is, in the country where they are doing business. In these cases, HR professionals might travel or relocate to the field to meet prospects, or they might use technology tools to recruit long-distance. Recruiters often travel extensively.

Skills and Training

Successful human resource managers must have high ethical standards. International human resources management also requires good language skills, cultural sensitivity, and diplomacy.

A bachelor's degree related to human resources, human resources administration, or industrial and labor relations is usually required.

✏️ English Language Arts/Writing

What personality types might be suited for this career? Why?

@ To learn more about human resource managers and their career paths, go to the International Business Online Learning Center through **glencoe.com.**

Career Data

Education: Bachelor's degree

Skills: Bilingual or multilingual and communication skills

Outlook: Growth faster than average in the next ten years

► **Strike Support**
    Did you know that
when workers go on
strike or are locked out
during bargaining in the
United States, they do
not receive any pay from
the company? Because of
this, some unions create
"strike funds" to help
union members during
those critical times.

As You Read

Question Are unions more
powerful in right-to-work
states or in non-right-to-
work states?

SHRM and Unions

When HR departments think about union-management relations, they consider unionization, bargaining, and grievances.

Unionization

Unions are beneficial to companies because they help standardize work quality. The procedures for hiring and firing workers are well established.

In the United States, some states are known as *right-to-work* states, where an employee can work in a unionized company but refuse to join the union.

Bargaining

The goal of bargaining is to agree on wages, working hours, pay raises, working conditions, methods for evaluating performance, methods to resolve grievances, and other issues. Many bargaining issues can be resolved by an arbitrator who offers compromise solutions.

Grievances

Grievances include complaints about unfair discipline, violation of a contract, unethical activities by a supervisor or coworker, or management failing to bargain in good faith. HR helps to establish grievance procedures and resolve problems.

International Union Issues

Human resource managers must know how unions operate in various international settings. Many nations, especially in Europe, have laws that create **accommodation**, the approach toward labor disputes in which unions and management are expected to cooperate.

In 1919, the *International Labor Organization* was founded in France and became an agency of the United Nations in 1946. It monitors working conditions and the quality of life internationally.

Quick Check 14.2

After You Read Respond to what you have read by answering these questions.

1. What is the human development index (HDI)? _____

_____

2. What three factors have an impact on managerial and leadership styles in a country? _____

_____

3. What forces affect labor unions in international settings? _____

_____

 **Academics** / *Mathematics*

4. If a country has a GNI of $22 billion and 15.5 million citizens, what is its per capita income?

_____

_____

Personality Traits

A job description may request a particular personality type for a position. Consequently, it is important to know your type and related traits. Read the characteristics below that describe people's personalities. Choose ten traits that best describe you, and then answer the questions that follow.

Personality Traits

_____ outgoing	_____ ambitious	_____ patient
_____ studious	_____ kind	_____ thoughtful
_____ neat	_____ strong	_____ intelligent
_____ quiet	_____ trustworthy	_____ respectful
_____ playful	_____ warm	_____ happy
_____ energetic	_____ persistent	_____ spontaneous
_____ serious	_____ organized	_____ worried
_____ easygoing	_____ rebellious	_____ sensitive
_____ caring	_____ stubborn	_____ sociable
_____ loyal	_____ responsible	_____ creative
_____ confident	_____ fair	_____ talkative
_____ cheerful	_____ calm	_____ inquisitive
_____ dependable	_____ brave	_____ funny
_____ generous	_____ helpful	_____ athletic
_____ shy	_____ imaginative	_____ competitive

Keeping in mind the traits that best describe your personality, what kind of work do you think would suit you? Which traits do you think a prospective employer would prefer? Why?

_____

_____

_____

ACADEMICS APPLIED Check off the academic knowledge you used to do this activity:

☐ English Language Arts ☐ Mathematics ☐ Social Studies ☐ Science

ACADEMIC AND CAREER PLAN Add this page to your Academic and Career Plan Portfolio.

CHAPTER SUMMARY

Section 14.1 **Managing Human Resources**

human resource management (HRM) (p. 328)

strategic human resource management (SHRM) (p. 329)

ethnocentric management (p. 329)

polycentric management (p. 329)

regiocentric management (p. 329)

geocentric management (p. 330)

- A strategic human resource management approach helps define and focus a company. It is a program of carefully planned strategies that lead to the hiring of home, host-, and third-country employees.

- Forms of management include: ethnocentric, polycentric, regiocentric, and geocentric.

- The most successful businesses do a good job of recruiting, selecting, orienting, and training employees. Recruiting involves actively looking for qualified people to fill jobs. Selection involves deciding which qualified applicant to hire. Orientation includes paperwork, tours, and introductions before a new employee begins the job. Training new employees includes on-the-job training, possibly with an experienced employee, and off-the-job training.

Section 14.2 **Union-Management Relations**

human development index (HDI) (p. 336)

paternalism (p. 337)

collective bargaining agreement (p. 338)

affirmative action (p. 338)

accommodation (p. 340)

- Successful international business operations adjust to local labor conditions and practices.

- A key factor that affects the relationship between union and management is the managerial and leadership styles that are most common in a country. Characteristics vary from paternalism and delegation of authority to worker-management antagonism.

- International HR managers should understand the quality of life and work in diverse regions when working with employees.

CONCEPTS REVIEW

1. **Define** strategic human resource management.

2. **Identify** three of the four human relations tasks.

3. **Describe** the difference between autocratic and democratic management styles.

4. **Explain** why international businesses must adjust to local labor conditions and practices.

5. **List** factors that determine managerial and leadership styles.

6. **Identify** factors HR managers should know about life and work in a country.

KEY TERMS REVIEW

7. Match each term to its definition.

_____ human resource management (HRM)

_____ strategic human resource management (SHRM)

_____ ethnocentric management

_____ polycentric management

_____ regiocentric management

_____ geocentric management

_____ human development index (HDI)

_____ paternalism

_____ collective bargaining agreement

_____ affirmative action

_____ accommodation

a. carefully planned strategies that lead to the hiring of home, host-, and third-country employees

b. the preference of an employer to use its own workers, both at home and abroad

c. a program designed to increase participation of various underrepresented groups in the workplace

d. a measure comparing the quality of life in different countries

e. the preference of an employer to hire only the best managers, regardless of their citizenship

f. the process of finding, selecting, training, evaluating, and helping employees

g. the preference of an employer to employ managers from a variety of countries in a region

h. the preference of an employer to use natives of the host country to manage operations there, but home-country residents to manage in the home country

i. the approach toward labor disputes in which unions and management are expected to cooperate

j. a contract created by a union and management that covers wages, hours, benefits, and working conditions

k. a system in which an authority fulfills the needs and regulates the conduct of the people under its control

Academic Vocabulary

8. On a separate sheet of paper, write a sentence or two related to human resource management using at least three of the academic terms you learned in the section openers:
- labor
- alternative
- commission
- debate
- interact
- conflict

Critical Thinking

9. The choices for practicing strategic human resource management are ethnocentric, polycentric, regiocentric, and geocentric. Identify situations in which it would be best to use each one.

Discussion Starter

10. Do you believe the HDI produces a reliable evaluation of the potential for human development? Express your opinion.

Point of View

11. Research and write an essay comparing the effects on personnel of hiring a CEO from inside vs. outside the company.

BUILDING REAL-WORLD SKILLS

12. Necessities of Life Having a job in a developing country means that you can purchase the necessities of life. The list of necessities varies from nation to nation. It also varies from state to state in the United States. For example, many states name food, clothing, and shelter as necessities. Others add a TV and a car.

Research and Share

a. Find out what items are considered necessities in one country in Asia, in Africa, in South America, and in Europe.

b. Discuss the differences.

13. Dispute Resolution One of the most vital areas of worker relations involves dispute resolution. Avoiding violence and the economic impact caused by work stoppages is very important. Consequently, the Departments of Justice and Treasury and other federal government agencies provide resources to settle such disputes. Private organizations also offer services to help resolve these problems.

Research and Write

a. Research the various alternatives for dispute resolution in the workplace.

b. Write a short paper comparing these various alternatives.

BUILDING ACADEMIC SKILLS

 English Language Arts

14. The presence of paternalism varies from company to company, and the desire for autonomy and empowerment varies from employee to employee. Write an essay on the style you would prefer.

MATH Mathematics

15. A "basket of goods" needed for living includes food, clothing, and shelter. In Indonesia it costs $150 (U.S. dollars) per month. A "basket" in Brazil costs $300 per month. See the graph for an average worker's hourly wage. Working 40 hours per week, which worker is better off?

Data Interpretation To solve this problem, you need to read a bar graph and understand the principles of division and subtraction.

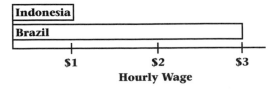

Hourly Wage

 Social Studies/History

16. Labor movements develop differently in different cultures and political structures. Consequently, a company's human resources department must tailor its relationships with unions to the models in the host countries. Research the histories of unions in three countries, one each in Europe, South America, and Asia. Write a report to the class on the differences between them.

SOC Social Studies/Geography

17. Find a world map. Note the locations of the countries you chose for exercise #16. Do you notice any correlation between the types of union-mangement relations and types of governments running these countries? Explain.

COMPETITIVE EVENT PREP

Location, Location, Location

18. Situation You are a sales representative for a large U.S. firm that wants to develop its position in the Middle East. You need to choose a country for your main office and create a plan of action to extend that presence to at least four additional offices. You must also decide whether to hire sales staff from that country or whether to ask U.S. sales personnel to relocate. You must also develop a training plan for that staff.

Activity Choose a country. Compare the cultural aspects of the country with nearby countries. Write a summary about the language, the primary religion, secondary religion, any subcultures or minority groups, and the issues you may have to deal with pertaining to gender and culture.

Evaluation You will be evaluated on how well you meet the following objectives:

a. Identify the influence religion has on doing business.

b. Consider the implications of the different languages of the region and whether you will specialize by country.

c. Detail cultural norms, the role of gender, values, and mores.

d. Describe how you will hire your sales force.

e. Reflect upon the best way to train your sales force.

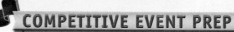

Internet Travels

Macedonia

Using the Internet, find a map of Macedonia. Study its geographical position and its neighboring states. Research and answer the following questions about Macedonia on a separate sheet of paper.

➤ What are the cultural and economic characteristics of Macedonia?

➤ What type of managerial style might be effective in Macedonia? Explain your answer.

@ For resources to help you do this exercise, go to the Online Learning Center through **glencoe.com.**

BusinessWeek online

19. Newsclip: The Future of Outsourcing Union leaders and workers are critical of outsourcing. But besides providing cheap labor, "transformational outsourcing" has advantages.

@ Go to the International Business Online Learning Center through **glencoe.com** to read an article about this topic. Then write a paragraph that explains why "transformational outsourcing" is changing the perception of offshoring.

Standardized Test Practice

20. Choose the best answer to the following fill-in question.

A company that prefers to use workers from its home country both at home and abroad is utilizing _____ _____.

○ ethnocentric management
○ polycentric management
○ regiocentric management
○ geocentric management

Test-Taking Tip Be careful when completing a statement. Use the process of elimination when you do not know the answer.

International Career Planning

Chapter Objectives

When you have completed this chapter, you will be able to:

Section 15.1

- Describe five assets an employee can offer to a company.

- Identify the steps of manager training.

- Explain on-the-job and off-the-job manager training programs.

Section 15.2

- Identify different career challenges.

- Discuss methods of stress management.

- Explain the necessary preparation for international travel.

- Identify three steps for career planning.

▶ BMW

BMW is a publicly owned corporation whose shares are traded on the stock exchanges. When you research this company through Standard & Poor's, you will find investment information such as this:

Index:	S&P Global 1200
Sector:	Consumer Discretionary
Company:	BMW
Symbol:	BMW
Country:	Germany
Price:	(varies)

Global Profile In 1916, *Bayerische Flugzeugwerke AG* was formed as a Munich airplane-engine manufacturing company. It became *Bayerische Motoren Werke AG,* or "Bavarian Motor Works" (BMW). BMW develops, manufactures, and sells automobiles and motorcycles. Its main brands are BMW, MINI, and Rolls-Royce. The three business segments are Automobiles, Financial Services, and Motorcycles.

Business Report BMW's brands belong to the premium sector of the international auto market. Built in 23 production plants, BMW vehicles are sold in more than 150 countries. With operations in America, Africa, Asia, Oceania, and Europe, and sales totaling more than 44.3 billion euros ($52.9 billion) annually, BMW provides steady returns to investors.

English Language Arts/Writing

A mainstay in the luxury automobile market, BMW targeted a different market by introducing the MINI in 2001. The retro design, high-tech engineering, and strong links to tradition made the car attractive to customers who wanted a lower-priced vehicle. BMW cultivated demand by showcasing the vehicle in the 2003 movie *The Italian Job. Write a paragraph about possible international careers at a luxury automobile company.*

@ To do this activity, go to the International Business Online Learning Center through **glencoe.com**.

Career Development

WHAT YOU'LL LEARN

- To describe five assets an employee can offer to a company
- To identify the steps of manager training
- To explain on-the-job and off-the-job manager training programs

WHY IT'S IMPORTANT

Great careers do not happen by accident. They take effort. Remember, success occurs when preparation meets opportunity.

KEY TERMS

- mentor
- superior-subordinate syndrome
- incremental manager training
- job-rotation manager training
- lateral-promotion manager training

Academic Vocabulary

You will find these words in your reading and on your tests. Make sure you know their meanings.

- identify
- achieve
- network

Reading Guide

Before You Read

What are your career goals?

MAIN IDEA
It takes preparation and planning to begin a career in international business.

GRAPHIC ORGANIZER
Draw this diagram. As you read this section, write in the five key employee assets and an example of each one.

1._____	2._____	3._____	4._____	5._____
_____	_____	_____	_____	_____
_____	_____	_____	_____	_____
_____	_____	_____	_____	_____
_____	_____	_____	_____	_____

Career Success

What is success? The answer might be quite different, depending on whom you ask. Many people measure success in dollars. Some believe success is measured by how many people they help. Others **identify** success with ranking in a company. No matter how you describe a successful career, it takes development and planning to have one.

Career development and planning have three main ingredients: improving the skills you have to offer to an employer, refining what the company has to offer to an employee, and dealing successfully with special career challenges.

What You Offer a Company

You can build your career by improving the things you have to offer to a company. Your cover letter and résumé (see **Figure 15.1**) reflect your career assets. There are five key employee assets:

- Work experience
- Education
- Special skills
- Personality characteristics
- Personal contacts

Work Experience

Early in your career, education may be your biggest asset. As time passes, experience becomes a more important factor. Experience is measured by two things: time and type.

Education

Employment application forms ask about a person's level of education. A high school diploma may be sufficient for entry-level jobs, but some companies may require a postsecondary degree.

Employers are interested in classes you have completed. For example, a retail firm may look for people who studied marketing and sales. For careers in international business, there are many classes designed to help people prepare, including world languages and classes in international business, economics, management, and finance.

Your educational background also includes your activities outside the classroom, such as the business club, sports, debate, or others.

Special Skills

Employers value many types of special skills. For example, physical labor requires physical strength and stamina. Attorneys must have analytical skills. International business skills include cultural sensitivity, adaptability, and language skills.

Figure 15.1

Résumé

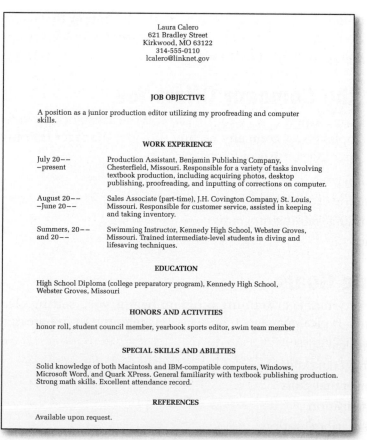

KEEP IT UPDATED A résumé includes your personal employee assets, such as education and experience. *Do you have a résumé ready for your next job search?*

Personality Characteristics

Desirable personality characteristics, or traits, include social skills, the ability to work well on teams and problem-solve, intelligence, and maturity. To **achieve** success, you should keep an open mind and be willing to try new experiences.

Contacts

The final asset that can become part of your personal balance sheet is a set of contacts, or people who help you with your career. These people are part of your **network**. One set of contacts is important when you look for a job. They are people you know who can refer you to employers and tell you about job openings. Employment applications typically ask for such references.

The other type of contact is a mentor. A **mentor** is a personal coach or counselor who helps an individual with his or her career. Mentors may be found within the company where you work. Individuals outside the company may also be professional contacts, such as an attorney working in one law firm who mentors an attorney who works in another firm. A mentor can be a supervisor, a friend, or a peer. Mentors offer advice about how to succeed in a company or a profession. They also help the new worker learn how to navigate company politics. As your career unfolds, it is wise to look for people who are willing to help you succeed.

What the Company Offers You

The second aspect of a successful career is the assistance provided by employers. A company usually provides manager training. Manager training consists of four steps:

1. Setting goals
2. Selecting candidates
3. Choosing training programs
4. Follow-up

Setting Goals

A quality manager training program begins with setting clear goals. Typical manager training goals are found in five areas:

1. Technical skills
2. Managerial skills
3. Conceptual skills
4. Socialization
5. Internationalization

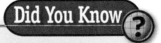

Role Playing

Did you know that almost every manager must deal with "superior-subordinate syndrome"? He or she will "have a boss" and "be the boss." Sometimes a manager takes orders. Sometimes a manager must give and enforce orders. It takes a different set of skills to adjust to each role.

Technical Skills

Technical skills are skills related to a particular job or occupation. Someone who is going to manage salespeople should learn how to motivate others or how to increase sales. A manager in the production department should know how the manufacturing system works. A computer manager must have highly-developed computer skills.

Managerial Skills

Managerial skills include a wide range of abilities. For example, managers need interpersonal skills to work with other people. A successful manager must also know how to resolve conflicts.

Conceptual Skills

Conceptual skills start with the ability to "see the big picture." This requires good analytical skills, creativity, and intuition. Using these skills, a successful manager can solve problems to the benefit of the whole company. A manager knows not only how he or she fits in with the larger company but also how all of his or her organization works.

Socialization

Socialization is the process of teaching people to accept the prevailing social standards of a group or culture. Socialization goals for managers are aimed at getting trainees to "think like a manager." A person who is promoted may have loyalty to past coworkers. The trainee must understand that he or she is playing a new role.

Managers also have supervisors. These individuals may experience **superior-subordinate syndrome**, a situation in which a manager will "have a boss" and "be the boss."

Internationalization

Internationalization skills include every aspect of preparing someone for an expatriate assignment. They include language, culture, and practical skills for working in other countries.

Selecting Candidates

One major responsibility assigned to the human resource (HR) department is to identify the people who will receive manager training. Most of the time, employees are selected for manager training programs because they have a solid "track record" combined with the right characteristics. A track record is the employee's history of success or failure in doing assigned tasks. Someone with a history of being promoted or of consistently taking on more responsibility has a good track record. An employee who consistently receives high performance evaluations may be selected.

Desirable personality characteristics of employees will vary by company. Some firms seek employees who have good people skills. Others look for well-organized employees. Certain companies want people who seem very motivated.

✓ Reading Check **Consider** Why is it important to develop a good track record?

Best Foot Forward

Your cover letter and résumé are a prospective employer's first impression of you. Naturally, you want to make the most of your abilities and accomplishments. This often means deciding what information to include, carefully wording your past job duties, and tailoring your résumé to the job description. However, it is not acceptable to lie or exaggerate. Common mistakes include inflating job titles, covering up periods of unemployment by fudging employment dates, and claiming unearned college degrees. *Describe two possible consequences of exaggerating your skills on your résumé.*

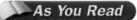
Choosing Training Programs

A key task for company leaders is choosing the right manager training program that will meet company goals and will be appropriate for trainees. These programs can be divided into two categories—on-the-job and off-the-job manager training.

On-the-Job Manager Training

To prepare people to move up in a company, businesses provide training on the job through incremental training, job-rotation training, and lateral-promotions training.

Incremental Training **Incremental manager training** is a form of training that gradually adds more managerial duties to a person's job. For example, someone who is selected to be a manager trainee in a grocery store may start out by being in charge of filling out daily reports and balancing cash register drawers. Over time, the person is given more responsibility until he or she is ready to manage the store.

Job Rotation **Job-rotation manager training** is a form of training in which the trainee learns different jobs by moving around in the company. A manager trainee at a retail store may be asked first to run a cash register, then to work in the electronics department, and finally in the credit office. As the trainee rotates, he or she learns whether he or she wishes to work as a department manager.

World Market   SPAIN

Camper Steps Up

When fourth-generation shoemaker Lorenzo Fluxá asked his grandfather if he could use the family tools and equipment to make casual footwear, it was a minor scandal. The family specialized in dress shoes, and the youngest Fluxá was proposing to make unisex slip-ons. He called them "Campers," named after the Spanish word for peasant. Luckily, the elder Fluxá granted permission, and the high-quality, low-pretention shoes were a hit among city folk in Barcelona who wanted to dress in the country style of Mallorca—the small town where the Fluxá family lived.

Ever since the family cobbled their first shoe in 1975, the company has sold quirky, stylish, and high-quality footwear around the world. Camper introduced innovations such as specially curved soles, breathable leather, and scrape-resistant finishes. Shoe-design interns come from as far as Japan and Scandinavian countries to train at Camper for a career in shoe design. Today Camper shoes sell in more than 50 countries.

THINK GLOBALLY *What factors might you consider before accepting an internship abroad?*

WALK DON'T RUN

@ To learn more about the country of origin for this global business, go to the International Business Online Learning Center through **glencoe.com**.

Figure 15.2

The Education-Income Connection

Highest Education Level	Annual Income
Doctoral degree	$89,400
Professional degree	$109,600
Master's degree	$62,300
Bachelor's degree	$52,200
Associate's degree	$38,200
Some college	$36,800
High School diploma	$30,400
No High School diploma	$23,400

Source: The U.S. Bureau of Labor Statistics

EDUCATION PAYS Higher levels of education pay off in annual and lifetime income. *What is the difference in yearly earnings between graduating from high school and dropping out?*

Lateral Promotions Lateral-promotion manager training is a form of job-rotation training that is enhanced by rewards for the trainee. The trainee receives a better title or a pay raise. Many large organizations and international businesses use this training.

Off-the-Job Manager Training

The other form of manager training takes place off the job. These programs include outside reading, additional in-house or out-of-house education, and leadership assignments. Additional education can pay career dividends, as illustrated in **Figure 15.2**.

Follow-Up

The company should follow up on the training program's strengths and weaknesses and make sure the program is identifying and training successful new managers.

Quick Check 15.1

After You Read Respond to what you have read by answering these questions.

1. What are five key employee assets? _____

_____

2. What are the four steps of manager training? _____

_____

3. What are the two main types of manager training? _____

_____

Academics / English Language Arts

4. Define the term *incremental* and how it relates to management training.

_____

Career Planning

WHAT YOU'LL LEARN

- To identify different career challenges
- To discuss methods of stress management
- To explain the necessary preparation for international travel
- To identify three steps for career planning

WHY IT'S IMPORTANT

A successful career takes careful planning to overcome career challenges such as stress, travel, and personal relationships.

KEY TERMS

- dual-career family
- travel itinerary
- passport
- visa
- work visa

Academic Vocabulary

You will find these words in your reading and on your tests. Make sure you know their meanings.

- commit
- attitude
- research

Reading Guide

Before You Read

What might be some career challenges in today's world?

MAIN IDEA

Awareness of the personal challenges of being an international businessperson can help you plan the right career path.

GRAPHIC ORGANIZER

Draw this diagram. As you read this section, identify the three steps of career planning and tools to complete those steps.

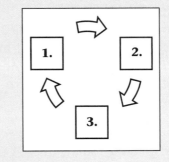

Career Challenges

Coping with career situations is easier when a company and the employee work together. Several challenging situations include: dual-career families, leaving an organization, and stress management.

Dual-Career Families

A **dual-career family** is a family arrangement in which both partners work. In the United States, the majority of families with two adults work. These families must address having and raising children, time management, and dealing with moving or relocation. In addition, a dual-career family may consist of two working adults who have no children. The acronym for this arrangement is *DINK,* or "double income/no kids."

Dual-Career Problems Conflicts can arise when both partners discuss having and raising children. Someone must be responsible for child care. Dual-career couples look for family-friendly businesses that provide day-care and flexible work scheduling.

Time management is another challenge. When a spouse travels or has a demanding job, the couple may have little time together. They must be willing to **commit** to solving the problem.

When one partner receives a promotion or new job offer, both partners are affected, especially if they are required to move. An international assignment also introduces stress. If possible, a company may help by finding the spouse a job in the host country.

Dual-Career Solutions Dealing with dual-career issues is easier when couples follow the three Cs: communication, cooperation, and commitment.

It is crucial to keep lines of communication open. Honesty is a key ingredient. Cooperation requires working around a partner's schedule. Spouses must help each other with household chores. Couples who succeed in dual careers try to be flexible and helpful. Commitment is vital.

Leaving an Organization

People leave companies for many reasons. Some reasons are positive, such as moving on to a better-paying job. However, when someone loses a job due to layoffs, the employee may harbor bad feelings. An employee may also feel angry if terminated.

Many HR departments deal with outplacement by offering access to training. The company may also help a former employee find a new job. The HR office may show a terminated employee how to apply for unemployment benefits.

HOME WORK Having dual careers can be a career challenge for both partners. *How might telecommuting help solve this problem?*

Stress Management

Stress is a problem that many workers encounter. Expatriate assignments can be especially stressful. Stress management requires recognizing that a situation can be overwhelming for an employee and addressing the problem. Some symptoms of stress manifest as physical, psychological, and social problems.

Many employers have programs designed to help with stress-related issues. These programs consist of four main activities:

- Placing employees in jobs they can handle
- Detecting people with stress-related problems
- Teaching stress-management techniques
- Reducing the stress levels of individual jobs

Employee Placement Employee placement is one way to prevent stress problems. Some workers can handle more challenges, excitement, or particular kinds of activity than others.

Detecting Stress Detecting stress is not always straightforward. Indeed, with e-mail, voice mail, cell phones, the Internet, and immediate 24/7 access to information, it may be a challenge to separate from the workplace and overcome stress. Some people with stress problems may develop a bad **attitude**, be argumentative, or appear tired because they are not sleeping well. Some become "workholics" and do not have a proper balance of work and leisure in their lives. Others show signs of substance abuse. HR personnel remind supervisors and managers to watch for these symptoms.

Stress-Management Training Many companies offer stress-management training in-house. Other companies hire consultants or send employees to seminars and training sessions to help them.

Reducing Stressors Company leaders can reduce stress in several ways. A job should be made as physically comfortable as possible. Discrimination, hazing, harassment, and conflict should not be tolerated in the workplace. If employees consistently "burn out" at a job, the job should be redesigned.

HR officers and others can help employees deal with these career challenges. Offering a strong, caring network for workers and their families makes a company a more inviting place to work.

Planning International Business Trips

Most employees find that some aspect of their job has an international element. They may have international customers, buy from international suppliers, and make contact with people from other countries. Traveling to other countries is part of everyday business for some employees. Advance preparations for travel include:

1. Learning about the destination country
2. Obtaining key documents
3. Working with governmental agencies

Learning about the Destination

To get ready for an international trip, it is important to research several factors about the country where you are going. Among the things you should examine are some basic issues:

- Safety
- Living conditions
- Immunization requirements
- Language barriers
- Local currency
- Time changes
- Other local arrangements

Safety issues relate to the levels of crime in a given area. In many parts of Europe, there are warnings about pickpockets. Unfortunately, kidnapping and terrorism take place in many areas around the world. It is crucial to know how to travel safely.

Culture Corner

Business Education, an American Original

Think About It Do you think of business as a trade or a profession?

With a culture that champions famous business icons, from Andrew Carnegie to Bill Gates, it is no surprise that business education got its start in the United States. In 1881, industrialist Joseph Wharton founded the University of Pennsylvania's prestigious Wharton School. It was the world's first collegiate school of business that was part of a larger university. At that time there were no textbooks, no curricula, and no professors of business. Today's Wharton offers 11 academic departments and the world's largest and most-published business school faculty. The college's 81,000 alumni include heads of state, ambassadors, founders of top companies, a Supreme Court judge, and winners of the Nobel Prize.

Wharton also offers an MBA program for executives in downtown San Francisco, California. Joseph Wharton would be proud. His vision of transforming business into a profession helped create an education industry.

Meeting and Greeting When doing business in the United States, handshakes are usually brief but firm. Use "Ms." to address a woman until you know if she prefers another title.

Business Etiquette Be on time for meetings, or five minutes early. Stand when being introduced. There is no set ritual for exchanging business cards.

Business Dress Proper dress varies by geographic region and company. Dress in a professional manner until you can observe what others are wearing.

English Language Arts/Writing

Describe a business course you would like to take as a high school course.

Be aware of living conditions in the country where you will be going. At the extreme end, living conditions might be difficult. There may not be quality transportation. The local water may not be suitable for drinking. Before traveling to another country, you may be required to get immunizations for polio, smallpox, or malaria. You will often face language barriers when you travel internationally, as described in Chapter 3. You will also need to carry local currency. Be aware of the exchange rate and any fees for converting the currency. Allow for jet lag and remember to make phone calls home at the proper times as you adjust to the local time.

As You Read

Question What are three factors to consider when planning an international business trip?

Other Advance Preparations

Identify the major transportation system that is used in a world city. For example, knowing how to ride the Metro while visiting or living in Paris, France, would be useful.

Advise your colleagues about your departure and arrival plans. A **travel itinerary** is a document that spells out travel times, transportation methods, and hotels or places where one will stay on a trip.

Set up housing arrangements in advance when possible. The Internet makes it easy to make hotel reservations around the world. You can also make reservations by telephone or fax.

Also, prepare a schedule of all your work assignments with times for meetings, lunches, dinners, social events, and time to rest.

Reading Check **Recall** Name three essential components of a travel itinerary.

Having What It Takes

A career in international business can be exciting, stimulating, and rewarding. However, it takes a special person to succeed in this ever-changing global world. Often the unknown is the norm in international business. Bridging the cultural gaps found in international business requires people who are flexible, can tolerate ambiguity, and will avoid negative judgments. Other character traits that are helpful include a curiosity about other cultures, an awareness of surroundings, and an ability to ask questions. *What traits do you possess that would serve you well in a multicultural environment?*

Key Documents

It takes time to obtain all of the necessary documents, so start preparations early. Travelers need four main documents: a passport, visa, work visa, and tickets and receipts.

Passport

A **passport** is a government document used to prove a person's citizenship in the country that issued it. U.S. citizens can apply for passports at designated post offices. You can also download forms and instructions from the Internet and apply by mail under certain circumstances. You must complete an application form and provide identification and a photo. Your passport may take four to six weeks to arrive. Always carry your passport with you.

Visa

A **visa** is a stamp of endorsement that allows the holder of a passport to enter a country. A visa is issued at the border as you enter.

Work Visa

A **work visa**, or work permit, is an official document that allows an individual to work legally at a job in a host country. Getting a work visa requires an application made to the foreign government's consulate, embassy, or other governmental agency. People entering the United States to work are regulated by the Department of Labor, State Department, and the Department of Immigration and Naturalization.

Tickets and Receipts

Hold onto all of your hotel reservations and payment receipts. With increasing concerns about security and terrorism, governments may ask a person to prove they have been staying in certain places.

Working with Customs Agencies

You should know what you can take into or out of a country. Customs agencies make these decisions. They work at protecting the public from disease and dangerous products, enforcing tariffs, and making sure illegal guns and drugs do not enter a country.

U.S. Customs and Border Protection

The U.S. Customs and Border Protection agency combines the Customs Service, which began in 1789, and the U.S. Border Patrol, which was established as part of the Immigration Bureau in 1924. The Department of Homeland Security was established after the attacks of 9/11 during 2001. Then in 2003, the U.S. Customs and Border Protection agency was added to that agency.

Crossing Borders

As you pass across a national border, you will be asked to declare all the items you have. Make sure you know what can be legally carried into or out of a country to avoid being detained.

CAREER/LIFE COACH

If you are lucky, you know exactly what you want to be and do. For some people, goals are crystal clear. Others experience doubt and uncertainty. Many adults find themselves wondering whether they are on the right career path. While soul-searching is important, an outside voice can help.

Job Description

Life coaches sit down with people to assess what they want and what they need, and to identify their strengths. They are not unlike psychologists in that they do a lot of listening and a small amount of talking, though they are not medical professionals.

A good life coach can help you give words to feelings and goals that you do not realize you have. Life and career coaches can help you articulate your goals, set priorities, become more effective at work, and balance family and work priorities. A life coach can help you realize exactly what you are meant to do.

Skills and Training

Life and career coaches should have a strong desire to help others while being ethical and trustworthy. They should have a high degree of emotional sensitivity.

School counselors must be certified, and other counselors must be licensed to practice in all but two states. A master's degree is usually required to become a licensed counselor. Life coaches are not accredited.

English Language Arts/Writing

How can life and career coaches help young people just starting out in the world of work? How can they help upper-level managers who have worked in international business for many years?

@ To learn more about life and career coaches and their career paths, go to the International Business Online Learning Center through **glencoe.com**.

Career Data

Education: High school diploma, bachelor's degree

Skills: Communication and stress-management skills

Outlook: Growth faster than average in the next ten years

How Do You Say?

Q: In Castilian Spanish, how do you say: "Thank you for your time"?

A: Gracias por su tiempo. (pronounced: Grăh-thēē-ŭs pŏhr soo tēē-ĭm-pō.)

@ To learn this phrase in other languages, go to the International Business Online Learning Center through **glencoe.com**.

Planning a Career in International Business

There are many sources of information to help you plan. Libraries, the Internet, government organizations, schools, employers, and members of your local community can all provide useful information. Planning a career involves:

1. Deciding what you want to do
2. Analyzing your options
3. Researching a career

What You Want

Deciding what you want to do means taking a good look at your interests, abilities, and goals. It is important to work at a job you find interesting. At the same time, make sure you have the aptitude and skills needed to do the job effectively. Think about how much money you want to make, how much free time you want, whether you are willing to travel, and how important it is to climb to the top of the career ladder.

Analyzing Your Options

Analyzing your options means acquiring good advice about a career. Talk to career counselors. Visit with people in the profession that interests you. Focus on choosing a career that will keep you employed, committed, and satisfied.

Researching a Career

Researching a career means finding information to help you match your level of education, experience, and personal characteristics to the job or profession. Find out how long it will take you to get established in a company or profession.

Quick Check 15.2

After You Read Respond to what you have read by answering these questions.

1. What special career challenges do many employees face? _____

_____

2. What are four main travel documents? _____

_____

3. What are the main goals of customs agencies? _____

_____

Academics / Social Studies

4. Explain the history of the formation of the U.S. Department of Homeland Security.

_____

_____

Mentor Relationships

Mentors provide needed wisdom, accurate information on company politics, beneficial assignments, and future prospects. Write a memo to yourself on how you would select and cultivate a relationship with a prospective mentor at your place of employment.

_____

_____

_____

_____

_____

_____

_____

_____

_____

_____

_____

_____

_____

_____

_____

_____

_____

_____

_____

_____

ACADEMICS APPLIED Check off the academic knowledge you used to do this activity:

☐ English Language Arts   ☐ Mathematics   ☐ Social Studies   ☐ Science

ACADEMIC AND CAREER PLAN Add this page to your Academic and Career Plan Portfolio.

(tl) Ulf Wallin/Getty Images; (tr) Royalty-free/David De Lossy/Getty Images; (b) Royalty-free/Getty Images

CHAPTER SUMMARY

Section 15.1 **Career Development**

mentor (p. 350)

superior-subordinate syndrome (p. 351)

incremental manager training (p. 352)

job-rotation manager training (p. 352)

lateral-promotion manager training (p. 353)

- There are five key assets that each employee can offer: work experience, education, special skills, personality characteristics, and personal contacts.

- Manager training consists of four steps: setting goals, selecting candidates, choosing training programs, and follow-up.

- Two approaches are used to prepare people to move up in a company: on-the-job training and off-the-job training. On-the-job training consists of incremental, job-rotation, and lateral-promotions training. Off-the-job training consists of outside reading, additional education, and specially designed methods, such as leadership assignments.

Section 15.2 **Career Planning**

dual-career family (p. 354)

travel itinerary (p. 357)

passport (p. 358)

visa (p. 358)

work visa (p. 358)

- Career challenges include dual-career families, leaving an organization, and stress management.

- Methods of stress management include placing employees in jobs they can handle, detecting people with stress-related problems, teaching stress-management techniques, and reducing the stress levels of individual jobs.

- Preparing for international travel requires doing three things: learning about the destination country, obtaining key documents, and working with governmental agencies.

- There are three steps to planning a career in international business: (1) deciding what you want to do, (2) analyzing your options, and (3) researching a career.

CONCEPTS REVIEW

1. **Describe** three of the five assets each employee can offer to her or his company.

2. **Explain** how a company develops its managers.

3. **Describe** the difference between on-the-job training and off-the-job training.

4. **Identify** three challenges usually found in a career.

5. **List** three things that must be done to prepare for international travel.

6. **Explain** the three steps to planning a career in international business.

KEY TERMS REVIEW

7. Match each term to its definition.

_____ mentor

_____ superior-subordinate syndrome

_____ incremental manager training

_____ job-rotation manager training

_____ lateral-promotion manager training

_____ dual-career family

_____ travel itinerary

_____ passport

_____ visa

_____ work visa

a. a form of training that gradually adds more managerial duties to a person's job

b. a form of job-rotation training that is enhanced by rewards for the trainee

c. a family arrangement in which both partners work

d. a form of training in which the trainee learns different jobs by moving around in the company

e. a personal coach or counselor who helps an individual with his or her career

f. a government document used to prove a person's citizenship in the country that issued it

g. a stamp of endorsement that allows the holder of a passport to enter a country

h. an official document that allows an individual to work legally at a job in a host country

i. a situation in which a manager will "have a boss" and "be the boss"

j. a document that spells out travel times, transportation methods, and hotels or places where someone will stay on a trip

Academic Vocabulary

8. On a separate sheet of paper, write a sentence or two related to international career planning using at least three of the academic terms you learned in the section openers:

- identify
- achieve
- network
- commit
- attitude
- research

Critical Thinking

9. Many couples with dual careers in management postpone having and raising children until their 30s. Evaluate the pros and cons of this approach.

Discussion Starter

10. Peace Corps volunteers serve their country by living and working in developing countries. Would this experience prepare you for a career in international business? Why or why not?

Point of View

11. Consider an international business career that interests you. What type of managerial training (incremental, job rotation, or lateral promotion) would you like to experience? Why?

BUILDING REAL-WORLD SKILLS

12. Business Card Etiquette You meet a new, important business contact in Japan. He hands you his business card. You slide it into your pocket and continue to introduce yourself. Suddenly, his attitude changes. His welcoming smile is replaced by a worried expression. He finds an excuse to leave your presence. Ultimately, the potential business is lost.

Research and Share

a. Research the importance of the exchange of business cards in other countries, such as Japan.

b. Draw conclusions as to what happened in the described meeting and how you would prevent such an occurrence.

13. Staying Current Careers have been ended by a person's failure to adapt to circumstances. One sign of this attitude is resistance to integrating new technology into business and interactions with other businesspeople.

Research and Write

a. Research and find out what types of technology businesses used 25 years ago.

b. Write a short paper about how differently a businessperson might function using that technology in today's world. Discuss the advantages and disadvantages of using technology today.

BUILDING ACADEMIC SKILLS

 English Language Arts

14. Pickpockets are a problem in many areas of Europe. Write a short essay on what it would be like to have your money, identification, and credit cards stolen while in another country. What would you do?

 Social Studies/Psychology

16. The concept of "face," the custom of gift giving and bowing at introductions, and the use of business cards are specific to Asian cultures. Why do you think American business practices are different from those in Asia?

MATH Mathematics

15. A person with an associate's degree in engineering may earn approximately $200,000 more over her or his lifetime than a high-school graduate. A person with a college degree in business may earn almost $400,000 more than someone with a high school diploma. Working 40 years, how much might someone with a college degree in business earn over someone with an associate's degree in engineering?

Computation and Estimation To solve this problem, you need to understand the principles of division and subtraction.

SOC Social Studies/Sociology

17. For years, the typical family in the United States consisted of a working father and a stay-at-home mom. But by 2000, 80 percent of the workforce was composed of dual-career couples with women comprising 60 percent of the workforce. Research whether other countries have experienced similar shifts and why. Report your findings to the class.

COMPETITIVE EVENT PREP

The Pocket Administrative Assistant

18. Situation You are the administrative assistant for the president of a large construction firm. Your boss is going to the Middle East. He has asked you to get sufficient foreign currency for his trip to Dubai, UAE, Egypt, Kuwait, and Turkey. He plans to spend a day relaxing in Greece.

Activity Design a wallet card similar in size to a credit card for each currency. This card should feature various denominations of both U.S. and the foreign currency so that he can tell at a glance approximately how much something costs. Add to this card other important conversion information related to weights, distances, and temperatures. Your boss should be able to easily determine the U.S. equivalent and the foreign designation.

Evaluation You will be evaluated on how well you meet the following objectives:

a. The card should be neat and clear to follow.

b. Detail appropriate denominations of money for cab fare, meals, hotels, and clothing purchases.

c. Convert distances between the airport and places of business and temperatures.

d. Role-play presenting the card to your boss.

BusinessWeek online

19. Newsclip: Get 'Em While They're Young Companies such as Deloitte & Touche LLP and Lockheed Martin are offering mentorships, internships, and college scholarships to high school students.

@ Go to the International Business Online Learning Center through **glencoe.com** to read an article about this topic. Then write a paragraph that describes how high school students can benefit from early recruitment.

Standardized Test Practice

20. Choose the best answer to the following multiple-choice question.

Which of the following statements is an opinion?

○ The U.S. Border Patrol was established as part of the Immigration Bureau in 1924.

○ The Customs Service began work in 1789.

○ The U.S. Customs and Border Protection agency was added to a larger agency, the Department of Homeland Security.

○ The most important job of the U.S. Customs and Border Protection agency is to collect tariffs.

Internet Travels

Estonia
Using the Internet, find a map of Estonia. Study its geographical position and its neighboring states. Answer the following questions about Estonia on a separate sheet of paper.

➤ Research the culture and lifestyle in Estonia.

➤ Using the text's list of things to consider before visiting a foreign country, prepare a memo for travelers to Estonia covering these topics.

@ For resources to help you do this exercise, go to the International Business Online Learning Center through **glencoe.com**.

Test-Taking Tip This question requires that you identify an opinion. An opinion is a statement of belief not a proven fact. Opinions often contain subjective words such as *most, easiest, best,* and *should.*

Chapter 16

Technology and the Future Global Economy

Chapter Objectives

When you have completed this chapter, you will be able to:

Section 16.1

- Identify the communication tools available to international businesspeople.
- Explain the difference between computer hardware and software.
- Describe types of internal and external communications.

Section 16.2

- Explain how e-commerce programs are used for international operations.
- Identify new technologies that can help employees reach career goals.

► HARMAN INTERNATIONAL

Harman International is a publicly owned corporation whose shares are traded on the stock exchanges. When you research this company through Standard & Poor's, you will find investment information such as this:

Index:	S&P Global 1200 and S&P 500
Sector:	Consumer Discretionary
Company:	Harman International Industries, Inc.
Symbol:	HAR
Country:	U.S.A.
Price:	(varies)

Global Profile Co-founded by Dr. Sidney Kardon in 1953, Harman International was the first company to design and manufacture hi-fi receivers. Since then the company has grown into the world's premiere audio manufacturer, designing and marketing high-quality, high-fidelity audio products for the consumer, professional, and automotive markets. Harman International's brands include Infinity, JBL, AKG, DigiTech, and Harman Kardon. Its loudspeakers and other equipment are used by professionals at concert halls, stadiums, airports, and other buildings, and for recording, broadcast, cinema, and music reproduction.

Business Report Harman employs more than 10,800 people. With sales exceeding $3 billion annually, analysts find that Harman also produces solid investment performance in the global stock markets.

English Language Arts/Writing

Today the home audio market is integrating DVD players, PCs, MP3 players, and phones—and Harman is embracing the changes. Its "Infotainment" products are designed to provide intuitive, interactive interfaces that combine sounds and technology. *Write a paragraph about why the use of technology and innovation has affected Harman's success.*

To do this activity, go to the International Business Online Learning Center through **glencoe.com**.

Technology and International Business

WHAT YOU'LL LEARN

- To identify the communication tools available to international businesspeople
- To explain the difference between computer hardware and software
- To describe types of internal and external communications

WHY IT'S IMPORTANT

The global marketplace changes continually. Business moves faster and faster every day, and depends on information technology.

KEY TERMS

- information technology (IT)
- hardware
- software
- intranet
- extranet

Academic Vocabulary

You will find these words in your reading and on your tests. Make sure you know their meanings.

- equip
- potential
- media

Reading Guide

Before You Read

How has information technology changed the nature of international business?

MAIN IDEA

Improvements in computers and telecommunications make the world "smaller" by providing access to fast communication worldwide.

GRAPHIC ORGANIZER

Draw a flow chart similar to this one. As you read this section, write in three types of software and two applications for each one.

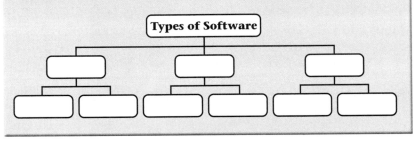

Information Technology and You

Most high school students in today's world have grown up using new technologies. Many of these same technologies play an important role in the world of international business. Technology helps create, manufacture, sell, and ship products around the world.

Communication Tools and IT

The computer is probably the most important technological advancement of the past 100 years. Computers have generated vast improvements in what is known as "information technology." **Information technology (IT)** is the hardware and software used in creating, processing, storing, and communicating information. This information has a wide variety of uses and users.

When computers were first developed in the 1940s and 1950s, they were large, slow, and noisy. Computers were once room-sized, but today everything from a phone to a car includes a small computer. Computers have two main components—hardware and software.

Computer Hardware

Computer **hardware** consists of the physical components of a computer system. There are four basic kinds of hardware parts:

- The processor
- Memory
- Input and output devices
- Storage devices

The Processor The processor is essentially the brain of the computer. A central processing unit (CPU) is the processor used in personal computers, which are more powerful than the earliest models. Improvements increased the speed of computer processors.

Memory Computer memory holds the data and the instructions required to operate the computer. One type of memory is known as *random access memory* (RAM). RAM stores information on a temporary basis. *Read-only memory* (ROM) is computer memory on which data has been pre-recorded and cannot be easily changed. A computer's capacity to store memory is measured in bytes, which include a kilobyte (KB) for one thousand pieces of information, a megabyte (MB) for one million, a gigabyte (GB) for one billion, and a terabyte (TB) for one trillion. Larger amounts of memory make it possible to process more information.

Input and Output Devices Input devices feed information to the computer. Common input devices include the keyboard, mouse, touchpad, joystick, camcorder, digital camera, and microphones. Output devices present data from the computer to the user. Output devices include the monitor, printer, speakers, modems, display projectors, and even robotic arms used in manufacturing.

Storage Devices Storage devices are places to save information. They include external hard drives, CD-ROMs, and flash drives, or memory sticks, which are portable storage devices.

Computer Software

Software is a computer program or application. Various forms of software contain the instructions that run a computer. Software **equips** computer users with the tools necessary to complete various tasks. There are many types of software:

- Word processing
- Desktop publishing
- Spreadsheets
- Accounting
- Database management
- Graphics
- Communication systems
- Groupware
- Web-page design

Word Processing You have probably used a word-processing program to write a school paper. In the business world, word-processing programs enable you to prepare letters, books, and mailings.

Desktop Publishing Desktop publishing allows a user to write, design, and lay out both text and graphics in publications in many languages to different markets.

TECH Trends

Mobile Communication Systems

The world is moving toward wireless connectivity. This means that people can carry and use most computers, PDAs, cell phones, and other devices practically anywhere in the world. U.S. Cellular is one provider of wireless access. The company's software is called "Novarra." It helps technology users across a range of computing devices. Intel's wireless technology is called "Centrino." This technology is licensed to and sold by Dell. IBM's product is called "Pervasive Wireless." No matter what company or what name, each device makes it possible to send messages and retrieve information without a physical connection such as a telephone line. The future of wireless technology will include many dramatic new innovations and products. *Research and write a paragraph about possible future wireless innovations.*

@ For links to help you do this activity, go to the International Business Online Learning Center through **glencoe.com**.

E-Commerce and Cultural Interdependence

The Internet has made buying and selling goods and services a world affair. With a click of a button, people from every part of the globe can perform business transactions. When making international e-commerce transactions from the comfort of your own home or office, it is easy to forget that you are dealing with different cultures in different places. Intercultural rules of communication and etiquette are as important as ever, even though you may never know the location of a transaction. E-commerce truly is the ultimate connection to a multicultural world. *Investigate an e-commerce site for a company such as IKEA or McDonald's. What are some strategies or Web-design techniques used to effectively serve a multicultural customer base?*

As You Read

Predict In what ways have communication systems innovations impacted international business?

Spreadsheets Spreadsheet programs calculate and store information, such as sales figures, product quantities, prices, and unit production costs for products. This makes it easy to calculate financial options for a business and to examine data quickly and logically.

Accounting Accounting software tracks payroll, pays bills, submits invoices, and computes taxes. It can also compute exchange rates and other international monetary variances.

Database Management Database programs store and analyze many kinds of information to help a business realize its **potential**. Marketing databases contain lists of people's names, addresses, and consumer characteristics, allowing database managers to determine who may be interested in their company's products. Production databases hold lists of supplies, products, inventory, and schedules. Employee databases keep track of workers, wage rates, and benefits.

Graphics Designers and other businesspeople use graphics programs to make visual presentations. These include graphs, charts, slides, animation, and video clips. Such programs can make a much more persuasive sales pitch than presentations using only text. Computer Aided Design (CAD), used in manufacturing, architecture, interior decorating, and other simulations, uses graphics to visually present detailed technical information.

Communication Systems Software packages improve a company's communication systems by helping computers communicate with each other globally. These systems can be programmed to assist with e-mail and to help an operator work with databases, accounts, and other shared files.

Groupware Groupware allows various types of software applications to enable team members to work together. It can be used to plan and implement a project by setting target goals.

Web-Page Design Web-page design programs assist in the design of Web sites. These Web sites are used to send and receive information to and from customers, suppliers, and others.

Technology and Communication Systems

Innovations in fiber optics, digital-processing programs, and broadband-cable systems have led to more sophisticated telephones, scanners, video and computer conferencing programs, and Webcast systems. Each innovation has had a profound effect on communications and international business.

Telephones The telephone used to be a simple, wire-connected device. Now, wireless cell phones allow users to talk to each other from remote locations. Because cell phones can also take photos and send text messages, access the Internet, play and store music and visuals, and transmit various kinds of data, cell phones are replacing other portable **media** players. These phones and their systems make it possible for travelers to stay connected almost anywhere.

Technology from Siemens

In 1842, Werner von Siemens received his first patent in Prussia for his method of plating gold and silver. When his brother Wilhelm found a way to market this technique in England, the seeds of a business empire were planted. Werner made further breakthroughs by developing a printer telegraph, copper-wire insulation, and the dynamo-electric principle, which made it possible to create and supply electricity to cities. By 1914, Siemens was a global company employing a workforce of 82,000.

Then came war. The first World War in 1914 wiped out 40 percent of the company. World War II in 1942 destroyed 80 percent of the remaining company.

Siemens had to rebuild. First, the company helped build a rail network, establish postal service, and generate and distribute power in Germany. Then it reorganized to do business in the global marketplace. Today the company is a major provider of information technology and telecommunication products, and power generation in more than 190 countries.

THINK GLOBALLY *Why would a technology-based company need to view business on a worldwide level to survive?*

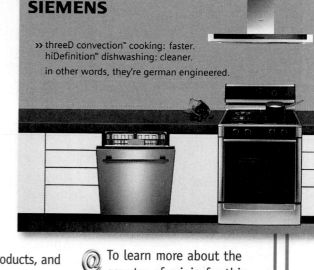

SIEMENS

» threeD convection™ cooking: faster.
hiDefinition™ dishwashing: cleaner.
in other words, they're german engineered.

@ To learn more about the country of origin for this global business, go to the International Business Online Learning Center through **glencoe.com**.

Faxes and Scanners Facsimile (FAX) machines and scanners have allowed for speed and convenience for both domestic and international business. Forms and other documents requiring a signature can be sent quickly by fax. Scanned documents can be sent via e-mail.

Conferencing Systems Video- and computer-conferencing systems make virtual face-to-face and computer-to-computer visits possible. In international business, being able to put a face with a name is extremely valuable. There may be a slight time delay with translation, but this technology promotes personalized business activity.

Webcasts Webcasts are broadcasts made over the Internet, similar to video and computer conferences. Businesspeople use this technology to talk to employees, companies, and customers.

Internal Company Communication

Data and information need to move in several directions in a successful business operation. Internal company communications are vital to keep things running smoothly. Information also moves to the outside world, including other companies, such as suppliers, retail organizations, and individual consumers. Information moves in three directions—downward, upward, and laterally. (See **Figure 16.1** on page 373.)

A I HEAR YOU International teleconferences may require translators. *What are the benefits of teleconferencing?*

Downward Communication

Downward communication takes place when managers give orders and directions. Managers also ask questions of or seek input from lower-level employees. Top managers have several communication choices. They can call subordinates on the phone, send memos, or use e-mail. *Group e-mail* is a form of communication in which the same message is sent to every employee by e-mail.

Upward Communication

Upward communication consists of all the questions, comments, ideas, and concerns that lower-level employees send to managers. Choosing the appropriate method for talking to the "people upstairs" can be a challenge for international businesspeople.

It is important to know and understand the culture of both the company and the region where the company operates. In some circumstances, directly contacting upper management would be viewed as insubordination.

Reading Check **Recall** Compare and contrast upward and downward internal communication.

Lateral Communication

Lateral communication is communication between people who are at a similar level or position in the company. Managers and others must stay in contact with each other to coordinate the activities of all departments.

For example, think about a sales representative who lands an important new account, takes a large order, and promises quick delivery. When that happens, he or she should contact the production and shipping departments to make sure the promise is kept.

E-mails, phone calls, faxes, teleconferences, and Web-based communication all assist in moving information back and forth between departments. A company's internal, Web-based communication system is an **intranet**. The intranet is usually unavailable to the public.

Potential Problems

High-tech communication introduces some unique problems. For example, many people experience a feeling called "information overload," or being so overwhelmed with communication that you lose important messages. The best way to manage information overload is to devise a system to prioritize your messages.

Another problem that occurs is the back-and-forth attempt to reach someone by phone by leaving a message when the caller does not reach a "live" person. This is known as *phone tag*. Because of portability, cell phones can reduce this problem.

Figure 16.1

Internal Communication

UPSTAIRS, DOWNSTAIRS Company communication can go through different channels, but the proper channel may differ from country to country. *Why might it be inappropriate for a Japanese salesperson to contact his or her company's CEO via e-mail?*

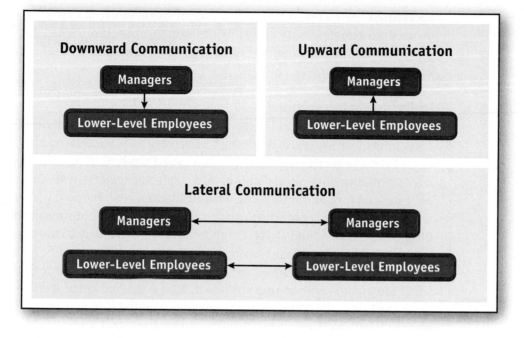

Internationally, callers need to remember differences in time zones. It helps to confirm this before making the call. All parties should communicate the time in their own time zone.

It is important to know how to properly greet someone. It helps to say "hello" in the native language of the person you are calling. Also, be aware of differences in formality.

Communication skills, both verbal and written, are vital in the world of international business. Business schools and other places that train international employees, including high schools, teach business communication skills, such as public speaking and writing business letters and memos.

External Company Communication

External communication includes messages to outside organizations and messages to individual consumers or customers. Different forms of communication are required for internal versus outside communication.

Outside Organizations

Outside (or external) organizations include suppliers, retail outlets, shipping companies, service organizations, and governmental organizations. Communication with these organizations is essential. Management must be sure that the proper communication channel is used to contact each group. For example, international shippers may use new electronic technologies to create a shipping manifest or bill of lading.

Internet The Internet has changed the nature of external communication with other organizations and individual consumers. A company's Web site can take orders, track shipping, and examine account balances. In the United States, any information generated on a company-owned computer is the property of the company.

Extranet An **extranet** system is a semiprivate network that allows more than one company access to the same information. The company can use the extranet to share information and collaborate on various projects.

Individual Consumers

Technology may also be used to communicate with individual consumers. Customers may phone a company to place orders, make complaints, or seek information. This is called "in-bound telemarketing." A high-quality phone system and a toll-free telephone number are essential for communicating with individual customers.

Many firms also contact consumers through e-mail. A business can direct current customers to its company Web site as a way to keep in contact with individual customers. However, customers should be able to opt out of receiving these messages if they wish. Remember that there are "spam" laws to prevent unsolicited e-mail advertisements.

A business's Web site can offer many functions. It can provide information, an open communication channel, and a method for making purchases.

Communication with other organizations and with individual customers has become much easier with the development and availability of information technologies. The Internet and other technologies make it possible to instantly send photos, illustrations, ads, charts, and other forms of information. In the world of global business, technology indeed "makes the world smaller."

Quick Check 16.1

After You Read Respond to what you have read by answering these questions.

1. What are the two main parts of a computer system? _____

_____

2. In what directions does information move within a company? _____

_____

3. What two main outside groups are reached using information technology? _____

_____

Academics / Mathematics

4. If your company's server has 4500GB of storage, how many MB of storage does it have?

_____

_____

The Future Global Economy

Reading Guide

Before You Read

What might be one defintion of the term *e-workforce*?

MAIN IDEA

Thanks to personal computers and telecommunications technology, a trip to the store or a trip to work can be as close as your home computer.

GRAPHIC ORGANIZER

Draw this table. As you read this section, write in three online catalog features and describe their benefits.

Online Catalogs	
Features	**Benefits**
1.	1.
2.	2.
3	3

WHAT YOU'LL LEARN

- To explain how e-commerce programs are used for international operations
- To identify new technologies that can help employees reach career goals

WHY IT'S IMPORTANT

The global economy is changing. To succeed in global business, you must use information technology, build multichannel markets, and utilize the workforce in innovative ways.

KEY TERMS

- e-commerce
- e-tail
- encryption
- e-workforce
- telecommuting

Academic Vocabulary

You will find these words in your reading and on your tests. Make sure you know their meanings.

- generate
- link
- cycle

The Future Is Now

The explosion of online commerce has created an entirely new landscape for both domestic and international business. The future global economy will include many new marketing and e-commerce programs. The global economy will also reflect technology's dramatic effects on the lives of employees and their jobs.

E-Commerce

The nature of marketing has changed. The driving force is e-commerce. **E-commerce**, or electronic commerce, is the marketing of goods and services over the Internet. E-commerce affects both domestic and international companies in many significant ways. Today eBay and other Internet-based, customer-to-customer Web sites enable online sales transactions. E-commerce also affects business-to-business (B2B) transactions. Two factors contribute to the impact of e-commerce:

1. E-commerce components
2. Effects of e-commerce on global business

E-Commerce Components

An e-commerce program makes it possible to reach customers in new ways. Stores known as *bricks and mortar* operations, or stores with a physical location, can now stay in contact with customers 24 hours a day, seven days a week by using features of the Internet. These businesses, which have both online and physical locations, are known as *click-and-mortar* operations. Another name for marketing in more than one way is *multichannel marketing.*

Marketers and businesspeople can use multichannel marketing to reach two customer groups—individual consumers and businesses. Web sites, online chat with technology support, e-mail programs, data-file sharing, and other technology-driven methods allow companies to expand lists of potential buyers and **generate** more business.

Retail e-commerce programs are also called **e-tail** operations. E-commerce programs have three main components:

- An online catalog
- The shopping cart
- The payment system

▼ **SHOPPING ONLINE A catalog is a key part of an e-commerce operation. What features make this Web-based catalog effective?**

The Catalog The online catalog lists the goods or services the company is offering for sale. A well-designed Web-site catalog is easy to access. Customers can quickly find the items that interest them. Customers also want to know prices, discounts, how long it will take to deliver the items, and other details.

An online catalog should have a "contact us" **link** to a contact Web page. Using this option, customers can reach the company via e-mail or telephone. Some sites include a "live chat" feature. Most Web sites also offer company history, investor information, and employment information.

Companies that have international customers usually provide additional options on an opening page. These typically include options for selecting a different language and for choosing your home country.

Shopping Cart A shopping cart is a virtual storage device. As customers view the catalog, they find items they wish to buy. They can compile a list of items and store the list in the shopping cart.

Culture Corner

Extraterrestrial Tourism in Russia

Think About It How important is technology to space travel?

In October 1957, the Soviet Union launched the first unmanned satellite, Sputnik 1, in orbit around the earth. The first human to orbit the earth was also a Soviet Russian, Yuri Gagarin, in 1961. His successful flight motivated the United States to declare a "space race." In July 1969, the United States succeeded in landing two men on the moon with the Apollo 11 spacecraft.

Countless space missions later, the world's first space tourist ventured into "the final frontier." In 2001, an American businessman paid $20 million to ride a Russian Soyuz rocket to the International Space Station for a one-week stay. A year later a South African Internet mogul took a similar trip. Trips like these might become a 21st-century industry. Companies around the world are ready to build passenger vehicles, lunar cruise ships, rotating hotels, and orbiting cities. Some have plans for virtual tours of space from the safety of Earth. Positioned on motion platforms, participants take a simulated drive across the moon's surface in a rover, exploring the moonscape through the "eyes" of robots.

Meeting and Greeting When doing business in Russia, shake hands firmly and say "good morning," "good afternoon," or "good evening." It is considered bad luck to shake hands over a threshold.

Business Etiquette Exchange business cards with one side translated into Russian. Meetings begin on time; negotiations can be lengthy.

Business Dress Businesspeople dress formally and conservatively, avoiding light or bright colors. Men wear suits. Women wear suits, dresses, or pantsuits.

English Language Arts/Writing

How might e-training integrate with space travel?

Payment Methods The most common payment method for individual e-commerce consumers is a credit card. Several credit card companies have created payment systems with additional security that allows consumers to make online purchases without worrying that their credit card information will be stolen. Creating consumer confidence in online credit card use was a major challenge for many companies when they began offering e-commerce programs.

Transactions are protected by encryption technology. **Encryption** is a form of code and signal scrambling that makes it nearly impossible for hackers to steal or alter sensitive information. Careful security and use of encryption technology are vital for e-commerce companies working to establish trust in international business relationships.

> **As You Read**
>
> **Relate** How does a virtual shopping cart differ from a physical shopping cart? Have you ever used a virtual shopping cart to purchase something over the Internet?

Reading Check **Recall** How does encryption technology affect e-commerce?

The Effects of E-Commerce

Using e-commerce offers major advantages to many types of companies. Retail stores, which were once limited to physical locations, can now reach customers globally.

Companies involved in business-to-business transactions benefit from e-commerce. They can order supplies from low-cost bidders around the world. Also, the number of potential new customers expands.

Businesses can use e-commerce programs to sell travel, credit, banking, insurance, and other services to a worldwide audience.

Other Uses of E-Commerce

A Web site provides a constant **cycle** of information: E-commerce allows the company to reach customers, and customers to reach the company. Marketers can also use Web-site technology to conduct surveys and perform other forms of market research. Research allows a company to better market products, adapt products, and refine advertising messages. It can also help identify new global trade opportunities.

The E-Workforce

Technology not only affects goods and services—it also affects jobs. The **e-workforce** is the population of workers who use computers to do business. This e-workforce is shaped by technology in two basic ways—how work is performed and where work is performed.

How Work Is Performed

Many jobs have changed due to upgrades in technology. These technological innovations include wearable computers, specialized software packages, and e-training programs.

Wearable Computers Wearable computers are small, lightweight computers that people can carry. Head mounts, PDAs, and cell phones make it possible to communicate anywhere.

Specialized Software Packages Specialized software packages may include expert systems. An *expert system* is computer software that stores and uses knowledge that a human expert would have.

E-Training Programs E-training programs can help new employees learn jobs quickly and effectively. One version of e-training uses "virtual reality," whereby a real situation is simulated using computer technology. Pilots, police trainees, and soldiers can practice handling dangerous situations through virtual reality programs. Students can simulate lab experiments without injury.

THE VIRTUAL WORLD Virtual reality is not just for gaming. Simulations help train employees around the world. *How does e-training aid international business managers and HR personnel?*

IT PROFESSIONAL

As businesses get larger, so do their computer networks. Multinational corporations must carefully plan to make sure all of their computers, in all of their different offices, can communicate with one another.

Job Description

Information technology professionals do more than just install computers. They have to create elaborate plans for making large-scale networks work together. There is a range of IT roles within an organization. IT professionals may plan and coordinate installation and upgrading of hardware and software, programming and systems design, development of computer networks, and performance of Internet and intranet sites. They are responsible for network security. They analyze the computer and information needs of their organizations and determine immediate and long-range personnel and equipment requirements.

IT professionals may travel to remote offices to take inventory of equipment, maintain lists of hardware and software in use, and come up with plans for upgrades and new installations. IT professionals are often "on call."

Skills and Training

IT professionals need strong communication skills for working with managers, vendors, and consultants. Advanced technical knowledge is essential. IT professionals also need leadership and management skills.

A bachelor's degree is usually required. Some candidates secure entry-level jobs with an associate's degree, but gain additional experience and further education. IT professionals who wish to take on management roles should consider an MBA with a technology component.

✏ English Language Arts/Writing

What roles do IT professionals play in internal and external company communications?

@ To learn more about IT professionals and their career paths, go to the International Business Online Learning Center through **glencoe.com.**

Career Data

Education: Associate's degree, bachelor's degree, MBA with technology component

Skills: Computer, technology, mathematical, and communication skills

Outlook: Growth faster than average in the next ten years

Where Work Is Performed

Due to new technologies, people can work remotely almost anywhere in the world. The benefit is that employees have data and information at their fingertips. The downside is that it is more difficult to "leave work at work."

Telecommuting Another growing trend in human resource management is **telecommuting**, a practice whereby the employees work at home aided by technology. The employee who is telecommuting sends work to the office via fax, telephone, e-mail, and rapid delivery services such as UPS or FedEx. Meetings can take place through teleconferencing. The employee visits the office when necessary.

Telecommuting is popular in the publishing industry. Writers, editors, and advertising sales representatives can work at home. This allows the company to save money on overhead.

The use of telecommuting will probably increase dramatically in the next few decades. It will also change the nature of international trade. Employees may be able to relocate around the world. The concepts of host-country employees and home-country employees may become less defined as a result.

The Impact of Technology

Computers and information technology are vital to the international business environment. Computer hardware and software allow businesspeople to quickly perform a wide variety of activities. Communication can move efficiently through upward, downward, and lateral channels internally as well as to those outside the company. E-commerce programs make it possible for businesses to reach more individual consumers and companies.

Quick Check 16.2

After You Read Respond to what you have read by answering these questions.

1. What are the three components of an e-commerce program? _____

   _____

2. What types of technology are used in performing work? _____

   _____

3. What is the definition of the term *telecommuting*, and what are its benefits? _____

   _____

Academics *English Language Arts/Writing*

4. Define the term *virtual reality* and describe how it relates to e-training programs.

   _____

   _____

E-Trusion vs. Solitude

The intrusion of some technologies (called "e-trusion") into a person's ability to find renewing solitude is troubling to psychologists. The connectivity offered by cell phones, e-mail, and pagers, as well as news, sports, and personal downloads onto wireless devices of all kinds tends to form a "habit structure." This habit structure makes people feel a lack of control, guilt, and loneliness when they cannot access or connect. Consider how e-trusion might affect you. Write a plan or schedule for well-balanced activities throughout the day and night.

_____

_____

_____

_____

_____

_____

_____

_____

_____

_____

_____

_____

_____

_____

_____

_____

_____

_____

_____

ACADEMICS APPLIED Check off the academic knowledge you used to do this activity:

☐ English Language Arts   ☐ Mathematics   ☐ Social Studies   ☐ Science

ACADEMIC AND CAREER PLAN Add this page to your Academic and Career Plan Portfolio.

CHAPTER SUMMARY

Section 16.1 Technology and International Business

information technology
    (IT) (p. 368)

hardware (p. 369)

software (p. 369)

intranet (p. 372)

extranet (p. 374)

- Numerous communication tools are available to international businesspeople. They include computer hardware and software of all kinds, telephones, faxes and scanners, conferencing systems, and Webcast systems.

- The physical components of a computer system are hardware. Software is a computer program or application used by the hardware.

- Various internal communication includes three types: downward, upward, and lateral. External communication systems include the Internet, extranet, Web sites, in-bound telemarketing, and e-mail.

Section 16.2 The Future Global Economy

e-commerce (p. 375)

e-tail (p. 376)

encryption (p. 377)

e-workforce (p. 378)

telecommuting (p. 380)

- E-commerce or electronic commerce is the marketing of goods and services over the Internet. It allows for businesses to use multichannel marketing to reach individual consumers and businesses globally through e-tail Web sites, online chatrooms, e-mail, data-file sharing, and other methods.

- The application of new technologies to e-commerce can provide opportunities for career-minded employees who can adapt to change quickly. New technologies include wearable computers, specialized software packages, and e-training programs.

CONCEPTS REVIEW

1. **Explain** how new technologies can play a role in international business.

2. **Provide** two examples of computer hardware.

3. **Distinguish** computer hardware from computer software.

4. **Describe** two examples of external communication.

5. **Define** the term *e-commerce.*

6. **Discuss** how new technologies can help employees' careers.

KEY TERMS REVIEW

7. Match each term to its definition.

_____ information technology (IT)

_____ hardware

_____ software

_____ intranet

_____ extranet

_____ e-commerce

_____ e-tail

_____ encryption

_____ e-workforce

_____ telecommuting

a. the marketing of goods and services over the Internet

b. a semiprivate network that allows more than one company access to the same information

c. retail e-commerce programs

d. a company's internal, Web-based communication system

e. a form of code and signal scrambling that makes it nearly impossible for hackers to steal or alter sensitive information

f. a computer program or application

g. the population of workers who use computers to do business

h. the physical components of a computer system

i. a practice whereby employees work at home aided by technology

j. the hardware and software used in creating, processing, storing, and communicating information

Academic Vocabulary

8. On a separate sheet of paper, write a sentence or two related to technology and the future global economy using at least three of the academic terms you learned in the section openers:
- equip
- potential
- media
- generate
- link
- cycle

Critical Thinking

9. When e-commerce first started, some experts believed that in a short time all buying and selling would take place online. Many normally realistic investors drove e-commerce company stock prices up. However, the prices soon fell. Discuss the lessons from this experience.

Discussion Starter

10. Information technology helps a company's upper management directly contact and survey its consumers. As an example, opinion data can be created by the recipient of every tenth cash register receipt validating a 2-for-1 coupon by taking a survey on line. Discuss the strengths and weaknesses of such systems in class.

Point of View

11. E-training that focuses on topics such as obscure company policies generally does not succeed. In a short essay, state and evaluate the factors that make e-training succeed or fail. Include any personal experiences.

BUILDING REAL-WORLD SKILLS

The GLOBAL WORKPLACE

12. Watch What You Input

Computer keyboards vary from country to country. The standard layout is called the "QWERTY" layout of 102 keys. However, in many cases, keys are added. In addition, QWERTY becomes QWERTZ in Central Europe, and AZERTY in France and Belgium. Special marks and accent keys are integrated for most languages. Chinese, Japanese, and Korean keyboards use a variety of ways to input their thousands of characters.

Research and Share

a. Research the impact of the standard for informational input globally.

b. Give a short report on the pros and cons of the keyboard method of input.

The U.S. WORKPLACE

13. Telecommuting Success Tips

Many people would like to work from home. Flexible scheduling, being able to sleep later, prioritizing your own tasks, and not having to dress in business attire are all good motivations. However, being successful at telecommuting requires the worker to overcome a lack of structure and the exposure to possible interruptions.

Research and Write

a. Research the various problems of telecommuting and proposed solutions.

b. Write a short paper giving your evaluation of telecommuting.

BUILDING ACADEMIC SKILLS

ELA English Language Arts

14. Some individuals open every e-mail they receive but have piles of unopened regular mail (snail mail). Others listen only to the first sentence or two of voice mails before deleting them. Research informational overload and its causes. Write a short essay on these topics and include solutions.

MATH Mathematics

15. According to recent statistics, each person receives on average 900 e-mail messages per month. About half are spam. Roughly 1 in 30 of these messages has a virus attached. Approximately how many messages containing viruses does a person receive per day in a 30-day month?

Computation and Estimation To solve this problem, you need to understand the principles of multiplication and division.

SOC Social Studies/Sociology

16. Different societies have different expectations regarding answering the phone. The verbal first impression may be vital. Whether you use electronically generated voices or Elvis impersonators saying "hello" for you, your choice of message conveys an impression. Research alternatives to the personal message and what they may convey to a caller. Report your findings to the class.

SOC Social Studies/History

17. The Internet began as a crude network used to connect research labs and grew into the information "mother lode" it is today. Prepare a short report on the history of the Internet.

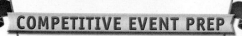

COMPETITIVE EVENT PREP

Product Business Plan

18. Situation A group of investors has asked you to prepare a business plan to sell your product abroad. You must look at the worldwide market for your product, and consider the expanded product lines you may want to offer in a specific country.

Activity After selecting a country and a product, develop a detailed business plan using all the components that your investors will expect to consider.

Evaluation You will be evaluated on how well you meet the following objectives.

  a. Prepare a succinct executive summary of your idea.

  b. Define your product, and the relevant facts about it.

  c. Review how you will market the product, to whom, and at what price point.

  d. Evaluate where you will produce your product, whether you will use management trained in the United States or locals, and other operational details.

  e. Discuss whether you will purchase or rent facilities and the reasoning behind your decision.

  f. Define the basic financial issues, and then prepare a financial statement.

  g. Create a professional business plan outline.

BusinessWeek online

19. Newsclip: How Otto Got an E-Commerce Head Start Germany's Otto Group is the world's second-biggest online retailer. Its Crate & Barrel brand is also one of the fastest-growing retailers in America. Michael Otto's early emphasis on e-commerce has driven this success.

 Go to the International Business Online Learning Center through **glencoe.com** to read an article about this topic. Write about how e-commerce and "t-commerce" drive sales.

Standardized Test Practice

20. Choose the best answer to the true/false question that follows.

Hardware equips users with instructions to run their computers to provide easy onscreen access.

○ True

○ False

Central African Republic

Using the Internet, find a map of the Central African Republic. Study its geographical position and its neighboring states. Answer the following questions about the Central African Republic on a separate sheet of paper.

➤ Research the history, political status, and economic position of the Central African Republic.

➤ Do you think IT has penetrated this country extensively? Why or why not? Compare your expectations with data on the number of radio and television stations, cell-phone users, and Internet hosts in the country.

For resources to help you do this exercise, go to the International Business Online Learning Center through **glencoe.com**.

Test-Taking Tip When choosing the correct answer to a true/false question, avoid answers that state a reason or justification. They tend to be false.

International Career Plan Sim

Success Model: **G.A.P ADVENTURES**
Country of Origin: **CANADA**
Business: **TOURISM**

In 1990, Bruce Poon Tip launched G.A.P Adventures with the vision that other people would share his desire to experience authentic global adventures that minimize environmental impact and help local economies. Imagine a camel trek with Berber tribesmen in Africa, a photo op with the penguins in Antarctica, or bargaining with the merchants in the bazaars of India. Traveling and experiencing the heart of a culture allow people to understand the world in ways never imagined, "outside the controlled environments of traditional tourism."

Founder Tip began planning and preparing for his career when he was in high school, participating in Canada's Junior Achievement (JA) organization. He learned the basics of business and took tourism courses. Since then his dream of G.A.P Adventures has grown into a company that offers tours on all seven continents. Bruce Poon Tip tells young entrepreneurs: "Have a lot of passion for your product or whatever you decide you want to start."

● Situation

Recently, you have been thinking about what you will do upon graduation from high school. After taking your International Business course, you feel certain that having the opportunity to travel will play an important role in your career planning decisions.

● Assignment

✓ Take a career interest inventory.
✓ Research two international business careers that interest you.
✓ Plan a trip to a country where you might like to work.
✓ Create a final report.

● Resources

SKILLS NEEDED

✓ *Academic Skills:* reading, writing, math, and social studies
✓ *Basic Skills:* speaking, listening, thinking, problem-solving, and interpersonal skills
✓ *Technology Skills:* word-processing, keyboarding, presentation, telecommunications, and Internet skills

TOOLS NEEDED

✓ Newspapers and magazines, such as *BusinessWeek* and *U.S. News and World Report*
✓ Access to the Internet and library
✓ Access to a career interest inventory (through the career center at school or Internet)
✓ Paper, pens, pencils, and markers
✓ Poster board and glue
✓ International food products (optional)
✓ Word-processing, spreadsheet, and presentation software

• Procedures

STEP 1 REAL-WORLD RESEARCH

A. Take a career interest inventory.

B. Research a country where you might like to work and find information about the:
- Geography
- Language(s)
- People and culture
- Religion and holidays
- Food, including a recipe for a native dish

STEP 2 COMMUNITY RESEARCH

Contact a travel agent or tour company to plan a trip to the country you are researching. Ask about the sights, the cost of the trip (including transportation), and information helpful to someone moving there.

STEP 3 INTERNET RESEARCH

Research two international business careers:
- Find out educational requirements.
- Find out the expected salary range.
- Match your career inventory to the careers.

STEP 4 CREATE IT

On a poster board, create a collage, drawing, or representation of the country where you might like to work one day. Represent the information researched in Step 1B.

STEP 5 GRAPHIC ORGANIZER

On a separate sheet of paper, create a diagram to organize the elements of your trip.

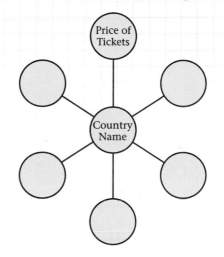

• Report

Prepare a report of your findings using the following tools, if available:
- *Word-processing program:* Prepare a 2-page report with results of the career interest inventory and how they relate to careers you researched.
- *Spreadsheet program:* Prepare a chart comparing careers you researched. Include educational requirements, experience, and salary range.
- *Presentation program:* Prepare a ten-slide presentation about the country where you might like to work. Include your trip plan.

• Evaluation

Present your report to the class and/or hand it in to your teacher. Use this chart to assess yourself before and after your presentation:

PRESENTATION SELF-CHECK RUBRIC	1 Needs Work	2 Average Quality	3 Good Quality	4 Excellent Quality	Totals
Knowledge of country researched					
Continuity of overall report					
Voice quality					
Eye contact with audience					
				TOTAL =	

0–6 Needs Work; **7–10** Average Quality; **11–14** Good Quality; **15–16** Excellent Quality

---

• Academic and Career Portfolio

Add this report to your Academic and Career Portfolio.

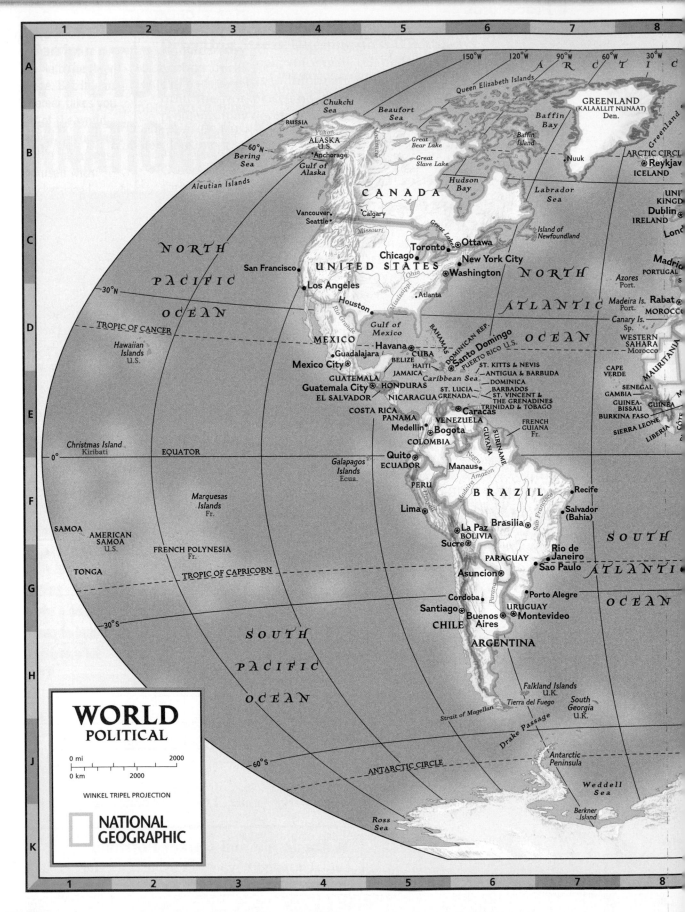

WORLD
POLITICAL

0 mi   2000

0 km   2000

WINKEL TRIPEL PROJECTION

NATIONAL
GEOGRAPHIC

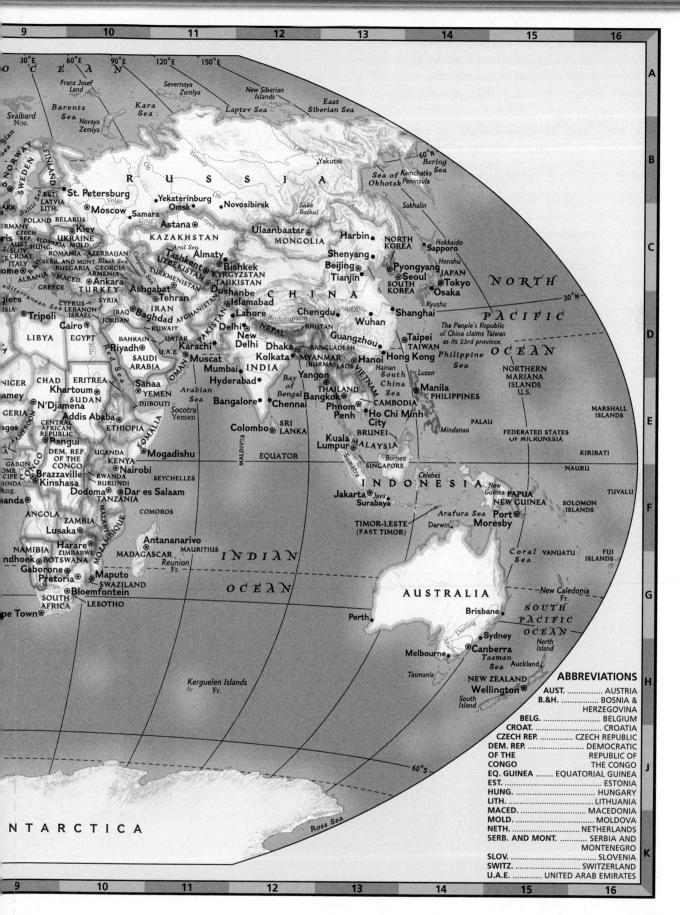

Units of Measurement

Historically, units of measurement were known as *Imperial units*, used in the British Commonwealth countries. They are similar but not identical to the units of measurement that are used mainly in the United States today.

The Metric System

The International System of Units (SI) is the most widely used system of units. SI is commonly known as the *metric system*. The metric system can be used legally in every country in the world. In many countries, use of the metric system is mandatory.

METRIC UNIT	U.S. UNIT	METRIC EQUIVALENT
WEIGHT		
metric ton (t)	short ton	0.907 metric tons
kilogram (kg)	pound (lb)	0.454 kilogram
gram (g)	ounce (oz)	28.350 grams
gram (g)	grain (gr)	0.0648 gram
VOLUME		
liter (l)	gallon (gal)	3.785 liters
liter (l)	quart (qt)	0.946 liters
milliliter (ml)	pint (pt)	473.176 milliliters
milliliter (ml)	fluid ounce (fl oz)	29.573 milliliters
cubic meter (m²)	cubic yard (yd²)	0.765 cubic meter
cubic meter (m²)	cubic foot (ft²)	0.028 cubic meter
cubic centimeter (cm²)	cubic inch (in²)	16.387 cubic centimeters
LENGTH		
kilometer (km)	mile (mi)	1.609 kilometers
meter (m)	yard (yd)	0.9144 meters
centimeter (cm)	foot (ft)	30.48 centimeters
centimeter (cm)	inch (in)	2.54 centimeters
AREA		
square kilometer (km²)	square mile (mi²)	2.590 square kilometers
square meter (m²)	acre (ac)	4047 square meters
square meter (m²)	square foot (ft²)	0.093 square meter
square centimeter (cm²)	square inch (in²)	6.452 square centimeters

A

accommodation the approach toward labor disputes in which unions and management are expected to cooperate (p. 340)

accounting the systematic process of recording and reporting the financial position of a business (p. 302)

accounting cycle the activities, or steps, that help a business keep its accounting records in an orderly manner (p. 307)

acculturation process of understanding, adapting to, and operating in a foreign culture (p. 66)

adaptation the process of adjusting or modifying a product to fit the needs of a particular market, country, or region (p. 231)

affirmative action a program designed to increase participation of various underrepresented groups in the workplace and government (p. 338)

arbitration a process to resolve disputes in which each side presents its case to an independent individual, the arbitrator, who makes decisions that are binding (p. 122)

audit a review of a company's accounting statements by an independent observer, or auditor (p. 306)

authority the right to direct with permission to act (p. 216)

B

balance of trade the difference between how much a country imports and how much it exports (p. 94)

balance sheet a report of the balances of all assets, liabilities, and owner's equity at the end of an accounting period (p. 303)

bargaining power a company's ability to achieve its bargaining goals without compromise (p. 310)

bond a corporation's written pledge to repay a specific amount of money, along with interest (p. 314)

bribe an item or money offered to entice the receiver to do something illegal or unethical (p. 66)

business any activity that seeks profit by providing goods or services to others (p. 7)

business ethics a set of ideas about how a company should conduct business in relation to legal, social, and environmental issues (p. 17)

C

C&F cost and freight, price quoted to the buyer signifying the buyer pays separately for insurance (p. 87)

capital money needed to establish a business and operate it for the first few months, or to expand an existing business (p. 163)

cartography the science or art of mapmaking (p. 141)

channel of distribution the path a product takes from the producer to the consumer (p. 289)

CIF the price quoted to the buyer, including cost, insurance, and freight (p. 87)

civil law a set of codes based on broad legal principles (p. 116)

code of ethics a statement that explains what a company or group believes is proper and improper conduct (p. 18)

collective bargaining agreement the contract created by union and management that covers wages, hours, benefits, and working conditions (p. 338)

command economy or planned economy, an economic system in which a central authority makes all key economic decisions (p. 132)

commercial risk or trade risk, a risk present in day-to-day buying and selling processes between companies (p. 167)

common law a set of laws based on local customs, traditions, and precedent (p. 115)

common stock a unit of ownership of a company that entitles the owner, or stockholder, to voting privileges (p. 313)

communication transmitting, receiving, and processing information (p. 53)

consumer promotions tactics used to sell products and services to end-users, or consumers (p. 270)

control to compare actual performance to the standards, and then making needed corrections (p. 220)

corporation a type of business ownership in which many people, whom the law treats as one person, own the business (p. 186)

cost accounting a method of accounting that adjusts the cost of goods to reflect a country's inflation rate (p. 305)

cultural baggage set of cultural attitudes that include the beliefs, values, and assumptions that people carry with them throughout life (p. 39)

cultural bias a preconceived attitude of favoring or disliking a particular culture (p. 40)

culture the set of beliefs, customs, and attitudes of a distinct group of people (p. 31)

culture shock a reaction that newcomers to a culture may experience; reactions may include feeling uncomfortable, afraid, resentful, and/or intrigued (p. 39)

currency the form of money used by a specific country (p. 156)

currency exchange rate the rate at which one country's currency can be traded for another country's currency (p. 156)

currency value fluctuation the change in value of one country's currency when it is traded for another country's currency (p. 158)

D

decentralization an arrangement whereby the delegation of authority is systematically built into a company's operations (p. 216)

demand the amount or quantity of goods and services that consumers are willing to buy at various prices (p. 131)

democracy a government system in which the nation's citizens hold political power (p. 109)

demographics statistics that describe a population in terms of personal characteristics such as age, gender, income, marital status, ethnicity, education, and occupation (p. 257)

Key Terms Glossary

dependency the practice of relying too much on one trading partner (p. 94)

differentiation a strategy of developing and delivering products that are different and better than others in the same industry (p. 213)

direct distribution channel a path used to sell products directly to consumers without the use of wholesalers or retailers (p. 290)

direct marketing the practice of contacting buyers directly (p. 290)

directing showing the way by leading or motivating (p. 217)

domestic company a company that conducts business in only one country (p. 7)

dual-career family a family arrangement in which both partners work (p. 354)

dumping the practice of selling goods in another country for less than the cost of manufacturing them, or for less than their market price (p. 97)

E

e-commerce or electronic commerce, the marketing of goods and services over the Internet (p. 375)

economics the study of how a society chooses to use resources to produce and distribute goods and services for people's consumption (p. 130)

encryption technology a form of code and signal scrambling that makes it nearly impossible for hackers to steal or alter sensitive information (p. 377)

entrepreneur a person who starts a new business (p. 193)

entrepreneurship the process of starting up a new company or business (p. 193)

e-tailing retail e-commerce programs (p. 376)

ethics a set of moral principles by which people conduct themselves, personally, socially, or professionally (p. 16)

ethnocentric management the preference of an employer to use its own workers, both at home and abroad (p. 329)

ethnocentrism the belief that one's own culture is better than all other cultures (p. 44)

e-workforce the population of workers who use computers to do business (p. 378)

exchange rate risk a risk that occurs when the currency exchange rate fluctuates as a transaction takes place (p. 167)

expatriate a person who relocates in a foreign country to live and/or conduct business (p. 66)

exports goods and services that people in one country sell to people in another country (p. 83)

extranet a semiprivate network that allows more than one company access to the same information (p. 374)

F

FOB free on board, or the ownership of merchandise in transit determines if freight charges are free (p. 87)

folkways and mores cultural customs that dictate how people act socially (p. 32)

free trade agreement a treaty between countries in which the countries agree to not charge taxes, duties, or tariffs on goods that they trade (p. 113)

free trade zone a place where people can buy goods from other countries without paying extra taxes (p. 113)

G

geocentric management the preference of an employer to hire only the best managers, regardless of their citizenship (p. 330)

gift an item given to convey good will (p. 66)

global dependence the concept that all countries depend on each other for trade (p. 12)

global entrepreneurship the process of selling new products, starting a new operating division, or starting up a new company in another country (p. 196)

globalization increasing integration of the world economy (p. 7)

good a tangible item that is made, manufactured, or grown (p. 83)

H

hard currency a currency that can be exchanged for other currencies at uniform rates in financial centers around the world (p. 157)

hardware the physical components of a computer system (p. 369)

human development index (HDI) a measure comparing the quality of life in different countries, using three measures (p. 336)

human resource management (HRM) the process of finding, selecting, training, evaluating, and helping employees (p. 328)

I

imports goods and services that people in one country buy from people in another country (p. 83)

income statement a report of the net income or net loss for an accounting period (p. 303)

incremental manager training a form of training that gradually adds more managerial duties to a person's job (p. 352)

indirect distribution channel a path that uses consumer agents or merchant middlemen to distribute products from producer to consumer (p. 289)

inflation the rise in the level of prices for goods and services over time (p. 304)

information technology (IT) the hardware and software used in creating, processing, storing, and communicating information (p. 368)

insurable risk a risk insurance companies will cover, including an "act of God" and other less-random events (p. 170)

intellectual property an original work fixed in a tangible medium of expression that can be copyrighted, patented, or trademarked (p. 118)

International Accounting Standards Board (IASB) an organization that creates accounting standards that businesses use around the world (p. 308)

international business any activity involving business across national borders (p. 7)

international company a company that conducts business across national borders (p. 7)

International Organization for Standardization (ISO) the world's largest developer of quality control standards (p. 241)

international trade all business activities conducted between individuals, companies, and governments from different countries (p. 82)

international trade documentation the papers and documents used to legally export or import goods (p. 60)

intranet a company's internal, Web-based communication system (p. 372)

intrapreneurship the process of starting a new business that is spun off from an existing business (p. 195)

J

job rotation manager training a form of training in which the trainee learns different jobs by moving around in the company (p. 352)

just-in-time (JIT) an inventory system used to make sure raw materials arrive at the plant just when the manufacturer needs them (p. 241)

L

language the medium of communication through words, symbols, numbers, characters, or nonverbal cues (p. 53)

lateral promotion manager training a form of job-rotation training that is enhanced by rewards for the trainee (p. 353)

leadership the ability to influence behavior in organizations (p. 219)

liability legal responsibility for the financial cost of another person's losses or injuries (p. 116)

limited liability company (LLC) a company whose owners and managers enjoy limited liability and some tax benefits (p. 187)

litigation a legal process used to resolve a dispute through the court system (p. 120)

M

management the process of getting things done through other people (p. 208)

market a set of people who share similar wants and needs who are capable of buying products (p. 256)

market economy an economic system in which economic decisions are made in the marketplace (p. 131)

market segmentation the process of analyzing and classifying customers in a market to create smaller, more precise market segments (p. 257)

marketing the process of planning, pricing, promoting, selling and distributing products to satisfy customers' needs and wants (p. 256)

mediation a process of intervention between conflicting parties that promotes resolution of their conflict outside the court system (p. 120)

mentor a personal coach or counselor who helps an individual with his or her career (p. 350)

mixed economy an economic system in which the marketplace determines some economic decisions, and the government makes some decisions (p. 133)

mode of entry the method a company uses to sell products in another country (p. 188)

money anything that people accept as a form of payment (p. 154)

motivation the cause of behaviors, what maintains behaviors, and sometimes what stops behaviors (p. 218)

multinational corporation (MNC) an organization that operates in more than one country (p. 188)

N

nonverbal communication sending messages without the use of words (p. 61)

norms social rules that affect behaviors and actions, and represent cultural values (p. 32)

O

organizational market or business market, a group of companies that buy and resell goods, and companies that use these goods to create other products (p. 259)

organizing a process that brings together people and materials or technology in an organization (p. 214)

P

partnership a type of business ownership in which two or more people own the business (p. 185)

passport a government document that is used to prove a person's citizenship in the country that issued it (p. 358)

paternalism a system in which an authority fulfills the needs and regulates the conduct of the people under its control (p. 337)

penetration pricing the practice of setting the price for a product as low as possible to quickly enter a market (p. 286)

personal selling any form of direct contact between a salesperson and a customer (p. 267)

planning outlining a course of action for the future (p. 210)

polycentric management the preference of an employer to use natives of the host country to manage operations there, but home-country residents to manage in the home country (p. 329)

population density a measurement of the number of people living in a geographic area (p. 141)

preferred stock a type of stock that gives the stockholder the advantage of receiving cash dividends before common stockholders receive cash dividends (p. 313)

Key Terms Glossary

process reengineering a program to improve a business through major changes to the production process (p. 242)

product differentiation an advertising approach whereby a company suggests its product is different from and better than similar products from competitors (p. 258)

promotional mix any combination of the four components of promotion: advertising, personal selling, sales promotion, and public relations and publicity (p. 262)

protectionism a system of imposing extra costs on imports to protect the interests of local businesses (p. 95)

proximity the physical nearness of one thing to another (p. 146)

public relations a program of activities that help an organization influence a target audience (p. 272)

Q

quality the level of excellence present in a product (p. 230)

quality circle a group of employees who meet regularly to discuss ways to increase quality (p. 242)

R

regiocentric management the preference of an employer to employ managers from a variety of countries in a region (p. 329)

risk the possibility of loss when there is uncertainty associated with the outcome of an event (p. 166)

role the part a person plays in a social situation (p. 33)

S

scarcity a situation in which there is a limited amount of a commodity (p. 136)

service an intangible benefit or task provided by a business to its customers (p. 84)

Six Sigma a quality management program designed to find ways to make products efficiently and without mistakes or variations (p. 242)

skimming pricing the practice of setting the price for a new or prestige product as high as possible (p. 286)

slang colloquial speech used on the street or in recreational situations (p. 55)

social institutions the organizations that represent the patterns of activity that express the culture of a country (p. 37)

social responsibility the duty to do what is best for society (p. 17)

soft currency an unstable currency that is not exchanged at major financial centers (p. 157)

software a computer program or application (p. 369)

sole proprietorship a type of business ownership in which one person owns the business (p. 185)

sourcing the process of locating and acquiring component parts for a final product (p. 235)

stakeholders individuals or groups of people who have a direct interest, involvement, or investment in something (p. 18)

standardization the practice of making a product the same, without modification, for all markets (p. 231)

stereotyping the practice of identifying a person or group by a single trait, or as a member of a group instead of as an individual (p. 40)

strategic human resource management (SHRM) carefully planned decisions that lead to the hiring of home-, host-, and third-country employees (p. 329)

strategic plan a company's long-term plan (p. 212)

Subchapter S corporation a corporation that is taxed like a partnership (p. 187)

subculture a smaller group or subset within a larger culture (p. 35)

superior-subordinate syndrome a situation in which a manager will "have a boss" and "be the boss" (p. 351)

supply the amount of goods and services that producers provide at various prices (p. 131)

T

teaching helping someone to learn new knowledge or acquire a new skill (p. 217)

telecommuting a practice whereby employees work at home aided by technology (p. 380)

theocracy a type of totalitarian government whose leaders claim to be inspired by divine guidance (p. 110)

theocratic law a set of laws based on religious teachings (p. 116)

topography the physical surface features of a geographic area (p. 141)

total quality management (TQM) a program in which all of management focuses on quality and quality improvement as the most important company goal (p. 242)

totalitarianism a type of government system in which citizens have no influence on governmental policies and laws (p. 109)

trade barriers restrictions that reduce free trade and limit competition from imported goods (p. 94)

trade promotions tactics used to sell products and services to other businesses (p. 268)

transaction risk the risk associated with a buyer making installment payments on a purchase (p. 168)

travel itinerary a document that spells out travel times, transportation methods, and hotels or places where someone will stay on a trip (p. 357)

V

value the degree of quality as compared to the price or cost of the product (p. 230)

values strongly held concepts that are present in a culture (p. 32)

verbal communication sending messages by using words that are either spoken or written (p. 53)

visa a stamp of endorsement that allows the holder of a passport to enter a country (p. 358)

W

work visa or work permit, an official document that allows an individual to work legally at a job in a host country (p. 358)

A

achieve to attain a desired end or aim

acquire to come into possession or control of something

adjust to adapt or conform

administration a group constituting the political executive in a presidential government

alternative one of two or more choices or courses of action

analyze distinguishing the parts of something in order to discover its true nature

appreciate to increase the value of something

approach the taking of preliminary steps toward a particular purpose

area a geographic region

assess to determine the importance, size, or value of someone or something

attitude a feeling or emotion toward a fact or state

automate to operate by use of a self-acting or self-regulating mechanism

B

benefit to be useful or profitable

C

civil code a systematic compilation of laws designed to comprehensively deal with the core areas of private law

commission a fee paid to an agent or employee for service

commit to obligate or pledge oneself

compensate to offset an undesired effect

component a constituent part; ingredient

concept an idea generalized from particular instances

conduct to direct or take pat in an operation or management

conflict competitive or opposing action of incompatibles

consist to be composed or made up

constant something invariable or unchanging

corporate formed into an association and endowed by law with the rights and liabilities of an individual; of, or relating to, or being the large corporations of a country or region considered as a unit

create to make or bring into existence something new

cycle an interval of time during which a sequence of a recurring succession of events is completed

D

database a large collection of information organized for rapid search and retrieval

debate to discuss a question by considering opposing arguments

demonstrate to prove or make clear by reasoning or evidence

distribute to give out or deliver

domestic of, relating to, or originating within a country

E

economy the structure and conditions of how material resources are used in a country or area

element one of the factors determining the outcome of a process

enhance to increase or improve in value, quality, desirability, or attractiveness

environment the aggregate of social and cultural conditions that influence the life of an individual or community

equate to make equal

equip to furnish appropriate provisions for service or action

establish to put on a firm basis; set up

estimate to judge tentatively or approximately something's value, worth, or significance

F

factor an active contributor to the production of a result

feature to have or to present something or someone as an important element

focus a center of activity, attraction, or attention

formula a general fact, rule, or principle expressed in mathematical symbols

G

generate to bring into existence

goal the end toward which effort is directed

I

identify to establish the identity of someone or something

impact a significant or major effect

income a gain or recurrent benefit, usually measured in money, that derives from capital or labor

individual something or someone existing as a distinct entity

infrastructure the underlying foundation or basic framework of a system or organization

interact to act upon one another

invest to commit money in order to earn a financial return

item an object of attention, concern, or interest

J

journal a record of current transactions

L

labor human activity that provides the goods or services in an economy; or workers available for employment

legal of or relating to law

link on a Web-site page, an identifier that permits connection to another Web-site page or element; also known as hyperlink

M

media methods of conveyance or expression; plural of medium

method a way, technique, or process of or for doing something

Academic Vocabulary Glossary

N

network a usually informally interconnected group or association of persons, often within professions

O

overseas of or relating to movement, transport, or communication over the sea

P

parameter any of a set of properties whose values determine the characteristics or behavior of something

partner one involved in a relationship with one or more other parties involving close cooperation and joint rights and responsibilities

perceive to attain awareness or understanding of something or someone

percent a value determined on the basis of a whole divided into 100 equal parts

policy an overall plan embracing general goals and acceptable procedures

potential possibility for development

precede to be, go, or come ahead of

predict to foretell on the basis of observation, experience, or

scientific reason

principle a comprehensive and fundamental law, doctrine, or assumption

process a continuous operation

purchase to obtain by paying money

R

range to change or differ within limits

ratio the relationship in quantity, amount, or size between two or more things

region a broad geographic area distinguished by similar features

register to secure official entry in a system of public records

regulate to bring under the control of law or constituted authority

require to call for as suitable or appropriate

research to search or investigate exhaustively

resource a source of supply or support

respond to show a reaction

role a function or part performed in a particular operation or process

S

seek to make an attempt

sequence a continuous or connected series

similar having characteristics in common; strictly comparable

statistic part of or a whole collection of quantitative data

structure something arranged in a definite pattern of organization

subordinate a person or thing occupying a lower class, rank, or position

survey to query in order to collect data for the analysis of some aspect of a group or area

T

target to set as a goal or mark

technology a manner of accomplishing a task using technical processes, methods, or knowledge

theory a belief, policy, or procedure proposed or followed as the basis of action

tradition an established or customary pattern of thought, action, or behavior

transfer to convey from one person, place, or situation to another

trend prevailing tendency or inclination

V

volume mass or the representation of mass

Index

Index

Index